Cartel Regulation

India in an International Perspective

Lovely Dasgupta

FOUNDATION
BOOKS

FOUNDATION BOOKS

Foundation Books is an imprint of Cambridge University Press, India.

Cambridge House, 4381/4 Ansari Road, Daryaganj, New Delhi 110 002

www.cambridgeindia.org

First published 2014

Digitally Printed at Replika Press Pvt. Ltd.

ISBN 978-93-82993-75-9 Hardback

Contents

Preface

This book is the outcome of sustained research conducted over a period of five years. Cartels provided the opportunity to explore and produce something uniquely Indian, but sprinkled with international flavours. The subject proved challenging, more so because of the kind of extensive scholarship on the topic available in advanced jurisdictions. It was indeed an arduous task to deliver a work good enough to further the cause of critical authorship in the field of competition law in India.

The book tries to give a detailed account of the Indian anti-cartel provisions that were brought into force in the year 2009. The critique is based on a comparative account of the anti-cartel provisions of the EU and the US. The idea is to suggest accommodation of Indian interest as well as incorporation of efficient structures from the jurisdictions under review. The thrust is also on the core idea of balancing the interest of a wider consumer base and not just the end consumer.

The book has benefitted a lot from the writings of Indian economist, Professor Dr Aditya Bhattacharjea, whose critique of the Indian competition law is remarkable. There are others too who have, through their criticisms and negative comments, helped spur new thought processes. One should also thank Cambridge University Press for not only agreeing to publish but also encouraging writing of the book.

The book deals with law as it prevailed up to October 28, 2013.

Abbreviations

AEA	Agricultural Engineers Association Ltd
AMTPP	The Association of Motion Pictures and TV Programme Producers
ASCAP	American Society of Composers, Authors and Publishers
ATF	Air Traffic Fuel
BIDS	Beef Industry Development Society Limited
BMI	Broadcast Music, Inc
BR	Butadiene rubber
CAG	Comptroller Auditor General
CAMs	Conditional access modules
CASNUB	CAst steel SNUBer equipped
CBS	Columbia Broadcasting System
CCI	Competition Commission of India
CJ	Chief Justice
CompAT	Competition Appellate Tribunal
CUTS	Consumer Unity and Trust Society
DG	Director General
DTH	Direct-to-home
EC	European Commission
ESBR	Emulsion styrene butadiene rubber
EU	The European Union
FENIN	Federación Española de Empresas de Tecnología Sanitaria
FTA	Free to air
FTC	Federal Trade Commission
FTPGI	The Film and Television Producers Gild of India Ltd.
HR	Hot rolled coils
IBA	Indian Bank Association
IDRA	The Industries (Development and Regulation) Act, 1951
IFSL	Indiabulls Financial Services Limited
ITR	India Tyre, Rubber Co
LAB	Linear alkaline benzene
MRTP	Monopolies and Restrictive Trade Practices Act, 1969
OECD	Organisation for Economic Cooperation and Development

PMAD	Paper Merchant's Association, Delhi
R&D	Research and Development Agreements
RBI	Reserve Bank of India
RGTI	Road Goods Transportation Industry
SIM	Subscriber identity module
STB	Set top box
TERI	The Energy and Resources Institute
TPPL	Tamil Nadu Petro Product Ltd
TRAI	Telecom Regulatory Authority of India
TRIPS	(The Agreement on) Trade Related Aspects of Intellectual Property Rights
UK	United Kingdom
UPDF	United Producers/Distributors Forum
US	The United States
USSR	Union of Soviet Socialist Republics
WTO	World Trade Organization

1 Introduction

Scope

This book is focused primarily on the interpretation and application of the anti-cartel provisions within the Competition Act, 2002. Although India had started on the path to industrialization and modernization soon after its independence from the British rule in 1947, to begin with and for quite some time it adopted and followed the so-called 'mixed economic policy' under which the state was the major player in industrialization and trade. Under this policy, very limited and restricted scope existed for the non-state actors to participate effectively and decisively in industrialization or international trade. In fact, the borders were not open for international investment or trade. Consequently, little or limited scope existed for free competition among private enterprises. Even then, precautions were taken in the Monopolies and Restrictive Trade Practices Act, 1969, against the misuse of freedom of trade by private actors. Nonetheless, the Monopolies and Restrictive Trade Practices Act was not geared to deal stringently with cartels. The reason was that the focus of the Act was to curb monopolies and dominant undertakings.

Accordingly, the anti-cartel provisions within the Monopolies and Restrictive Trade Practices Act were weak. Cartels were not prohibited *per se*; they were declared void only if they harmed public interest. Further, there was no mechanism for the detection of cartels. This was a major lacuna within the Monopolies and Restrictive Trade Practices Act, since cartels are usually secretive in nature. In the absence of any deterring substantive as well as procedural provisions, cartels thrived within the Indian economy. This is amply substantiated by the surveys conducted by CUTS (Consumer Unity and Trust Society). Moreover, writers have extensively analysed the provisions of the Monopolies and Restrictive Trade Practices Act and highlighted the weaknesses within the Act.[1] Specifically, it is evident from their writings that the Monopolies and Restrictive Trade Practices Commission had failed to take any concrete steps against cartels. At the beginning of the last decade of the last millennium, specifically in 1991, India changed its path by introducing the so-called 'new economic policy'.

The new economic policy, which replaced the mixed economy by a market economy, opened up and encouraged participation in industrialization and trade not only to domestic enterprises but also to foreign ones. India also opened its international borders for cross-border trade. This change in India's policy was closely connected with the politico-economic changes that took place in Europe, starting in 1989 with the fall of the Berlin Wall and disintegration of the Soviet Union that removed the Iron Curtain between the market and state-controlled economies and led the process of economic globalization. A few years later, India became a member of the WTO (World Trade Organization) and as such had to establish trade practices consistent with the WTO standards. In pursuance of those standards as well as other TRIPS (trade-related aspects of Intellectual Property Rights) requirements, India had to modify many existing laws and enact many new ones—the Competition Act, 2002 is one of them. With the lessons learnt from the failures of the Monopolies and Restrictive Trade Practices Act, it became necessary that cartels be dealt with stringently. However, the Competition Act's full operation and application is yet to be experienced. It is important for the Act's success and the achievement of its purpose that it is read and understood in its proper perspective.

The present enquiry, however, is not about every aspect or provision of the Act. It proceeds on the argument that the protection of consumer interests is the main objective of the Act and cartels or agreements in restraint of trade are inimical to that objective and defeat it. Therefore, cartels in any form that have the natural tendency of operating against the interest of the consumer cannot be permitted or justified under the Act. The Monopolies and Restrictive Trade Practices Act never furthered consumer interests with its weak anti-cartel provisions. Furthermore, as will be explained later, the use of the public interest standard allowed the cartelists to escape any sort

---

1 See for example, A N Oza, "Monopolies and Restrictive Trade Practices Act", *EPW* 5, no. 9 (1970): 413–424; A. N. Oza, "Recent Amendments to the MRTP Act", *EPW* 17, no. 42 (1982): 1697–1705; H.K. Paranjape, "The MRTP Amendment Bill: A Trojan Horse", EPW 19, no. 17 (1984): 715–729; Hansavivek, "Companies: Thwarted by MRTP Act?" *EPW* 6, no.23 (1971): 1124–1126; Jaivir Singh, "Monopolistic Trade Practices and Concentration of Economic Power: Some Conceptual Problems in MRTP Act", *EPW* 35, no.50 (2000): 4437–4444 et al.

of prohibition that the Monopolies and Restrictive Trade Commission was empowered to impose. The Competition Act does away with the public interest standard. However, being a comparatively recent legislation meant dealing with the challenges of a liberalized economy, it needs to be seen whether the anti-cartel provisions in the Act are an improvement over the previous law. Importantly, any effective anti-cartel provision needs to lay down the parameters for dealing with cartels. Any anti-cartel provisions, accordingly, will have to choose between the *rule of reason* approach or the *per se* approach.

The consequence of falling foul of anti-cartel provisions should be deterring. Therefore, the provision for fines has to be clear and the amount substantial. Finally, the method of detection of cartels has to be clearly specified. This is important as cartels usually operate in secret. The anti-cartel provisions within all competition laws incorporate these parameters. The provisions of the Competition Act, 2002 has been analysed from different perspectives by several writers.[2] However, the efficacy of the anti-cartel provisions in furthering consumer interest has yet to be analysed comprehensively. This book is an attempt to fill in this void in the existing literature. The reason why this book deals only with cartels is evident from the nature of cartels themselves. To elaborate a little bit at this point, in all existing competition law regimes they have been regarded as anti-competitive behaviour.[3] Yet, they are different from other anti-competitive behaviour because of their inherent nature.

They are the anti-thesis of the objectives pursued by competition law regimes world over. The objective of competition laws is to protect the process of competition and maximize consumer welfare[4] by forcing producers to offer the consumer a greater choice of high-quality products and services at low prices.[5] Cartels, on the other hand, are cooperative arrangements

---

2 For example, see Arjun Kapoor, 'Competition Law and the Liberalization of Legal Services Sector in India', http://www.cci.gov.in/images/media/ResearchReports/ArjunIntern280111.pdf (accessed October 21, 2011); Sowmya Suman, 'Competition Law and Cartelization', http://www.lawyersclubindia.com/articles/COMPETITION-LAW-amp CARTELIZATION-543.asp (accessed November 21, 2011); Sanchit Aggarwal, "Competition Law and Protection of Consumer Interest", http://www.cci.gov.in/images/media/ResearchReports/SanchitInt260811.pdf (accessed November 20, 2011)

3 Maher M. Dabbah and Barry E. Hawk, ed., *Anti-Cartel Enforcement Worldwide* (CUP, 2009)

4 Richard Whish, *Competition Law* (6th ed., OUP, 2009) 1.

5 R. Shyam Khemani, "Competition Law Policy-Exemptions, Exceptions, and Differential Application", in *Competition Law Today-Concepts, Issues, and the Law in Practice,* Vinod Dhall, ed. (OUP, 2007) 153.

between competitors to raise prices and reduce choices to the disadvantage of the consumers. They also curtail incentive for innovation and quality[6] at the expense of consumers.[7] Cartels, therefore, obtain complete monopoly in the market.[8] They affect the quality of products and services in the absence of any competitive pressure to innovate.[9] In essence, these arrangements are aimed at fixing prices, sharing markets and fixing production quotas to maximize profits. The whole idea of earning profits through cartelization is therefore to harm the interests of both the public and the consumers.[10] Cartels also represent the aggregate of the bargaining power of large corporate entities that are in a position to dictate the terms of the market. This is possible because a combination of large corporate entities enable cartels to dominate the market.[11]

The compulsion to cooperate is driven by self-interest. Corporate entities want to protect their market shares and consumer base by stabilizing prices. The price competition is consequently substituted by agreements to fix prices. The lack of price competition automatically deprives the consumers of choices and forces them to abide with the existing supplier or seller. Cooperative arrangements assure corporate entities that their business quota will not be poached. On the whole, cartels are formed primarily to maintain *status quo* among the participants. This feature of cartels also helps one in distinguishing cartels from other horizontal cooperative arrangements. Corporate entities do cooperate for other purposes than merely raising prices or maintaining *status*

---

6 *Union of India and Ors vs Hindustan Development Corpn. and Others, SCC* 3 (1993): 499; SCR 3, no. 128 (1993): 167. [The Supreme Court of Indian defines cartels as "an association of producers who by agreement among themselves attempt to control production, sale and prices of the product to obtain a monopoly in any particular industry or commodity". Analysing the object of formation of a cartel, cartels, in other words, amount to an unfair trade practice which is not in the interest of the public.]

7 Dabbah and Hawk, (n 3) 1.

8 Debora L. Spar, *The Cooperative Edge-The International Politics of International Cartels* (Cornell University Press, 1994) 2. [Spar explains that '[c]artels are a particular form of cooperation and contain some characteristics that are not shared by other cooperative endeavours.']

9 See Report prepared by the International Competition Network (ICN) Working Group on Cartels, 'Defining Hard Core Cartel Conduct, Effective Institutions, Effective Penalties', http://www.internationalcompetitionnetwork.org/uploads/library/doc346.pdf (accessed 28 April 2011)

10 Massimo Motta, *Competition Policy-Theory and Practice* (CUP, 2004) 19. [Motta states that in case of cartels the decrease in total welfare also decreases consumer welfare and vice versa.]

11 Christopher Harding and Julian Joshua, *Regulating Cartels in Europe-A Study of Legal Control of Corporate Delinquency* (OUP, 2003) 4.

quo. For example, corporate entities may enter into cooperative agreements for research and development.

In these types of cooperative agreements, the main purpose is to develop better technologies or better production facilities or products or services. The restraint imposed is ancillary to the main purpose. The outcome of such cooperative arrangements furthers the object of competition law. There is consequently provision of quality products or services at lesser prices. In this respect, therefore, a research and development agreement is different from cartels since it is not a cooperative agreement to avoid competition. The object of cartels is raising prices by curbing competition while other cooperative arrangements may or may not have an anti-competitive effect. Therefore, cartels are regarded as naked restraints in contrast to other horizontal cooperative agreements.[12] The only purpose of or justification for cartels for their cooperative agreement is the detrimental effect on competition. One may argue that cartels are for the benefit of the competitors at the cost of the consumers.[13]However, that is no justification for their existence, especially when they disregard the interests of society in general and of the consumer in particular.[14] The lack of justification springs from the very fact that cartels thrive on exploiting unequal bargaining power. The weaker party—the consumer, who lacks bargaining power against the cartels—gets to bear the burden of the raised prices or lack of choices.

Defining consumers

As the book examines the impact of cartels on consumers, let us define and explain the terms consumer and consumer interests, just as the term cartel was defined and explained above. The 'consumer' referred to in 'consumer welfare', as understood in neo-classical economics, signifies society at large and not just the end user. Accordingly, the emphasis of neo-classical economics is on efficiency viz. efficient utilization of resources that enhances the 'economic wealth of the society' at large. This definition of consumer welfare is also termed as total welfare or economic welfare.[15] Evidently, within this

12 Whish (n 4) 572.

13 Dabbah and Hawk (n 3) 1–2.

14 OECD Policy Brief, "Hard Core Cartels- Harm and Effective Sanctions" (May 2002) http://www.oecd.org/dataoecd/30/10/2754996.pdf (accessed November 2, 2011)

15 Barry J Rodger and Angus MacCulloch, *Competition Law and Policy in the European Community and United Kingdom* (2nd ed., Cavendish Publishing, 2001) 7.

notion, bargaining concerns are not factored in.[16] Leading scholars emphasize consumer interest as 'consumer well-being', distinguishing it from consumer welfare or welfare of the society at large.[17] For example, Buttigieg's consumer interest concerns the interest of the end user, i.e., the final consumer. His justification for defining consumer interest in terms of end user interest is that efficient allocation of resources need not always benefit the end consumer. For example, a merger may be efficient in terms of utilization of resources; however, it may lead to increase in prices for the end consumer. The emphasis therefore is on keeping the prices low while providing quality goods and services.[18]

Buttigeig belongs to a group of scholars who argue against the efficiency view point. They argue that the goal of any competition law should be to prevent firms with market power from harming the end consumer.[19] These arguments defining consumer interest in terms of end consumer interest however are not suited to the Indian scenario where apart from the end consumer there are other groups whose interest may be equally jeopardized due to unequal bargaining power. Accordingly in this book, the term 'consumer interest' has been used to represent the interest of a broader category of entities—it includes all who are beset with unequal bargaining power vis-à-vis large corporate entities. The term 'consumer' includes the end user as well as any intermediary who is directly or indirectly affected by an anti-competitive conduct. Understood specifically in the context of cartels, therefore, consumer interest in this book denotes the interest of this wide consumer base with weak bargaining power.

This broadening of the definition of consumer will also help in overriding the problem faced with the term 'public interest'. The term 'public interest', being ambiguous, does not fit into any precise definition. It may override bargaining concerns in favour of market power. On the other hand, using

---

16 See for example Kenneth G. Elzinga, "The Goals of Antitrust: Other than Competition and Efficiency, What Else Counts?', *University of Pennsylvania Law Review* 1191 125 (1977): 6.

17 Eugène Buttigieg, *Competition Law: Safeguarding the Consumer Interest: A Comparative Analysis of US Antitrust Law and EC Competition Law* (Kluwer Law International, 2009) 1–16.

18 *Ibid.* 6–7.

19 See, for example, Joseph F. Brodley, "The Economic Goals of Antitrust: Efficiency, Consumer Welfare, and Technological Progress", *N.Y.U.L. Rev.* 62 (1987): 1020; Robert H. Lande, "Wealth Transfers as the Original and Primary Concern of Antitrust: The Efficiency Interpretation Challenged", *Hastings L.J.* 34 (1982–1983): 65; Eleanor M. Fox and Lawrence A. Sullivan, "Antitrust-Retrospective and Prospective: Where Are We Coming From? Where Are We Going?", *N.Y.U. L. Rev.* 62 (1987): 936.

the broad definition of consumer ensures that the market power of corporate entities is not allowed to overpower the smaller players in the field. Thus, the concerns of small suppliers, distributors and end consumers are taken into account on the touchstone of unequal bargaining power. These concerns are different in developing countries from the concerns of developed countries with respect to determining the goals of competition law. Developing countries do have specific needs and the goals of competition law should accommodate these needs.[20] Importantly, developing countries have their peculiar concerns which warrants different goal setting for competition law.[21] On the whole, competition law of different jurisdictions will have different goals that may range from economic to the political.[22]

The relevance of the domestic set-up in designing the goals of competition law cannot thus be ignored.[23] The compulsions of the domestic economy

---

20 Ajit Singh and Rahul Dhumale, "Competition Policy, Development and Developing Countries", 1999, http://www.icrier.org/pdf/wto7.pdf (accessed 1 January 2011).

21 Eleanor M. Fox, "World Competition Law: Conflicts, Convergence, Cooperation" in Vinod Dhall, ed. (n 5) 224.

22 Maher M. Dabbah, *International and Comparative Competition law* (CUP, 2010) 39.

23 See Christopher Bellamy, "Some Reflections on Competition Law in the Global Market", New England Law Review 15, 34 (2000):1 http://www.nesl.edu/userfiles/file/lawreview/vol34/1/BELLAMY.PDF (accessed 1 July 2011). [An example is the South African Competition Act of 1998. Section 2 of the South African Competition Act spells out a number of objectives which the competition law is required to achieve. It states that: 'The purpose of *this Act* is to promote and maintain competition in the Republic in order – (a) to promote the efficiency, adaptability and development of the economy; (b) to provide consumers with competitive prices and product choices; (c) to promote employment and advance the social and economic welfare of South Africans; (d) to expand opportunities for South African participation in world markets and recognize the role of foreign competition in the Republic; (e) to ensure that small and medium-sized enterprises have an equitable opportunity to participate in the economy; (f) to promote a greater spread of ownership, in particular to increase the ownership stakes of historically disadvantaged persons; (g) to detect and address conditions in the market for any particular goods or services, or any behaviour within such a market, that tends to prevent, restrict or distort competition in connection with the supply or acquisition of those goods or services within the Republic; and (h) to provide for consistent application of common standards and policies affecting competition within all markets and sectors of the economy'. The Vietnam Competition Law on the other hand emphasizes the protection of the interest of the state, public interests, interest of the business entities as well as consumers, as its goals. Accordingly, the Competition Law, 2004, Article 4 states that '1. Enterprises enjoy freedom to competition within the legal framework. The State protects the lawful right to business competition. 2. Competition must be implemented on the principles of honesty, non-infringement upon the interests of the State, public interests, legitimate rights and interests of enterprises, consumers and compliance with the provisions of this Law']

will accordingly shape the competition law.[24] Following a similar approach, India's Competition Act of 2002 emphasizes the need to protect consumer interests as its major goal.[25] The Raghavan Committee Report which preceded the enactment of the Act also noted that the 'ultimate raison d'être of competition is the interests of the consumer'.[26] Although the Raghavan Committee's consumer was the end consumer, the Act has adopted a broader definition of 'consumer'. In the author's opinion, within the Indian competition law framework, a broad definition of consumer is well justified and needed.

In the light of the foregoing explanation of the concept of cartels and consumer interest, this book tries to establish why competition law provides the best framework to deal with cartels. Cartels being horizontal agreements are equally amenable to remedy by contract law. This is because agreements between competitors eschewing competition in favour of cooperation may be regarded as an agreement in restraint of trade. Accordingly, the agreements become unenforceable among the parties to such cartel agreements. However, the problem with the doctrine of restraint of trade is that being a contractual remedy, it comes into play only when the parties to the contract challenge the agreement. This will therefore ensure that if the cartelists want, they can continue with their cooperation without any fear of legal intervention. The limitation in the reach of the restraint of trade doctrine emanates from the inherent nature of the contract, which is a private law invoked only by the parties to the agreement. In contrast, competition law is a public law which is mandated to interfere with any conduct that is defined as anti-competitive. Therefore, the cartel agreement can be interfered with, overriding the concerns for contractual sanctity.

The doctrine of restraint of trade has relevance for identifying the norms governing the condemnation of an agreement in restraint of trade. These

---

[24] See Kim Kampel, "The Role of South African Competition Law in Supporting SMEs", http://www.competition regulation.org.uk/conferences/ southafrica04/kampel.pdf (accessed 1 October 2011).

[25] The long title of the Competition Act, 2002 is 'An Act to provide, keeping in view the economic development of the country, for the establishment of a Commission to prevent practices having adverse effect on competition, to promote and sustain competition in markets, to protect the interests of consumers and to ensure freedom of trade carried on by other participants in markets, in India, and for matters connected therewith or incidental thereto'.

[26] S.V.S. Raghavan Committee Report, "Report of the High Level Committee on Competition Policy Law", para 1.1.9 http://www.globalcompetitionforum.org/regions/asia/India/Report_of_High_Level_Committee_on_Competition_Policy_Law_SVS_Raghavan_Committee29102007.pdf (accessed 25 May 2011) .

norms have distinguished the ancillary restraint from the naked restraint. Any restraint which is ancillary to the main contract does not render the contract as an agreement in restraint of trade. Understanding the process leading to the separation of an ancillary restraint from the naked restraint will help in better appreciating the pernicious character of cartels. This understanding will also help in meaningfully engaging with the *per se* or the *rule of reason* debate within the competition law framework. Taking a call on this debate is essential to assess the response of the Indian competition law towards cartels. The *per se* or the *rule of reason* debate within the competition law framework is similar to the debate that existed for long in the common law with respect to the treatment of agreements in restraint of trade. Therefore, the study of the doctrine of restraint of trade helps in better analysing the anti-cartel provisions within Indian competition law.

The object of this book in analysing the above-mentioned provisions is to ascertain the effectiveness of these provisions in deterring the formation of cartels. The focus therefore is exclusively on domestic cartels. Accordingly, the book does not include any discussion on international cartels and export cartels. The primary purpose is to assess the extent to which the anti-cartel provision within the Competition Act, 2002 accommodates consumer interest. For this purpose, extensive reference has been made to the two most influential anti-cartel models—that of the United States and the European Union. The research also takes into account the extent to which the Competition Act, 2002 differs in its treatment of cartels from the erstwhile Monopolies and Restrictive Trade Practices Act, 1969. It examines the extent to which the norms evolved within the contract law framework inform the response to cartels.

Overview of the chapters

The book begins by analysing the etymology of cartels. Thus, the first chapter begins by defining cartels and distinguishing the cartel arrangement from other cooperative agreements. The focus then shifts to a historical overview of the socio-political context in which cartels came to be regarded as anti-competitive. The chapter then outlines the reason which necessitates a stringent approach in anti-cartel measures. Herein, the chapter elucidates the arguments of the lack of any pro-competitive outcome of a cartel arrangement. As cartels are anti-competitive agreements among competitors, their interaction with contract law also needs to be analysed. In particular, the role of the doctrine of restraint of trade in anti-cartel regulation is sought to be analysed. The doctrine of restraint of trade prohibits any agreement which restrains a party from carrying on his/her trade, profession, business or occupation. A cartel is an agreement in restraint of trade since it restricts a party from independently carrying on his/her trade. Hence, logically, cartel agreement appears susceptible to the applicability of the doctrine of restraint of trade. Further, from the consumer interests' perspective, it is necessary to understand the effectiveness of the doctrine as a private law remedy against cartels. The chapter concludes by reiterating the need to take a pro-consumer approach while dealing with cartels.

The treatment of cartels in the more advanced competition law regimes, viz., US and EU is undertaken in the second and third chapter of the book. The study of the US's anti-cartel law assumes importance because of its impact on the way similar laws have developed world wide including India.[27] Important principles like the *per se* rule, the *quick look rule of reason* and the *rule of reason* have all been the outcome of the debate over cartels in the US. Apart from these principles, the use of the leniency programme as an important anti-cartel measure makes the study anti-cartel law of the US important. In addition, the US has also pioneered private enforcement of the anti-cartel law.[28]

The second chapter begins by analysing the debate surrounding the interpretation of Section 1 of the Sherman Act. Through various case analyses, the chapter outlines the progression of the debate that marked the evolution of the approach of the US towards cartels. The focus is on the pro-consumer approach developed by the US Supreme Court in laying down the theoretical framework for anti-cartel measures. The chapter then identifies the federal authorities who are in charge of enforcing the anti-cartel law. Again, the chapter outlines the pro-consumer approach pursued by the authorities while enforcing the anti-cartel law. The third chapter then analyses the enforcement of the anti-cartel provisions within the EU. The chapter analyses the decisions of the EU Competition Commission and the European Court of Justice to establish the pro-consumer approach of the EU anti-cartel law. The chapter also analyses the rule applied by the EU authorities, viz., *per se* or *rule of reason* in enforcing anti-cartel measures. In addition, the chapter analyses the various EU Competition Commission's directives, reports and notifications to establish the pro-consumer approach.

The chapter also uses the example of crisis cartels to highlight the zero-tolerance approach of the EU towards cartels. The chapter further analyses the

---

[27] Dabbah (n 22) 227.

[28] Dabbah (n 22) 256.

EU leniency programme as well as the EU regulations relating to imposition of fines on cartels, in order to understand their deterrent effect on cartels. Finally, the chapter highlights the ongoing debate within the EU on private enforcement of competition rules. The debate reflects the effort taken by the EU to factor in consumer interest in the enforcement of the anti-cartel law. The fourth and fifth chapters focus on the main theme of the book. In other words, these two chapters provide comprehensive analyses of the anti-cartel law in India. They portray the two phases in the development of the anti-cartel law in India. The first phase, as detailed in chapter four, deals with the pre-liberalization era. It was the time when the Monopolies and Restrictive Trade Practices Act, 1969 used to deal with all types of anti-competitive conduct. The chapter analyses the debate preceding the enactment of the Monopolies and Restrictive Trade Practices Act, 1969 in order to contextualize the response of the Indian law towards cartels.

In the process, the chapter addresses the question as to whether cartels were regarded as injurious to consumer interest under the Monopolies and Restrictive Trade Practices Act, 1969. The chapter also identifies the nature of cartel activity prevalent in India. This is done to assess the extent of cartelization in the domestic market. The fifth chapter deals with the post-liberalization response towards cartels. The chapter analyses the development preceding the passage of the Competition Act, 2002. The purpose is to contextualize the reasons for repealing the Monopolies and Restrictive and Trade Practices Act, 1969. The chapter then analyses the anti-cartel provisions within the Competition Act, 2002. It compares and contrasts these provisions with the repealed Monopolies and Restrictive and Trade Practices Act, 1969. The purpose is to identify the change in approach towards cartels. The chapter then analyses the various decisions on cartels made by the Competition Commission of India. The purpose is to ascertain pro-consumer approach in the enforcement of the provisions. The last chapter of the book draws conclusions from the entire discussion relating to cartels, consumer interests and the approach of the anti-cartel provisions within Indian law. The book concludes with a series of suggestions regarding the manner in which anti-cartel provisions can better reflect a pro-consumer approach.

2 Cartels: Understanding the Sum and Substance of the Concept

Context

In order to understand why cartels are bad for consumer interests, it is important to first understand the concept of cartels. The conceptual analysis will also give an overview of the socio-political context in which cartels operate. The distinction between cartels and other horizontal agreements needs to be understood. The common law doctrine of restraint of trade is also to be analysed in order to understand the nature of restraint that cartels impose on their members. This will also help in recognizing the difference between freedom to trade versus freedom to contract. However, cartels challenge the efficacy of this doctrine. In addition, the doctrine is also inadequate to protect the consumer from the harm caused by cartels. The mapping of the drawbacks in the doctrine of restraint of trade vis-à-vis cartel conduct will help explain the same. The question of ancillary restraint as distinguished from naked restraint also gets addressed in the process. The argument that the co-conspirator is *in pari delicto*, i.e., both the parties to the agreement are equally guilty, has also been dealt with. Furthermore, the difficulty that a consumer faces in overcoming the problem of *privity of contract* while challenging a cartel activity is nuanced herein. In this context, the chapter highlights the arguments that justify a pro-consumer approach in anti-cartel regulation. By doing so, the chapter looks into both the legal and economic understanding of cartels.

Concept of cartels

The conceptual analysis of a cartel needs to be first done at the definitional level. This will help in distinguishing between cartels and other types of cooperative arrangements. *Oxford's Advanced Learner's Dictionary*[1] defines cartel as:

> 'a group of separate companies that agree to increase profits by fixing prices and not competing with each other'.

Black's Law Dictionary[2] defines a cartel as:

> '[a] combination of producers or sellers that join together to control a product's production or price; [a]n association of firms with common interests, seeking to prevent extreme or unfair competition, allocate markets, or share knowledge'.

Harding and Joshua state:

> 'The word cartel has a complex etymology. The basis of its modern usage is in the idea of a suspension of hostilities (or, by analogy, rivalry)'.[3]

They substantiate their observations by referring to the meaning of cartels, as understood by international lawyers, viz., 'the terms of agreement between belligerents for the exchange or ransom of prisoners'.[4] Similarly, the Organisation of Economic Co-operation and Development (OECD) defines cartels as:

> 'a formal agreement among firms in an oligopolistic industry. Cartel members may agree on such matters as prices, total industry output, market shares, allocation of customers, allocation of territories, bid rigging, establishment of common sales agencies and the division of profits or combination of these'.[5]

It is therefore evident that the concept of a cartel refers to an agreement of cooperation amongst firms with similar interest. It is primarily a case of firms combining to protect their mutual interests instead of competing with each other. In other words, it is a horizontal agreement among competitors to cooperate. The underlying assumption of such cooperative arrangements appears to be the fear of competition. According to Spar, cartels

> 'arise because the competitors realize that they can advance their own self-interest by working with each other. Together they can dominate the market and dictate the price that consumers must pay'.[6]

---

1 A.S. Hornby, *Oxford Advanced Learner's Dictionary of Current English,* 6th ed., (OUP, 2000).

2 Bryan A. Garner (ed.), *Black's Law Dictionary,* 8th ed.(Thomson West, 2004).

3 Harding and Joshua (n 11 of Chapter 1) 12.

4 *Id*

5 Available at http://stats.oecd.org/glossary/detail.asp?ID=3157 (accessed 20 August 2013).

6 Spar (n 8 of Chapter 1) 2.

As stated by Professor Robert Liefmann, cartels are 'voluntary agreements between-or … associations of independent enterprises of similar type to secure a monopoly of the market'.[7]

Although the concept of cartels have been prevalent for a long time, it was only in the beginning of the twentieth century, that the word 'cartel' came to be widely used in the English language. As Clark points out,

> 'The word "cartel" as currently used in the context of modern industrial economics, was not in general circulation in the English speaking world in 1890. The Oxford English Dictionary's earliest reference to the meaning of "cartel" in the industrial organization context is dated 1902'.[8]

Notwithstanding the late entry of the word 'cartel' in the English vocabulary, its meaning remains the same as that understood by the Germans. This is evident if one compares the definition of cartel as given by Professor Liefmann vis-à-vis the one given in the Oxford and Black's dictionaries. All these definitions describe cartels as cooperative arrangements to restrict or eliminate competition by monopolizing the market to maximize profits.[9]

Cartels in this sense are regarded as sinister or evil. In contrast to other cooperative arrangements like joint ventures, cartels are naked restraints. According to Monti, cartels

> 'restrict competition without producing any objective countervailing benefits…In cartel cases the positive side of the equation is zero'.[10]

It is therefore evident that all horizontal cooperative arrangement among competitors are not per se anti-competitive. According to Whish,

> 'there may be circumstances in which competitors cooperate with one another in a way that delivers economic benefits, not just for themselves, but for consumer welfare as well'.[11]

---

7 Robert Liefmann, *Cartels, Concerns and Trusts* (Batoche Books, 2001), 37.

8 Nolan Ezra Clark, 'Antitrust Comes full Circle: The Return to the Cartelization Standard', Vand. L. Rev. 1125, 1136 (1985): 38.

9 But See Liefmann (n 7) 39. [According to Prof Liefmann, cartels are not profit maximizing arrangements; they 'may be used not to increase the profits of their members but to prevent them falling below a certain level — a thing which may easily happen in open competition'.

10 Mario Monti, 'Why should we be concerned with cartels and collusive behaviour?', Third Nordic Competition Policy Conference on Fighting Cartels: Why and How, held in Stockholm on September 11–12, 2000, http://www.kkv.se/upload/filer/eng/publications/3rdnordic010412.pdf (accessed 10 October 2010)

11 Richard Whish,, 'Control of Cartels and other Anti-competitive Agreements' in VinodDhall, ed. (n 5 of Chapter 1) 55.

The distinction between anti-competitive cartels and pro-competitive cooperative arrangements thus is important. The term 'cartels', for the purpose of this book, thus refers to hard core anti-competitive horizontal agreements which neither benefit the public in general nor the consumers in particular. In fact, there are several horizontal cooperative arrangements which are either not regarded as anti-competitive or are specifically exempted from the operation of competition law. For example, state-promoted cooperative arrangements may be treated as an exception and thus excluded from the operation of the anti-cartel provision of the competition law. Crisis cartels or rationalization cartels are also examples of such exceptions. The EU has exempted R&D agreements and specialization agreements.[12] Similarly, the US grants anti-trust immunity to small business joint venture agreements with notification and prior approval of the Attorney General.[13]

Context and purpose of cartels: A historical overview

From the above discussion, it is evident that cartels are the opposite of competing business entities. It is therefore interesting to study the socio-political context which influences business rivals to form cartels. For this purpose, a historical review of three different jurisdictions will give an inkling of why cartels get formed and what possible reasons lead to their condemnation. We will first observe the US jurisdiction—a historical review of its cartelization will enable us to get an idea of the socio-political context that fostered and later denounced cartels. The other two jurisdictions to be studied will be Germany and Japan. These two countries were historically regarded as highly cartelized. It will thus be informative to examine the socio-political situations in these countries that encouraged cartelization.

---

[12] Specialization agreements are essentially agreements that are entered into for the purpose of rationalizing production. Thus, the parties agree to specialize in manufacture by allocating the manufacture of certain products among themselves. The justification given for exempting such horizontal arrangements is that it lowers prices. See (2011) OJ C 11/1 (the EU Competition Commission Guidelines on the applicability of Article 101 of the Treaty on the Functioning of the European Union to Horizontal Co-operation Agreements) http://eur-lex.europa.eu/LexUriServ/LexUriServ.do?uri=OJ:C:2011:011:0001:0072:EN:PDF (accessed 12 October 2011)

[13] R. ShyamKhemani, 'Applications of Competition Law: Exemptions and Exceptions', UNCTAD (2002), 15–16 http://www.unctad.org/EN/docs/ditcclpmisc25_en.pdf (accessed October 12, 2011). See also 'Statutory Provisions and Guidelines of the Antitrust Division', in *Antitrust Division Manual,* 4th ed. (US Department of Justice, Antitrust Division, 2008) II-20-II-21 http://www.justice.gov/atr/public/divisionmanual/atrdivman.pdf (accessed 12 October 2011)

US and cartels

In the US, a unique socio-political and economic scenario fashioned its response to the cartels. To begin with, historically the common law doctrine of restraint of trade, advocating freedom of the individual to trade, was exported by the English to their American colonies. Soon this belief in freedom to trade and free competition became part of the United States legal system.[14] There was an unwavering belief in the spirit of free competition within the Amercian society. Being largely a society of small entrepreneurs and farmers, there was an overwhelming aversion towards authoritarianism and trade monopolies.[15]

This belief in social, economic and political laissez-faire ensured that individuals competed freely and without restraint. There was thus an environment of freedom of contract, of trade and of unrestrained individual competition.[16] Competition and not cooperation was part of the American way of life. The increasing economic prosperity was accompanied by technological improvements and innovations. As a result, means of communications like railways and telegraph, witnessed dramatic improvements. These developments resulted in the opening of wider markets, creating a large single domestic market.[17]

The creation of a large domestic market resulted in dramatic developments in the way business was being done. Business enterprises, which were earlier operated by owners, were transformed into large corporate structures operated by managers. Consequent to this transformation, managers became the principle decision makers, thereby relegating the owners to the fringes of the corporate structures.[18] The new corporate structures emphasized the need for centrally managed corporations that would strive to achieve economies of scale.[19] Consequently, importance was given to the bigness

---

14 Mark R. Joelson, *An International Antitrust Primer: A Guide to the Operation of United States, European Union and Other Key Competition Laws in the Global Economy, 3rd ed.* (Kluwer Law International, 2006) 2.

15 Richard Hofstadter, 'What Happened to the Antitrust Movement?' in *The Political Economy of the Sherman Act: The First One Hundred Years,* ed. E. Thomas Sullivan, (OUP, 1991), 20–31.

16 *Id.*

17 Motta (n 10 of Chapter 1) 1–3.

18 Tony A. Freyer, *Regulating Big Business: Antitrust in Great Britain and America 1880–1990* (CUP, 1992), 1–10.

19 Economies of scale refer to the reduction in the per unit cost of manufacture through expansion of the scale of the firm's operation. For example, bulk purchase is said to be cost effective than single purchase.

of the corporation, capable of mass production. The incentive to achieve size was the huge domestic market that these corporations tried to capture through cut throat competition.

In their efforts to be ahead of the competition, the corporations followed an integrated business model. Thus, the giant corporations built efficient marketing organizations controlling their buying and selling, as well as controlling the means of production and channels of distribution. As a result, they slowly pushed small enterprises to the brink of extinction. Thus, there was a shift in American capitalism from that which emphasized individual entrepreneurial skills to that which emphasized managerial capitalism.[20] The growth of these big corporations led to their inevitable dominance of the market and the whittling down of free competition.

The first to undergo consolidation were the railways. It was believed that a large railway system will run more efficiently than small ones. Further, the cost of establishing and running the railways were so high that competition was felt to be ruinous to the interest of the industry.[21] Thus, economies of scale were the credo for running the railways. Nonetheless, the consolidation of the railways turned them into monopolies that rigged prices and charged the public heavily in order to ensure profitable returns on investments.[22] These tactics of the railways adversely affected the American farmers, among others—they had to pay excessive railroad freight charges for transporting their produce.[23]

As a result, organized movements started protesting the exploitative practices of the railways. These movements, collectively known as the Granger movement, primarily demanded government intervention through anti-monopoly legislations.[24] The creation of trusts finally caused the US Congress to legislatively intervene against cartels. As noted from the above review, the main problem facing the small entrepreneurs and the end user consumers in the US was that of monopoly of the giant corporations. One of the methods by which the corporations increased their size was through mergers.[25] In order to beat their competitors, the corporations indulged in price cutting.

---

20 See generally Butler Shaffer, *In Restraint of Trade: The Business Campaign against Competition 1918–1938* (Associated University Presses, 1997).

21 Charles R. Geisst, *Monopolies in America: Empire Builders & Their Enemies From Jay Gould to Bill Gates* (OUP, 2000), 15.

22 *Id.*,18.

23 *Id.*, 21.

24 *Id.*

25 *Id.*

As a result of excessive price cutting, it was felt that the industry which involved heavy capital investments and huge fixed costs will suffer. Therefore, the American corporations started entering into pooling agreements. Through these agreements, the minimum price was fixed so as to ensure profits. In the US, pooling agreements were not legally enforceable. Therefore, the corporations devised a new form of doing business in the guise of trusts.[26] John D. Rockefeller pioneered the idea of business trusts which were legally enforceable under the common law.[27] As a result, the Standard Oil Trust was created, controlling the stock certificates and voting rights of over forty companies.[28] Even before the formation of the Standard Oil Trust, Rockefeller had convinced other smaller oil refineries to enter into a cartel agreement with the railways. The purpose of such agreements understandably was to ensure that the oil companies had to pay the cheapest possible freight charges for transporting their goods. The formation of the Standard Oil Trust was the next logical step in this game of maximizing profits.[29]

These exploitative tactics of the big companies in collusion with the railways continued to hurt the farmers. Though the Granger movement had been successful in convincing certain state legislatures to regulate the railways, the trust remained in the loose. Finally, under pressure from the farmers, the federal government of the US passed the Interstate Commerce Act. However, it was not meant to regulate trusts.[30] The growing power of trusts was soon regarded as a threat to democracy and good governance. The legislators in the US realized that they had to act to deal with the trusts. The common law doctrine of restraint of trade, which had been successfully used against private restraints and other restrictive practices, could not counter the trusts. Hence in 1890, the Sherman Act, bearing the name of Senator John Sherman of Ohio, was passed. The Sherman Act till date is regarded as the 'Magna Carta' of all anti-trust movements.[31]

---

[26] William A. Wines, *Ethics, Law and Business* (Routledge, 2006), 235–236.

[27] A trust is a concept whereby the owner of the property, by agreement, transfers the legal title to a person called the trustee. The trustee is to manage the property for the benefit of a third party called the beneficiary. This kind of an agreement suited the interests of big corporations like Standard Oil as it helped in maximizing profits and reducing cut throat competition.

[28] See Paul S. Boyer and others, *The Enduring Vision: A History of the American People, 6th ed.* Vol.2 (Wadsworth Cengage Learning, 2010), 409.

[29] *Id.*, 409.

[30] The Interstate Commerce Act was passed to regulate the railways that were using discriminatory pricing tactics to exploit farmers, small entrepreneurs and end user consumers.

[31] See David J. Gerber, *Global Competition: Law, Markets and Globalization* (OUP, 2010), 123.

On reviewing the scenario in the US, it is evident that trusts were a greater problem in the US than cartels. While both cartels and trusts are examples of cooperation, they each have their distinctive features. As explained before, cartels are the most obvious forms of cooperation wherein markets and prices are fixed by agreement amongst the competing firms. In the case of business trusts, there is one shell company that decides on behalf of all the member companies. Nonetheless, since both cartels and trusts harmed the end user consumers, the farmers and the small entrepreneurs, there was a gradual realization to bring in regulations.[32] The size of the corporation was not the problem because they provided benefits to the larger public. The problem was with their exploitative tactics which overshadowed the benefits. On the whole, the unique socio-economic and political events within the US shaped its legislative attitude towards cooperation, competition and consumer interest.

Germany and cartels

Germany was known as the land of cartels, with a large number of industrial cartels in existence.[33] The country's fascination for cartels was a reaction to the disappointment with free competition. Like many other European countries, Germany witnessed excessive growth due to rapid industrialization. However, with the beginning of the economic depression in 1873, the euphoria associated with free competition fizzled out. The producers felt that unrestrained competition was not conducive for profitable business. It led to overproduction, low prices and low demand, giving a clouded view of competition.[34]

The rapid industrialization led to large-scale disruption of societal organizations. Artisans and agriculturists were faced with the prospect of large-scale displacements and disruptions. In addition, the industrialization in Germany witnessed the growth of large industries. These industries completely dominated and stifled the growth of small-scale industries. The large industries of Germany not only controlled factories, but also the whole process from production to the sale of the finished goods. Thus, the dominance of the big industry was all-prevailing and left no space for other smaller entrepreneurs.[35]

---

[32] See David J. Gerber, *Law and Competition in Twentieth Century Europe: Protection Prometheus* (OUP, 2003), 32–37.

[33] Liefmann (n 7) 60. [According to Prof Liefmann, the number of cartels existing in Germany in the year 1923 amounted to more than 1000.]

[34] Gerber (n 32) 70–71.

[35] *Id.*

As a result of these outcomes of free competition, there was a realization among the Germans, that competition had to be regulated. While the public regulation was expectedly done by the intervention of the government, private regulation took the form of cartels. In course of time, cartels became a permanent feature of German economy; they were prominent and prolific in their growth. The extensive growth of cartels in Germany was due to socio-political reasons that were unique to the country. One factor was the rapid growth of the German industry which resulted in expanded industrial capacity. This ensured that sharing markets helped the industries protect their profits while competition would have ruined them.[36]

Another factor was that the type of industry which gained prominence involved goods that was most suitable for cartelization, viz., coal, iron and chemicals. Further, since the industry was dependent on financing from banks, there was always a tendency by the banks to foster cartelization. This was done in order to ensure that the markets stabilized and chances of default in the payment of loans were reduced. Moreover, political reasons like protectionism and endeavour to attain military might helped the process of cartelization to attain permanency in Germany. Finally, the German ethos for cooperation helped the community at large to prefer cartels over competition, which symbolized individualism.[37]

Overall, the benefits from cartels were well expounded by the Germans who perceived them as natural and necessary. Cartels seemed to be the only answer to over-production and economic instability. Though the process of cartelization within the German economy led to increase in prices and hardship for the consumers, this was regarded as necessary in the larger public interest.[38]

The cultural quotient also conditioned the response of Germany towards cartels. They were regarded as symbols of cohesion and cooperation in German society. This was welcomed in an environment where excessive industrialization had led to social displacement.[39]

It was against this background that, in 1897, the legality of a cartel agreement was evaluated by the highest court of the German Empire, the Reichsgericht, in the case of *B. v. Saon Woodpulp Manufacturers Ass'n*.[40] This

---

36 Gerber (n 32) 74–75.

37 *Id.*, 76.

38 *Id.*, 88.

39 Harding and Joshua (n 11 of Chapter 1) 69.

40 See Ivo E. Schwartz, 'Antitrust Legislation and Policy in Germany: A Comparative Study', *U. Pa. L. Rev.* 617, 626 (1956–1957): 105.

case was heard under the then prevailing trade legislation, viz., the Trade Regulation Act of 1869. The Saxon wood pulp manufacturers had entered into a joint selling agreement. Accordingly, all the members had agreed to sell through a central sales agency. However, one of the members breached the agreement and was accordingly sued by the other members. In defense, the defendant challenged the validity of the agreement. The ground of challenge was that the agreement was in violation of the principle of the freedom of business as enshrined in the 1869 Act.[41]

The court applied the relevant provision of the 1869 Act which aimed (a) to protect the larger public interest and public welfare and (b) to protect the freedom of the individual to conduct his business in the manner he wants.[42] It applied the *rule of reason test* in determining whether *the object or the effect* of the cartel agreement defeated any of the stated aims of the 1869 Act. On the protection of the interest of society issue, in general, the court declared that a cartel formed to protect competitors from ruinous competition is reasonable and hence valid. The justification given was that ruinous competition will decrease the prices to an unreasonably low level thus driving out business persons as the industry could not then be profitably operated. This would not only harm the individual business person but also affect the economic health of the society at large. Hence, the court held that cartels were the best mechanism to avoid the catastrophic consequences of unreasonably low prices and wasteful over-production.[43]

On the individual's freedom to do business without contractual interference in the form of cartels, the court declared that such interference will be prohibited only if the cartel contract permanently destroyed the freedom of the member. In other words, if the cartel agreement placed temporary restrictions on the freedom of an individual to do business that will not *per se* void the cartel agreement. Interestingly, on the protection of public welfare issue, the court declared that if the *object or effect* of a cartel agreement is creation of monopoly and *exploitation of consumers*, then such agreements can be objected to under the 1869 Act and declared void.[44] Thus the court, to a limited extent, recognized the importance of consumer interest in regulation of cartels. Nonetheless, this decision of the court established

---

41 Harding and Joshua (n 11 of Chapter 1) 70.

42 See John M. Kleeberg, 'German Cartels: Myths and Realities' http://www.econ.barnard.columbia.edu/~econhist/papers/Kleeberg_German_Cartels.pdf (accessed 11 October 2011).

43 Schwartz (n 40) 627.

44 *Id.*, 628.

the *rule of reason* approach by which cartel contracts were valid unless they were proven to be unreasonable.[45]

The legal recognition of cartels added to the socio-political support existing for cartels. Nonetheless, there were groups that demanded some form of legislative intervention to deal with the abuses of cartels.[46] In the absence of any strong institutional support for consumer interests, it was left to the other stakeholders, viz., immediate purchasers from cartels, sellers to cartels and small- and medium-sized companies, to voice their concern about the dominance of cartels.[47] However, it was only after the end of the First World War that Germany enacted its competition law. The main reason behind the enactment was the high inflation faced by the German economy.[48] The other main reason was the tendency of cartels to pass on the hardship of the economic downturn to the consumer.[49]

The enactment was passed in the form of an Ordinance and titled *Ordinance against the Misuse of Economic Power*.[50] The legislative enactment of 1923, however, was a loose attempt at freeing the market from unproductive restraints with objective of increasing production.[51] The legislation created a special Cartel Court and insisted that

> '"Contracts and resolutions which involve undertakings in respect of production or marketing policy, or which prescribe conditions of trading, or methods of price fixing or the prices to be demanded (syndicates, cartels, conventions and the like agreements) must be in writing'.[52]

The special Cartel Court was created as an appellate body to which the parties to a cartel agreement as well as the parties challenging the validity of the cartel agreement could appeal. Thus for example under §4 of the 1923 Act it was stated that

> 'If a contract or resolution of the kind specified in §1, or a particular method of applying such a contract or resolution endangers the national economic system or the public interest, then the Reich Minister of

45 Kleeberg (n 42) 48.

46 Harding and Joshua (n 11 of Chapter 1) 72.

47 Harding and Joshua (n 11 of Chapter 1) 72

48 See Knut WofgangNorr, 'Franz Bohm and the Theory of the Private Law Society', in *The Theory of Capitalism in the German Economic Tradition-Historism, Ordo-Liberalism, Critical Theory, Solidarism*, ed. Peter Koslowski, (Springer, 2000), 153–154

49 *Id.*, 154

50 Liefmann (n 7) 213. The legislation was published on 2 November 1923.

51 Gerber (n 31) 124.

52 Liefmann (n 7) 214. [§1of the Ordinance]

> Economic Affairs (1) may apply to the Cartel Court for a declaration that the agreement is null and void or for an injunction restraining the parties from applying it…'.[53]

Thus, the Cartel Court was expected to review the validity of the cartel contract.

The reading of the various provisions of the 1923 legislation including the preamble gives a clear indication that the purpose of the legislative intervention was not to eliminate cartels. The only objective was to regulate the cartels in a manner that they can be better used for economic development. Thus, for example, in §4, it is further stated that

> '[T]he Reich Minister of Economic Affairs … (2) may order that any party to the [cartel] contract or resolution shall be free at any time without notice to denounce the contract or withdraw from the agreement; or (3) may order that a copy of all agreements and instructions which have been adopted for the purpose of giving effect to the contract or resolution shall be forwarded to him, and that such agreements or instructions shall not take effect until this has been done. It will be held that the public interest is endangered especially to an extent that is economically unjustifiable where production or marketing is restricted, or where prices are raised or prevented from falling, or, in case of prices based on an index number, where a "risk-premium" has been added to the price, or where there is inequitable interference with freedom of exchange through buyer's or seller's boycotts or through the fixing of differential prices or conditions of trading'.[54]

The presence of more than 3000 cartels after the enactment of the 1923 legislation further establishes that the cartel friendly environment was not affected.[55] Notwithstanding the semblance of cartel regulation that the 1923 legislation sought to introduce, the onset of the Great Depression in 1929 diluted the enactment.[56] With the onset of the Great Depression, the voices of the industrialists got stronger in their demand to weaken the 1923 regulation. The industrialists expectedly felt that the regulation was a nuisance. They received support in their criticism from lawyers, bureaucrats and economists.[57] One explanation for this alliance between the industry and other opinion makers appears to be the existing turmoil within German society. There was then prevailing in Germany widespread political disintegration. All the

---

53 *Id.*, 215.

54 *Id.*

55 *Id.*,141.

56 *Id.*, 137.

57 *Id.*, 144.

so-called opinion makers had to protect their *status quo* and their financial and intellectual interests. Industry provided the viable alternative for protecting this *status quo*. Hence, it was most beneficial to form an alliance with the industry.[58]

The political disintegration within Germany disenchanted the people—they had lost their faith in politicians and democratic ideals. The situation was ripe for the coming into power of Hitler. With the arrival of Hitler on the scene, the whole regulatory regime relating to cartels was overturned. The emphasis was now on mandatory cartelization and state control of the cartels. Thus, the process of cartelization reached its completion during the Nazi period. The end of the Second World War however witnessed a radical change in the competition law regime within Germany. To start with, Germany had to unconditionally surrender to the allied forces. The defeat in the Second World War finally resulted in the redrawing of the map of Germany—it was divided into West Germany and East Germany. West Germany was occupied by the US, the UK and France, while East Germany was solely under the control of Soviet Russia.[59] Expectedly, political ideologies played a major role in shaping Germany's response to cartels. The US took the lead and consequently determined the approach West Germany should have towards cartels.

Consequently, the emphasis was on complete ban of cartels without exception. This was intended to break the legal foundation on which cartels had been sustained in Germany. Meanwhile, the process of handing over the power back to the Germans, i.e., the West Germans started. One important condition that was especially laid down by the Western allies, primarily the US, was the enactment of a viable German competition law. This was agreed to and on January 1, 1958 the new German competition law was enacted.[60] The law did not completely prohibit cartels. Instead, it prohibited all agreements which did or intended to distort competition.[61] This prohibition was subject to a number of exemptions like those agreements intended to rationalize the concerned economic activity or which provided a fair share of benefits

---

[58] *Id.*, 145.

[59] See F.M. Scherer, *Competition Policies for an Integrated World Economy* (The Brookings Institution, 1994), 26.

[60] Harding and Joshua (n 11 of Chapter 1) 98–99.

[61] §1 of the Act against Restraints of Competition (hereinafter the Act). [Agreements between undertakings, decisions by associations of undertakings and concerted practices which have as their object or effect, the prevention, restriction or distortion of competition, shall be prohibited.]

to the consumers.[62] The re-unification of Germany on 3 October 1990[63] ensured that the 1958 Act was applied across the entire Germany. However, the original Act has over the years undergone several reforms in view of the requirement to comply with the EU competition law. Hence at present the amended Act is in tune with the provisions of the EU competition law.[64]

Japan and cartels

Another jurisdiction which evolved its own unique take on cartels is Japan. Historically, Japan followed a 'closed country' policy (*Sakoku*).[65] According to this policy, Japanese were to live in international isolation. All contact with the outside world, except for China and Korea, were prohibited. The only other country which was allowed to maintain trading relations with Japan was Holland. This policy of international isolation was followed because of the perceived threat from foreign religious practices, especially Christianity. Trade was the other reason for following a 'closed country' policy, as it was not considered worthwhile to exchange precious metals with expendable foreign goods. This policy of international isolation, which was in place for over two hundred years, starting from 1639 onwards, led Japan to devise its own development model which was driven by national identity. It also helped Japan escape the fate of colonialism, unlike many other Asian countries.[66]

Political developments at the international level however forced Japan to open up—mainly, the defeat of China by Great Britain in the Opium Wars.[67] As a consequence of this defeat, China was forced to provide greater market access to Britain and other Western countries through an arrangement called the treaty port system. This was primarily an instrument by which Britain and other Western powers enjoyed fixed low tariffs for the goods entering and leaving selected Chinese ports. Further, the treaty included a most

---

[62] See §2 and 3 of the Act.

[63] See the history of re-unification at http://74.125.153.132/search?q=cache:http://www.cybergerman.addr.com/east_west.html (accessed 4 October 2009).

[64] On April 20, 2009, the Act was further amended to bring it in tune with the EU competition law. The amended Act is available at http://www.bundeskartellamt.de/wEnglisch/download/pdf/GWB/110120_GWB_7_Novelle_E.pdf (accessed 11 October 2011)

[65] Marius B. Jansen, *The Making of Modern Japan* (Harvard University Press, 2002), 91–93.

[66] R. H. P. Mason and J. G. Caiger, *A History Of Japan* (Tuttle Publishing, 1997), 202–207. However there are historians who believe that the international seclusion was a tragedy for Japan and hence disastrous. For a detailed discussion see *Id* at 94–95.

[67] The Opium Wars started because of the Chinese protest over the illegal trading of opium by British merchants. It lasted from 1839 to 1842 and 1856 to 1860.

favoured nation clause by which a benefit received by one Western power was to be automatically extended to other Western countries. As a result of these forced concessions by China to the Western powers, there were far more ships in the Japanese waters, then ever before. Consequently, Western powers like Britain, Russia, France and the US, had the means to militarily intervene in Japan.[68]

The Western powers however preferred to request rather than wage war in order to convince Japan to open up its markets. The Japanese ruler knew that they had little option but to bow down to the foreign pressure. It was however left to the US to force the Japanese to open up their markets and subsequently provide access to other western powers.[69] Soon, the Japanese were forced to sign oppressive treaties with the Western powers that not only opened up Japan but also erased its policy of international isolation.[70] These treaties caused a lot of discontentment among the Japanese for they felt that their sovereignty had been undermined. The domestic dissensions led to a regime change and ultimately to a change in the economic policy.[71] One of the tasks that the new regime undertook was to re-negotiate the oppressive treaties on more equitable terms. This was the beginning of the modernization of Japan and the introduction of a market economy. However, Japan never endorsed the concept of 'laissez faire' or freedom of trade or contract, as understood by the common law. There, thus, continued state intervention in business transactions as well as adoption of nationalistic policies.[72] As a consequence, monopoly and combinations were encouraged over free market competition.

The adoption of measures like tariff protection, subsidies to domestic industries and other such schemes was favoured by both the private enterprise and the government. Further, Japanese businessmen strongly believed that cooperative agreements and business associations were the best way of ensuring economic development. The concept of free trade, according to the Japanese, was not suited for their society. Hence, the Japanese government

---

68 W. G. Beasley, *The Rise of Modern Japan: Political, Economic, and Social Change since 1850,* 3rd ed. (Palgrave Macmillan, 2000), 26–27.

69 W.G. Beasley, 'The Foreign Threat and the Opening up of Ports', in *The Cambridge History of Japan, Vol. 5: The Nineteenth Century,* eds. John W. Hall, Marius B. Jansen, Madoka Kanai & Denis Twitchett (CUP, 1996), 267–269.

70 Conrad Totman, *A History of Japan* (Blackwell Publishers, 2001), 279–282.

71 Richard Sims, *Japanese Political History since the Meiji Renovation 1868–2000* (Palgrave Macmillan, 2001), 1–2.

72 Harald Baum and Eiji Takahashi, 'Commercial and Corporate Law in Japan: Legal and Economic Developments after 1868', in *History of Law in Japan since 1868,* ed. Wilhelm Rohl, (Brill, 2005), 337–338.

introduced regulatory measures to restrict competition. Japan further ensured that while Western technology and know-how was being used in the development of its industries, the domestic market remained protected from foreign competition.[73] The Japanese government thus favoured, encouraged and enforced cartel agreements. The pro-cartel policy of the Japanese suited their militaristic endeavours and established them as an imperial power.[74]

Japan thus developed, through cartels, a unique model of economic development which continued till the end of the Second World War.[75] After the war, however, Japan was forced to re-orient its economic policies from that of cooperation to that of competition, as dictated by the US.[76] The changes in the economic policy were not supported by the Japanese, as they felt that the idea of free competition was a luxury for rich nations and detrimental to the need of a resource-scarce country like Japan.[77] Nonetheless, change was forced upon Japan with the dissolution of Zaibatsu[78] and the dismantling of various cartels. The aim of the post-war efforts of the US was to 'democratize' the Japanese economy by ensuring deconcentration of the Japanese economy. They firmly believed that, overseas, big was bad and that the Japanese business organizations were responsible for Japan's military adventures.[79] As a result, they forced the Japanese government to enact anti-monopoly legislation patterned along the lines of their own anti-trust law.[80]

---

73 B.K. Marshall, 'Private Entrepreneurs and the Meiji Government', in *Meiji Japan: Political, Economic and Social History, 1868–1912*, ed. Peter F. Kornicki (Routledge, 1998), 281–294.

74 Mansel G. Blackford, *The Rise of Modern Business in Great Britain, The United States, and Japan,* 2nd ed. (UNC Press, 1998), 158.

75 Tony A. Freyer, *Antitrust and Global Capitalism 1930–2004* (CUP, 2009), 100–101.

76 TakemaeEiji, *The Allied Occupation of Japan* (Continuum International Publishing Group, 2002), 307.

77 Wyatt Wells, *Antitrust and the Formation of the Postwar World* (Columbia University Press, 2002), 175–176.

78 It was a tightly knit family-owned group of companies. For details of the organizational structure of Zaibatsu, see generally, Hiroyuki Odagiri, *Growth through Competition, Competition through Growth; Strategic Management and the Economy in Japan* (OUP, 2002). After the dissolution of Zaibatsu under American pressure, Japanese economy saw the growth of *Keiretsu.* These are horizontal groupings of companies who organize for the purpose of cooperating with each other and own shares of each other's stock. Hence the *Keiretsu* can be regarded as a Japanese form of cartel. See Gregory K. Bader, 'The Keiretsu Distribution System of Japan: Its Steadfast Existence despite Heightened Foreign and Domestic Pressure for Dissolution', *Cornell Int'l L.J.* 365, 368–372 (1994): 27.

79 See Yoshiro Miwa and J. Mark Ramseyer, 'Does Ownership Matter? Evidence from the Zaibatsu Dissolution Program', (2001), http://papers.ssrn.com/sol3/papers.cfm?abstract_id=262440 (accessed 10 August 2009).

80 Blackford (n 74) 179.

Things however changed with the beginning of the Cold War era between the US and the Communist Bloc led by the USSR. The US realized that an economically strong Japan will prove to be a useful ally against the Communist Bloc.[81] As a result, the anti-monopoly programmes were diluted. Rationalization cartels were permitted in 'depressed industries' like coal mining, textiles, etc., to counter excessive competition.[82] Nonetheless, the enactment of anti-monopoly legislation led the Japanese economy to imbibe the principles of competition. However, strict compliance with unrestrained competition could never have been possible for Japan. This is so because of the political realities in which Japan was placed. With most Asian countries limiting their trade with Japan, post-Second World War Japan had to survive economically and therefore cooperation rather than competition was preferred.[83] By the 1990s, Japan transformed itself from an economically struggling country to a developed country.

However, Japanese consumers felt that the cartel regulating policy was largely producer driven rather than consumer driven. As a consequence of the growing dissatisfaction of the Japanese consumer, there was a re-orientation in the Japanese policy and emphasis was laid on competition-based deregulation.[84] Consequently, promotion of cartels was replaced by stricter enforcement of anti-monopoly principles.[85] The enforcement, however, has been primarily driven by Japan's domestic interests leading to the accusations by Western scholars that Japan has failed to enforce the competition principle in its true spirit.[86] In other words, Japanese anti-monopoly legislation continues to be far less effective than the anti-trust laws of the US. The main reasons, according to the critics, are weak enforcement and penalty measures provided within the anti-monopoly legislation.[87] Notwithstanding these

---

[81] See Alex Y. Seita, Jiro Tamura, 'The Historical Background of Japan's Antimonopoly Law', *U. Ill. L. Rev.* 115, 185 (1994).

[82] Blackford (n 74) 183.

[83] Blackford (n 74) 186.

[84] See generally AkinoriUesugi, 'How Japan is Tackling Enforcement Activities against Cartels' *Geo. Mason L. Rev.* 349 (2005): 13.

[85] Jacqueline Bos, 'Antitrust Treatment of Cartels: A Comparative Survey of Competition Law Exemptions in the United States, the European Union, Australia and Japan', Wash. U. Global Stud. L. Rev. 415, 424, (2002): 1. See also Toshiaki Takigawa, 'The Prospect of Antitrust Law and Policy in the Twenty-First Century: In Reference to the Japanese Antimonopoly Law and Japan Fair Trade Commission', *Wash. U. Global Stud. L. Rev.* 2 (2002): 1.

[86] See generally James D. Fry, 'Struggling to Teethe: Japan's Antitrust Enforcement Regime', *Law &Pol'y Int'l Bus.* 825 (2001): 32.

[87] *Id.,* 312–313.

criticisms, the Japanese continue to implement the principles of competition law according to their domestic economic requirements and interests.[88]

Doctrine of restraint of trade and cartels: A study

While the historical survey of cartels reveals that cartel regulation was determined by each jurisdiction's domestic compulsions, the common law traditionally resorted to the doctrine of restraint of trade to deal with these restrictive arrangements. Hence, in comparing and contrasting the doctrine with the cartels, it would be first relevant to do a conceptual analysis of the doctrine. This would help in understanding the inherent nature of the doctrine. Further, it will also help in nuancing the difference in the Indian and the common law approaches. Finally, it will also explain the futility of using this doctrine to challenge the validity of a cartel agreement.

Doctrine of restraint of trade: The concept

The doctrine of restraint of trade is defined in section 27 of the Indian Contract Act, 1872 (hereinafter called the Act).[89] The term 'restraint of trade' means to restrict the choices of an individual to engage in the trade, occupation or profession of one's own liking. For example, such restrictions are imposed by the legislative enactments,[90] in furtherance to the state's public policy concerns. However, when the restrictions on trade are sought to

---

88 See Hiroshi Iyori, 'A Comparison of US–Japan Antitrust Law: Looking at the International Harmonization of Competition Law', *Pac. Rim L.* (1995): 4 and *Pol'y J.* 59, 90–91. See also Ki Jong Lee, 'Culture and Competition: National and Regional Levels', *Loy. Consumer L. Rev.* 33(2008): 21.

89 The Indian Contract Act, section 27 [Agreement in restraint of trade, void: Every agreement by which any one is restrained from exercising a lawful profession, trade or business of any kind, is to that extent void.]

90 For example, Article 19 (g) of the Constitution of India, 1950 guarantees the fundamental right to 'practice any profession, or to carry on any occupation, trade or business'. However, this right is subject to Article 19 (6) which makes it clear that ['Nothing in sub-clause (g) of the said clause shall affect the operation of any existing law in so far as it imposes, or prevents the State from making any law imposing, in the interests of the general public, reasonable restrictions on the exercise of the rights conferred by the said sub-clause, and, in particular, [nothing in the said sub-clause shall affect the operation of any existing law in so far as it relates to, or prevents the State from making any law relating to (i) the professional or technical qualifications necessary for practicing any profession or carrying on any occupation, trade or business, or (ii) the carrying on by the State, or by a corporation owned or controlled by the State, of any trade, business, industry or service, whether to the exclusion, complete or partial, of citizens or otherwise'].

be imposed through private agreements, it is problematic. The reason is that such agreements may be the result of unequal bargaining power.[91] In terms of contract, a bargain means the price one pays for receiving performance from the other party to the contract.[92] However, when the party is forced to pay a price due to lack of choice, it implies an unequal bargaining power between the parties to the contract. For example, between the employer A and the employee B, greater bargaining power is presumed to be with A. This presumption is based on the choices available to each individual. The employer is the job provider and has the luxury to impose conditions on the employee who is seeking employment.[93] The existence of unequal bargaining power among the parties to contract defeats the requirement of free consent, cherished by the traditional contract law.[94] In other words, though there is an apparent free consent, the same gets skewed substantively due to lack of choices.

Common law and section 27 of the Indian Contract Act: The contrast

The concern regarding unequal bargaining is reflected in the *Act* which declares all agreements in restraint of trade as *per se void.* This approach is based on the traditional English law that also regarded all agreements in restraint of trade as *per se* void. The *per se* void approach in the English law was enforced so stringently that infringement of the same attracted imprisonment for persons who sought to enforce such restrictive agreements.[95] Nonetheless, this policy of the English law of rendering such contracts as *per se* void threatened

---

91 On the importance of bargain principle within the law of contract, see generally Melvin Aron Eisenberg, 'The Bargain Principle and its Limits', *HLR* 741 (1982): 95.

92 *Id.* at 742.

93 One may counter this argument by referring to the high attrition rate in the IT sector. However, even in those sectors where the workforce has flexibility in movement among organizations, the service conditions are determined by their prospective employers. On the point of inequality between the employer and the employee, see for example, *Central Inland Water Transport Corpn Ltdv BrojoNathGanguly*, AIR 1986 SC 1571, *SCC* 156 (1986): 3.

94 According to the classical theory of contract, the law of contract is regarded as an instrument for the implementation of a basic moral principle that autonomous individuals can choose to impose obligations on themselves by an exercise of free will which the State and its courts are bound to respect. See P.S. Atiyah, 'Contract as Promise: A Theory of Contractual Obligation by Charles Fried', *HLR* 509 (1981): 95.

95 See for example, G.H. Treitel, *The Law of Contract*, 10th ed. (Sweet & Maxwell, 1999), 415.

existing commercial and economic structures.[96] For this reason the *per se* void rule under the English law was replaced with the rule of *per se* valid. The *per se* valid rule implied that a contract in restraint of trade was *per se* valid, provided it was formed with adequate consideration and the restraint was not effective throughout the country, but limited within a specified region.[97] This qualified approval of the restraint of trade covenant was introduced in the *Mitchel* case[98] by Chief Justice Parker. He classified restraints as general and partial/particular.[99] General restraints would disallow a person from carrying trade anywhere in the country. On the other hand, partial restraint would only prevent trading in a certain specified territory, leaving the other regions of the country wide open.

According to Chief Justice Parker, all general restraints are *per se void* for they create monopoly. On the other hand, partial or particular restraints, supported by adequate consideration do not create monopoly.[100] In giving his reasons for declaring general restraints void *per se*, Chief Justice Parker by implication refers to the inequality of bargaining power. He uses the example of a master who can force the apprentice to sign non-competing bonds.[101] In other words, according to him, general restraints are naked restraints with no other purpose. On the contrary, in partial/particular restraints, restraint is ancillary, as their main purpose is to further the larger interest of society and the individual. He states that

> 'there may happen instances wherein they may be useful and beneficial, as to prevent a town from being overstocked with any particular trade, or in the case of an old man finding himself in such circumstances either of

---

96 Thus it would be difficult for a master to employ and train an apprentice if he could not impose a non-competing clause on the apprentice after the apprenticeship is over. Similarly, it would be difficult for a businessman to sell his business if after the sale he decides to compete with the purchaser—there is no means of restraining such competition.

97 The rule of *per se valid* was established by the decision of *Mitchel v. Reynolds*, [1558-1774] All ER Rep 26. This case was about a lease of bakery business by the defendant to the plaintiff for a term of five years. The defendant covenanted that he would not carry on the trade of a baker for the said term, within the concerned area. Furthermore, in case of a breach of this covenant he would compensate the plaintiff. There was a breach by the defendant of this undertaking and the plaintiff sought to enforce the covenant. The defendant challenged the covenant as *per se* void being in restraint of trade.

98 *Id.*

99 *Id.*, 30.

100 *Id.* This is subject to the qualification that the partial restraint should not be unreasonable, i.e., more than what is required to promote the interest of the party in whose favour the restraint is.

101 *Id.*,31.

> body or mind that he is likely to be a loser by continuing his trade, it will be better for him to part with it for a consideration, that by selling his custom he may procure to himself a livelihood which he might probably have lost by trading longer'.[102]

This analysis by Chief Justice Parker consequently provides an explanation as to why it became necessary in English law to shift the emphasis from declaring all restraints as *per se void* to all restraints being *per se valid* provided they are ancillary in nature.

The approach of the *per se* valid rule was subsequently modified by the courts of England in the case of *Thorsten Nordenfelt v The Maxim Nordenfelt Guns and Ammunition Company, Limited*[103]. In this case, the appellant (original defendant) had a flourishing business of guns and ammunitions. In 1886, he sold off the same to a company for a large sum. The business of this company was taken over by the respondents (original plaintiff) in the year 1888. Accordingly, the respondents entered into an agreement with the appellant, which was in substitution of the agreement between the appellant and the previous company. The new agreement contained the following clause:

> 'The said Thorsten Nordenfelt shall not, during the term of twenty-five years from the date of the incorporation of the company, if the company should so long continue to carry on business, engage, except on behalf of the company, either directly or indirectly in the trade or business of a manufacturer of the guns, gun-mountings, or carriages, gun-powder, explosives, or ammunition, or in any business competing or liable to compete in any way with that for the time being carried on by the company; provided that such restriction shall not apply to explosives other than gunpowder, or to subaqueous or submarine boats or torpedoes, or castings or forgings of steel or iron, or alloys of iron or of copper…'.[104]

Mr Nordenfelt challenged the validity of the covenant alleging that it was a covenant in restraint of trade which is unlimited in space. Thus, he was challenging the covenant on the ground that it was a general restraint of trade. In the lower court, Justice Romer declared that the covenant was

---

102 *Id.*

103 [1894] A.C. 535.

104 *Maxim Nordenfelt Guns and Ammunition Company v. Nordenfelt* [1893] 1 Ch. 630, 633–634.

unreasonable and thus void because the restraint was unlimited as to space.[105] In the Court of Appeal, this decision was reversed.

The Court of Appeal unanimously held that though the distinction between general and partial restraints holds true, there can be exceptional situations where a general restraint will be held valid. The underlying test that needs to be applied to assess the validity of a general restraint is whether the same is in consonance with public policy and is reasonable. In other words, the Court of Appeal established a two-tiered test to assess the validity of a restraint of trade doctrine, viz., public policy and reasonableness. In order to satisfy both these conditions, the restraint should be

> 'only to afford a fair protection to the interests of the party in favour of whom it is given, and not so large as to interfere with the interests of the public…'.[106]

According to the Court of Appeal, the said covenant, satisfied these two conditions.[107]

The House of Lords affirmed the decision of the Court of Appeal and emphatically dismissed the distinction between partial and general restraints stating that with the development of trade and commerce

> 'the time for a new departure has arisen and that it should be now authoritatively decided that there should be no difference in the legal considerations which would invalidate an agreement whether in general or partial restraint of trading'.[108]

Accordingly, the House of Lords declared that the only test to evaluate the validity of a restraint of trade clause will be the test of reasonableness. The House of Lords echoed the two-tiered approach developed by the Court of Appeal and stated that a restraint of trade clause should be

> 'reasonable, that is, in reference to the interests of the parties concerned and reasonable in reference to the interests of the public, so framed and so guarded as to afford adequate protection to the party in whose favour it is imposed, while at the same time it is in no way injurious to the public'.[109]

---

105 *Maxim Nordenfelt v. Nordenfelt* (n 103) 637–638.

106 *Id.*, 673.

107 One of the main reasons for upholding the validity of the covenant, according to the Court of Appeal, was that the restriction applied to only one type of business carried on by the defendant, viz., guns and ammunitions. The defendant was, as per the Court of Appeal, free to trade in other types of businesses like submarines, torpedoes etc.

108 [1894] A.C. (n 103) 575, as per Lord Morris.

109 *Id.*, 565, as per Lord Macnaghten.

The *Nordenfelt* case thus turned the tide of the English law towards the test of reasonableness. The *Act* though retained the *per se* void approach towards a restraint of trade clause. Further, according to the *Act,* if there is a contract which contains a clause that is restrictive in nature, the offending clause shall be struck down. The remaining parts of such a contract will continue to be enforceable. This is evident from the reading of section 27 which renders only the restrictive clause void and not the whole contract.[110]

The exception, as appears from the language of section 27, is when a person sells the good will of his business.[111] The seller here agrees with the purchaser not to compete with him. In other words, there is a restraint imposed on the seller that he shall not compete with the purchaser under the same name and in the same business, within a specified area. Such agreements in restraint of trade are enforceable provided they are reasonable. The Supreme Court of India has reiterated the *per se void* approach in *Superintendence Company of India (P) Ltd. v Sh. Krishan Murgai.*[112] In this case, Justice Sen emphatically declared that

> 'Neither the test of reasonableness nor the principle that the restraint being partial was reasonable are applicable to a case governed by section 27 of the Contract Act, unless it falls within Exception 1'.[113]

Similarly, in *Gujarat Bottling Co. Ltd. and others v. Coca Cola Co and others*[114], it was unanimously declared by the Supreme court that

> 'an enquiry into reasonableness of the restraint is not envisaged by section 27...instead of being required to consider two questions as in England, the courts in India have only to consider the question whether the contract is or is not in restraint of trade'.[115]

---

[110] This is however subject to the doctrine of severability according to which only if the rest of the contract can be severed from the offending clause and still be enforced, will the contract be valid. In the restraint of trade cases, it is possible to severe the offending clause from the rest of the contract.

[111] Indian Contract Act, 1872, section 27 Exception 1: Exception 1 [Saving of agreement not to carry on business of which goodwill is sold. One who sells the goodwill of a business may agree with the buyer to refrain from carrying on a similar business, within specified local limits, so long as the buyer, or any person deriving title to the goodwill from him, carries on a like business therein, provided that such limits appear to the court reasonable, regard being had to the nature of the business.]

[112] MANU/SC/0457/1980.

[113] *Id.,* para 51.

[114] (1995) 5 SCC 545.

[115] *Id.,* para 24.

Doctrine and cartel: Identifying the fault line

Notwithstanding the differences between the English law and the Indian law, the effectiveness of the doctrine of restraint of trade from the perspective of anti-cartel regulation needs to be analysed. The first task thus is to assess the effectiveness of the doctrine when used by a cartelist to challenge the validity of a cartel agreement. As explained above, the clause in restraint of trade is incorporated by the parties to the agreement. The purpose of such a clause is that one of the parties agrees, in lieu of consideration, not to compete with the other party. As was explained in the above discussed cases, the party in whose favour the covenant is given wants to gain maximum benefit from the transaction. Thus, if it is a case of sale of goodwill, the seller covenants not to compete so as to give maximum commercial advantage to the buyer. The same logic applies in any other commercial transaction wherein the non-competing clause adds value to the product.

The problem occurs when the restrictive covenant turns out to be so oppressive that it deprives the covenantor of any benefit. This is so because the law needs to balance between freedom to trade and freedom to contract. While parties are free to contract on any term they want, they cannot usurp others' freedom to trade . Under the Indian law, once it is established that the restrictive clause is such that it operates beyond the period of contract, the same is proven to be in restraint of trade. Hence, by applying the doctrine of restraint of trade, the contract law seeks to confine non-competing covenants to the tenure of the contract and not beyond. Further, since the non-competing clause is part of the contract, any challenge to its validity will have to come from the party to the contract. This is premised on the concept of privity by which only the parties to the contract can sue or be sued. Further, while evaluating the challenge of restraint of trade, the interest of the claimant is of primary concern. The court, like in any other matter relating to contracts, looks into the nature of the clause and is not required to evaluate the competitive process or market structure. The court will rather evaluate issues like quality of consent and bargaining power.

As explained before, a cartel is an agreement between competitors not to compete. Hence in this regard it is also an agreement in restraint of trade. As with any other contract, here too the restrictions are agreed upon in lieu of considerations like sharing of the market, fixing prices, quota restrictions etc. Thus, the doctrine of restraint of trade can be useful if a party to such a cartel agreement wants to challenge the cartel contract as in restraint of trade. The party though, under section 27, will have to prove that the agreement imposes restrictions beyond the period of contract. However, in view of the fact that the Competition Act, 2002 has prohibited cartels, a party challenging a cartel agreement using the doctrine of restraint of trade can face a serious challenge. This is so because under section 23 an agreement whose consideration or object is illegal is *void ab-initio.*[116] Moreover, any party to such an agreement will be held to be *in pari delicto.*[117]

Thus. for a party challenging the validity of a cartel agreement on the basis of restraint of trade doctrine, the argument of *in pari delicto* can defeat the claim. For example, in *Bernard Crehan v Inntrepreneur Pub Company CPC,*[118] the plaintiff claimed damages for losses suffered due to an anti-competitive agreement, to which he was a party.[119] The claim was filed under Article 101 (1) of the EU competition law,[120] claiming a violation of the competition law

---

[116] Indian Contract Act, section 23 [What considerations and objects are lawful, and what not: The consideration or object of an agreement is lawful, unless: It is forbidden by law, or is of such a nature that, if permitted, it would defeat the provisions of any law; or is fraudulent; or involves or implies, injury to the person or property of another; or the Court regards it as immoral, or opposed to public policy. In each of these cases, the consideration or object of an agreement is said to be unlawful. Every agreement of which the object or consideration is unlawful is void.]

[117] See for example, *Kuju Collieries Ltd v. Jharkhand Mines Ltd and others* AIR 1974 SC 1892, 1894, para 8

[118] [2004] EWCA Civ. 637.

[119] The plaintiff, Mr Crehan, had taken on lease two pubs from the defendant. As part of the lease agreement, it was made mandatory that Mr Crehan will have to buy beers from Courage Ltd., a beer company. Courage Ltd. was also a share holder in the defendant's company. Mr Crehan suffered immense financial loss in the course of his pub business. Consequently, he found it difficult to pay for the purchases of beer and other goods, made from Courage Ltd. Accordingly, Courage Ltd sued him, to which he counter-claimed. In his counter-claim, Mr Crehan challenged the beer tie clause in the lease agreement as anti-competitive. He also filed for damages.

[120] Article 101 (1) provides: The following shall be prohibited as incompatible with the internal market: All agreements between undertakings, decisions by associations of undertakings and concerted practices which may affect trade between Member States and which have as their object or effect, the prevention, restriction or distortion of competition within the common market, and in particular those which:

(a) directly or indirectly fix purchase or selling prices or any other trading conditions;

(b) limit or control production, markets, technical development, or investment;

(c) share markets or sources of supply;

(d) apply dissimilar conditions to equivalent transactions with other trading parties, thereby placing them at a competitive disadvantage;

(e) make the conclusion of contracts subject to acceptance by the other parties of supplementary obligations which by their nature or according to commercial usage, have no connection with the subject of such contracts.

provisions. The Court of Appeal referred the matter to the European Court of Justice to determine whether a party to an anti-competitive agreement can claim damages as a result of such an agreement. In other words, the Court of Appeal wanted the European Court of Justice to determine whether the rule of *in pari delicto* will apply in such a situation. Accordingly, the European Court of Justice in *Courage v Crehan*[121] noted that

> 'any individual can rely on a breach of [Article 101(1)] of the Treaty before a national court even where he is a party to a contract that is liable to restrict or distort competition within the meaning of that provision'.[122]

However, the European Court of Justice ruled that entitlement to damages of a person party to an anti-competitive agreement can be debarred if such a claimant or plaintiff is 'found to bear significant responsibility for the distortion of competition…'.[123] The European Court of Justice thus emphasized on the bargaining capability of the claimant. Hence, if the claimant was capable of exercising choices but nonetheless willingly participated in the anti-competitive agreement, he or she would be rightly precluded from taking advantage of his or her own illegality. In other words, the European Court of Justice applied the rule of *in pari delicto*.

On the other hand, if the claimant/plaintiff is found to be of weaker bargaining power and hence was coerced to abide by the anti-competitive agreement, then such a person, according to the European Court of Justice, was entitled to claim damages.[124] The Court of Appeal applied this analysis to the case and found for the plaintiff, declaring that

> '[t]here was no equality of bargaining power in any real sense. Mr. Crehan was in a markedly weaker position than Inntrepreneur: if he wanted to lease the pubs he had to agree to the tie. In practice Inntrepreneur imposed the tie on him'.[125]

Interestingly, if such a question relating to the applicability of the rule of *in pari delicto* comes before Indian courts, they too will be convinced of the inequality of the bargaining power argument. However, considering the typology of cartels (as discussed later in the second chapter), bargaining issues may not always come to the rescue. Challenging a cartel agreement

[121] Case C-453/99, [2001] ECR I-6297.
[122] *Id.*, para 24.
[123] *Id.*, para 31.
[124] *Id.*, para 33.
[125] [2004] EWCA (n 118) 153.

on the basis of restraint of trade doctrine is more likely to be hit by the applicability of *in pari delicto* then saved by the argument of inequality of bargaining power.

Consumers, cartels and the doctrine of restraint of trade: The problem of privity

The discussion so far explained the limitation of the doctrine for the purpose of challenging the validity of a cartel agreement. The usefulness of the doctrine in promoting consumer interests vis-à-vis cartels also needs to be studied. A consumer challenging a cartel on the basis of the doctrine of restraint of trade would be non-suited on the basis of privity of contract. As explained before, this concept implies that no stranger can either sue or be sued on a contract. The consumer in a cartel scenario is the stranger as he or she is not a party to the cartel agreement. The utility of the doctrine as a contract law remedy against cartels is thus negated. The *Mogul Steamship* case will help highlight these limitations.[126] In this case, the defendants, who were owners of ships, entered into an agreement amongst themselves, for the purpose of securing the shipping trade exclusively for themselves.

In order to successfully enforce the agreement, the defendants promised rebates to those customers who would commit to ship their freight exclusively with the defendant's ships. Further, they threatened to ban all firms/customers who would ship their freight with non-members. In other words, all firms shipping their freight with ships not owned by the defendants were to face collective boycott by the defendants for the purpose of future shipments. The agreement also provided regulation of the number of ships to be sent to ports for loading the cargo. Finally, the agreement also provided measures for dividing the cargo amongst the members and fixing freight charges. The plaintiffs were also ship owners who were interested in carrying their business in the same routes as that of the defendant. However, they were excluded by the defendant from their association and consequently they decided to openly compete with the defendants for the cargo and the customer.[127]

The defendants in order to meet the challenge of competition posed by the plaintiffs indulged in predatory pricing of freight charges. In other words, the defendants charged excessively low freight rates, which forced the plaintiffs to

---

[126] *The Mogul Steamship Company Limited v McGregor, Gow, & Co., and Others* [1892] A.C. 25.

[127] *Id.*, 27–29

match the price war. The same however made it impossible for the plaintiffs to carry on their business profitably. Further, the defendants threatened to dismiss any agent who acted for the plaintiffs in helping them load cargo.[128] The plaintiff accordingly sued the defendants alleging a conspiracy to injure them. In effect, the plaintiff was claiming damages for tort of conspiracy. A tort of conspiracy is defined as an agreement between two or more persons to do an unlawful act or to do a lawful act by unlawful means, causing damage to the plaintiff.[129] It is important to note that a tort of conspiracy comprises those acts which if done by an individual will not amount to any breach of legal duty, whereas if done in combination will amount to an unlawful act.[130]

For example, instructions by a combination of two or more persons to dockyard workers to refuse to handle goods imported by the plaintiff were alleged to be a conspiracy.[131] This could not be so alleged if the same instruction was given by an individual. For an individual to be liable for such instructions, it has to be shown that the individual has procured the breach of contract by so instructing the dock workers. This is so because a persuasion or inducement on its own does not amount to a breach of legal duty and hence a tort. However, acts done to induce a person to breach contract is a breach of legal duty, as there is a duty on the part of a third party not to interfere with the performance of a contract. Hence, in the Mogul case, the plaintiff relied on this tort to claim that acts of fixing freight price, dividing cargo, regulating the number of ship and predatory pricing/underbidding the plaintiff, were a conspiracy to injure the plaintiffs in their trade.

In addition, the plaintiff also claimed that as the association of the defendant was an agreement in restraint of trade, it was illegal and thus void. However, this argument based on restraint of trade was taken primarily to establish the main allegation of tort of conspiracy. As noted above, the plaintiffs could not have challenged the validity of the defendant's agreement as they were not privy to the same. Nonetheless, for establishing the tort of conspiracy, the plaintiffs had to establish that there was (a) an agreement between the defendants (b) for affecting an unlawful purpose and (c) the same resulted in damage to the plaintiff. Hence the plaintiff had to establish not only an agreement but also the fact that the agreement was to further an illegal objective which caused injury to the plaintiff. It was to establish the

---

[128] *Id.*, 29.

[129] See for example, G.J.Hughes, 'The Tort of Conspiracy', MLR, 209 (Apr., 1952) 15:2,.

[130] *Id.*, 210.

[131] See for example, *Crofter Hand Woven Harris Tweed Company, Limited, and Others v Veitch and Another* [1942] A.C. 435.

illegality of the agreement that the argument of restraint of trade was brought up. The defendant countered the allegation of tort of conspiracy by stating that neither was their agreement to form the association illegal in itself nor did they use any illegal means to further the objective of their association, and thus they were not responsible for the injury suffered by the plaintiff.[132]

While the facts did reveal an agreement, the courts found it hard to get convinced about the illegality of the objective. This is because for an act to be actionable as a tort, it must be either done '*wrongfully and maliciously*' or it should be done in furtherance of a '*wrongful and malicious combination*', thereby causing injury to the claimant/plaintiff. [133] In the lower court, Lord Coleridge held that the defendants 'have a right to endeavour by lawful means to keep their trade in their own hands and by the same means to exclude other from its benefits...'.[134] In other words, the judge approved the policy of collective boycott and price rigging indulged in by the association. He justified these acts as reasonable and legitimate pursuance of the selfishness of traders.[135] This reflects the position of the common law on anti-competitive practices.[136] The plaintiff could not have complained of the illegality of anti-competitive practices *per se* under tort since such practices were not on their own regarded as malicious or unlawful. The practices needed to be proven to have been done with the aim of causing injury to the plaintiff. Neither could the plaintiff have pleaded the illegality of the act on the ground that the combination was in restraint of trade since an agreement in restraint of trade is merely regarded as void and not illegal.

The plaintiff's case based on tort of conspiracy accordingly failed because of the above stated reasons. The courts refused to recognize that inducing customers through discounts or agreeing to fix prices and divide markets and cargo so as to create barriers for competitors was unlawful in itself. The requirement was to show that all these acts were done with the aim of injuring the plaintiff. Further, the link between the acts and the injury suffered by the plaintiff had to be established. On their own, these practices were regarded as part and parcel of conducting trade and commerce. Further, as stated earlier, there could not have been an action on the basis of contract as the plaintiff

---

[132] *The Mogul Steamship Company, Limited v. Mcgregor, Gow, & Co., and Others,* (1888) L.R. 21 Q.B.D. 544, 548.

[133] *Id.*, 552, Lord Coleridge's judgment.

[134] *Id.*, 552.

[135] *The Mogul Steamship* (n 132) 554.

[136] See Alexander Kamerling and Chris Goodwill, *Restrictive Covenants under Common and Competition Law,* 6[th]ed. (Sweet & Maxwell, 2010) 347.

had no contractual relation with the defendants. In the Court of Appeal, Lord Esher in his dissenting judgment, however, held an agreement in restraint of trade as illegal.[137] He stated that since such an illegal agreement was entered into to interfere with the trade of the plaintiff, it was actionable as tort of conspiracy.[138] Lord Esher emphasized the need to maintain fair competition and thus to him the acts of the defendants

> 'in lowering their freights far beyond a lowering for any purpose of trade—that is to say, so low that if they continued it they themselves could not carry on trade—was not an act done in the exercise of their own free right of trade, but was an act done evidently for the purpose of interfering with, i.e., with intent to interfere with, the plaintiffs' right to a free course of trade…'.[139]

The majority though affirmed the decision of Lord Coleridge and regarded the practices of the defendant as legitimate persuasion of trade. Thus, Lord Justice Bowen observes that the defendants have, by indulging in the practices complained of by the plaintiff,

> 'done nothing more against the plaintiffs than pursue to the bitter end a war of competition waged in the interest of their own trade'.[140]

He rejected the argument of fair competition on the ground that unless the act complained of falls within any of the known examples of tort of conspiracy, viz., through coercion, intimidation, fraud, obstruction, et al., it is not actionable merely on grounds of unfair competitive practices.[141] The argument of the plaintiffs that the defendant's agreement was in restraint of trade and thus illegal, was also rejected by Lord Justice Bowen. He stated that

> 'combination of capital for purposes of trade and competition is a very different thing from such a combination of several persons against one, with a view to harm him, as falls under the head of an indictable conspiracy. There is no just cause or excuse in the latter class of cases. There is such a just cause or excuse in the former'.[142]

For an anti-competitive practice, like the one complained of by the plaintiff, to be actionable as tort of conspiracy, the test was (a) whether it was intentional

---

[137] *The Mogul Steamship Company, Limited v. Mcgregor, Gow, & Co., and Others* (1889) L.R. 23 Q.B.D 598, 605.

[138] *Id.*, 606.

[139] *Id.*, 610.

[140] *Id.*, 614.

[141] *Id.*, 615.

[142] *Id.*, 617.

and (b) even if it was intentional, whether it had a just cause or excuse. If the latter was satisfied, then notwithstanding the detrimental effect of such an act on the third party, under common law, there was no relief.

Evidently, therefore the doctrine of restraint of trade can never be used to sue a cartel. To reiterate, agreements in restraint of trade are void in so far as they are not enforceable among the parties to the agreement. However, they do not amount to illegality in the sense that the parties cannot be acted against for having committed a civil wrong or a crime.[143] Lord Justice Fry also concurred with Lord Justice Bowen and held that

> 'competition was in substance the only weapon which the defendants intended to use against their rivals in trade. No thought of using violence, molestation, intimidation, fraud, or misrepresentation was entertained by the defendants'.[144]

He accordingly insisted that for an act of one to injure another's business by use of mere competition is not actionable as tort of conspiracy.[145] Thus he too rejected the argument of fair competition. These sentiments of the majority got reflected in the judgment of the House of Lords.[146] They unanimously rejected the claim of the plaintiff based on illegality of the restraint of trade agreement and the consequent claim of tort of conspiracy.[147]

Making a case for pro-consumer orientation of the anti-cartel law

The foregoing discussions brought forth both the detrimental effect of cartels on consumer interest as well as the limitations of the traditional common law concepts in dealing with cartels. Evidently, consumer interest was relegated to the background. The question then is: why should consumer interest take precedence over all other interests when it comes to anti-cartel regulation? The answer to this question lies in first identifying the other interests. The definition of cartels and the discussion on cartels so far, clearly establishes that cartel is a grouping of private business entities with strong bargaining power.

---

[143] *Id.*,619 [As Lord Justice Bowen declared, 'Contracts, as they are called, in restraint of trade, are not, in my opinion, illegal in any sense, except that the law will not enforce them. It does not prohibit the making of such contracts; it merely declines, after they have been made, to recognise their validity. The law considers the disadvantage so imposed upon the contract a sufficient shelter to the public'.]

[144] *Id.*, 622.

[145] *The Mogul Steamship* (n 137) 630.

[146] *The Mogul Steamship* (n 126) 37.

[147] *Id.*, 39–40.

Irrespective of whether these groupings or agreements are formed overtly or covertly, they continue to have as their objective the earning of profit at the cost of the consumer.[148]

This view of cartels is not confined to Western scholars alone. Those from the Third World also view cartels as detrimental to consumer interests. Bhattacharjea thus notes that

> 'Cartels harm consumers while seldom yielding any efficiency gains, and therefore in most countries evidence of a cartel agreement is sufficient to condemn it, without further investigation of its effects'.[149]

Similarly, Bhatia notes that

> 'There is worldwide recognition and consensus that Cartels harm consumers and damage economies'.[150]

According to Nanda and Pham,

> 'Other than causing some loss in consumer welfare, cartelisation also hampers the development of developing countries and growth of their firms…'.[151]

The Report of the Twelfth Five Year Plan of the Planning Commission of India also notes that one of the objectives of the competition policy is to

> 'forestall other forms of market failure, such as formation of cartels, leading to collusive pricing, division of markets and joint decisions to reduce supply'.[152]

---

[148] See for example, Maher M. Dabbah, *EC and UK Competition Law: Commentary, Cases and Materials* (CUP, 2004), 233. [Dabbah states that 'Somewhere on the spectrum of horizontal agreements…such cooperation will have no pro-competitive object or effect at all, but is rather, purely intended to maximize the profits of the parties to the agreement at the expense of consumers…In the world of competition law, this type of collusion is generally known as cartel'.].

[149] Aditya Bhattacharjea, 'Of Omissions and Commissions: India's Competition Laws', *EPW* 31 (2010) 45:35.

[150] G.R. Bhatia, 'Combating Cartel in Markets – Issues & Challenges', http://www.competition-commission india.nic.in/speeches_articles_presentations/GR.BhatiaArticle.pdf (accessed 12 October 2011).

[151] Nitya Nanda and Alice Pham, 'Multilateral Competition Framework: Where and How?',*CUTS* (2004) www.cuts-international.org/view-2.doc(accessed October 12, 2011).

[152] See 'Consumer Protection and Competition Policy', in Planning Commission (Government of India), *Eleventh Five Year Plan (2007–2012) Inclusive Growth, Vol. 1* (OUP, 2008), 246 http://planningcommission.nic.in/plans/planrel/fiveyr/11th/11_v1/11th_vol1.pdf (accessed 13 October 2011)

These views thus reinforce the detrimental effect of cartels on both the consumer and public at large.[153] Nandi Mokoena, member of the South African Competition Commission notes that cartels ensure that 'consumers cannot "shop around" to obtain the best prices'.[154]

Hence the impression would be that not only consumers but all sectors are affected by cartels—specifically, intermediate buyers who end up paying high prices to cartelists, the sellers or manufacturers who are forced to sell at the price fixed by the cartelists, the small and medium enterprises that are forced out of the market because of the cartelists. Interestingly, these are the very same stake holders who raised their concerns against cartels in such pro-cartel jurisdictions as Germany.[155] All these stake holders will protest or will be affected because they are not in a position to counter the bargaining power of cartels. This lack of bargaining power of the stake holders makes them as vulnerable to cartel abuses as are consumers. Hence, one can argue that there exists a commonality of interest between consumers and other small business entities.[156]

If that be the case, then it can further be argued that pitching a pro-consumer rhetoric for anti-cartel provision will end up benefitting all. This is so as according to the Indian competition law, the term consumer is wide enough to include both intermediary buyers and sellers as well as end consumers. According to the Competition Act 2002, a consumer is

> 'any person who (i) buys any goods for a consideration which has been paid or promised or partly paid and partly promised, or under any system of deferred payment and includes any user of such goods other than the person who buys such goods for consideration paid or promised or partly paid or partly promised, or under any system of deferred payment when such use is made with the approval of such person, whether such purchase of goods is for resale or for any commercial purpose or for personal use; (ii) hires or avails of any services for a consideration which has been paid or promised or partly paid and partly promised, or under

[153] However an opposite view on the detrimental effects of cartel has been given by leading Third World economist (Professor) Ajit Singh who notes that 'economic theory does not have such a black and white attitude towards cartels'. For a detailed discussion see Ajit Singh, 'Multilateral Competition Policy and Economic Development. A Developing Country Perspective on the European Community Proposals', *UNCTAD* (2004) http://www.unctad.org/en/docs/ditcclp200310_en.pdf (accessed October 12, 2011).

[154] Report on the Proceedings of the Third Anti-Corruption Summit, 'Chapter 7: Price-Fixing and its Impact on Communities' http://www.nacf.org.za/anti-corruption-summits/third_summit/UnitedNationsReport_summit3_Chapter7.pdf (accessed October 12, 2011).

[155] Harding and Joshua (n 11 of Chapter 1) 72.

[156] Singh (n 153)

> any system of deferred payment and includes any beneficiary of such services other than the person who hires or avails of the services for consideration paid or promised, or partly paid and partly promised, or under any system of deferred payment, when such services are availed of with the approval of the first-mentioned person whether such hiring or availing of services is for any commercial purpose or for personal use'.[157]

Further commenting upon the broad notion of the consumer under the EU law, Monti observes that the consumer interest element is 'implicitly incorporated in the economic freedom value'.[158] Since it is evidently the lack of bargaining power that enables cartels to harm the consumer, anti-cartel measures needs to correct this imbalance. It, therefore, justifies a pro-consumer approach in anti-cartel enforcement.

Looking forward

The foregoing discussion reveals that cartels fall within the spectrum of horizontal cooperation. However, with cartels the problem is that they are formed to avoid the cost of competition and not for any other purpose. The idea of such a cooperative arrangement is always to benefit of the producer or the cartelists. The loss inevitably has to be borne by the consumer. Interestingly, notwithstanding all the socio-political justifications for promoting cartels, it has hardly ever been benevolent to the consumer. The hard core cartel essentially feeds on the weaker bargaining power of the consumer. Hence with respect to cartels, a pro-consumer approach is justified. This is more so in the context of India where the law itself recognizes a broader definition of consumers who are to be the focal point of the competition law. The question then would be: how the Indian competition law addresses this concern of the consumer? The study of two of the most advanced competition law jurisdictions, viz., US and EU may provide insights into the challenges facing an effective regulation of cartels. The two chapters that follows suit will review the law on cartels in existence in these two jurisdictions.

---

[157] Section 2 clause (f) of the Competition Act, 2002.

[158] Giorgio Monti, *EC Competition Law* (CUP 2007) 99.

3 Cartels and Consumer Interests in the US

Context

This chapter is an evaluation of the theoretical framework that has developed in the US for the purpose of dealing with cartels. The examination begins by outlining the debate that preceded the passage of the Sherman Act. This would help in identifying the approach of the legislators towards cartels. Thereafter, the interpretation of the Sherman Act by the US Supreme Court will be evaluated in order to cull out the various approaches developed towards cartels. This is important in understanding the reasons that led to the development of the different approaches. It will also highlight the method used to distinguish between legitimate horizontal cooperation and cartels. Further, it will also be educative in understanding how far the interest of different stake holders, like the small and medium enterprises and the end consumers got factored in while developing the appropriate response towards cartels. Finally, the approaches of various enforcement agencies against cartels will be evaluated to find out how much importance consumer interest receives. In the process, the chapter answers the following questions: does the application of the ancillary restraint concept helps in distinguishing a cartel from other cooperative horizontal agreements? which approach, viz., the *per se* or the *rule of reason*, best accommodates consumer interest?

The Sherman Act and cartels: The beginning of the story

The consumer movement forced legal intervention in the US against trusts which were the cartels of America.[1] The legislation that epitomizes this intervention is the *Sherman Act* (hereinafter called the Act). The Sherman

[1] For a detailed discussion please refer to Chapter 1.

bill, as envisioned and mentored by Senator John Sherman of Ohio, had the following operative language:

> "That all arrangements, contracts, agreements, trusts, or combinations... made with a view, or which tend to prevent full and free competition... or which tend to advance the cost to the consumer...are hereby declared to be against public policy, unlawful, and void'.'[2]

This anti-trust bill, after several sessions of debate in the US Congress, was referred to a committee for further deliberations. The outcome was a new bill substituting Senator Sherman's bill. The language of this new bill was completely different from the original. For example, the words 'full and free competition' and 'cost to the consumer' were replaced with 'contract... in restraint of trade' and 'monopolize or attempt to monopolize...trade'.[3] The new bill was passed by the 51st Congress, without an elaborate debate, bringing into existence the Sherman Act of 1890.[4]

Bork argues that this drastic difference in the language between the original bill (as proposed by Senator Sherman) and the new bill (which got enacted) did not affect the 'consumer welfare' value of the Act.[5] Peritz however argues that neither 'history nor logic' supports the view that the Act embodied the consumer welfare policy as envisioned under the original bill.[6] On the contrary, what came forth as a common concern between the supporters and opponents of the original bill was the need to ensure that all 'commercial endeavour' should lead to 'fair price'.[7] Senator Sherman was concerned about the harmful effect of combinations like cartels on consumers. These concerns were patterned on the lines that cartels will lead to higher prices and lack of choices for the consumer. They were also based on the superior bargaining power of large combinations like cartels as against the consumer or small businesses.[8] As argued above, this concern for bargaining power justifies a pro-consumer approach in anti-cartel regulation.

On the other hand, the opponents sought the enforceability of agreements in reasonable restraints that would protect fair prices for the producers in

---

2 Rudolph J.R. Peritz, *Competition Policy in America: History, Rhetoric, Law*, revised edition,(OUP, 2000), 13.

3 *Id.*, 13–14.

4 *Id.*, 14.

5 Robert H. Bork, 'Legislative Intent and the Policy of the Sherman Act', *Journal of Law and Economics* 7, 11 (Oct. 1966): 9.

6 Rudolph J.R. Peritz (n 2) 14.

7 *Id.*, 17.

8 *Id.*, 15.

'face of ruinous competition'.[9] Peritz notes that the opponents of the original bill harped on the liberty of an individual to enter into private agreements.[10] This emphasis on liberty to enter into contract is akin to the classical contract argument which emphasized the sanctity of contracts based on procedural fairness disregarding the issues concerning substantive fairness arising out of inequality of bargaining power.[11] This insistence on the liberty to enter into private contracts impliedly justified price fixing cartels. The argument also favoured the producers as against the end consumers and other groups with lesser bargaining power. It was this divided Congress that passed the 1890 Act, uncertain about the contours of the new legislation.

There were however two unique features that became an inseparable part of the Act. These were the (a) threat of imprisonment and the power of the government to confiscate property in cases of cartels and other combinations and (b) the remedy of treble damages available to the injured party (including third party). These remedies proved that, notwithstanding the debate, there was an undisputed realization that anti-competitive behaviour causes harm.[12] The mix of civil and criminal penalties and the usage of the common law language make the 1890 Act a unique piece of legislation. However, with the Congress being divided in its understanding of the role of the Act, it was left to the US courts to come up with norms. The US courts thus were required to play around with a sparsely drafted statute and determine the approach that was appropriate towards cartels.[13] The US Supreme Court was responsible for developing the theoretical framework within which the cartels had to be dealt with. The questions that need to be answered are: what was this framework? What were the guidelines or norms that were developed within this framework to distinguish legitimate horizontal cooperation from cartels? Whose interests were given primacy when it came to dealing with cartels, viz., the producers or the consumers (both intermediary as well as the end user)?

---

9 *Id.*

10 *Id.*, 16

11 See e.g. Richard Stone, *The Modern Law of Contract* (8th edn. Routledge-Cavendish, 2009) 469-470; See also Mindy Chen-Wishart, 'The O'Brien Principle and Substantive Unfairness' (1997) 56:1 The Cambridge law Journal 60; See also Ewan Mckerndrick, *Contract law-Text, Cases, And Materials* (2nd ed. OUP, 2005) 792

12 Rudolph J.R. Peritz (n 2) 25-26. The original section 7 of the Act, which provided for treble damages later got converted into the Clayton Act with further amendments.

13 Gerber (n 31of Chapter 2) 123–124

Naked restraint: Cartels and consumer interests

In the absence of any new institutional or procedural or methodological framework, the implementation of the Act was through the suits initiated by either the federal government or private litigants.[14] For instance, the US Supreme Court in the *United States v. E. C. Knight Co. et al.*[15] clarified the ambit of the Act.[16] In this case, the court had to determine the constitutional validity of the Act, as the challenge was that the Congress exceeded its constitutional mandate in ratifying the Act.[17] In other words, the question had to be resolved as to whether the Act applied to intra-state restraints or was confined only to inter-state restraints and monopolies. If it was applicable only to inter-state restraints, then the Act was within the power granted to the Congress under the commerce clause.[18] The Act comprises seven sections, of which section 1 of the Act reads as follows:

> 'Every contract, combination in the form of trust or otherwise, or conspiracy, in restraint of trade or commerce among the several States, or with foreign nations, is hereby declared to be illegal. Every person who shall make any contract or engage in any combination or conspiracy hereby declared to be illegal shall be deemed guilty of a felony, and, on conviction thereof, shall be punished by fine not exceeding $ 100,000,000 if a corporation, or, if any other person, $ 1,000,000, or by imprisonment not exceeding 10 years, or by both said punishments, in the discretion of the court.'[19]

---

14 *Id.*, 124.

15 156 US 1 (1895), 15 S.Ct. 249. It was decided on January 21, 1895. See also 'Sherman Anti-Trust Act (1890)' at http://www.ourdocuments.gov/doc.php?flash=old&doc=51# (accessed October 13, 2011).

16 In this case, the allegation was that the American Sugar Refining Company monopolized the manufacture as well as sale of the refined sugar in the US, and controlled the prices of sugar. This monopoly was achieved by the American Sugar Refining Company through purchase of the majority shares of its competitors, one of them being E.C. Knight. It was therefore argued by the government that the American Sugar Company had conspired with its competitors to restrain trade in refined sugar, among the various states and with foreign nations. It was further averred by the government that this conspiracy was entered into for the purpose of raising prices of refined sugar. Hence, it was argued by the government that the acts of the American Sugar Refining Company and its co-conspirators was in violation of the Sherman Act. The issue thus was to decide whether the Act extended to monopoly in the manufacturing of sugar, which was a local activity.

17 See Article 1 Section 8 clause 3 of the US Constitution ('The Congress shall have power… To regulate commerce with foreign nations, and among the several states, and with the Indian tribes').

18 *Id.*

19 15 USCS §1.

Thus to proceed under section 1 of the Act, there has to be a proof of a contract, combination or a conspiracy in restraint of inter-state trade or commerce. This clearly covers horizontal agreements among competitors.

Cartels are therefore the subject matter of the section. Importantly, cartelization has to restraint *inter-state trade or commerce.* The second section makes the act of monopolization illegal. The language of this section also uses the expressions 'conspiracy or combination' to mean monopolizing trade and commerce. Thus, cartels which aim at monopolizing the market appear to be covered by this section.[20] The remaining five sections of the Act deal with the question of procedure, jurisdiction and exemption.[21] In the *E.C. Knight case*[22], the US Supreme Court had to decide whether the conduct complained of was in restraint of *inter-state trade or commerce.*[23] Delivering the majority opinion, Chief Justice Fuller held that

> 'the contracts and acts of the defendants related exclusively to the acquisition of the Philadelphia refineries and the business of sugar refining in Pennsylvania, and bore no direct relation to commerce between the states or with foreign nations.'[24]

It thus emphasized that intra-state restraints or conspiracies were not within the mandate of the Congress and the Act will not apply in such situations. In other words, only when the objective of the conspiracy or collusion affects inter-state trade and commerce, does the Act come into play.[25] Justice Harlan dissented from this conclusion and declared that the acquisition of monopoly

---

20 See 15 USCS §2: 'Every person who shall monopolize, or attempt to monopolize, or combine or conspire with any other person or persons, to monopolize any part of the trade or commerce among the several States, or with foreign nations, shall be deemed guilty of a felony, and, on conviction thereof, shall be punished by fine not exceeding $100,000,000 if a corporation, or, if any other person, $ 1,000,000, or by imprisonment not exceeding 10 years, or by both said punishments, in the discretion of the court'.

21 See generally 15 USCS §3–7.

22 156 US 1 (1895) (n 15).

23 *Id.*, 11.

24 *Id.*, 17.

25 The interpretation distinguishing inter-state and intra-state commerce is based on the fact that the US Congress cannot pass any law regulating intra-state commerce. Thus, to regulate anti-competitive practices within a state, the concerned state has to pass its own anti-competitive legislation. In the E.C. Knight case, the constitutional validity of the Sherman Act was challenged, and negated by the majority through interpretation, stating that the Act did not cover intra-state commerce. For an overview of the US anti-trust law see generally 'Antitrust: An overview' http://topics.law.cornell.edu/wex/Antitrust (accessed 5 August 2011).

in the refining of sugar had the effect of restraining *inter-state trade and commerce* and hence was within the ambit of the Act. His dissent was based on the dominant market share of the defendant through its acquisition of almost all the sugar refineries in the US. As the defendant owned almost all the sugar refineries, it could fix the prices of sugar.[26] This abuse of a dominant position clearly affected *inter-state trade and commerce.*

The reason was that though the refining of sugar may be done within Philadelphia, the sugar so manufactured would be bought 'to be sold to persons in other states, or to be carried to other states'.[27] Nonetheless, this decision established a dichotomy between manufacture and commerce.[28] The question then was: what could be the impact of this dichotomy on developing a response to cartels? The majority opinion conveyed an impression that if there was proof of an 'intention to put a restraint upon trade or commerce', then the Act would apply, overriding the dichotomy between manufacture and commerce.[29] The next problem then would be that notwithstanding the nakedness of the restraint, if the intention to affect inter-state trade and commerce is not proven, the Act will be of no use. Even though the *E.C. Knight case* was primarily on monopolization through mergers and only tangentially related to cartels, the principles evolved on what would amount to restraint on *inter-state trade and commerce* became relevant for furthering the evaluation of the US response to cartels.[30]

Cartels: The initial response vis-à-vis consumer interests

The first case which laid down the norms of the theoretical framework dealing with cartels was the *United States v. Trans-Missouri Freight Ass'n.*[31]

---

[26] 156 US 1 (1895) (n 15) 37–38.

[27] *Id.*, 33. As stated by Justice Harlan.

[28] See Boris I. Bittker, *Bittker on the Regulation of Interstate and Foreign Commerce* (Aspen Publishers, 1999), 3–26.

[29] *Id.*, 17.

[30] Mark S. LeClair, *Cartelization, Antitrust and Globalization in the US and Europe,* (Routledge, 2011), 3.

[31] 166 US 290, 17 S.Ct. 540. It was decided in March 22, 1897. 'In this case large number of railway companies entered into an agreement to form an association called the Trans-Missouri Freight Association. The agreement laid down the rules binding on the parties, outlining the purpose of the agreement which was mutual protection by establishing and maintaining reasonable rates, rules, and regulations on all freight traffic. In order to accomplish the said objectives, the agreement amongst other things provided the following: Each railway company shall identify a person who shall 'be held personally responsible for rates on that road'; That 'committee shall be appointed to establish rates, rules, and regulations on the traffic subject to this association, and to consider changes therein,

This case involved a horizontal agreement between railway companies[32] with the sole purpose of fixing freight charges. The agreement among the railway companies thus confirmed to the typology of a straightforward price fixing cartel.[33] In this sense, it was a naked restraint. The agreement was challenged by the US government as violating section 1 of the Act. Expectedly, the defendant, i.e., Trans-Missouri Freight Association denied the allegations and claimed that the agreement was necessary to protect the interests of the companies.[34] The justification sought for the cartel arrangement was thus based on necessity. Implicit in this argument was the contention of reasonability, viz., that the price-fixing arrangement was reasonable as it was needed to protect the interest of the producer. The question therefore was: could ruinous competition be used as a justification for cartels whose sole purpose was to fix price, i.e., ensure price stability? Hence, the US Supreme Court had to interpret the Act to decide whether the test of reasonableness is permitted.

The manufacture and commerce dichotomy, established in the *E.C. Knight* case did not raise a problem here. This was so because the US Supreme Court declared that transportation of goods and persons from one state to another by the railway companies amounts to *inter-state trade and commerce.*[35] Furthermore, the defendants herein admitted that they were engaged in *inter-state trade and commerce.* The only ground in which they argued for the exclusion of the Act was that the railway companies were governed by

---

and makes rules for meeting the competition of outside lines'; That 'at least five days written notice prior to each monthly meeting shall be given the chairman of any proposed reduction in rates'; That at 'each monthly meeting, the association shall consider and vote upon all changes proposed, of which due notice has been given, and all parties shall be bound by the decision of the association'; That 'By unanimous consent, any rate, rule, or regulation relating to freight traffic may be modified at any meeting of the association without previous notice'; That 'It shall be the duty of the chairman to investigate all apparent violations of the agreement, and to report his findings to the managers, who shall determine, by a majority vote (the member against whom complaint is made to have no vote), what, if any, penalty shall be assessed, the amount of each fine not to exceed one hundred dollars, to be paid to the association.' Thus the chief concern of the association was rate fixing, as a measure of protecting the members from unrestrained competition.

32 In the US, railways continue to be privately operated, with the help of government support and regulation. For information on the structure of the United States railway system, please see www.nationalatlas.gov/mld/railrdl.html (accessed 9 November 2010). Also see http://www.fra.dot.gov/. (accessed April 9, 2010)

33 See Alan J. Meese, 'Liberty and Antitrust in the Formative Era', *B.U. L. Rev.* 1,13 (1999): 79.

34 166 US 290 (n 31) 308.

35 I*d.*, 312–313.

the *Interstate Commerce Act of 1887*.[36] The US Supreme Court rejected this argument stating that the special statute did not exclude the application of the Act as the special statute does not authorize '[c]ompeting and nonconnecting [rail] roads... to make an agreement like this one.'[37] On the argument of ruinous competition as a justification of cartels, the majority led by Justice Peckham declared that the language of the Act does not make any distinction between reasonable and unreasonable restraint of trade.[38]

The only investigation required to be made under the Act was whether a particular agreement was in restraint of *inter-state trade and commerce*. The US Supreme Court consequently rejected all justifications including that of ruinous competition, which were given to establish the reasonability of the cartels. It declared that the sole purpose of the agreement was to fix freight rates and hence notwithstanding the necessity to fix the rates,

> 'the direct, immediate, and necessary effect [of the agreement] is to put a restraint upon trade or commerce as described in the act.'[39]

This reading of the Act by the majority thus laid down *per se illegality* of all agreements in restraint of *inter-state trade and commerce*. Accordingly, all cartels are agreements in restraint of trade and hence *per se illegal* under the Act. In a dissenting opinion, Justice White, however, insisted that the Act does permit a distinction between reasonable and unreasonable restraint of trade. He feared that such universal applicability will render the Act 'unreasonable and as violative of the elementary principles of justice'. [40] According to him, this wide interpretation would then cover all contracts which have the effect of restraining trade. As all trading or commercial transactions require the imposition of some restraint, this interpretation will ban all trade.[41] Furthering his line of argument, Justice White evaluated the common law distinction between partial and general restraints, arguing thereby that agreements in partial restraint were no longer covered by the definition of restraint of trade.

One may doubt this proposition, in view of the discussion in the second chapter. Nonetheless, Justice White's thrust was that the Act covers only unreasonable restraint of trade because restraint of trade means nothing but

---

36 *Id.*, 314–315. The Interstate Commerce Act of 1887 was a federal statute enacted by the US Congress to regulate the railroad industry.

37 *Id.*, 315.

38 *Id.*, 328–329.

39 *Id.*, 342.

40 *Id.*, 344.

41 166 US 290 (n 31) 351–352.

unreasonable restraint of trade.[42] To substantiate his point, Justice White refers to the title of the Act—it reads as 'An act to protect trade and commerce against unlawful restraints and monopolies'. Justice White accordingly stated that the use of the word 'unlawful' explains that the Act does make a distinction between unreasonable and reasonable restraint of trade agreements. Further, Justice White insisted that the legislative intent in passing the Act was 'to protect the liberty of contract and the freedom of trade'.[43] According to him, the interpretation of the Act adopted by the majority

> 'frustrates the plain purpose intended to be accomplished by congress, but also makes the statute tend to an end never contemplated, and against the accomplishment of which its provisions were enacted.'[44]

Having thus argued for the *rule of reason* test, Justice White then holds that the *Interstate Commerce Act of 1887* did authorize the railway companies to fix freight rates in order to avoid the consequence of ruinous competition.[45] Consequently, for Justice White, this established the reasonability of the price-fixing cartel.

One may however note that the majority did save certain agreements like those entered for the sale of good will or partnership agreements or property—the main subject of most of these agreements was the sale of good will or partnership or sale of property. The restraint imposed was collateral to the main agreement. Therefore, if a partnership agreement prohibits the partners to take up a competing business, that restraint would be collateral to the main agreement. Such agreements were therefore exempted from the purview of the language of the Act.[46] This approach of the majority led by Justice Peckham reflected their deep concern for the effect of price-fixing agreements on competition. The rejection of the common law reasonability test therefore was in order to make a distinction between restrictive agreements which hamper competition from those which are necessary to conduct business and trade.[47] In this sense, the majority attempted, though did not elucidate, to

42 *Id.*, 348–349

43 *Id.*, 355.

44 *Id.*, 356.

45 *Id.*, 369–373.

46 *Id.*, 329.

47 See for example, Robert H. Bork, 'The Rule of Reason and the Per Se Concept: Price Fixing and Market Division', *Yale L. J.* 775, 790 (1965): 74. [According to Bork, 'Peckham was redefining "restraint of trade" to refer to the elimination of competition in the general market… thus, the contrast between an agreement collateral and subordinate to the sale of property and an agreement between railroads to set rates. One was probably perceived as very unlikely to affect competition generally; the other as almost certain to…']

point out certain types of ancillary restraint which were outside the purview of the Act. Overall though, we see a tussle between *per se illegality* of cartels and the *rule of reason* approach towards cartels in the initial days of the Act.

For example, in *Joint-TrafficAss'n*[48], the US Supreme Court was re-visited with the question as to whether the Act admits the test of reasonableness. Factually, the case was similar to the *Trans-Missouri Freight Association* one. Here too the agreement was entered into between railway companies for the purpose of fixing freight rates, passenger fares and other conditions relating to the conduct of their business, viz., inter-state railroad transportation.[49] The US Supreme Court followed the rationale of the *Trans-Missouri Freight Association case* and reiterated that the Act treats all agreement in restraint of trade as *per se illegal.*[50] The majority led by Justice Peckham noted that in both the cases, viz., *Trans-Missouri* and *Joint-Traffic*

> '[the] natural and direct effect of the two agreements is the same, viz. to maintain rates at a higher level than would otherwise prevail…'[51]

The defendant challenged the constitutional validity of the Act on the ground that by rendering all contracts in restraint of trade as *per se illegal*, it threatens the existence of trade itself. [52]

The majority rejected this argument by declaring that

> 'the statute applies only to those contracts whose direct and immediate effect is a restraint upon interstate commerce…'[53]

The US Supreme Court reiterated the distinction between ancillary and naked restraint pointed out in the *Trans-Missouri* case. The US Supreme Court here too clarified that ancillary restraints or incidental restraints are not covered by the concept of restraint of trade as used under the Act.

The majority accordingly noted that a lease contract or a contract for the purpose of sale of goodwill are not regarded as contracts in restraint of *inter-state trade and commerce* within the meaning of the Act.[54] It is thus clear that for the US Supreme Court the word 'restraint of trade' as used in the Act had a different meaning from that understood under the common law.

[48] *United States v Joint-TrafficAss'n*, 171 US 505, 19 S.Ct. 25. It was decided on October 24, 1898.

[49] *Id.*, 506.

[50] *Id.*, 565.

[51] *Id.*

[52] *Id.*, 566–567. Evidently this argument was based on the analysis of Justice White in the *Trans-Missouri* case

[53] *Id.*, 568.

[54] *United States v Joint-TrafficAss'n*, (n 48) 567–568.

This is so because under the Act, the word 'restraint of trade' is enlarged to mean '*restraint of trade or commerce among the several states*'. The implication was that all contracts which directly restrained *inter-state trade and commerce* are illegal under the Act. This manner of reading the Act and the concept of restraint of trade helped in distinguishing cartels from say a partnership agreement or any other ordinary contract.

The *per se illegality* of cartels was also reiterated in the *Addyston Pipe & Steel Company et al. v. United States.*[55] The case related to a price-fixing cartel formed between six corporations who were in the business of manufacture and sale of cast iron pipes.[56] The defendants admitted the existence of such a combination but denied that the same was in restraint of *inter-state trade or commerce.*[57] Interestingly, the justification provided for such a price-fixing arrangement was the avoidance of ruinous competition.[58] The argument of ruinous competition appears to be a common refrain in all the three cases analysed so far. Like the previous cases, here too, the US Supreme Court dismissed the argument of ruinous competition given to establish the reasonability of the cartel. It affirmed the lower court Judge Taft's ruling, wherein he held that

> 'the association of the defendants was void at common law, because in restraint of trade... and tending to a monopoly... that the attempted justification of this association is without foundation.'[59]

Interestingly, there appears to be a shift in the stance of Justice Peckham when he affirms the ruling of Judge Taft. The reasoning applied by Judge Taft for declaring the combination or conspiracy of the defendant as unlawful within the Act was based on the common law distinction between reasonable and unreasonable restraint. It was on the basis of this distinction that he holds the defendant's agreement as a naked restraint with the

> 'the sole object... to restrain competition, and enhance or maintain prices... nothing to justify or excuse the restraint... it would necessarily have a tendency to monopoly, and therefore would be void.'[60]

On the other hand, Justice Peckham's analysis, prior to the *Addyston* case had been to hold that under the Act, all agreements in restraint of trade are

---

[55] 175 US 211, 20 S.Ct. 96. It was decided on December 4th, 1899.

[56] *Id.*, 213.

[57] *Id.*, 214.

[58] *Id.*

[59] 46 L.R.A. 122, 85 F. 271, 291.

[60] *Id.*, 282–283.

declared void and illegal. Further, according to him, partnership contracts etc. were not to be regarded as in restraint of trade since in these cases, the restraint was ancillary or collateral. This conclusion was arrived at with denial of the fact that the Act co-opts the common law principle on restraint of trade, viz., the difference between naked and ancillary. In the *Addyston* case, by affirming Judge Taft's ruling on the legality of the defendant's combination, Justice Peckham seems to have acknowledged the fact that the Act renders illegal only unlawful restraint.[61] This also appears to be the opinion of Justice White, as evident from his dissent in the *Trans-Missouri* case.

In the *Addyston* case, the US Supreme Court also declared that the defendant's association, though comprising manufacturers, was distinguishable from the *E.C. Knight* case. The reason being that in the latter case, the combination's sole purpose was to control the manufacture of sugar. There was no proof of the combination's objective to further dispose of the manufactured product among several states. In the absence of the element of *inter-state trade and commerce,* the combination was rightly held to be out of the purview of the Act. On the other hand, in the *Addyston* case, the manufacturer's combination involved 'contracts for the sale and transportation to other states of specific articles'.[62] This thus took the case out of the manufacture and commerce dichotomy. The *Addyston* case defendants were not merely controlling the manufacture of cast iron pipes but they were also determining the price at which 'all contracts for the delivery of pipe' were being entered into. This aspect relating to the fixing of prices at the stage of delivery and restriction of competition amounted to 'a restraint upon interstate commerce'. Hence the Act clearly applied here.[63]

The cases analysed so far establish the *per se illegality* of price-fixing cartels. They clearly fall within the definition of cartels whose sole purpose are to fix prices at the cost of the public including the consumer. Further, the justification of ruinous competition was disregarded as reasonable ground for determining the legality of cartels. In analysing the harmful nature of

---

61 *Id.,* 279. [Judge Taft states that 'Contracts that were unreasonable restraint of trade at common law were not unlawful in the sense of being criminal, or giving rise to a civil action for damages in favor of one prejudicially affected thereby, but were simply void, and were not enforced by the court. The effect of the act of 1890 was to render such contracts unlawful in an affirmative or positive sense, and punishable as a misdemeanour, and to create a right to civil action for damages in favour of those injured thereby, and a civil remedy by injunction in favour of both private persons and the public against the execution of such contracts and the maintenance of such trade restraints.']

62 175 US 211 (n 55) 240.

63 175 US 211 (n 55) 241

price-fixing cartels, the US courts resorted to the common law doctrine of restraint of trade.[64] The courts tried to adapt the doctrine for the purpose of its applicability under the Act. However they outlined the fact that all unreasonable restraint upon *inter-state trade and commerce* will be covered by the Act and declared illegal. Further, the essential nature of cartels was established as a conspiracy. Judge Taft considered that price-fixing cartels committed fraud on the public by creating an impression that competition existed among the cartel members. They accordingly tried to conceal their *modus operandi* from the public. This was evident in the *Addyston* case where the defendants indulged in bid rigging, ensuring that a cartel member wins the bid in a public auction.[65] Finally, the dichotomy between manufacture and commerce is not relevant when a price-fixing cartel also indulges in the sale of the products that it manufactures. The only condition being that the sale has to be among several states, viz., *inter-state*—then it will be regarded as part of commerce.[66]

Unsettling the per se rule? The Standard Oil and thereafter

The legal position on price-fixing cartels however became doubtful with the *Standard Oil* case.[67] The *Standard Oil* case was about monopolization which was the result of the creation of a trust called the Standard Oil Company of New Jersey.[68] In order to decide upon the legality of the trust agreement, the US Supreme Court revisited the question concerning the correct 'conception of the meaning' of section 1 and section 2 of the Act.[69] Chief Justice White led the majority opinion in holding that the sections have to be to read as incorporating the *rule of reason.* In essence it meant that the US Supreme Court by a majority of 8:1 established that in order to determine the infringement of section 1 or section 2, the court needs to apply the rule of reason as understood in the common law. This meant that only those contracts which were in unreasonable restraint of trade would be

---

64 See Tony Freyer, 'The Sherman Antitrust Act, Comparative Business Structure, and the Rule of Reason: America and Great Britain, 1880–1920', *Iowa L. Rev.* 991, 1004 (1989): 74.

65 85 F. 271 (n 59) 293. [The term 'conspiracy' was defined by Judge Taft as 'a combination of two or more persons to accomplish an unlawful end by lawful means or a lawful end by unlawful means.']

66 175 US 211 (n 55) 247–248.

67 *Standard Oil Company of New Jersey et al. v. United States*, 221 US 1, 31 S.Ct. 502. The judgment was delivered 8:1, with Justice Harlan partly dissenting.

68 For the detailed facts see *Id.*, 30–43.

69 *Id.*, 48–49.

illegal under the Act.[70] The above conclusion led the majority to reject the contention of the government that the Act covers all agreements in restraint of trade, notwithstanding its reasonability or unreasonability. Chief Justice White reiterates his assertion in the *Trans-Missouri* dissent that such a reading would make the Act unreasonable, destroying all contractual transactions. Accordingly, he justifies that use of *rule of reason* as the only plausible approach envisioned by the Act to determine its infringement.[71]

The majority further held that both the *Trans-Missouri* and *Joint-Traffic* cases were decided by applying the *rule of reason.* It was the applicability of the *rule of reason* that led the courts in the stated cases to hold the cartel agreement as *per se illegal.*[72] This determination of the majority was correct, as is evident from the afore stated analysis of these two decisions. In both the decisions, the emphasis was on direct and immediate effect of the restraint on *inter-state trade and commerce.* These decisions also distinguished between naked restraints and ancillary or collateral restraint which indirectly affected *inter-state trade and commerce.* In fact, Chief Justice White did hold that there was a commonality between the rule of direct and indirect effect of restraint and the *rule of reason.* He supported this conclusion by reasoning that 'the history of the act and the analysis of its text' clearly establish

> 'that in every case where it is claimed that an act or acts are in violation of the statute, the *rule of reason*, in the light of the principles of law and the public policy which the act embodies, must be applied.'[73]

By applying this theoretical framework to the impugned trust agreement, the majority declared it to be in violation of both section 1 and 2 of the Act. The US Supreme Court deduced that the creation of the trust was with the intention to completely dominate the oil industry. There was accordingly a combination or conspiracy for the purpose of monopolizing the oil industry and hence directly restraining *inter-state trade and commerce.*[74]

This *rule of reason approach* was dissented to by only one of the nine judges, viz., Justice Harlan. His dissent was that by reading into the Act, the *rule of reason*, the majority had indulged in *judicial legislation.*[75] Accordingly, he reiterated the *Trans-Missouri* opinion which according to him unequivocally declared that the Act

---

70 *Id.*, 60–62.

71 *Id.*, 63–64.

72 *Id.*, 65–66.

73 *Id.*, 66.

74 *Standard Oil* (n 67) 73–77.

75 *Id.*, 90.

> '[prohibits] and [makes] illegal not only every contract or combination, in whatever form, which was in restraint of interstate commerce, without regard to its reasonableness or unreasonableness, but all monopolies or attempt to monopolize "any part" of such trade or commerce'.[76]

As held by the majority, this reading of the *Trans-Missouri* judgment, nevertheless, cannot lose sight of the fact that the said judgment also referred to the direct and indirect effect of restraint. In the *Addyston* case also, Judge Taft based his opinion on the common law understanding of the word 'restraint of trade'. Hence it seems that Justice Harlan may not be correct in accusing the *Standard Oil* bench for introducing the *rule of reason* test within the Act. The *Standard Oil* decision embodying the *rule of reason* was re-affirmed in the *American Tobacco* case.[77] This case was on mergers and the resulting monopolization. Chief Justice White reiterated that the *rule of reason* as applied to the Act, proscribed those

> 'acts or contracts or agreements or combinations which operated to the prejudice of the public interests by unduly restricting competition, or unduly obstructing the due course of trade, or which, either because of their inherent nature or effect, or because of the evident purpose of the acts, etc., injuriously restrained trade…'.[78]

Bork argues that Chief Justice White thus established a three-tier test, wherein an agreement will either be on its face restrictive in nature or will have its objective or effect as restraint of trade. Accordingly, all cartel agreements will be *per se illegal* as they are inherently anti-competitive and prejudicial to public interest.[79] This three-tier test, according to Bork, was similar to the test of direct or indirect restraint developed by Justice Peckham and the test of ancillary and non-ancillary restraint developed by Judge Taft.[80] The development of the *rule of reason* approach evidently did not have any effect on the *per se illegality* of cartels. The analysis used by Chief Justice White in the *Standard Oil* and the *American Tobacco* case established a common link between these two cases and the *Trans-Missouri* and the *Joint Traffic* cases.

---

76 *Id.*, 94.

77 The same year, i.e., 1911, another important case was resolved. The case, *American Tobacco Company and Others v US*, 221 US 106, 31 S.Ct. 632, was decided subsequent to the decision in the Standard Oil case. Here too, the majority decision was given by Chief Justice White who expectedly reiterated the rule of reason approach evolved in the preceding case. As in the Standard Oil case, here too, the lone dissenting opinion was given by Justice Harlan, and the dissent was on the same lines as before.

78 *Standard Oil* (n 67) 179.

79 Bork (n 47) 804.

80 *Id.*, 805.

This analysis meant that an agreement entered into solely for the purpose of fixing prices, dividing markets, dividing customers, bid rigging and collecting boycotts will be held to be *per se illegal.* These agreements will be treated as inherently prejudicial to the competitive process and the public interest which includes the consumer interest. As will be seen in the next chapter on EU competition law, all these agreements were treated as having their *objective* as anti-competitive and hence declared to be *per se illegal.* A review of cartel cases post the *Standard Oil* and *Amercian Tobacco* decision needs to be therefore done to gauge the extent to which the *per se illegal* approach is established in the US anti-cartel regulation.

Post-*Standard Oil* scenario, cartels and consumers

One of the first cases on price-fixing agreements that came up before the US Supreme Court in the post-*Standard Oil* era was the case of *Board of Trade of City of Chicago et al. v. United States.*[81] This case dealt with a challenge to the rules adopted by the Board of Trade of the City of Chicago.[82] The impugned rule adopted by the Board prohibited the members from purchasing or offering to purchase, during the intervening period starting from the close of the call to the opening of the session on the next business day, any grain at a price other than the one fixed at the closing of the call. The position prior to the adoption of this rule was that the members were free to fix their prices throughout the day as they respectively saw fit. After the adoption of the rule though, the prices at which the members bid, had to be fixed at the day's closing bid on the call until the opening of the next session.[83] On the face of it, this arrangement among the members of the Chicago Board of Trade does not appear to be a naked restraint. The members merely agreed to be bound by the prices that were fixed at the close of the business hours till the opening of the next business hours. There was nothing in the agreement which deprived the members or coerced them to perpetually give up their freedom in fixing the bid price.

Justice Brandeis too noted the apparent lack of any hard core restraint of the price-fixing arrangement. He criticized the government for basing its case on the simplistic notion that any

81 246 US 231, 38 S.Ct. 242. (Decided on 4 March 1918).

82 See *Id.*, 235–36. ['The Board of Trade was the commercial centre through which most of the trading in grain was done. Its 1600 members included brokers, commission merchants, dealers, millers, maltsters, manufacturers of corn products and proprietors of elevators. Grains there dealt in were graded according to their kind and quality...'.]

83 246 US 231(n 81) 237.

> 'rule or agreement by which men occupying positions of strength in any branch of trade, fixed prices at which they would buy or sell during an important part of the business day, is an illegal restraint of trade under the Anti-Trust Law'.[84]

This argument of the government reflects the long ensuing debate regarding the reasonable interpretation of the Act. By this argument, the government appears to be reverting back to the old stance that the Act renders illegal all agreements in restraint of *inter-state trade and commerce.* Justice Brandeis rejected this stance of the government and went on to apply the *rule of reason* test to the facts of the case. He further elaborated the *rule of reason* by declaring that

> 'The true test of legality is whether the restraint imposed is such as merely regulates and perhaps thereby promotes competition or whether it is such as may suppress or even destroy competition'.[85]

Justice Brandeis further fine-tuned this doctrinal reiteration by specifying the factors that the courts needed to take note of to assess the illegality of the restraint. Accordingly, the courts needed to evaluate the facts peculiar to the business to which the restraint is applied. Further requirement was the assessment of the conditions before and after the restraint was imposed. Additionally, the courts were required to consider the nature of the restraint and its effect, actual or probable. The history of the restraint and the evil in existence also needed attention. In the final assessment, the courts had to look into the reason for adopting the particular remedy and the object that the restraint sought to attain.[86] Applying these standards to the existing facts, Justice Brandeis led the US Supreme Court in unanimously concluding that the rule adopted by the Board was reasonable and necessary to promote the business of selling and purchasing the grains.[87] This decision furthered the distinction, established in the US anti-trust law, between naked and ancillary restraint.[88] It also clarified that all ancillary restraint is subject to the *rule*

---

84 *Id.*, 238.

85 *Id.*

86 *Id.*, 238.

87 *Id.*, 239.

88 In fact, it has been noted by US anti-trust scholars that the restraint on prices imposed by the Board was ancillary to the main operation of the Board, which was to efficiently run a joint venture 'among its members to create an efficient, partial integration of their activities as buyers and sellers of grains'. See for example, Peter C. Carstensen, 'Lost in (Doctrinal) Translation: The Misleading Retelling of the Supreme Court's Antitrust decisions on Restraints of Trade', *SMU L. Rev.* 525 (2009): 62.

of reason analysis. Finally, this case also established that not all horizontal cooperative arrangements are *per se illegal.*

The distinction between horizontal agreements on the basis of hard core naked restraints and ancillary restraints can be seen in the case of *United States v. Trenton Potteries Co. et al.*[89] This case involved a challenge to the agreement entered into between twenty individuals and twenty-three corporations for fixing the prices of sanitary pottery. Further, it was also alleged by the government that by virtue of the said agreement, the sale of pottery was limited to a special group of customers, thereby depriving others of the products.[90] The type of arrangement alleged in the case therefore reflected only one purpose, i.e., fixing of prices. This, therefore, appears to fall in line with the kind of price-fixing agreements that were declared illegal in the *Trans-Missouri* and the *Addyston* cases. In other words, the impugned agreement appears to be a naked price-fixing horizontal restraint. Justice Stone too declared the impugned agreement as a naked price-fixing arrangement. Accordingly, he went along with the precedence and held the agreement to be *per se illegal.* He reasoned that price-fixing agreements cannot be made the subject of *rule of reason* analysis because

> '[t]he reasonable price fixed today may through economic and business changes become the unreasonable price of to-morrow'.[91]

The price-fixing arrangement in this case was also distinguished from the *Chicago Board of Trade* case on the ground that the latter was merely a regulation of a board of trade and not a price-fixing agreement among competitors.[92] The court emphasized that while the *rule of reason* standard may hold true for other types of anti-competitive acts, it certainly does not apply to naked restraints like cartels. Price-fixing cartels had to be regulated by the *per se* standard, which according to the court was best suited for furthering the public and consumer interests.[93] This opinion clearly established that the determination of a naked restraint had to be based on the inherent character of the agreement and on the effect or objective of the agreement. For example in the *Trenton* case, the objective of the agreement was to fix price. This theoretical framework was further applied in the *Socony-Vacuum Oil Co., Inc., et al. v. United States*[94] case. The case—which involved a price-fixing

[89] 273 US 392, 47 S.Ct. 377 (decided on February 1927).

[90] *Id.*, 394.

[91] *Id.*, 397.

[92] 273 US 392 (n 89) 401.

[93] *Id.*, 397.

[94] 310 US 150, 60 S.Ct. 811 (decided on May 6, 1940).

agreement among certain major oil companies with Socony-Vacuum Oil Company being one such conspirator— further assumed significance in understanding the US response to cartels because it reviewed past decisions and reiterated the doctrinal underpinnings of the anti-cartel law.[95]

In the US Supreme Court, Justice Douglas delivered the majority judgment by approving the *per se illegal* standard for price-fixing cartels. He declared that

> 'for over forty years this Court has consistently and without deviation adhered to the principle that price-fixing agreements are unlawful per se under the Sherman Act and that no showing of so-called competitive abuses or evils which those agreements were designed to eliminate or alleviate may be interposed as a defense'.[96]

By making this declaration, the court was affirming that both the *Trenton Potteries* case and the *Chicago Board of Trade* case were part of the same tradition. It thus placed Brandeis, Peckham and White on the same plane, by insisting that they all declared naked restraints like cartels as *per se illegal.* It was therefore inevitable that Justice Douglas explained the *Chicago* case as one which involved rules that

> 'was somewhat akin to rules of an exchange limiting the period of trading...No attempt was made to show that the purpose or effect of the rule was to raise or depress prices... Since it was not aimed at price manipulation or the control of the market prices and since it had "no appreciable effect on general market prices", the rule survived as a reasonable restraint of trade.'[97]

This case also clarified the standard of proof required to establish the violation of section 1 of the Act. Mr Justice Douglas declared that the act of conspiring is enough to establish the *per se illegality* of price-fixing cartels. Hence the ability of the conspirators to affect the market or to successfully execute the conspiracy need not be assessed under section 1 of the Act. Neither is it material that the conspiracy had a partial effect on the *inter-state trade and commerce.* In essence, therefore to establish *per se illegality*, it is enough to

---

95 'The method adopted by the conspirators, viz., the oil companies was that they would spot buy gasoline at high prices fixed by them and not by the sellers (who were largely independent refineries). Subsequently, they would sell the oil to the downstream market, viz., the retailer, again at the price fixed by them. By buying large quantities of gasoline at high prices, they were able to ensure that the prices of gasoline stabilize. Consequently, consumers ended up paying more for the gasoline then they would have otherwise paid'.

96 310 US 150 (n 94) 218.

97 *Id.*, 217.

show the existence of an agreement or conspiracy amongst competitors to fix prices. Their market power need not be assessed.[98]

The lone dissenting judgment was given by Justice Roberts who held that there was no evidence that the defendants conspired to fix prices. According to him, an agreement to remove a harmful practice from an industry, so as to ensure free competition was not *per se illegal.* He may have been adhering to the argument of ruinous competition. In his assessment, any agreement that would remove a 'harmful' practice of price war or competition is reasonable. Thus, it was reasonable for the defendants to agree to purchase excess or surplus gasoline at high prices which in turn increased the prices of the gasoline as sold to the retailers and consumers.[99] Notwithstanding this lone divergent opinion, the majority judgment had, in this 1940 case, unequivocally re-affirmed the *per se illegality* of price-fixing cartels. The *Socony* case settled the position so far as cartels are concerned. For example, in the *Leegin* case[100], the US Supreme Court declared that

> 'Restraints that are per se unlawful include horizontal agreements among competitors to fix prices...or to divide markets...'.[101]

Thus, all type of cartels, viz., for fixing prices, for dividing markets, for dividing customers and for bid rigging will be covered by the *per se illegal* rule. Notwithstanding the classification of the cartels as *per se illegal,* being in naked restraint, the problem in identifying a naked restraint as against an ancillary restraint continues to be ambiguous.

The per se or rule of reason: Rise of a non-dichotomous approach to cartels

An example of such a confusion would be the *Broadcast Music, Inc., et al., v. Columbia Broadcasting System, Inc., et al.* case[102]. Justice White delivered the majority judgment, applying the *rule of reason* test to an agreement that had cartel-like features. The case involved the question as to whether the issuance by ASCAP and BMI to CBS, of blanket licences to copyrighted musical compositions at fees negotiated by them is price fixing *per se* unlawful

[98] *Id.,* 224 (footnote number 59 of the case).

[99] *Id.,* 260.

[100] *Leegin Creative Leather Products, Inc., Petitioner v. Psks, Inc., Dba Kay's Kloset . . . Kay's Shoes,* 551 US 877,127 S.Ct. 2705 US (decided in 2007).

[101] *Id.,* 886.

[102] 441 US 1, 99 S.Ct. 1551.

under the anti-trust laws.[103] In other words, the US Supreme Court had to decide whether the granting of an all-encompassing licence to use the entire package of copyrighted music, for a price agreed among the said licencng organizations should be declared illegal *per se* for being a naked restraint. If one refers to the test evolved by Justice Douglas in the *Socony-Vacuum Oil* case, then all price-fixing agreements should be unlawful *per se* under the Act. Further, no justification can be given as a defence.[104] Broadcast Music sought to distinguish this case from other price-fixing precedents, thereby justifying the applicability of the *rule of reason* based analysis. Justice White, while accepting the usefulness of a *per se* approach, disagreed with the scope of its application. According to him

> 'This per se rule is a valid and useful tool of antitrust policy and enforcement. And agreements among competitors to fix prices on their individual goods or services are among those concerted activities that the Court has held to be within the per se category. But easy labels do not always supply ready answers.'[105]

Justice White then went on to explain why not all price-fixing agreements can be termed as *per se* illegal. He used the example of partners fixing the price of their goods which will not be regarded as *per se illegal.* Justice White apparently alluded to the ancillary restraint test developed earlier. He explained that while certain practices are established to be within the ambit of *per se illegality*, for others, such *per se* classification can be done only after having considerable experience with that particular business relationship.[106] Justice White used this argument as a justification to take the Broadcast Music case out of the ambit of a *per se* analysis, stating that '[we] have never examined a practice like this one before…'[107] The emphasis of his argument was on the fact that the blanket licencing arrangement was essential to effectuate the rights of the copyright owners, as envisaged under the Copyright Act.[108] This was also a way to highlight the fact that the price-fixing arrangement was ancillary to the need to protect the rights of the musical composition owner.

---

[103] *Id.*, 4. Here CBS stands for Columbia Broadcasting System, Inc.; ASCAP stands for American Society of Composers, Authors and Publishers; BMI stands for Broadcast Music, Inc.

[104] 310 US 150 (n 94) 218.

[105] 441 US 1 (n 102) 8.

[106] *Id.*, 9–10.

[107] *Id.*, 10.

[108] *Id.*, 19.

The court referred to reports of the Department of Justice and the opinions of various experts to highlight the need for issuing blanket licences. It emphasized the unique nature of copyrighted music whose public performance would require the permission of the copyright owner. The court noted that the system of blanket licence ensured that all the copyright owners could pool their compositions at one place and millions of users could access the music through one licence. Hence, a user of the blanket licence gets access to all the compositions covered by the licence, thereby avoiding the costs involved in negotiations for individual compositions. This savings of costs and conferring of benefits was regarded by the court as one of the pro-competitive and pro-consumer benefits of the blanket licence.[109] The court admitted that the pricing of the blanket licence was not the result of competition, nonetheless the fixing of the blanket licence fee by the defendants did not deprive individual copyright owners from selling their compositions in other markets.[110] These reasons convinced the majority that the challenged conduct of the defendant should be subject to the *rule of reason* analysis.[111]

Finally, the court insisted that the application of the *per se* approach to a price-fixing arrangement among competitors must be guided by the following concerns, viz.,

> 'whether the effect and... the purpose of the practice are to threaten the proper operation of our predominantly free-market economy... whether the practice facially appears to be one that would always or almost always tend to restrict competition and decrease output, and in what portion of the market, or instead one designed to increase economic efficiency and render markets more, rather than less, competitive.'[112]

Consequently, in this case, the US Supreme Court re-formulated the *per se illegal* approach by insisting that even though an arraignment may on the face of it appear to be akin to a price-fixing cartel, one needs to look into the effect of such restraint on the output. This is true in case of horizontal agreements, fixing prices in new areas, wherein the courts have not had considerable experience of the challenged conduct. Justice Stevens dissented on the ground that the blanket licence agreement was violative of the Act under the *rule of reason* analysis. He however agreed with the majority that the blanket licence agreement is subject to a rule of reason approach.[113] On

---

[109] *Id.*, 20–23.

[110] *Id.*, 23–24.

[111] *Id.*, 24–25.

[112] 441 US 1 (n 102) 19–20.

[113] *Id.*, 26.

the whole, the theoretical framework developed in this case appears to be a continuation of the previous decisions, and probably can be said to further fine-tune the test of distinguishing a naked restraint from an ancillary one.[114] Hence, one can say that a naked restraint would be one where the tendency to restrict output will always be presumed. This presumption can be rebutted by the defendant by showing that the arrangement or agreement in fact does not restrict the output. Though, it is evident from the cases discussed so far, that in the case of a naked restraint, the defendant can never rebut the presumption of illegality.

Against this backdrop, it is easier to understand that in the *Broadcast Music* case, the non-exclusive licence granted by individual copyright owners to ASCAP and BMI, redeemed the blanket licence agreements. It was because of the nature of this arrangement between the copyright owners and ASCAP and BMI, that the majority distinguished the *Socony-Vacuum* case, stating that the said arrangement did not threaten the 'central nervous system of the economy'.[115] Notwithstanding the fine-tuning of the *per se illegal* approach, it seems obvious that through the *Broadcast Music* judgment, the US Supreme Court has moved from an irrebuttable presumption of illegality to a rebuttable presumption of illegality in certain situations.[116] The question from a consumer perspective is: when will the court use the rebuttable presumption test and where will it use the irrebuttable presumption test? This is a pertinent question as the parameters taken into account for rebutting the presumption will determine the extent to which the interest of the consumer is taken into account.

The *Broadcast Music* case shows that one of the parameters used to rebut the presumption of illegality is the benefit conferred upon the consumer by the restraint—this is the reason why the court had insisted that any restriction on output will be *per se* illegal. It also follows from the *Broadcast Music* case that

---

[114] *Cf* Joseph W. deFuria, Jr., 'Reasoning Per Se and Horizontal Price Fixing: An Emerging Trend in Antitrust Litigation?',*Pepperdine. L. Rev.* 39 (1986): 14. [The author believes that there is a break with the earlier US Supreme Court decision, in the sense that in the *Broadcast Music* case, the court looked for justification before condemning the agreement. It did not concentrate merely on the fact that price has been fixed. The court rather looked into the fact as to 'whether the practice [also] facially appear[ed] to be one that would always or almost always tend to restrict competition and decrease output . . . or instead one designed to "increase economic efficiency and render markets more, rather than less competitive"'. This to the author establishes the contradistinction with the *Socony-Vacuum* case.]

[115] 441 US 1 (n 102) 23.

[116] Charles J.Goetz and Fred S. McChesney, *Antitrust Law: Interpretation and Implementation,* 3rd ed. (Foundation Press, 2006), 173.

the US Supreme Court had done away with the strict distinction between a *rule of reason* analysis and a *per se illegal* analysis of a cartel. The court will declare a naked restraint as *per se illegal* but if the challenged conduct has any redeeming feature like pro-consumer benefit, then the court will apply a *truncated rule of reason analysis*. This approach, developed by the US Supreme Court is also labelled as the *quick look* approach. In this, if the court has any doubt about the perniciousness of the agreement it can quickly consider, based on the pleading, affidavits and other evidence, whether the conduct is to be declared *per se illegal*. If the court comes to a negative conclusion as to the pro-competitive aspect of the arrangement, it will declare the conduct as *per se illegal*. However, on a positive assessment of the conduct as pro-competitive, it will go into a detailed *rule of reason* analysis to determine the desirability of the arrangement. In other words, this is a preliminary review of the facts to decide the approach to be adopted in a particular case.[117] Finally, it also seems that where the alleged price-fixing conduct pertains to a new area or practice, the courts will more likely apply the *quick look* approach.

The *quick look* approach thus can also be regarded as an attempt by the US Supreme Court to take the middle-of-the-road approach.[118] If, for example, a price-fixing cartel has some redeeming feature, then the preliminary inquiry or quick look can lead to a detailed rule of reason analysis. The only question for a reader of this book then would be: has the *Broadcast Music* judgment overruled the *Socony-Vacuum* case? There is no indication to this effect in the BMI judgment and hence one can reconcile the two approaches as part of the evolutionary process to distinguish cartels from genuine joint venture collaborations.[119] This evolution is necessary in the absence of any specific exemption under the Sherman Act. The *Arizona v. Maricopa County Medical Society et al.*[120] case is an example of this evolutionary process in the post-BMI scenario. In this, the US Supreme Court by a majority held the price-fixing

---

[117] *Id.*, 172–174.

[118] Adam Weg, 'Per Se Treatment: An Unnecessary Relic of Antitrust Litigation', 60 *Hastings L.J.* 1535, 1542 http://www.uchastings.edu/hlj/archive/vol60/Weg_60-HLJ-1535.pdf (accessed August 29, 2011).

[119] Accordingly, practices which have over the years been declared consistently to be *per se illegal* will not then be subject to *quick look* analysis. Cartel arrangements like price fixation, output restriction, market division etc. are always treated as *per se illegal*. This means that the plaintiff does not have the burden of proof to show market power or anti-competitive effect. See Thomas B. Leary, 'A Structured Outline for the Analysis of Horizontal Agreements', http://www.ftc.gov/speeches/leary/chairsshowcasetalk.pdf (accessed August 29, 2011)

[120] 457 US 332, 102 S.Ct. 2466.

schedule of a non-profit organization as *per se* illegal. The case involved a non-profit organization, viz., the Maricopa Foundation, comprising licenced doctors who were engaged in private practice. The arraignment provided for a schedule of maximum fees that the participating doctors agreed to accept as payment in full for services performed for the patients insured under various insurance plans approved by the foundation. It was this fee schedule which was challenged as a price-fixing agreement among competitors in restraint of trade. It needs to be noted that the doctors who were party to the impugned agreements, were however free to charge any fees, beyond the scheduled maximum or below the said schedule, from the non-insured patients. One could therefore argue that this agreement was a non-exclusive arrangement.[121]

Nonetheless, the majority led by Justice Stevens held that over the years, the stance of the US Supreme Court has placed

> 'horizontal agreements to fix maximum prices on the same legal—even if not economic—footing as agreements to fix minimum or uniform prices'.[122]

He reiterated the *per se illegality* rule established in the *Trenton* and *Socony-Vacuum* cases holding that the US Supreme Court has never 'wavered in… enforcement of the per se rule against price fixing'.[123] Accordingly for him, the maximum fee schedule amounted to a price restraint and thus was *per se illegal.* The reason for holding it so was the lack of incentive to the medical practitioners to innovate and experiment resulting in stagnation within the medical field—all the doctors were bound by the maximum fee schedule irrespective of their skill, talent, training and experience. This kind of an arrangement was also likely to discourage new practitioners to enter the field. Consequently, it was not only anti-competitive but also detrimental to the public'.[124] As Justice Stevens notes:

> 'The price-fixing agreements in this case, however, are not premised on public service or ethical norms'.[125]

Further, rejecting the argument of lack of judicial experience in dealing with issues relating to the health industry for the purpose of applying the *per se rule,* Justice Stevens declared that the same would be 'quite obviously…

---

[121] *Id.*, 339–341.

[122] *Id.*, 348.

[123] *Id.*, 347.

[124] *Id.*, 348.

[125] *Id.*, 349.

inconsistent with *Socony-Vacuum.*'[126] This declaration may appear to be in contradiction with the court's decision in the BMI case, where they insisted that until the judiciary gained sufficient experience with an industry, it should not apply the *per se* rule.[127] Yet a look at footnote number 19 of the majority opinion clears this impression. The court does admit that

> 'a new per se rule is not justified until the judiciary obtains considerable rule-of-reason experience with the particular type of restraint challenged'.[128]

As a further clarification of its stance, the majority declared that

> 'The anticompetitive potential inherent in all price-fixing agreements justifies their facial invalidation even if procompetitive justifications are offered for some'.[129]

From this approach of the majority, it is evident that the practices which have, over the years, been declared to be manifestly anti-competitive or naked restraints will be always presumed to be *per se illegal.* The court supported its position by distinguishing BMI. It declared that in BMI, what the licencors were selling was a different product in the form of the blanket licence. This was not the same thing as sale by the individual composers of their composition in different markets. In these other markets, they were free to compete with each other on prices and customers. In other words, the blanket licence was a separate product in itself which did not restrain the

> 'the right of any individual copyright owner to sell his own compositions separately to any buyer at any price'.[130]

Furthermore, the court emphasized that the price of the blanket licence in the BMI case was not fixed through a horizontal agreement among competitors. Hence, if there was price fixing it was only in the literal sense and not in the sense as understood for the purpose of the *per se rule.* In contrast, in the Maricopa case, the member doctors of the challenged foundation were competitors, competing for patients (customers) and prices (fees). They all sold the same product, i.e., medical services, and as members of the foundation, they did not sell any other product. In other words, unlike ASCAP and BMI, the Maricopa Foundation was selling the same product as

---

[126] *Id.*, 349.

[127] 441 US 1 (n 102) 10.

[128] 457 US 332 (n 120) 349–351.

[129] *Id.*, 351.

[130] 457 US 332 (n 120) 355.

the individual members. The formation of the foundation was thus a method adopted by the doctors

> 'to sell their services to certain customers at fixed prices and arguably to affect the prevailing market price of medical care'.[131]

This also meant that the price fixed by the combination of doctors was not ancillary to the main purpose but the main purpose for which they formed the combination. This convinced the court that there was no *necessary* requirement for the doctors to fix the price for selling their product, viz., medical services. Thus, the crucial difference in the BMI situation where the protection of the interest of the copyright owners was regarded as the main reason for the granting of the non-exclusive licence to ASCAP and BMI was established.[132] The court further distinguished the combination of doctors from a legitimate joint venture or a partnership. The court said

> 'The foundations are not analogous to partnerships or other joint arrangements in which persons who would otherwise be competitors pool their capital and share the risks of loss as well as the opportunities for profit. In such joint ventures, the partnership is regarded as a single firm competing with other sellers in the market. The agreement under attack is an agreement among hundreds of competing doctors concerning the price at which each will offer his own services to a substantial number of consumers... the fee agreements disclosed by the record in this case are among independent competing entrepreneurs. They fit squarely into the horizontal price-fixing mold'.[133]

The dissenting opinion of Justice Powell insisted on a more discerning approach. In effect, he argued that the court did not have enough experience to apply the *per se rule* in the Maricopa case.[134] He insisted that an analysis of pro-competitive justifications needs to be done when the practice is novel and has no precedent of *per se illegality*.[135] He did admit that all agreements which on the face of it or from the record appear pernicious are to be categorized as *per se illegal.* Accordingly, Justice Powell states that

> 'It is settled law that once an arrangement has been labeled as 'price fixing' it is to be condemned per se. But it is equally well settled that this characterization is not to be applied as a talisman to every arrangement

[131] *Id.*,356.
[132] *Id.*
[133] *Id.*, 356–357.
[134] *Id.*, 364.
[135] *Id.*, 363–364.

> that involves a literal fixing of prices. Many lawful contracts, mergers, and partnerships fix prices. But our cases require a more discerning approach.'[136]

Justice Powell accordingly dismissed the distinction sought to be drawn by the majority with the BMI case. For him, both were similar arrangements and like in the BMI case, here too the combination, i.e., Maricopa Foundation was formed to provide 'medical services that in fact benefits rather than injures persons who need them'.[137]

On the whole, the Maricopa reiterates the shift in the approach of the US Supreme Court as is evident from the *quick look* presumptions. For traditional categories of *per se illegal* conduct, the presumption is conclusive or irrebuttable but for newer types of conduct, the presumption is rebuttable.[138] In the Maricopa case itself, the court did explain the anti-competitive harm of the arrangement, thus negativing the pro-competitive justifications provided by the defendants. It will not be wrong therefore to contend that in the case of cartels even a shift to rebuttable presumption will not help the defendants. Further, all cases of cartels will be governed by the *per se rule.* So far as determining whether the conduct is a naked restraint or not, the court is likely to resort to the *quick look* approach. This again reverts to the rebuttable presumption theory, with the defendant getting a chance to show the combination's pre-competitive values.[139] In cases of cartels, this is never possible. Hence, based on the review of the US Supreme Court's judgments, cartels are always *per se illegal.*[140] It is also evident that the pre-BMI cases did not allow defendants to show any pro-competitive justifications for their conduct as is evident from the *Socony-Vacuum* case. The present position of the US Supreme Court though appears to show a bent towards the quick look approach.[141]

---

136 *Id.*, 361–362.

137 *Id.*, 367.

138 DolphSchimdt, 'Antitrust—Application of Per Se Rule against Price Fixing for Doctors' Maximum Fee Schedules: Arizona v. Maricopa County Medical Society', *U. Kan. L. Rev.* 479, 488–489, (1983): 31.

139 See generally Edward Brunet, 'Streamlining Antitrust Litigation by "Facial Examination" of Restraints: The Burger Court and the Per Se Rule of Reason Distinction', *Wsh. L. Rev. 1* (1984): 60.

140 See, for example, the statement of Justice Kennedy in Leegin (n 100) 893, where he emphasizes that 'A horizontal cartel among competing manufacturers or competing retailers that decreases output or reduces competition in order to increase price is, and ought to be, per se unlawful'.

141 Recent trends show that US courts have developed another approach termed as the *inherently suspect rule.* It is interchangeably used with the *quick look* approach. While in

Anti-cartel movement: Strengthening the pro-consumer approach

The above discussion thus establishes that the US Supreme Court has rendered all cartels *per se illegal.* In order to ensure that this declaration of the highest court translates into reality, the US Congress has created an agency responsible for enforcing the anti-cartel law. This is the Federal Trade Commission (hereinafter called the FTC) which was established in the year 1914 for the purpose of conducting investigations and capturing conduct that may not strictly fall under the Act.[142] The FTC thus is empowered under the FTC Act 1914 to '(a) prevent unfair methods of competition, and unfair or deceptive acts or practices in or affecting commerce; (b) seek monetary redress and other relief for conduct injurious to consumers; (c) prescribe trade regulation rules defining with specificity acts or practices that are unfair or deceptive, and establishing requirements designed to prevent such acts or practices; (d) conduct investigations relating to the organization, business, practices, and management of entities engaged in commerce; and (e) make reports and legislative recommendations to the US Congress'.[143] The FTC specifically derives its power to deal with cartels and other anti-competitive practices from section 5 of the FTC Act.[144]

It is in pursuance of this section that the FTC through its Bureau of Competition takes measures against cartels. The FTC as part of its anti-cartel measures conducts investigations and frames charges against offenders. It issues subpoenas[145] for the purpose of forcing the offending parties to

the *quick look* approach, the plaintiff is required to show actual anti-competitive effects, the *inherently suspect* approach presumes anti-competitiveness on the basis of the nature of the restraint. However, in both the approaches, the presumption is rebuttable. For a detailed discussion on the similarity and difference between the quick look approach and the inherently suspect approach, see Tiffany Lena Lee, 'Anticompetitive Exclusion and the "Inherently Suspect" Framework: The Viability of the Federal Trade Commission's Analysis in Realcomp II', *U.C. Davis Bus. L.J.* 375 (2011): 11.

142 IoannisKokkoris and Rodrigo Olivares-Caminal, *Antitrust Law amidst Financial Crises* (CUP, 2010), 48–51.

143 The objectives have been taken from the Federal Trade Commission website http://www.ftc.gov/ogc/stat1.shtm (accessed August 30, 2011)

144 Section 5 of the FTC Act [15 USC. § 45]: Unfair methods of competition unlawful; prevention by Commission (a) Declaration of unlawfulness; power to prohibit unfair practices; inapplicability to foreign trade (1) Unfair methods of competition in or affecting commerce, and unfair or deceptive acts or practices in or affecting commerce, are declared unlawful. (2) The Commission is empowered and directed to prevent persons, partnerships or corporations…from using unfair methods of competition in or affecting commerce and unfair or deceptive acts or practices in or affecting commerce…

145 Subpoena is a writ commanding a person designated in it to appear in court under a penalty for failure http://www.merriam-webster.com/dictionary/subpoena (accessed 31 August 2011).

produce all evidence related to the matter under investigation.[146] The party, who is issued the subpoena, has an option of raising an objection to the subpoena by filing a petition for getting it quashed. The said petition will be heard by the Commissioner appointed for the purpose. From his or her order, an appeal is laid before the full Commission. In case the party fails to respond to the subpoena either by complying with it or getting it quashed, or if the petition for quashing is denied, the Bureau of Competition will get the subpoena judicially enforced through the courts having jurisdiction. Failure to comply with such a court order of compliance with the subpoena will amount to contempt of court. In addition to the power of issuing the subpoena, the Bureau also has the power to enforce filing of information by different commercial entities regarding their internal management and business practices.[147] As is in the case of subpoenas, here too, the same options are available to the addressee of the inquiry and the Bureau of Competition.

In addition to these investigative powers, the FTC through its Bureau of Competition has certain enforcement powers. The FTC can challenge anti-competitive conduct like cartels by initiating administrative adjudicatory proceedings under section 5(b) of the FTC Act.[148] The orders issued as part of these proceedings by the FTC is subject to appeal. The FTC in these proceedings can issue cease and desist orders against the offending business entities. It also has the rule-making power to enforce anti-cartel provisions along with other competition provisions of section 5 (a) of the FTC Act. This power is vested under section 18 of the FTC Act. Further, under section 13 (b) of the FTC Act, the FTC has the power to obtain preliminary and permanent injuctive reliefs. The FTC can also obtain disgorgement of unjust enrichment, restitution for injury suffered by consumers and other equitable

---

146 See Section 9 of the FTC Act.

147 See Section 6 (b) of the FTC Act.

148 The administrative trials of the FTC are similar to court trials. These proceedings are usually commenced after the conclusion of the investigation by the FTC. Once the investigation is over, the investigating staff may recommend that the Commission challenge the anti-competitive conduct. If the Commission decides by a majority to challenge the conduct, it will send the matter for adjudication to an administrative law judge, who is independently appointed by the Office of Personnel Management. Thus the administrative law judge is not an employee of the FTC. Interestingly, however, the determination of the administrative law judge will be binding only if the Commission approves the decision. It is only then, depending upon the decision of the administrative law judge, that the FTC will pass a cease and desist order. For a critique on FTC proceedings see Diana Gillis, 'Closing an Administrative Loophole: Ethics for the Administrative Judiciary', *Geo. J. Legal Ethics* 863 (2009): 22.

reliefs. Further, it can also initiate civil suits for imposing penalties against violators of cease and desist orders. The FTC is therefore empowered with litigating powers. [149] As to the exact nature of the anti-competitive activities that the FTC can take note of under section 5, the US Supreme Court has provided clarifications.

For example, in the *FTC v Indiana Federation of Dentists*[150] case, the court explained the scope of section 5 of the FTC Act. The case dealt with the Indiana Dental Association's decision not to share the dental x-rays of a patient with his or her insurers—to enable the insurers to evaluate the desirability of the treatment performed by the dentist (who were members of the said association).[151] As result of the non-submission of the dental x-rays by the association members, the insurers were forced to adopt alternative methods to determine the desirability of the treatment. The same however proved to be expensive and left the insurers with no option but to abandon such evaluation.[152] This agreement of the association's members was regarded as anti-competitive and the FTC passed a cease and desist order.[153] Subsequently, thereafter another association of the Indiana dentists was formed, viz., the Indiana Federation of Dentists. They decided to prohibit all their members from submitting the dental x-rays to the insurers.[154] The FTC issued a complaint against the federation for indulging in 'unfair method of competition' in violation of section 5 of the FTC Act.[155]

At the conclusion of the proceedings before an administrative law judge (who conducts the proceedings under section 5 (b)), the FTC passed a cease and desist order.[156] The Commission decided that the act of the federation's members to refuse to submit the dental x-rays was a conspiracy in restraint of trade and unreasonable, as per the standards laid down by the US Supreme Court while interpreting section 1 of the Act.[157] In judicial review, the Court

[149] Information available at the FTC website http://www.ftc.gov/bc/about.shtm (accessed August 31, 2011).

[150] 476 US 447, 106 S.Ct. 2009 (decided in 1986).

[151] *Id.*, 450.

[152] *Id.*

[153] *Id.*

[154] 476 US 447 (n 150) 451.

[155] *Id.*

[156] As explained in n 333, the cease and desist order is passed by the full Commission on approving the determination of the administrative law judge. The FTC Commissioners are granted dual prosecutorial and adjudicative roles under the Administrative Procedure Act of the US.

[157] 476 US 447 (n 150) 452.

of Appeal (7th Circuit) reversed the order of the Commission, and declared that the findings of the Commission were erroneous.[158] On appeal, the US Supreme Court held that the practice of the federation was akin to group boycotts, viz., an agreement or conspiracy resulting in a concerted refusal to deal with suppliers or end consumers, and hence *per se illegal.*[159] Nevertheless, they decided not to extend these categories to the case as it involved a rule of a professional group. For this reason, the case was decided by applying the *rule of reason* analysis. Accordingly, the court declared the rule of withholding the dental x-rays as unreasonable.[160] The court also clarified that the

> '[t]he standard of "unfairness" under the FTC Act is, by necessity, an elusive one, encompassing not only practices that violate the Sherman Act and the other antitrust laws, but also practices that the Commission determines are against public policy for other reasons'.[161]

The FTC therefore is empowered to take note of any act that appears to be anti-competitive. Since violations of the Act are part of the FTC's enforcement mandate, all cartel activities will be investigated and proceeded against by the FTC. The US Congress further strengthened its anti-trust laws by passing the Clayton Act in 1914.[162] The Clayton Act listed the conduct which will be regarded as illegal under the Act. Acts such as price discrimination (§ 2, 15 USC. § 13), predatory pricing (§ 2 (a), 15 USC. § 13 (a)) and tying and exclusive dealing agreements (§ 3, 15 USC. § 14) were rendered illegal. Additionally, under section 11 of the Clayton Act, the FTC is authorized to initiate proceedings for violations of the Clayton Act by using both administrative and judicial remedies.[163] Along with the FTC, there is another important organ of the US Government that is responsible for the enforcement of the anti-trust laws including the anti-cartel laws. It is the Anti-trust Division of the Department of Justice of the US Government. It differs from the FTC, in that it is the sole agency of the US Government empowered to criminally prosecute cartels.[164] One of the effective methods

158 *Id.*, 453 [The Court of Appeal agreed with the Federation that its rule against sharing of dental x-rays was merely a moral and ethical rule having no bearing on competition or the welfare of the patients].

159 *Id.*, 458.

160 *Id.*, 461–463.

161 *Id.*, 454.

162 1914, 15 USC. § § 12–27.

163 1914, 15 USC (n 162) Sec 11 (15 USC. § 21).

164 See John M Connor, 'Anti-Cartel Enforcement by the DOJ: An appraisal', *Comp. L. Rev.* 89 (2008): 5 (1). The Division can start investigation on the basis of information received from various sources, for example, individuals or businesses. The attorneys of the Division

used by the Division to detect cartels is by providing incentives to cartel members to become whistleblowers. This, in effect, means that cartel members are incentivized to break ranks and become informers against the cartels. The breaking of ranks or whistleblowing not only ensures that the whistleblower gets protection from prosecution but also helps in the effective detection and speedy conviction of other cartel members.[165] The Division follows an automatic amnesty policy, in the sense that the whistleblower will be granted amnesty automatically if there is no pre-existing investigation against him or her. This automatic amnesty is thus available to a corporate entity who comes forward and reveals the existence of a cartel before any investigation has been started by the Division. The amnesty is certain to be granted without being subject to the discretion of the prosecutors.[166]

In addition to the automatic amnesty programme, the Division also has an alternative amnesty programme. This is available to a corporate entity that breaks ranks and blows the whistle after the Division has received information about the cartel activity, irrespective of whether the entity does so before or after the investigation has begun. One of the conditions which the grant of alternative amnesty is dependent on is whether the said grant would not be unfair to others considering the nature of the cartel activity, the nature of the role played by the confessing corporation and the time when the confessing corporation comes forward. The earlier the corporation confesses, the easier it is to convince the Division as to the fairness of the amnesty. Further, in granting alternative amnesty, only the individuals who come forward with the corporation is eligible for the amnesty.[167] In contrast, under the automatic amnesty programme, along with the confessing corporation, all directors,

---

must develop the necessary legal and factual basis for getting an approval for formal investigation. This approval is granted by the Director of Criminal Enforcement and also the FTC. There is first a preliminary inquiry and then a grand jury investigation which will establish the criminal conspiracy of the cartel members. The conspirators will be formally charged which be followed by a trial. For information about the grand jury investigation procedure, please see the Antiturst Division (Department of Justice) 'Grand Jury Manual' http://www.justice.gov/atr/public/guidelines/4371.htm (accessed October 21, 2011). See also DabbahandHawk (n 3) 1258–1262.

[165] Jason D. Medinger, 'Antitrust Leniency Programs: A Call for Increased Harmonization as Proliferating Programs Undermine Deterrence', *Emory L.J.* 1439, 1441 (2003): 52.

[166] See Scott D. Hammond, 'Detecting and Deterring Cartel Activity through an Effective Leniency Program', http://www.justice.gov/atr/public/speeches/9928.pdf (accessed 1 September 2011).

[167] Scott D. Hammond and Belinda A. Barnett, 'Frequently Asked Questions Regarding the Antitrust Division's Leniency Program and Model Leniency Letters', http://www.justice.gov/atr/public/criminal/239583.pdf (accessed 1 September 2011)

officers and employees who come forward as part of the corporate confession and agree to cooperate, also receive automatic amnesty.[168] In addition to the corporate leniency programme, the Division also has an individual leniency programme. Here too there is an automatic amnesty programme which is available to an individual before the investigation has begun. In the alternative amnesty programme however, an individual will be entitled to a statutory or informal immunity from criminal prosecution based on prosecutorial discretion, on a case-by-case basis.[169]

One of the key features of the US leniency programme is that only the first confessor is eligible for immunity from criminal prosecution and criminal conviction. The idea is to encourage cartelists to be the first to break ranks and report the conspiracy to the Department of Justice.[170] The incentives for being the first to be at the door of the Department of Justice are many. Since cartelists are prosecuted criminally, the consequence of a criminal conviction is quite severe. Prior to June 22, 2004, a cartelist (be it a company or individual) when convicted, was liable to be punished, in case of corporations, with a fine up to $10 million, and in case of individuals, with a fine up to $ 350,000. In addition, an individual was also liable to be punished with an imprisonment of three years.[171] After June 22, 2004, corporate fines have been increased to $100 million and individual fines to $ 1 million. Further, the jail term for individual offenders have been increased to ten years.[172] In addition to these punishments, cartelists (corporations and individuals) are subject to the alternative fine provision under the US Criminal Procedure.[173] According to 18 USC. § 3571 (d), in case of pecuniary gains resulting from an offence or loss being suffered by any one other than the defendant, as a result of the offence, the fines imposed will be up to twice the gross gain or twice the gross loss. This thus puts a cartel member at enormous risk and consequently makes the amnesty option attractive. The confessor not only gets immunity

---

168 See Department of Justice, Corporate Leniency Policy, http://www.justice.gov/atr/public/guidelines/0091.htm (accessed 1 September 2011).

169 See Department of Justice, Leniency Policy for Individuals, http://www.justice.gov/atr/public/guidelines/0092.htm (accessed 1 September 2011).

170 See Gary R.Spratling, 'Detection and Deterrence: Rewarding Informants for Reporting Violations', *Geo. Wash. L. Rev.* 798, (2001): 69.

171 In effect an individual was liable to be punished with both the fine and imprisonment or only the fine or only the imprisonment.

172 See Antitrust Division (US Department of Justice), 'An Antitrust Primer for Federal Law Enforcement Personnel' (2005) http://www.justice.gov/atr/public/guidelines/209114.htm (accessed 2 September 2011).

173 See 18 USC. § 3571 [The section deals with sentence of fines].

from criminal prosecution but also has to pay zero fines.[174] The exemption from fines is tremendously attractive considering the huge amount of fines that the corporation and the individuals end up paying.[175] Further, for the directors and employees of the company, the fear of incarceration also acts as an incentive to confess.[176]

The success of the US leniency programme is thus largely based on the strong detection and enforcement measures carried on by both the FTC and the Department of Justice.[177] As is understandable, in the absence of fear of detection, there will be no incentive for a cartelist to break ranks. This fact has made the US leniency programme the most effective tool for disbanding cartels.[178] Though the leniency programme is based on the philosophy of winner takes it all, there is an alternative formulae called amnesty plus which is applied in the case of a corporation that is not the first to confess. Amnesty plus essentially is a method of encouraging conspirators to come forward and apply for leniency with regard to the cartel activity being carried out in other markets. For example, in an investigation conducted in pursuance of a leniency application, the Division proceeds against a company called ZYZ. In the meantime, ZYZ, through its internal review gets information that it is a participant in an arrangement which is nothing but a cartel relating to some other product market (sprockets). The Division having no knowledge of the same, ZYZ can confess and inform about the said cartel. If ZYZ satisfies all the conditions of the corporate leniency programme, it will be given automatic amnesty in respect to the cartel activity in the sprocket product market.[179] As far as the ongoing investigation is concerned,

---

[174] See Thomas O. Barnett, 'Seven Steps to Better Cartel Enforcement', (2006) 11th Annual Competition Law and Policy Workshop European Union Institute Florence, Italy http://www.justice.gov/atr/public/speeches/216453.pdf (accessed 21 October 2011).

[175] For example, till the year 2005, the largest fine that a corporation ended up paying was $500 million and that for an individual has been $10 million.

[176] Scott D. Hammond (n 167) 4–5.

[177] One needs to note that the FTC and the Division together clear all proposed grand jury investigations in order to avoid overlapping of investigations. In essence, the FTC and Division need to ensure that they do not end up investigating the same conduct. Thus FTC can investigate cartel conduct but is not empowered to prosecute criminal anti-trust violations. See Dabbah and Hawk (n 3 of Chapter 1) 1258. See also 'Antitrust Division Manual: Chapter III-Investigation and Case Development- B(3)', 4th edition, (2009), http://www.justice.gov/atr/public/divisionmanual/chapter3.pdf (accessed 21 October 2011).

[178] *Id.*, 1.

[179] This implies that the company's internal review brought forth the fact that the company is part of a cartel in the second product market. Hence they decide to confess to the Division before anyone else or any of their employees does so.

the Division would recommend the sentencing court to substantially reduce the fine for ZYZ's combined cooperation in the ongoing investigation as well as for revealing the other cartel. It follows, therefore, that even the second to the door can obtain reduction in fines (though no protection from criminal prosecution and conviction), if they cooperate with the Division in its investigation.[180] However there is also a system of penalty plus. If the corporate or individual under investigation for cartel offence fails to report its participation in a second anti-trust offence, not known to the Division, then the consequences are severe. If the Division discovers the second offence and successfully prosecutes the offenders, then it will urge the sentencing court to consider this failure to report as a ground for aggravated sentencing.[181]

As far as the pro-consumer approach in anti-cartel measure is concerned, the US appears to be quite active. That protection of consumer interest is one of the main aims of the US anti-trust law is evident from the various documents issued by the FTC and the Department of Justice. For example, in its primer on cartel behaviour, prepared by the Department of Justice, it is declared that

> 'American consumers have the right to expect the benefits of free and open competition — the best goods and services at the lowest prices.'[182]

Further, the motto of FTC, as declared in its website is 'Protecting America's Consumers'.[183] The FTC proudly declares that its Bureau of Competition champions the rights of American consumers.[184] Importantly, the pro-consumer approach of the US anti-trust law is evident from the fact that amnesty is granted only against criminal sanctions. A cartel member continues to be liable for civil actions for treble damages.[185] The civil action can be

[180] See Gary R.Spratling (n 170) where Spartling argues that the second at the door too ends up getting huge financial advantages. See also Scott D. Hammond, 'Measuring the value of second in cooperation in corporate plea negotiations'. (2006), The 54th Annual American Bar Association Section of the Antitrust Law Spring Meeting http://www.justice.gov/atr/public/speeches/215514.htm (accessed 21 October 2011).

[181] See Scott D Hammond, 'An Overview of the Recent Developments in the Antitrust Division's Criminal Enforcement Programme', (2005), Before the American Bar Association Midwinter Leadership Meeting http://www.justice.gov/atr/public/speeches/207226.htm (accessed 21 October 2011).

[182] See Department of Justice, 'An Antirust Primer- Price Fixing, Bid Rigging, and Market Allocation Schemes: What They are and what to Look for'. http://www.justice.gov/atr/public/guidelines/211578.pdf (accessed 2 September 2011).

[183] For information visit http://www.ftc.gov/ (accessed 2 September 2011).

[184] For information visit http://www.ftc.gov/bc/index.shtml (accessed 2 September 2011).

[185] However with the Antitrust Criminal Penalty Enhancement and Reform Act, 2003, the civil penalties are no more trebled for those who effectively participate in the leniency

instituted both by the Department of Justice under 15 USC. § 15 (a) [section 4a][186], as well as any private parties (which will include both consumers as well as state or local government), under 15 USC. § 15 [section 4][187]. Further, under the leniency programme, it is mandatory for the applicants to give full, continuing and complete cooperation that furthers the investigation. One of the specific obligations that have to be complied with by the applicant to satisfy the requirement of complete cooperation with the Department of Justice is restitution to the victims of the cartel activity.[188] Non-fulfillment of such specific obligations will result in revocation of the amnesty granted by the Department of Justice.[189] This again reflects concern for the consumer who would end up as a victim of the cartel.

Looking forward

The above review of the US anti-cartel law reveals several interesting points. First, it was established in the early years of the Sherman Act that price-fixing cartels are bad and need to be treated as *per se illegal*. Secondly, the ensuing debate in the US Supreme Court was and has been about determination of ancillary restraint as compared to a hard core restraint. Thirdly, notwithstanding the evolution of the *quick look* approach, the identification of the ancillary from

programme. However for non-participants, the treble damages continue to apply. Thus the cartelists participating in leniency programme will be liable to pay only single damages. See Bridget C. Kevin, 'The Antitrust Criminal Penalty Enhancement and Reform Act of 2003', http://luc.edu/law/academics/special/center/antitrust/pdfs/b_kevin.pdf (accessed October 21, 2011). On May 27, 2010, the 2003 Act was extended for another ten years as it was felt that the damages limiting provision was successful in uncovering and prosecuting cartels. The information is available at http://legaltimes.typepad.com/blt/2010/05/senate-extends-criminal-antitrust-amnesty-law.html (accessed October 22, 2011)

186 As per Section 4a of the Clayton Act: ['Whenever the United States is hereafter injured in its business or property by reason of anything forbidden in the antitrust laws it may sue therefore in the United States district court for the district in which the defendant resides or is found or has an agent…and shall recover threefold the damages by it sustained…']

187 As per Section 4 of the Clayton Act: ['[A]ny person who shall be injured in his business or property by reason of anything forbidden in the antitrust laws may sue therefore in any district court of the United States in the district in which the defendant resides or is found or has an agent…and shall recover threefold damages by him sustained…']

188 See Morrison Foerster, 'Antitrust Report: Department of Justice Amnesty Program Takes Another New Turn', (2005) http://www.mofo.com/pubs/xpqPublicationDetail.aspx?xpST=PubDetail&pub=7064 (accessed October 22, 2011).

189 This is so because usually no final leniency is granted till the completion of the investigations and the resulting prosecutions of the co-conspirators. See *Id.*, p 23–24.

the core continues to be problematic. Fourthly, in the case of horizontal agreements to divide markets, customers, bid rigging, price fixing, etc., the courts will rely on precedents and hold them as *per se illegal.* Fifthly, in the case of new emerging fields where there is lack of prior experience, the courts will apply the *quick look* or its variant, the *inherently suspect* approach test and decide whether to declare it *per se illegal* or not. Sixthly, the *per se* approach towards cartels is part and parcel of the enforcement policy of the FTC and the Anti-trust Division of the Department of Justice. Consequently, all measures, rules and guidelines are issued to ensure a highly successful anti-cartel policy. The leniency programme designed to deal with both corporates as well as their personnel, is aimed at encouraging a race to the Division. The individual leniency programme makes it seem wise for corporations to be the first to the door least their employees or directors overtake them. In case an employee overtakes the corporation in the race, the corporation will lose the benefit of automatic amnesty. Seventhly, automatic amnesty from criminal liability does not grant immunity from civil actions by private parties like consumers. Finally, the anti-cartel law in the US is geared to further the interest of both the end consumer as well other intermediaries who are injured by cartels. The *per se illegality* of cartels is a proof of this consumer-oriented approach. The US Supreme Court has, as discussed above, rejected the *rule of reason* approach towards cartels as their inherent pernicious nature negates any justification. Thus, the justification provided in the form of ruinous competition argument has also been rejected. It is time now to move on and review the next jurisdiction, viz., EU, in order to properly grasp the complexities of enforcing an anti-cartel law that furthers consumer interest.

4 EU, Cartels and Consumer Interests

Context

With the signing of the Treaty of Rome, the competition law became an important chapter of the Treaty. This was a significant step since major European economies like Germany were largely cartelized.[1] The Treaty of Rome was subsequently amended by the Treaty of Maastricht in 1993 and then by the Treaty of Amsterdam in 1997. The Amsterdam Treaty re-numbered the Treaty of Rome, which effectively meant that the provisions relating to competition were also re-numbered.[2] Thus, Articles 81–89 embodied the entire European competition law (hereinafter called the EU competition law).[3] The Treaty of Rome has been further amended and re-numbered by the Treaty of Lisbon, signed on December 13, 2007 in Lisbon.[4]

Accordingly, the EU competition law, in its entirety, is embodied in Chapter I of Title VII of the Treaty of Lisbon. Furthermore, the Articles 81–89 have been re-numbered as Articles 101–109. As in this book we are concerned with cartels, our focus will be on the relevant provisions relating to cartels. The interpretation of the relevant provisions by EU institutions

---

1 See generally, Giorgio Monti (n 158 of Chapter 2) 1–6. See also the discussion on Germany and cartels in Chapter I, Section 2.2.2.

2 Article 81 was previously numbered as Article 85 under the Treaty of Rome.

3 See generally Whish (n 4 of Chapter 1) 48–49.

4 The Treaty of Lisbon, known as the 'Reform Treaty' came into force on December 1, 2009, upon ratification by all the EU members. 'Europa - Treaty of Lisbon - Taking Europe into the 21st Century' http://europa.eu/lisbon_treaty/take/index_en.htm (accessed September 20, 2010). The details of the Treaty of Lisbon can be downloaded from http://bookshop.europa.eu/is-bin/INTERSHOP.enfinity/WFS/EU-Bookshop-Site/en_GB/-/EUR/ViewPublication-Start?PublicationKey=FXAC08115 (accessed 20 September 2010). The Treaty of Lisbon has re-named the Treaty of Rome (also called the Treaty on the European Union) as the Treaty on the Functioning of the European Union (TFEU).

will be analysed in this chapter. This analysis will help us understand the theoretical response of the EU to cartels. The questions that are sought to be addressed in the process are: which approach, viz., the *per se* or the *rule of reason*, best accommodates the consumer interest (both intermediary and end consumer), and how is the objective of an agreement assessed for the purpose of categorizing it as a cartel conduct? As the role of EU institutions in both framing and implementing the anti-cartel law is of paramount importance, the chapter will begin with a review of the structural schema of these institutions. It is herein important to note that the Treaty of Lisbon has not brought about any structural changes within the EU institutions.

EU institutions: An overview

The EU comprises the European Parliament, the European Council, the Council of the European Union, the Commission, the Court of Justice of the EU, the European Central Bank and the Court of Auditors. However, it is the European Parliament, the Council of the European Union and the European Commission which produces the policies and the law that are applicable across the EU. The Court of Justice of the EU plays the role of upholding the rule of the EU law and is assisted by the General Court (earlier called the Court of First Instance). In the order of hierarchy and importance, both the European Parliament and the Council of the European Union occupy a place of equal importance. Both the institutions exist to complement each other in the matter of framing policies and enacting laws.

The European Parliament is a directly elected body having representatives from all the twenty-seven member countries. Along with the Council of the European Union, the European Parliament is empowered to adopt, in a procedure known as 'co-decision', draft legislations proposed by the European Commission. The European Parliament also has the power to force the European Commission to resign. When it comes to formulating and adopting the EU competition laws, the European Parliament has to be consulted by the Council of the European Union.[5] In other words, the European Parliament is assigned the role of a consultant and not that of a framer as far as the EU competition law is concerned. The responsibility and

[5] See The Treaty of Lisbon (n 4) Article 103 (1) (It states that the 'The appropriate regulations or directives to give effect to the principles set out in Articles 101and 102 shall be laid down by the Council, on a proposal from the Commission and after consulting the European Parliament'.)

power to frame EU competition laws have been vested with the Council of the European Union.

The Council of the European Union therefore becomes the highest legislative body for formulating EU competition laws. This function, as mentioned above, will nonetheless have to be discharged, in consultation with the European Parliament. In its role as a legislature, the Council of European Union is assisted by the European Commission. The Council of the European Union thus vets the various proposals on competition and issues regulations or directives, for ensuring 'compliance with the prohibitions laid down in Article 101(1) and in Article 102 by making provision for fines and periodic penalty payments'.[6] In addition, the Council of the European Union also defines the scope of Articles 101 and 102 as well as the respective function of the European Commission and the Court of Justice of the European Union.

Of the two, i.e., the European Commission and the Court of Justice of the European Union, it is the former which is responsible for the enforcement of the competition laws. So the European Commission is the executive branch and is responsible for administering the anti-cartel laws. One however needs to note that the competition laws form only a part of the several other laws that the European Commission has to enforce. The European Commission, as an institution essentially comprises 27 Commissioners (from each member country of the EU) and several thousand civil servants, who together are split into several departments called the Director General and Services. Competition thus is the subject matter of one such Director General and Services (in other words, department).

Through the respective Director General and Services, the Commission prepares the proposals for legislative acts, viz., regulations, directives and decisions, relating to various fields. Only the European Commission has legislative initiative within the EU, thereby ensuring that no legislation originates from the legislative branches of the EU. In addition to the monopoly over preparing formal proposals for legislations, the European Commission also has the sole power to ensure the implementation of the legislations. Further, the European Commission also holds executive power along with the Council of European Union. The Court of Justice of the European Union comprises the entire judicial system of the EU. The European Court of Justice, the General Court and the Civil Service Tribunal form part of this system.

---

6 The Treaty of Lisbon (n 4) Article 103 (2) (a).

The Court of Justice of the European Union tests the legality of the EU laws, ensures that the EU laws are properly interpreted and applied, that the member states observe the EU laws and interprets the EU law at the request of the various national courts and tribunals. Of the three wings of the Court of Justice of the European Union, the Civil Service Tribunal, as the name suggests, is created specially to deal with disputes between the EU and its civil service. The General Court, on the other hand, is the Court of First Instance, from whose decision appeal lies at the last wing of this institution, viz., the European Court of Justice. Having briefly discussed the various EU institutions, we will now move on to an in-depth study of the area of EU competition law in connection with the regulation of cartels and protection of consumer interests.

Historically, cartels were regarded as an accepted practice of doing business in Europe. It was the Second World War and the dominance of the US in world politics that forced the European nations to re-think their approach on cartels. Therefore, clause 1 and clause 2 of Article 101 (formerly Article 81/ Article 85) of the EU Treaty (Lisbon) lay down the law for dealing with cartels in the EU. As stated before, it is the European Commission that is responsible for enforcing these Articles. It was however only during the late 1960s that the European Commission became active in taking action against cartels. The enforcement machinery gained further momentum in the 1980s and the 1990s. At present, the European Commission's cartel regulation aims at maximum deterrence of cartels. [7]

The European Commission's jurisprudence on cartels has evolved over the years, thereby establishing norms subject to which a cartel is declared illegal.[8] As mentioned above, clauses 1 and 2 of Article 101 defines the practices prohibited by the EU law. Article 101, thus, is the embodiment of the common objectives stated in the Preamble of the Lisbon Treaty. The Preamble of the Lisbon Treaty emphasizes the need to have an internal market for the purpose of furthering economic integration and economic progress.[9] The need to have an integrated internal market is further reiterated in Article 3, clause 3 of the Lisbon Treaty which states that

> 'The Union shall establish an internal market. It shall work for the sustainable development of Europe based on balanced economic

---

7 Christopher Harding and Julian Joshua (n 11 of Chapter 1) 117–119.

8 See generally http://ec.europa.eu/competition/cartels/overview/index_en.html (accessed 20 September 2010)

9 See The Treaty of Lisbon (n 4), the Preamble.

> growth and price stability, a highly competitive social market economy (emphasis added) aiming at full employment and social progress…'.[10]

Clause 1 of Article 101 is worded in a manner that can be interpreted to enforce the objectives mentioned in the Lisbon Treaty. It states that

> 'The following shall be prohibited as incompatible with the internal market: all agreements between undertakings, decisions by associations of undertakings and concerted practices which may affect trade between Member States and which have as their object or effect the prevention, restriction or distortion of competition within the internal market and in particular those which:
> (a) directly or indirectly fix purchase or selling prices or any other trading conditions;
> (b) limit or control production, markets, technical development, or investment;
> (c) share markets or sources of supply;
> (d) apply dissimilar conditions to equivalent transactions with other trading parties, thereby placing them at a competitive disadvantage;
> (e) make the conclusion of contracts subject to acceptance by the other parties of supplementary obligations which, by their nature or according to commercial usage, have no connection with the subject of such contracts'.[11]

Clause 2 of Article 101 adds that

> 'Any agreements or decisions prohibited pursuant to this Article shall be automatically void…'.[12]

Since the language of Article 101 is the same as that of the former Article 81, the interpretation, application and the scope of Article 101 will also be the same.[13] Therefore, like the former Article 81, Article 101 will also apply

---

10 *Id.*, Article 3 Clause 3 of Lisbon Treaty at C 115/17.

11 See Article 101 (1).

12 *Id.* Article 101 (2).

13 This statement is supported by the fact that the series of amendments to the EU/EC Treaty has never amended the competition articles. The only change that has taken place over the years, as part of these amendments, is the re-numbering of the Articles. Hence, Article 81 is to be now referred to as Article 101. The EU institutions, viz., the Courts as well the Commission and the Council's statements and decisions further support the fact that substantively there has been no change in the competition law articles. For example, in the European Council Regulation [2003] OJ L 1/1, while referring to Article 81 and 82, it is clarified that 'The title of Regulation…has been adjusted to take account of the renumbering of the Articles of the EC Treaty, in accordance with Article 12 of the Treaty of Amsterdam; the original reference was to Articles 85 and 86 of the Treaty'. The title of the Regulation was further adjusted taking into account the re-numbering brought about

across all sectors of the economy except for those which have been expressly exempted[14] by Article 101 (3).[15] For example, there is no exemption for sports which applies across the sector. However, if the activity is of a purely sporting nature and interest and has no bearing upon any *economic activity*,[16] it falls outside the scope of the EU competition rules.[17]

For the purpose of evaluating cartel regulation in the EU, it will be pertinent to thus understand the interpretation, scope and application of

by the Lisbon Treaty. Accordingly, all references to Article 81 and 82 have been replaced with Article 101 and 102. For details, visit http://europa.eu/legislation_summaries/competition/firms/l26092_en.htm and http://eur lex.europa.eu/LexUriServ/LexUriServ.do?uri=OJ:L:2003:001:0001:0025:EN:PDF (accessed October 24, 2011). See also Case C-439/09, *Pierre Fabre Dermo-Cosmétique SAS v. Président de l'Autorité de la concurrence Ministre de l'Économie, de l'Industrie et de l'Emploi*, [2011] ECR 0000, where the 'ECJ was required to give a preliminary ruling on the question, referred to it by the French Court of Appeal;. The referred question was framed as follows: 'Does a general and absolute ban on selling contract goods to end-users via the internet, imposed on authorised distributors in the context of a selective distribution network, in fact constitute a "hardcore" restriction of competition by object for the purposes of Article 81(1) EC [Article 101(1) TFEU] which is not covered by the block exemption provided for by Regulation No 2790/1999 but which is potentially eligible for an individual exemption under Article 81(3) EC [Article 101(3) TFEU][?]'. This clearly establishes that for interpreting Article 101 or 102, the jurisprudence developed under the former Article 81 and 82 are applicable. In other words, the substantive competition law of the EU remains the same notwithstanding the amendments. Also see Tables of Equivalences referred to in Article 5 of the Treaty of Lisbon [2007] OJ 306/13 http://eur-lex.europa.eu/LexUriServ/LexUriServ.do?uri=OJ:C:2007:306:0202:0229:EN:PDF (accessed October 24, 2011)

14 Jonathan Faull and Ali Nickpay, ed., *The EC Law of Competition,* 2nd ed. (OUP, 2007), 183.

15 To be discussed.

16 In case C-519/04, *David Meca-Medina and Igor Majcen v Commission of the European Communities,* [2006] ECR I-06991, 'the ECJ declared that only when a sporting activity results in a gainful employment or to the provision of services for a remuneration will it be regarded as an *economic activity* and subject to the EU law. Further as per the ECJ if the challenged sporting rule/activity concerns movement of workers within the European Community or freedom to provide services or issues relating to competition, it is to be regarded as an *economic activity* and not merely confined to sporting activity. The ECJ further emphasized that even if a sporting activity/rule is not concerned with freedom of movement of workers or freedom to provide services, it still needs to be assessed under the EU competition law to see if there are any anti-competitive issues involved. Accordingly the ECJ evaluated the anti-doping rules adopted by the International Olympic Committee (IOC) and the International Swimming Federation (FINA) under Article 101/102 to determine whether they were anti-competitive or not. The ECJ upheld the anti-doping rules on the ground that they are framed to achieve a legitimate objective, viz. clean sports. Hence there was nothing inherently anti-competitive about the rules neither was their effect anti-competitive in nature'.

17 Jonathan Faull and Ali Nickpay (n 14) 186.

Article 101, clause 1, which will be on the same lines as that of Article 81 clause 1. Nonetheless, the review undertaken here will primarily focus upon the manner in which the EU has protected consumer interests, while regulating cartels. As will be evident, it is the European Competition Commission, the General Court (formerly the Court of First Instance) and the Court of Justice of the European Union, which has over the decades, laid down the norms subject to which cartel regulation has taken place and continues to take place. One thus needs to ascertain as to how far these norms have been influenced by the idea of consumer protection.

EU cartel law

To begin with, Article 101, clause 1 provides that

> 'all agreements between undertakings, decisions by associations of undertakings and concerted practices which may affect trade between Member States and which have as their object or effect the prevention, restriction or distortion of competition within the common market…'[18]

This formulation of the anti-competitive principle is evidently wide enough to cover all kinds of transactions that distort the competitive process. Accordingly, all anti-cartel measures are based on this Article. In particular, sub-clause (a) of Article 101, clause 1 mentions fixing of prices '*directly or indirectly*' as one of the proscribed activities.[19] Furthermore, sub-clauses (b) and (c) of Article 101, clause 1 appear to complete the picture in so far as anti-cartel measures are concerned.[20] Therefore, any arrangement relating to price-fixing and/or market sharing and/or sharing of customers and products or just products and/or imposing quotas and/or rigging bid and/or exchange of information has been included in the definition of cartels.[21]

Undertaking, associations of undertakings: Meaning

Undertaking

To fall foul of Article 101, clause 1, it thus has to be established that there exists an '*agreement*' between '*undertakings*' or that there exists '*concerted practices*'. Importantly, these '*agreements*' or '*concerted practices*' should result

18 Article 101 (1).

19 *Id.*

20 Article 101 (1).

21 Van Bael and Bellis, *Competition Law of the European Community*, 5th ed. (Kluwer Law International, 2010), 341.

in '*fixing of prices*' or '*any other trading conditions*'. Accordingly, the European Competition Commission and the various EU courts have had to interpret these terms to determine the existence of a cartel.[22] To begin, the scope of the term '*undertaking*' has to be understood before determining the scope of the other terms. This is so because, as is evident, Article 101, clause 1 applies only to anti-competitive practices carried on by *undertakings* or *associations of undertakings*. As maintained by the European Court of Justice

> 'in the context of competition law...the concept of an undertaking encompasses every entity engaged in an economic activity, regardless of the legal status of the entity and the way in which it is financed...'[23]

The determination of whether an entity is an undertaking or not, depends upon, whether it, carries on an economic activity or not. Therefore, the applicability of the competition law in general and cartel laws in particular, depend upon the interpretation given to the nature of the activity by the EU courts. Thus, for example, in *Federación Española de Empresas de Tecnología Sanitaria (FENIN) v. Commission of the European Communities,*[24] the European Court of Justice held that

> 'purchases intended for use in noneconomic activities are... not subject to competition law... a purchase falls within the scope of competition law only in so far as it forms part of the exercise of an economic activity...'.[25]

This reflected the sentiment of the Court of First Instance which declared that only the act of selling goods and services in a given market amounts to economic activity and not the act of purchasing—the act of purchasing has to be necessarily evaluated with the subsequent act to which the purchased goods are put to. If they are put to economic use, i.e., further offered to be sold in a given market, then it will be regarded as part of the economic activity.[26]

---

22 Jonathan Faull and Ali Nickpay (n 14) 188.

23 Case C-41/90, *Klaus Höfner and Fritz Elser v. Macrotron GmbH,* [1991] ECR I-1979, at 21. The case dealt with the issue of monopoly conferred on a public employment agency by the state for the purpose of procurement of employment. The specific question raised was whether the public employment agency is amenable to EU competition laws, notwithstanding the statutory monopoly granted to it by the national law. It was in this context that the European Court of Justice had to define the word 'undertaking' as understood under EU competition law. The Court held that employment procurement is an economic activity.

24 Case C-205/03, [2006] ECR I-06295.

25 *Id.,* 64–65.

26 See also Case T-319/99, *FENIN v. Commission of the European Communities,* [2003] ECR-II 357 at 36. The case involved a complaint against twenty-six public bodies, including

It is evident therefore that the determination of economic activity is dependent upon the purpose to which the original goods and services are put to. For this reason, mere buying for consumption is not an economic activity unless it is subsequently used to further an economic activity. The EU courts have also upheld that if an economic activity was inseparable from the public service/exercise of public powers, it would fall outside the ambit of the EU competition law.[27] It follows from this that if the economic activity can be severed from the exercise of the public power/ public service, the entity will be an undertaking according to the EU competition law.[28] As a consequence,

three ministries, which ran the national health system (Sistema Nacional de Salud) ('the SNS') on the ground that they were abusing their dominant position. This in effect was a breach of the EU competition law. The complaint was rejected by the EU authorities, i.e., the EU Competition Commission, on the ground that the SNS management bodies were not an *undertaking* within the meaning of the EU competition law as they were not carrying on any economic activity. The complaint was filed by FENIN which was an association of the majority of the undertakings which market medical goods and equipment, particularly medical instruments, used in Spanish hospitals. The members of that association sold those goods, inter alia, to the SNS management bodies. The sale of medical goods and equipment to the SNS management bodies represented more than 80% of the turnover for the undertakings who were members of FENIN. FENIN alleged that since the SNS bodies have a dominant position in the Spanish market for medical goods and equipment, FENIN could not exercise any commercial pressure. It was in this context that the Court of First Instance held that mere purchasing of medical goods and equipments from FENIN did not render the activity of SNS as an economic activity for the purpose of EU competition law, as they were providing the medical service free of charge. However, the ECJ reversed this finding, though upholding the definition of economic activity, given by the Court of First Instance. The ECJ noted that the Court of First Instance had failed to identify whether the private sector had a role to play in providing health care or whether it was purely within the control of the public health sector. Further, the dominance of the principle of solidarity in providing free health care also had to be looked into. The principle of solidarity is a fundamental principle of EU law which is used to exclude an activity from the ambit of the EU competition law on the ground that their pre-dominant objective is to provide social protection/security and benefit to the public. In this sense, the activity is regarded as a social and not an economic activity. Article 2 of the Treaty of Lisbon embodies the principle of solidarity as one of the values on which the EU is founded. See [2008] OJ C 115/17.

27 See Case T-155/04, *SELEX SistemiIntegratiSpA v. Commission of the European Communities*, [2006] ECR II-4797. The case involved the question as to whether the challenged activities of Eurocontrol, i.e., standardization, research and development and assistance to the national administrations for air traffic management, are economic activities and that Eurocontrol must, therefore, be regarded as an undertaking within the meaning of Article 82 [102].

28 *Id.*, 54 [The Court of First Instance, i.e., the General Court holds that "since the Treaty provisions on competition are applicable to the activities of an entity which can be severed from those in which it engages as a public authority, the various activities of an

in the *Sistemi* case[29], the Court of First Instance/the General Court found that of the various activities of the Eurocontrol challenged as being anti-competitive, only one could be regarded as an economic activity. The court found that

> 'the activity of assisting the national administrations is separable from Eurocontrol's tasks of air space management and development of air safety'.[30]

To bring the said activity out of the ambit of the public service task of Eurocontrol, the Court of First Instance had to underline its economic nature. It thus declared that the

> 'activity of assistance is...in no way an activity which is essential or even indispensable to ensuring the safety of air navigation'.[31]

The reason for this conclusion was that the assistance was with respect to the tendering procedure for procuring air traffic management equipments. Therefore, the impact on safety was only indirect. Further, since the assistance was offered only on the request of the national administration, it was the same as offering goods or services in the market. Thereby, the act of assistance was an economic activity.[32] By relying on past cases, the court held that

> 'the fact that activities are normally entrusted to public offices cannot affect the economic nature of such activities, since they have not always been, and are not necessarily, carried out by public entities... in this case, this means that the fact that the services in question are not at the current time offered by private undertakings does not prevent their being described as an economic activity, since it is possible for them to be carried out by private entities'.[33]

The European Court of Justice however revised the finding of the Court of First Instance and held that the activity of providing assistance to national administrations was typical to a public authority and cannot be regarded as an economic activity. After referring to the various provisions of the Convention

---

entity must be considered individually and the treatment of some of them as powers of a public authority does not mean that it must be concluded that the other activities are not economic".]

29 *Id.*

30 *Id.*, 86.

31 *Id.*, 86.

32 *Id.* at 86–87.

33 *Id.*, 89.

on the Safety of Air Navigation, which confers power on Eurocontrol, the court declared that

> 'in order for there to be a connection with the exercise of public powers, it is not necessary for the activity concerned to be essential or indispensable to ensuring the safety of air navigation, since what matters is that the activity is connected with the maintenance and development of air navigation safety, which constitute public powers'.[34]

Criticizing the Court of First Instance for having erred in law and declared that since the act of assisting governments for maintaining air safety is an exercise of public power and hence not in itself an economic activity, the Eurocontrol cannot, therefore, be regarded as an *undertaking* for the purpose of Article 101 and 102.[35] In the end, though, the judgment of the Court of First Instance was merely revised and not set aside, as the overall findings of that court were 'well founded in law'.[36]

Association of undertakings

The EU courts, as noted above, also had to define the term 'association of undertakings'. In *J. C. J. Wouters, J. W. Savelbergh and Price Waterhouse Belastingadviseurs BV v. Algemene Raad van de Nederlandse Orde van Advocaten*,[37] Advocate General Léger thus defined the term 'association of undertakings':

---

[34] Case C-113/07, *SELEX SistemiIntegratiSpA v Commission of the European Communities and Organisation Européenne pour la Sécurité de la Navigation Aérienne (Eurocontrol),* [2009] ECR I-2207, at 79.

[35] *Id.* at 82.

[36] Case C-113/07 (n 34) 83.

[37] Case C-309/99, [2002] ECR I-1577. The case involved the question concerning the legality of a regulation adopted by the Netherlands Bar Association. The regulation in issue prohibited lawyers practicing in the Netherlands from entering into multi-disciplinary partnerships with members of the professional category of accountants. The Court was required to decide whether the Treaty provisions on competition are applicable and, if necessary, whether they preclude such a prohibition of cooperation. The European Court of Justice thus had to decide whether the Netherlands Bar Association can be regarded as an association of undertaking within the meaning of Article 101, clause 1. The court decided in the affirmative holding that since the association exclusively comprised lawyers and took decisions exclusively concerning the lawyers and the legal services market, it was an association of undertakings. This conclusion was further supported by the fact that lawyers, in their individual capacity were regarded as undertakings within the EU competition law. Moreover, it was established that the association while adopting any regulation was not bound by any public interest notions.

> 'an association consists of undertakings of the same general type and makes itself responsible for representing and defending their common interests vis-à-vis other economic operators, government bodies and the public in general'.[38]

Thus a grouping of independent economic operators, for example, professionals will be regarded as an *association of undertakings,* as individual members of the group can be regarded as *undertakings.* Thus, for example, lawyers in their capacity as independent professionals are to be regarded as undertakings because they offer services in the market of legal services. Further, the inclusion of the term *association of undertaking* within Article 101, clause 1

> 'prevent[s] undertakings from being able to evade the rules on competition on account simply of the form in which they coordinate their conduct on the market. To ensure that this principle is effective, [Article 101 clause 1] covers not only direct methods of coordinating conduct between undertakings (agreements and concerted practices) but also institutionalised forms of cooperation, that is to say, situations in which economic operators act through a collective structure or a common body'.[39]

Having thus reviewed the definitions given to the terms *undertaking* and *association of undertakings,* one needs to now move into the discussions involving cartels. Importantly, one needs to understand how the EU courts have defined the terms *agreement, decisions and concerted practices,* while dealing with cartels.

Agreement, decisions and concerted practices: Proof of cartels

In cartel cases, understandably, the detection is tougher than the application of the law as cartels are secretive in nature.[40] The European Competition Commission further emphasizes the adverse effect of cartels on consumers.[41]

[38] *Id.,* 61of the opinion Mr Advocate General Léger delivered on July 10, 2001.

[39] *Id.,* 62 of the opinion of Mr Advocate General Léger delivered on July 10, 2001.

[40] Incardona, Rossella, 'The Fight against Hard-core Cartels and the New EU Leniency Notice', *The European Legal Forum(E),* 39–42 (2007): 1/2, at http://www.simons-law.com/library/pdf/e/686.pdf (accessed April 28, 2011).

[41] In his speech on recent developments and future priorities of the EU competition law, on April 8, 2011, JoaquínAlmunia, Vice President of the European Commission responsible for Competition Policy, said that, 'on… the fight against cartels, let me say that I consider them as the single most serious and dangerous infringement of competition law. In this regard I will continue to adopt a policy of zero tolerance'.

Accordingly, the EU courts have interpreted the terms *agreements, decisions and concerted practices* broadly to catch the maximum number of cartel practices.[42] Cartel practices can be broadly categorized depending upon the nature of the agreement. In the context of Article 101, clause 1 such agreements should 'affect trade between Member States' (the EU members) and *their object or effect* should be the *prevention, restriction or distortion of competition* within the internal market of EU. The case law reveals that cartel agreements are treated as agreements which have as their *object* the *prevention, restriction or distortion of competition.*[43] In *SC Belasco and others v. Commission of the European Communities*[44], the EU Competition Commission found that the agreement entered into between the members of Belasco[45] by which they allocated quotas, adopted a price list fixing the minimum selling price, allocated customers, determined the market share to be held by each member, adopted defensive mechanisms against outside competition, fixed prices of ancillary products etc. was in breach of Article 101, clause 1.

The Commission found that Belasco members had formed a cartel with the clear *object* of restricting competition. Hence the *effect* of such cartel agreements need not be looked into for the purpose of Article 101, clause 1.[46] Both the *object* and the *effect* of the cartels need to be examined when the quantum of fines/penalty have to be assessed. The European Court of Justice affirmed the decision of the Commission. It declared that the fact that the cartel may be operating in a single member country does not 'exclude the possibility that trade between Member States might be affected'.[47] As a result, the EU courts looks only into the intent/object of the agreement and not the actual effect when dealing with cartels. Similarly, in the case of *Montedipe*

---

http://europa.eu/rapid/pressReleasesAction.do?reference=SPEECH/11/243&format=HTML&aged=0&language=EN&guiLanguage=en (accessed April 28, 2011).

42 See Alison Jones and Brenda Sufrin, *EU Competition Law: Text, Cases, and Materials*, 4th ed. (OUP, 2011) 798.

43 See Jonathan Faull and Ali Nickpay (n 14) 747.

44 Case 246/86, [1989] ECR 2117.

45 Belasco was a cooperative association set up in 1955, comprising a number of Belgian roofing felt manufacturers.

46 [1986] OJ L 232/15, at 76 [The Commission noted that 'In assessing an agreement or concerted practice in the light of Article 85 (1), it is not necessary to consider the effect the agreement or practice had if it has been established that it had the object of restricting or distorting competition. However, not only the restrictive intent, but also the effects, of a cartel must be taken into consideration when it comes to assessing the gravity of the infringements.']

47 Case 246/86 (n 44) 33.

SpA v. Commission of the European Communities,[48] the General Court/Court of First Instance upheld the finding of the Commission whereby fifteen producers of polypropylene were fined for infringement of Article 101, clause 1. The Commission found, through investigations, that these fifteen producers had over a period of time colluded to fix prices, allocate quota and share the market. The General Court/Court of First Instance affirmed the findings of the Commission and held that once it is established that the agreement has as its *object* the restriction of competition, the *effect* needs to be looked into only for the purpose of fixing the fine.[49] The case also dealt with the meaning of *agreement* and *concerted practices*, a discussion which is relevant considering that many cartel practices involve both anti-competitive agreements as well as concerted practices.[50] The Court relied on the definition of *agreement* given in *ACF Chemiefarma NV v. Commission of the European Communities*[51] (the Quinine Cartel)[52].

In that case, the European Court of Justice held that the 'gentlemen's agreement' entered into between the quinine and quinidine producers, was an agreement within the meaning of Article 101, clause 1 as the

> 'document… amounted to the faithful expression of the joint intention of the parties to the agreement with regard to their conduct in the common market'[53].

Accordingly, the General Court/Court of First Instance in the *Montedipe* case declared that

> 'in order for there to be an agreement within the meaning of Article [101 clause 1]… it is sufficient that the undertakings in question should have expressed their joint intention to conduct themselves on the market in a specific way'.[54]

---

48 Case T-14/89, [1992] ECR II-1155.

49 *Id.,* 264 [The Court thus states that 'the Commission has proved to the requisite legal standard that the agreements and concerted practices held to have existed had an anti-competitive object for the purposes of [Article 101 clause 1] of the EEC Treaty. The question whether they were anti -competitive in effect is therefore relevant only to assessment of the amount of the fine…']

50 The Montedipe case is a good example of such cartel practices.

51 Case 41/69, [1970] ECR 661.

52 The cartel comprised producers of quinine and quinidine who, by agreement, decided to fix prices, share domestic markets, determine sales quotas and prohibit manufacture of synthetic quinidine.

53 Case 41/69 (n 51) 112.

54 Case T-14/89 (n 48) 230.

This definition of *agreement* has now become the 'classic' definition of the term with respect to the applicability of Article 101, clause 1.[55] Take, for example, the case of *Bayer AG v. Commission of the European Communities.*[56] The case concerned the ban on parallel exports, imposed by Bayer, on its whole sellers in Spain and France, of its medicinal product, trade named Adalat.[57] The company had accordingly banned parallel imports of the same product by its whole sellers in the United Kingdom.[58] In its defence, one of the arguments made by Bayer was that its decision to ban parallel exports and imports was a unilateral decision and not the result of an *agreement* between itself and the concerned whole sellers. There being no *agreement*, the EU Competition Commission erred in applying Article 101, clause 1 to its conduct. It was in the light of this contention that the General Court/Court of First Instance was required to revisit the concept of *agreement.*

The court first held that

> 'where a decision on the part of a manufacturer constitutes unilateral conduct of the undertaking, that decision escapes the prohibition in [Article 101 clause 1] of the Treaty'.[59]

After that, it went on to reiterate the definition of *agreement* as given in the previous cases tried in the EU courts. Consequently, the court held that an *agreement* is evidenced by the existence of a joint intention amongst the undertakings to operate in a certain manner within the internal market.[60] It further held that the manner of expression of the joint/common intention can be through a

> 'stipulation to be the expression of the parties' intention to behave on the market in accordance with its terms... without its having to constitute a valid and binding contract under national law'.[61]

---

55 Alison Jones and Brenda Sufrin (n 42) 142.

56 Case T-41/96, [2000] ECR II- 3383, affirmed on appeal in Cases C-2/01, joined with C-3/01, [2004] ECR I-23.

57 Bayer AG (hereinafter Bayer or the Bayer Group) is the parent company of one of the main European chemical and pharmaceutical groups and has a presence through its national subsidiaries in all the member states of the Community. For many years, it had manufactured and marketed under the trade name Adalat or Adalate, a range of medicinal preparations whose active ingredient was nifedipine, designed to treat cardio-vascular disease.

58 Parallel exports from Spain and France to United Kingdom were taking place because the price of the said medicinal preparation in Spain and France was forty per cent lower than those in the United Kingdom.

59 Case T-41/96 (n 56) 66.

60 *Id.,* 67.

61 *Id.,* 68.

Having thus re-emphasized the concept, relying on the previous case law, the court pointed out that the essence of proving an agreement under Article 101, clause 1 is the concurrence of wills of two or more undertakings irrespective of the form in which that concurrence is embodied.[62] Hence the unilateral conduct of an undertaking

> 'adopted in the context of the contractual relations which it maintains with his dealers, may in reality form the basis of an agreement between undertakings within the meaning of [Article 101 clause 1] of the Treaty, if express or implied acquiescence by the other contracting parties in the attitude adopted by the manufacturer is established'.[63]

With respect to the meaning of *concerted practices*, the General Court/Court of First Instance in *Montedipe* explained that

> 'any direct or indirect contact between...operators the object or effect whereof is either to influence the conduct on the market of an actual or potential competitor or to disclose to such a competitor the course of conduct which they themselves have decided to adopt or contemplate adopting on the market'.[64]

amounts to *concerted practices* within the meaning of Article 101, clause 1. In the reverse, therefore, it is mandatory under the EU competition law, that

> 'each economic operator must determine independently the policy which he intends to adopt on the common market'.[65]

This though will not preclude the undertakings from taking such decisions as is necessary to face competition. For example, a joint venture agreement between competitors, operating at the same level of market, can be highly beneficial for consumers and the economy. This is so because it enables these parties to pool-in their resources like know-how and finances. It also enables them to share the financial risk of the venture. In other words, not all horizontal cooperation is bad or prohibited by the EU competition law.[66] It is evidently only cartel practices which are banned by virtue of Article 101, clause 1. This is so because a cartel has only one objective—to maximize the 'joint profits' of the parties to the agreement or concerted practices.[67] In the

---

62 *Id.*, 69.

63 *Id.*, 111.

64 Case T-14/89 (n 48) 232.

65 *Id.*

66 Alison Jones and Brenda Sufrin (n 42) 784.

67 See also Case T-1/89, *Rhône-Poulenc SA v. Commission of the European Communities*, [1991] ECR II-867. [The General Court/Court of First Instance affirmed the definition of

Montedipe case, another interesting concept was discussed by the General Court/Court of First Instance. The concept was that of *single continuing infringement,* a concept which was earlier used by the EU Competition Commission in one of its previous decisions.[68]

Affirming the test used by the EU Competition Commission for proving the breach of Article 101, clause 1, the General Court/Court of First Instance, in the *Montedipe* case, held that the EU Competition Commission was justified in *treating* the series of *concerted practices and agreements* as part of the same infringement, since they all were aimed at one economic agenda, i.e., fixing of prices, allocating quota and sharing the market. For this reason, all anti-competitive activities indulged in by the concerned undertakings at different periods of time were treated as part of a *single continuous infringement/agreement.*[69] This concept thus enabled the Commission to apply Article 101, clause 1 to all those cartels which developed over a period of time, and tried to mask their activities through sophisticated means, as is evident in the *Montedipe* case. [70] Another point that was clarified in the *Montedipe* case, with regard to cartels, was that since there was a clear infringement of Article 101, clause 1, the application of the *rule of reason* was therefore clearly precluded 'assuming such a rule to be applicable in Community competition law'[71]; cartels were to be regarded as 'an infringement per se of the competition rules'.[72] This approach appears to be the settled law as far as the EU competition regime is concerned. In other words, cartels are to be treated as a *per se* infringement of Article 101, clause 1, as their *object* is anti-competitive.[73] This approach also reminds one of the US approach to cartels.

---

concerted practices given by the EU Competition Commission, according to which 'there is a concerted practice as soon as there is concerted action having as its purpose the restriction of the autonomy of the undertakings in relation to one another, even if no actual conduct has been found on the market'. Further, the EU Competition Commission defined the word 'practice' so as to include the 'mere act of participating in contacts, provided that they have as their purpose the restriction of the undertakings' autonomy'. These findings of the EU Competition Commission were re-affirmed in the Montedipe case.]

68 *Id.*, 94

69 Case T-14/89 (n 48) 203 [According to the EU Competition Commission, 'the whole complex of schemes and arrangements decided on in the context of a system of regular and institutionalized meetings constituted a single continuing "agreement" within the meaning of Article 85(1)'].

70 Alison Jones and Brenda Sufrin (n 42) 146.

71 Case T-14/89 (n 48) 265.

72 *Id.*

73 See also Case T-374/94, joined with Cases T-375/94, T-384/94 and T-388/94, *the European Night Services Ltd (ENS), Eurostar (UK) Ltd, formerly European Passenger Services Ltd (EPS), Union Internationale des Chemins de fer (UIC), NV NederlandseSpoorwegen (NS)*

As noted in the previous chapter, the US had witnessed a long-drawn debate with regard to whether cartels should be treated as *per se* void or should be subject to the *rule of reason test*.[74]

Article 101, clause 3 and cartels: Justification of ruinous competition

Coming back to the EU competition law, while cartels are treated as *per se* void, there does arise a question as to whether Article 101, clause 3 will be made applicable to them. The *European Night Service* judgment refers to the application of the *rule of reason* approach while dealing with cartels under Article 101, clause 3. One will therefore need to look into the criteria used to apply Article 101, clause 3 and determine whether the same is applicable to cartels under the EU competition law. In this again the recurring theme of the book needs to be the referral point of discussion, *viz.*, consumer interest.[75]

---

and SociétéNationale des Chemins de ferFrançais (SNCF) v. Commission of the European Communities, [1998] ECR II-3141, 136. [Herein the General Court/Court of First Instance held that 'Before any examination of the parties' arguments as to whether the Commission's analysis as regards restrictions of competition was correct, it must be borne in mind that in assessing an agreement under [Article 101 clause 1] of the Treaty, account should be taken of the actual conditions in which it functions, in particular the economic context in which the undertakings operate, the products or services covered by the agreement and the actual structure of the market concerned... unless it is an agreement containing obvious restrictions of competition such as price-fixing, market-sharing or the control of outlets... In the latter case, such restrictions may be weighed against their claimed pro-competitive effects only in the context of [Article 101 clause 3] of the Treaty, with a view to granting an exemption from the prohibition in [Article 101 clause 1]'. In the European Night case, the contested agreement was a joint venture agreement and hence it became necessary to assess its effect on competition.]

[74] For a detailed discussion refer to Chapter 3 of the book.

[75] Here one needs to reiterate that within the EU competition law, the concept of a consumer includes both intermediaries as well as end consumers. Hence when accommodating consumer interests within the EU competition law, one needs to take into account the interests of all and not only the end consumers. See the EU Competition Commission guidelines on the application of Article 81, clause 3 (Article 101, clause 3) of the Treaty, [2004] OJ C 101/97, para 84 http://eur-lex.europa.eu/LexUriServ/LexUriServ.do?uri=CE LEX:52004XC0427(07):EN:HTML (accessed 2 May 2011) ['The concept of "consumers" encompasses all direct or indirect users of the products covered by the agreement, including producers that use the products as an input, wholesalers, retailers and final consumers, i.e., natural persons who are acting for purposes which can be regarded as outside their trade or profession. In other words, consumers within the meaning of Article 81(3) are the customers of the parties to the agreement and subsequent purchasers. These customers can be undertakings as in the case of buyers of industrial machinery or an input for further

In the *Hachette SA v. Commission of the European Communities*[76], the General Court/Court of First Instance held that under the EU competition law

> 'no anti-competitive practice can exist which, whatever the extent of its effects on a given market, cannot be exempted, provided that all the conditions laid down in [Article 101 clause 3] of the Treaty are satisfied and the practice in question has been properly notified to the Commission.'[77]

Technically, therefore there exists no *per se* void rule under the EU competition law.[78] It follows that even cartels can be granted exemption under Article 101, clause 3. It also means that under the EU competition law, even if a practice is found to be anti-competitive under Article 101, clause 1, it will be further analysed under Article 101, clause 3. On reading Article 101, clause 3[79], it is evident that for an agreement caught under Article 101, clause 1, the defence of Article 101, clause 3 will be available if the agreement

> 'improves the production or distribution of goods or services or promotes technical or economic progress, allows consumers a fair share of the benefit, does not contain any indispensable restrictions, and does not eliminate competition in a substantial part of the products in question'.[80]

It is to be noted here that for the purpose of claiming benefit under Article 101, clause 3, all the four conditions have to be complied with. If the impugned agreement fails to satisfy any one of the four conditions, the rest will not

---

processing or final consumers as for instance in the case of buyers of impulse ice-cream or bicycles'.]

[76] Case T-17/93, [1994] ECR II-595.

[77] *Id.*, 85 [This was held in the context of a challenge to the EU Competition Commission's decision granting exemption under Article 101, clause 3, to a joint venture agreement.]

[78] Van Bael and Bellis (n 21) 345.

[79] Article 101, clause 3 thus states:
'The provisions of paragraph 1 may, however, be declared inapplicable in the case of:
— any agreement or category of agreements between undertakings,
— any decision or category of decisions by associations of undertakings,
— any concerted practice or category of concerted practices,
which contributes to improving the production or distribution of goods or to promoting technical or economic progress, while allowing consumers a fair share of the resulting benefit, and which does not:
(a) impose on the undertakings concerned restrictions which are not indispensable to the attainment of these objectives;
(b) afford such undertakings the possibility of eliminating competition in respect of a substantial part of the products in question'.

[80] Alison Jones and Brenda Sufrin (n 42) 190.

be examined at all. As a result, the fact that consumer welfare appears to be one of the conditions of this clause of Article 101, may make it difficult for a hard core cartel to justify itself and seek exemption. The EU Competition Commission guidelines on the application of Article 81, clause 3 (Article 101, clause 3) of the Treaty states that

> 'severe restrictions of competition are unlikely to fulfil the conditions of [Article 101 clause 3]. Such restrictions are usually...identified as hardcore restrictions in Commission guidelines and notices. Agreements of this nature generally fail (at least) the two first conditions of [Article 101 clause 3]. They neither create objective economic benefits nor do they benefit consumers. For example, a horizontal agreement to fix prices limits output leading to misallocation of resources. It also transfers value from consumers to producers, since it leads to higher prices without producing any countervailing value to consumers within the relevant market. Moreover, these types of agreements generally also fail the indispensability test under the third condition.'[81]

One therefore needs to reiterate that the EU competition law is geared towards achieving consumer welfare while dealing with cartels. For example, in its report on the Competition Policy 2008, the EU Competition Commission, for the first time, devoted a separate chapter on '*Cartels and consumers*'.[82] Therein it showed that of all anti-competitive practices, cartels are the worst, having no pro-consumer effect.[83] This zero-tolerance approach of the EU Competition Commission to cartels is evident with respect to '*crisis cartels*'[84]

---

81 See the EU Competition Commission guidelines (n 75) para 46 [The commission adds that 'Any claim that restrictive agreements are justified because they aim at ensuring fair conditions of competition on the market is by nature unfounded and must be discarded'. Hence it is only the four conditions which determine the case for a restrictive agreement under the EU competition law.]

82 See Report on Competition Policy 2008, COM (2009) 374 final, para 1, http://eur-lex.europa.eu/LexUriServ/LexUriServ.do?uri=COM:2009:0374:FIN:EN:DOC (accessed 2 May 2011).

83 See generally the opinion of the European Economic and Social Committee on the 'Report from the Commission: Report on Competition Policy' 2008, [2011] C 44/24, http://eur-lex.europa.eu/LexUriServ/LexUriServ.do?uri=OJ:C:2011:044:0143:0147:EN:PDF (accessed 2 May 2011).

84 'The term "crisis cartel" is used in two ways in economic literature. First, it can refer to a cartel that was formed during a severe sectoral, national, or global economic downturn without state permission or legal sanction. A second use of the term "crisis cartel" has been to refer to situations where a government has permitted, even fostered, the formation of a cartel among firms during severe sectoral, national, or global economic downturns, or when national competition law allows for the creation of cartels during such downturns. For antitrust considerations, a crisis is generally defined as deterioration in economic

as well.[85] There have been cases, though, where exemptions under Article 101, clause 3 have been granted to crisis cartels (also called restructuring agreements).[86] For example, in the Synthetic Fibers[87] case, the agreement to reduce the production capacity amongst producers of synthetic fibres in an industry that was facing the crisis of over-capacity, was exempted by the EU Competition Commission under Article 101, clause 3. This was clearly a producer's cartel but the EU Competition Commission justified the capacity reduction agreement or the restructuring agreement by stating that

> 'In a free market economy it ought to be principally a matter for the individual undertaking to judge the point at which overcapacity becomes economically unsustainable and to take the necessary steps to reduce it. In the present case, however, market forces by themselves had failed to achieve the capacity reductions necessary to re-establish and maintain in the longer term an effective competitive structure within the common market'.[88]

The EU Competition Commission further noted that in the long run, the agreement will benefit the consumers as it will improve the overall competitiveness of the undertakings which means better quality of products. The producers will also benefit as there will be increase in profitability due to increase in efficiency.[89]

The present philosophy of the EU Competition Commission, however, may make it difficult for a crisis cartel to get exempted under Article 101, clause 3. This is largely because of the guidelines on applicability of Article 101, clause 3 issued by the EU Competition Commission[90]. As discussed

---

performance indicators, such as demand, beyond that associated with a typical business cycle downturn. During the last century, such cartels have appeared in times of crisis, with most characteristic examples being the 19th century German crisis, the post-war era Japanese crisis, the US crisis during the great depression of the 1930s, and the East Asian financial crisis in 1998.' See LiaVitzilaiou, 'Crisis Cartels: For Better or For Worse?', *Antitrust Chronicle* (2011), https://www.competitionpolicyinternational.com/crisis-cartels-for-better-or-for-worse/ (accessed 2 May 2011).

85 See generally the report of the EU submitted to the Organization for Economic Cooperation and Development (OECD) on Crisis Cartels, http://www.oecd.org/officialdocuments/publicdisplaydocumentpdf/?cote=DAF/COMP/GF/WD(2011)20&docLanguage=En (accessed 2 May 2011).

86 Jonathan Faull and Ali Nickpay (n 14) 748, para 8.04.

87 [1984] OJ L207/17.

88 [1984] OJ (n 87) para 30 and 31.

89 *Id.*, para 39. Alison Jones and Brenda Sufrin (n 42) 246.

90 The EU Competition Commission guidelines (n 75) para 46.

above, the same requires that the impugned agreement need to comply with all the four conditions cumulatively. Moreover, it will be difficult for a crisis cartel, whose purpose is to artificially raise prices, to establish any pro-consumer benefits. Furthermore, in its report on crisis cartels to the OECD[91], the EU Competition Commission also reiterated that no economic crisis justifies the formation of cartels.[92] The possibility of getting exemption for a crisis cartel, of the Synthetic Fibers type, i.e., agreement to reduce over-capacity, is also unlikely under the present EU system. This is so because of the entry into force of the European Council Regulation No. 1/2003.[93] Prior to this regulation, an anti-competitive agreement needed to be notified to the EU Competition Commission, for the purpose of being considered for an individual exemption under Article 101, clause 3. For example, in the *Montedipe* case, rejecting the argument of the applicants, who wanted their agreement to be exempted, as it was a crisis cartel, the General Court/Court of First Instance held that Article 101, clause 3 cannot be applied since '[t]he applicant did not notify the agreements and concerted practices found to have existed'.[94] On the other hand, the 2003 regulation has abolished the notification system. As a result, the situation for over-capacity reduction agreements of the type dealt with in the Synthetic Fibers case is highly unfavourable.[95]

---

91 The report of the EU (n 85) para 62. (The EU Competition Commission concludes the report thus: 'The Commission will have to make a detailed assessment under Article 101(3) TFEU of the causal link between the agreement and the pro-competitive benefits, the likely "pass on" of the claimed pro-competitive benefits to consumers and of the indispensability of the agreement for obtaining those pro-competitive benefits. Industrial restructuring agreements imposing restrictions on output or entry barriers are very unlikely to fulfil conditions of 101(3) TFEU'.

92 *Id.*, para 5.

93 [2003] OJ L1/1, COUNCIL REGULATION (EC) No 1/2003 of 16 December 2002 on the implementation of the rules on competition laid down in [Articles 101 and 102] of the Treaty, http://eur-lex.europa.eu/LexUriServ/LexUriServ.do?uri=OJ:L:2003:001:0001:0025:EN:PDF (accessed 3 May 2011). [As per Article 1, clause 1 of the regulation, 'Agreements, decisions and concerted practices caught by [Article 101 clause (1)] of the Treaty which do not satisfy the conditions of [Article 101 clause (3)] of the Treaty shall be prohibited, no prior decision to that effect being required'. According to Article 1, clause 2 of the regulation, 'Agreements, decisions and concerted practices caught by [Article 101 clause (1)] of the Treaty which satisfy the conditions of [Article 101 clause (3)] of the Treaty shall not be prohibited, no prior decision to that effect being required'.]

94 Case T-14/89 (n 48) para 271.

95 Thus once it is found that an agreement is infringing Article 101, clause 1, the burden will be on the undertaking/undertakings to establish that they satisfy all the four conditions of Article 101, clause 3 cumulatively. In other words, the present scheme is based on self-assessment whereby each undertaking/undertakings will have to determine whether their

EU, crisis cartels and consumer interests: An example

An analysis of the *Irish Beef Industry* case[96] would further explain the position of crisis cartels that intend to reduce over-capacity vis-à-vis the application of Article 101, clause 3. In a study conducted by McKinsey, in 1998, it was established that the beef processing industry of Ireland was suffering from an over-capacity crisis, which was affecting its competitiveness. Accordingly, it was suggested, both by the McKinsey report, as well as by the Irish government that the members of the beef processing industry should enter into an over-capacity reduction agreement (called rationalization agreement). The concerned industry members formed the Beef Industry Development Society Limited (BIDS). It effectively meant a reduction in the processing capacity of the industry by closing down certain undertakings. The logic being that the existing undertakings could then efficiently match the capacity with the actual requirement of the product, i.e., processed beef. The Irish Competition authority found the rationalization agreement of BIDS in violation of the requirement of Article 101, clause 1. In addition, it found that the agreement failed to comply with the requirements of Article 101, clause 3. The lower court rejected the findings of the competition authority, though interestingly on the applicability of Article 101, clause 3, it found that the BIDS had not satisfied the condition on consumer benefit. The court nonetheless went on to assess the other conditions of Article 101, clause 3 and ruled in favour of BIDS.[97]

agreement will meet the standard set by Article 101, clause 3 or not. Hence, a crisis cartel for reducing over-capacity will no longer be in a position to be treated as an exception. They will have to satisfy the burden of proof, which is as difficult for them as for any other cartel. See also the speech of NeelieKroes, the former EU Commissioner for Competition and presently the EU Vice-President for Digital Agenda, who, on October 8, 2009, thus expressed her opinion on crisis cartels: 'If I may quickly mention the issue of so-called "crisis cartels"… There may be many temptations in 2009 to cut corners, but encouraging cartelists and others would be guaranteeing disaster. It would drag down recovery, increase consumer harm and create more cartel and cartel cases into the future. No-one wins – today's softness is tomorrow's nightmare'. http://europa.eu/rapid/pressReleasesAction.do?reference=SPEECH/09/454&format=HTML&aged=0&language=EN&guiLanguage=en (accessed 3 May 2011).

96 [2009] IESC 72.

97 This is interesting because, as discussed above, all the four conditions of Article 101, clause 3 have to be satisfied cumulatively. Hence if the infringer fails to satisfy any one of the four conditions, Article 101, clause 3 will not be applicable and there is no need to assess the other conditions.

In appeal, the Irish Supreme Court decided to refer the matter for a preliminary ruling under Article 267 (former Article 234)[98] to the European Court of Justice. The question that the Irish Supreme Court wanted the European Court of Justice to answer was

> 'whether agreements with features such as those of the BIDS arrangements are to be regarded, by reason of their object alone, as being anti-competitive and thus prohibited by [Article 101 clause 3] or whether, on the other hand, it is necessary, in order to reach such a conclusion, first to demonstrate that such agreements may have anti-competitive effects'.[99]

The European Court of Justice rejected the argument of BIDS that its rationalization agreement does not have the *object* or the *effect* of restricting competition, as required by Article 101, clause 3.[100] It held that

> 'to determine whether an agreement comes within the prohibition laid down in Article[101 clause 1] EC, close regard must be paid to the wording of its provisions and to the objectives which it is intended to attain. In that regard, even supposing it to be established that the parties to an agreement acted without any subjective intention of restricting competition, but with the object of remedying the effects of a crisis in their sector, such considerations are irrelevant for the purposes of applying that provision. Indeed, an agreement may be regarded as having a restrictive object even if it does not have the restriction of competition as its sole aim but also pursues other legitimate objectives'.[101]

---

98 According to Article 267 of the Treaty of Lisbon, 'The Court of Justice of the European Union shall have jurisdiction to give preliminary rulings concerning:
(a) the interpretation of the Treaties;
(b) the validity and interpretation of acts of the institutions, bodies, offices or agencies of the Union;
Where such a question is raised before any court or tribunal of a Member State, that court or tribunal may if it considers that a decision on the question is necessary to enable it to give judgment, request the Court to give a ruling thereon.
Where any such question is raised in a case pending before a court or tribunal of a Member State against whose decisions there is no judicial remedy under national law, that court or tribunal shall bring the matter before the Court.
If such a question is raised in a case pending before a court or tribunal of a Member State with regard to a person in custody, the Court of Justice of the European Union shall act with the minimum of delay'.

99 [2009] IESC 72 (n 96).

100 Case C-209/07, *Competition Authority v. Beef Industry Development Society Ltd and Barry Brothers (Carrigmore) Meats Ltd.*, [2008] ECR I-8637, para 20.

101 *Id.*, 21.

BIDS further argued that its agreement cannot be regarded as in violation of Article 101, clause 1, because it was not for the purpose of fixing prices or sharing markets or fixing quotas or sharing customers. The agreement was entered into for the purpose of reducing over-capacity in the beef processing industry. In other words, BIDS claimed that its agreement was not a cartel for the purpose of naked restraint but a crisis cartel.[102] The European Court of Justice rejected this argument, stating that Article 101, clause 1 does not provide an exhaustive list of prohibited agreements.[103] The European Court of Justice held that the BIDS agreement

> 'conflicts patently with the concept inherent in the EC Treaty provisions relating to competition, according to which each economic operator must determine independently the policy which it intends to adopt on the common market. [Article 101 clause 1] is intended to prohibit any form of coordination which deliberately substitutes practical cooperation[104] between undertakings for the risks of competition'.[105]

Thus the European Court of Justice ruled that the BIDS agreement had as its objective, 'the prevention, restriction or distortion of competition within the meaning of [Article 101 clause 1]'.[106]

In the light of these findings of the European Court of Justice, the Irish Supreme Court had to decide whether the BIDS agreement satisfied the requirement of Article 101, clause 3. The Irish Supreme Court distinguished between a cartel and a crisis cartel formed for the purpose of reducing over-capacity. In other words, the BIDS arrangement, according to the Irish Supreme Court, was the result of years of detailed studies, showing the existence of a severe crisis in the beef processing industry. Further, the BIDS formation was with the knowledge of the Irish Competition Authority. In this way, the BIDS arrangement was different from a cartel which is secretively formed and with no other purpose but to harm consumers. For the court,

[102] *Id.*, 22.

[103] *Id.*, 23.

[104] The term practical cooperation has been used in the European Court of Justice's decisions while defining the concept of *concerted practice.* It means that though there is no proof of agreement or no agreement has been arrived at between the parties, yet they coordinate their behaviour/conduct which is in the form of cooperating with each other on matters relating to their conduct of business. Thus, exchange of price information or quota target met is an example of such cooperation. This term is used to distinguish a concerted behaviour from parallel conduct. Parallel conduct is the conduct of a business entity which is out of an independent economic decision and not the result of any coordination with the competitors, even though the conduct mirrors the behaviour of the competitor.

[105] Case C-209/07 (n 100) para 34.

[106] *Id.*, para 40.

the latter (BIDS crisis cartel) therefore need to be treated differently. It may though be reiterated here, that, as discussed, irrespective of the nature of a crisis cartel, the conditions of Article 101, clause 3 has to be cumulatively satisfied, according to the 2004 guidelines. The Irish Supreme Court acknowledged this fact and thus referred the matter back to the lower court for analysing the case in light of the requirement of Article 101, clause 3. It however noted that so far as showing the beneficial effect on consumers was concerned, it was enough if the same can be positively established without showing the '*exact value or magnitude*' of that benefit. In other words, the proof of benefit is enough without quantifying the same. One cannot but reiterate here that notwithstanding the standard required, a crisis cartel will have to show that the concerned agreement has a beneficial effect on the consumer. The Irish case thus demonstrates the difficulty faced by a crisis cartel seeking exemption under Article 101, clause 3. This is primarily so because of the harm that cartels cause to consumer interests, apart from the other negative impacts.[107] Technically, it is possible for a crisis cartel to overcome Article 101, clause 1 if it can demonstrate pure reduction of over-capacity without compromising on any of the requirements of Article 101, clause 3. It is nonetheless a difficult task as the EU competition law is uniform in its application to cartels, irrespective of the existence of a crisis or not.[108]

Cartel typology: Changing shape to dupe consumers

Having seen how the EU cartel law is geared towards protecting consumer interests, it will be educative to review the different types of cartels that the EU Competition Commission and the EU courts have, over the years, identified and severely dealt with. Cartels are like amoeba—they change their shapes with only one agenda and that is to maximize 'supra-competitive'[109] profits at the cost of consumers. They can thus be formed with the agenda to fix prices and/or impose quota restrictions and/or share markets and/or share consumers and/or pull off collusive tendering/bid rigging and/or manage

[107] An example, which will further establish the fact that a crisis cartel like any other cartel hardly has any pro-consumer effect, is the recent decision of the Helenic Republic Competition Commission to impose fines on the crisis cartel formed by companies from the fish farming sector. The Commission reiterated the European Court of Justice's and the European Competition Commission's stance that 'the existence of an economic crisis cannot justify restriction of competition'. http://www.epant.gr/img/x2/news/news338_1_1298558886.pdf (accessed 3 May 2011). See NeelieKroes (n 95).

[108] The report of the EU (n 85) para 58.

[109] Jonathan Faull and Ali Nickpay (n 14) 753.

collective boycotts and/or exchange commercially sensitive information. What follows will be a review of cases, used herein, as examples of such behaviour of cartels.

Imperial Chemical Industries Ltd. v. Commission of the European Communities[110] is an example of a cartel which was formed with the objective of fixing prices. In this case, the producers of dyestuffs formed a cartel for the purpose of increasing the prices of the dyes and pigments, within the EU common market. The EU Competition Commission took action against the cartel, and fined them for their anti-competitive behaviour. The European Court of Justice upheld the decision of the EU Competition Commission by emphasizing that the

> 'function of price competition is to keep prices down to the lowest possible level and to encourage the movement of goods between the Member States, thereby permitting the most efficient possible distribution of activities in the matter of productivity and the capacity of undertakings to adapt themselves to change. Differences in rates encourage the pursuit of one of the basic objectives of the Treaty, namely the interpenetration of national markets and, as a result, direct access by consumers to the sources of production of the whole Community'.[111]

Such types of price-fixing cartels clearly violate both the clauses of Article 101. As is evident from the cases discussed so far, price-fixing arrangements are further supported by other types of arrangements.[112]

For example in the *Kaučuk v Commission*[113] case, the European Competition Commission fined the cartel formed by producers of butadiene rubber (BR) and emulsion styrene butadiene rubber (ESBR), both of which are types of synthetic rubber used in tyre production. The aim of the cartel, which operated from 1996 to 2002, was

> 'fixing price targets for the products, sharing customers by non-aggression agreements and exchanging sensitive commercial information relating to price, competitors and customers'.[114]

---

110 Case 48/69, [1972] ECR 619.

111 *Id.,* para 115–116.

112 See for example Case T-14/89 (n 48).

113 Case T-44/07, [2011] ECR 00000.

114 COMP/F/38.638 – Butadiene rubber and emulsion styrene butadiene rubber, para 249 of the EU Competition Commission's decision, http://ec.europa.eu/competition/antitrust/cases/dec_docs/38638/38638_826_1.pdf (accessed 4 May 2011).

This exemplifies the combination of anti-competitive practices that cartels can indulge in.[115] Furthermore, irrespective of the sector that cartels operate in, their behavioural pattern remain the same. For example, the EU Competition Commission found that between 1993 and 2000, Christie's International PLC (hereinafter Christie's) and Sotheby's Holdings, Inc. (hereinafter Sotheby's) had formed a cartel with the objective of fixing the terms and conditions at which they paid commission to the sellers as well as the terms and conditions at which the buyers purchased from them.[116] The EU Competition Commission also found that

> 'in order to implement and/or modify the agreements as required, the parties concerted and exchanged information during regular meetings or (telephone) contacts on any subject or matter (auctions, vendors, dealers, buyers) which might give rise to or encourage competition between them or otherwise conflict with or endanger their agreement not to compete'.[117]

The EU Competition Commission found that the agreement was in infringement of Article 101, clause 1, as the objective was to fix prices and other terms and conditions, which together ensured the success of the cartel. The Commission imposed a fine, though subsequently, reduced the same in view of its leniency measures.[118]

In the case of professional services also the EU Competition Commission has taken stringent action under Article 101, clause 1, for anti-competitive price fixing.[119] The best case exemplifying the EU Competition Commission's

---

[115] The EU Competition Commission imposed a fine of € 519 million. See the press release of the Commission at http://europa.eu/rapid/pressReleasesAction.do?reference=IP/06/1647&format=HTML&aged=0&language=EN&guiLanguage=en (accessed 4 May 2011). However the General Court/Court of First Instance annulled the decision of the EU Competition Commission, in so far as it concerned *Kaučuk* on the grounds that the Commission was not able to establish that *Kaučuk* participated in the BR cartel. See Case T-44/07 (n 113) para 68.

[116] [2005] OJ L 200/92, Fine Art Auction Houses.

[117] COMP/E-2/37.784 Fine Art Auction Houses, at para 77. http://ec.europa.eu/competition/antitrust/cases/dec_docs/37784/37784_8_4.pdf (accessed 4 May 2011).

[118] Accordingly, Christie's fine was reduced to zero, as part of its arrangement with the EU Competition Commission.

[119] For a detailed discussion on the EU Competition Commission's role in ensuring that no cartelization happens in the liberal professions, see supra Alison Jones and Brenda Sufrin (n 42) 807. See also COM (2004) 83 final, the Communication from the Commission Report on Competition in Professional Services, http://eur-lex.europa.eu/LexUriServ/LexUriServ.do?uri=COM:2004:0083:FIN:EN:PDF (accessed 4 May 2011). This report was followed up by COM(2005) 405 final, Communication from the Commission to the

approach is the case of the Belgian Architects' Association.[120] Here the National Council of the Belgian Architects' Association had adopted, by resolution, a scale of minimum fees 'due to an architect for services performed in independent practice in Belgium'.[121] The EU Competition Commission, on June 24, 2004, adopted a decision by which it declared that the scheme to establish a minimum scale

> 'is a decision of an association of undertakings which has the restriction of competition as its object. This is despite the fact that the Association has described the scale as a "guideline", and despite the fact that not all architects have treated it as compulsory'.[122]

The EU Competition Commission differentiated this case from the *Wouters*[123] case, stating that the

> 'the establishment of a (recommended) minimum fee scale by the Architects' Association cannot be considered as necessary in order to ensure the proper practice of the architect's profession'.[124]

It is important to note here that the EU Competition Commission acknowledges that some sort of regulation or restriction is indispensable in the liberal professions.[125] However, as is evident from the Belgian Architect's Association case decision, the Commission is intolerant about any kind of price fixation/fee fixation and/or regulation in advertisement and/or entry regulations and/or regulating business structures and/or multidisciplinary

---

Council, the European Parliament, the European Economic and Social Committee and the Committee of the Regions Professional Services - Scope for more reform; Follow-up to the Report on Competition in Professional Services, COM(2004) 83 of February 9, 2004, http://eur-lex.europa.eu/LexUriServ/LexUriServ.do?uri=COM:2005:0405:FIN:EN:PDF (accessed May 4, 2011).

120 [2005] OJ L004/10.

121 *Id.*, para 6.

122 *Id.*, para 8.

123 See Case C-309/99 (n 37) para 107–110 [In this case, the European Court of Justice held that the 1993 regulation of the Bar of Netherland, which prohibited partnership between lawyers and accountants, was 'necessary in order to ensure the proper practice of the legal profession, as it is organised in the Member State concerned'. The court held that the Bar of Netherland was justified in deciding that 'the objectives pursued by the 1993 Regulation cannot… be attained by less restrictive means'.] In the Belgian Architect decision *Id.*, para 11, the Commission rejected the desirability of the minimum fee scale.

124 *Id.*

125 *Id.*, para 2. The Commission defines liberal profession as 'occupations requiring special training in the liberal arts or sciences'. See COM (2004) 83 final (n 119) Executive Summary.

practices.[126] It can be argued that the kind of regulation that the *Wouters case*[127] dealt with might not be palatable to the EU Competition Commission.[128]

Another type of practice which would definitely fall foul of Article 101, clause 1 is the cartelization of the tendering process, known as collusive tendering or bid rigging. One good example to study this kind of cartel behaviour is the case of the *Pre-insulated Pipe cartel.*[129] Pre-insulated pipes are commonly used to transport heated water to supply heat to residential and commercial buildings, primarily in those EU countries which face extreme weather conditions.[130] During the 1990s, four Danish producers of pre-insulated pipes got together to form a cartel, whereby they agreed to fix prices, fix quota, share the market and customers and importantly decided to rig the tendering process. Thus, the members decided who among them should win a bid. The chosen member had to inform the others about the price that it would quote in the bid/tender; accordingly, the others would always quote a higher price so as to ensure the success of the designated cartel member.[131] Soon, producers from other countries joined in the cartel, raising the number of members to seven.[132]

The cartel agreement covered the whole of the EU common market.[133] Another part of this cartel arrangement was to eliminate the only competitors who refused to join the cartel.[134] This was done by forcing the competitor to be confined to its domestic market. In addition, the cartel took all measures to completely damage the competitor's business by poaching the competitor's employees and by interfering with their contracts with the customers.[135] The cartel also tried to enforce a collective boycott of the competitor so that the

[126] [2005] OJ L004/10 (n 120) para 3.

[127] Case C-309/99 (n 37). Even though the decision went in favour of the regulation, it can still be challenged and each case will be treated on its merit.

[128] Alison Jones and Brenda Sufrin (n 42) 808.

[129] [1999] OJ L24/1 Commission Decision of October 21, 1998 relating to a proceeding under [Article 101] of the EC Treaty (Case No IV/35.691/E-4: — Pre-Insulated Pipe Cartel) http://eur-lex.europa.eu/LexUriServ/LexUriServ.do?uri=OJ:L:1999:024:0001:0070:EN:PDF (accessed 5 May 2011).

[130] *Id.*, 4

[131] *Id.*, 14 and 29, para 33 and para 75, respectively.

[132] *Id.*, 26, para 66. Later three more producers joined in bringing the total number of cartel members to ten.

[133] *Id.*, 4, para 2.

[134] Power Pipe was the only competitor that refused to join the cartel. The company was based in Sweden and was one of the major producers of pre-insulated pipes. It was also Power Pipe who filed a complaint against the cartel. See *Id.,* 9 para 20.

[135] [1999] OJ L24/1 (n 129) 9 para 20.

competitor would be unable to fulfil its contractual obligations.[136] It was on the complaint of the competitor, that the EU Competition Commission investigated and finally adopted its decision on the cartel activity according to Article 101, clause 1. The Commission held that the cartel behaviour through agreements and concerted practice had the *object* as well as the *effect* to restrict competition, as per the requirement of Article 101, clause 1.[137] The Commission found that

> 'Price being the main instrument of competition, the various collusive arrangements and mechanisms adopted by the producers, including the common plan to eliminate or damage Powerpipe, were all ultimately aimed at an inflation of the price to their benefit and above the level which would be determined by conditions of free competition'.[138]

Accordingly, the Commission imposed fines in excess of € 92 million on all the ten undertakings.[139] From the review of the aforementioned examples, one can deduce that cartels are largely formed to fix prices, so that the members can earn profits, which will be more than what they will earn under free competition. Furthermore, one may note that all types of cartel behaviour, viz., market sharing, customer sharing, collusive tendering/bid rigging, collective boycott, quota restrictions, exchange of price sensitive information et al. is primarily aimed at raising prices at the cost of consumer benefits. Sometimes, however, the particular behaviour may be, on its own, found to be in violation of Article 101, clause 1, without the need to show price fixing.

For example in the *UK Agricultural Tractor Registration Exchange*[140] case, the EU Competition Commission held that the information exchange agreement

---

[136] To enforce collective boycott, the cartel passed resolutions wherein it was decided that no raw material be supplied to Power Pipe, no sub-contractor shall work for Power Pipe and all kind of supplies to Power Pipe be prevented. See *Id.*, 36–40, para 98–107.

[137] *Id.*, 54, para 146.

[138] *Id.*

[139] In appeal before the General Court/Court of First Instance, the fines imposed on two of the ten cartel members were reduced. See 'The 'Pre-insulated pipes' judgment: The European Court of Justice confirms the legality of the Commission's Guidelines on fines', *Competition Policy Newsletter* vol.3 (2005): 78–79, http://ec.europa.eu/competition/publications/cpn/2005_3_78.pdf (accessed May 5, 2011). On subsequent appeal, the European Court of Justice affirmed the judgment of the General Court/Court of First Instance. See Case C-189/02, *Dansk Rørindustri A/S* (C-189/02 P), *IsoplusFernwärmetechnikVertriebsgesellschaftmbH and Others* (C-202/02 P), *KE KelitKunststoffwerk GmbH* (C-205/02 P), *LR af* 1998 A/S (C-206/02 P), *BruggRohrsysteme GmbH* (C-207/02 P), *LR af* 1998 *(Deutschland) GmbH* (C-208/02 P) and *ABB Asea Brown Boveri Ltd* (C-213/02 P) v *Commission of the European Communities*, [2005] ECR I-5425.

[140] [1992] OJ L-68/19.

entered into by eight manufacturers and importers of agricultural tractors, concerning the exchange of information identifying the volume of their retail sales and their market shares, amounted to an infringement of Article 101, clause 1.[141] The eight undertakings were members of the Agricultural Engineers Association Ltd (AEA), the United Kingdom trade association of manufacturers and importers of agricultural machinery. The Commission reasoned that the exchange of information on retail sales and market shares restricted competition by creating a transparency of information among the competitors. Since there were only eight major players in the market, any such exchange of data meant that all of them were able to maintain their status quo in the market by coordinating their business decisions. This also meant that a new company would find it very hard to penetrate the market which was completely dominated by the eight undertakings.[142]

---

[141] *Id.,* para 37–48.

[142] *Id.* The Commission notes that 'The Exchange restricts competition because it creates a degree of market transparency between the suppliers in a highly concentrated market which is likely to destroy what hidden competition there remains between the suppliers in that market on account of the risk and ease of exposure of independent competitive action… Uncertainty and secrecy between suppliers is a vital element of competition in this kind of market. Indeed active competition in these market conditions becomes possible only if each competitor can keep its actions secret or even succeeds in misleading its rivals… This market knowledge allows each member and dealer to react immediately and thus to neutralize whatever initiative any one of the members / dealers… would take to increase its sales…the result in practice is that few such initiatives will be taken precisely because every supplier knows very well that the position of each of the others is and that, thanks to the transparency created by the system, any initiative on his part can be detected at once by the others'. On price competition, the Commission notes that the information exchange limits 'price competition as far as possible by allowing suppliers and dealers to react to any price-cutting or other market strategies selectively by limiting their response to the absolute minimum degree necessary in terms of product and territory and by being sure to hit the right target'. On how the information exchange restricts entry of new players in the market, the Commission notes that 'If a supplier chooses not to become a member of the Exchange, he is disadvantaged by the fact that he does not have available the detailed and accurate market information about other suppliers which is available to members of the Exchange. Detailed knowledge of the sales pattern for tractors on the United Kingdom market improves the members' ability to defend their positions vis-à-vis non-members… If a supplier chooses to become a member of the Exchange, he must reveal his exact retail sales by product and by every small geographic territory with the result that the Exchange then permits the established suppliers with considerable market shares and extensive dealer networks to become aware of the existence of new entry and to instantly detect the market penetration by any such new member. This market information on any new member will permit the established suppliers to defend their acquired positions by placing selective actions designed to contain the new member… As a result, for a small supplier it is neither advantageous to become a member of the Exchange nor to stay outside the Exchange'.

In this case, therefore, the fixing of a supra-competitive price was not the focal point. The focus was rather on the exchange of information which enabled the members to maintain high prices at the cost of the consumers. The Commission, in this case, held that since price competition was eliminated by such information exchange, all the members would be able to maintain a high price, thus depriving the farmers of effective choices among the products, viz., tractors.[143]

Having thus reviewed the various examples of possible cartel behaviour, one needs to finally determine what measures have been taken by the EU Competition Commission, to enable consumers to play a definite role in protecting their interest against cartels. The following section will review the various pro-consumer steps taken by the EU Competition Commission.

Pro-consumer measures: Reviewing the EU Competition Commission's effort

The EU Competition Commission, as noted above, has been driven by the consumer's welfare in its drive against cartels.[144] Over the years, it has initiated measures which not only attempt to deter cartel formation, and therefore harm consumers, but also ensures that consumers can have a direct remedy against the harm caused by the cartel behaviour. It is with this aim that on May 1, 2004, the EU Competition Commission adopted new enforcement measures against cartels.[145] By the new regulation, the Commission acquired the powers needed for investigation and collection of evidence against cartels.[146] Further, in order to ensure the effective enforcement of the competition rules

[143] *Id.* The Commission notes that 'for farmers, the purchase of a tractor represents a very high financial investment. Therefore, in the farmer's final choice, the price of the tractor remains an important element, in particular since all tractors of the members of the Exchange, however differentiated they may be, fulfill the same functions and are compatible with all other agricultural machines to be attached to a tractor. Reliability and brand loyalty are therefore not the only elements taken into account by a farmer. Price competition still plays an important role in this market… By increasing the transparency in a highly concentrated market and by strengthening the cohesion between the major suppliers in that market through regular and secret contacts, it is possible to maintain a general high price level in the market concerned in spite of price differences between the various products offered on the market'.

[144] On 'EU Competition Law and Consumers', see generally Giorgio Monti (n 158 of Chapter 2) 99–102.

[145] Alison Jones and Brenda Sufrin (n 42) 801.

[146] For a critical analysis on the working of the regulation, see Julian Joshua, 'The European Cartel Enforcement Regime Post-Modernization: How is it Working?', *Geo. Mason L. Rev.*, (2006) 13: 1247–1271.

against cartels, the regulation also provides for coordination with national competition authorities.[147] Importantly, the regulation identifies mechanisms by which cartels can not only be detected and proceeded against but also that have a deterrent effect on cartels, preventing their formation. The EU Competition Commission can, for example, impose fines[148] on cartels and grant amnesty to 'whistle blowers' under its leniency programme. From a consumer perspective, however, the most important development has been the private enforcement of the EU competition law against cartels. In addition, the EU Competition Commission also provides for a settlement procedure which gives an option to a cartel member to get the fine reduced.[149]

Fining cartels

The whole idea of imposing fines is to act as a deterrent for any entity which may have the intention of forming cartels.[150] The EU Competition Commission has, accordingly issued two guidelines, with respect to the method of calculating fines.[151] Of the two, it is the 2006 guidelines that are presently in force. It reiterates the deterrent objective of fines. The new guideline allows the EU Competition Commission to set the basic minimum of fine at thirty per cent of the value of the sale affected by the cartels. Furthermore, the Commission has the discretion to further increase the basic minimum of fine if the infringement continues. The maximum fine that can be imposed by the Commission shall

> 'not, in any event, exceed 10% of the total turnover in the preceding business year of the undertaking or association of undertakings participating in the infringement…'.[152]

---

[147] [2003] OJ L1/1 (n 93) Art 12. It makes provision for exchange of information amongst the EU Competition Commission and the national competition authorities. See also Maher M. Dabbah (n 23) 194–197.

[148] *Id.* Article 23, clause 2.

[149] COM (2009) 374 final (n 82) 7–8.

[150] Alison Jones and Brenda Sufrin (n 42) 1100.

[151] See [1998] OJ C 9/3, Guidelines on the method of setting fines imposed pursuant to Article 15 (2) of Regulation No 17 and Article 65 (5) of the ECSC Treaty, http://eur-lex.europa.eu/LexUriServ/LexUriServ.do?uri=OJ:C:1998:009:0003:0005:EN:PDF (accessed 9 May 2011); Also see [2006] OJ C 210/2, Guidelines on the method of setting fines imposed pursuant to Article 23(2)(a) of Regulation No 1/2003, http://eurlex.europa.eu/LexUriServ/LexUriServ.do?uri=OJ:C:2006:210:0002:0005:EN:PDF (accessed 9 May 2011).

[152] *Id.*, para 32.

Notably, after the coming into force of the 2006 guidelines, the EU Competition Commission has been imposing record high fines on cartels.[153] From 2007 to 2011, the EU Competition Commission has imposed a total of € 10.390.701.432 fine on cartels, approximately.[154] For example in April 2011, the EU Competition Commission adopted a decision by which it fined consumer product giant Unilever and Proctor & Gamble a total of € 315.2 million.[155] In 2008, the Commission imposed on car glass producers, a record fine totalling €1.3 billion.[156] One can therefore see that the trend is to use fines as a principal means to sanction cartels and make them pay for the harm that they had caused the consumers.[157]

Leniency programme of EU

The other manner in which the EU Competition Commission deals with cartels is to offer an incentive by which cartel members are induced to break ranks and blow the whistle.[158] The leniency programme is designed to help the Commission detect cartels with the help of insiders.[159] In return for their cooperation, the insiders/whistle blowers are promised lenient treatment.[160] The objective of such a programme is to instill fear in the cartel members that any one of them might break ranks and turn against them. This will

---

153 See generally 'GCR EU Cartel Survey: An analysis of cartel fines from 2005–2010' http://www.globalcompetitionreview.com/indepth/444/eu-cartel-survey/ (accessed 9 May 2011).

154 See Cartel fine statistics, http://ec.europa.eu/competition/cartels/statistics/statistics.pdf (accessed 9 May 2011).

155 See IP/11/473, Washing powder cartel, http://europa.eu/rapid/pressReleasesAction.do?reference=IP/11/473&format=HTML&aged=0&language=EN&guiLanguage=en (accessed 9 May 2011).

156 See IP/08/1685, 'Antitrust: Commission fines car glass producers over €1.3 billion for market sharing cartel', http://europa.eu/rapid/pressReleasesAction.do?reference=IP/08/1685&format=HTML&aged=0&language=EN&guiLanguage=en (accessed 12 August 2011).

157 On a critical appraisal of whether the fines imposed by the EU Competition Commission reflects consumer harm or not, see generally Cento Veljanovski, 'Cartel Fines in Europe-Law, Practice and Deterrence' (2007)30:1 World Competition, 65-86. See also SPEECH/11/268, JoaquínAlmunia, Vice President of the European Commission responsible for Competition Policy, 'Cartels: the priority in competition enforcement' http://europa.eu/rapid/pressReleasesAction.do?reference=SPEECH/11/268&format=HTML&aged=0&language=EN&guiLanguage=en (accessed 9th May 2011)

158 See Mark Furse, *Competition Law of the EC and UK* (6thedtn. OUP, 2008) 126–128.

159 Jonathan Faull and Ali Nickpay (n 14) 799, para 8.107

160 See Valentine Korah, *An Introductory Guide to EC Competition Law and Practice* (9thedtn, Hart Publishers, 2007) 280-281

act as a deterrent to any future attempt at forming cartels. The Commission published the first leniency notice in 1996, wherein it made clear that the leniency programme was applicable only in the case of cartels.[161] The Commission justified the adoption of such a programme as necessary for the protection of consumer interest.[162] Accordingly, the 1996 notice guaranteed a reduction of fine to the extent of seventy-five per cent or

> 'even from total exemption from the fine that would have been imposed if they had not cooperated'.[163]

The notice however did not guarantee complete immunity from legal proceedings. The whistle blowers were liable to 'civil law consequences of its participation in an illegal agreement'.[164] The 1996 notice was subsequently amended by the 2002 notice.[165] By this amendment, the Commission guaranteed hundred per cent immunity from fines to the undertaking which is first to arrive at the 'Commission's door'[166] and blow the whistle.[167] This increased the attractiveness of the leniency programme.[168] Subsequently, in 2006, the Commission replaced the 2002 notice with a new leniency notice.[169] This notice amended the grounds on which immunity from fines would be

---

161 [1996] OJ C 207/4, Commission Notice on the non-imposition or reduction of fines in cartel cases http://eur-lex.europa.eu/LexUriServ/LexUriServ.do?uri=CELEX:31996Y0718(01):EN:NOT (accessed 9 May 2011)

162 *Id.*at part A, point 4, [The Commission, in the introductory part of the 1996 notice states that "it is in the Community interest in granting favourable treatment to enterprises which cooperate with [the Commission]… The interests of consumers and citizens in ensuring that such practices are detected and prohibited outweigh the interest in fining those enterprises which cooperate with the Commission, thereby enabling or helping it to detect and prohibit a cartel."]

163 *Id.*, part B.

164 *Id.*, part E, point 4. Civil law consequences essentially mean claim for damages by the party injured due to the cartel conduct. See, for example, Case C-453/99 (n 121). See also Caroline Cauffman, 'The Interaction of Leniency Programmes and Action for Damages', *The Competition Law Review*, 181–220 (2011) 7:2, http://www.clasf.org/CompLRev/Issues/Vol7Issue2Art1Cauffman.pdf (accessed 26 October 2011).

165 [2002] OJ C 45/3, Commission notice on immunity from fines and reduction of fines in cartel cases, http://eur-lex.europa.eu/LexUriServ/LexUriServ.do?uri=CELEX:52002XC0219(02):EN:NOT (accessed 9 May 2011).

166 Alison Jones and Brenda Sufrin (n 42) 1122.

167 See Luiz Ortiz Blanco, *EC Competition Procedure,* 2nd ed. (OUP, 2006), 219–243.

168 The grant of immunity is however subject to the stringent conditions that have been laid down in the 2002 guideline.

169 [2006] OJ C 298/17, Commission notice on immunity from fines and reduction of fines in cartel cases, http://eur-lex.europa.eu/LexUriServ/LexUriServ.do?uri=CELEX:52006XC1208(04):EN:NOT (accessed 9 May 2011).

granted. Further, the notice also laid the grounds for reducing fines, if the undertaking reveals its participation in a cartel but fails to meet the criteria required for immunity. However, the 2006 notice reiterates the stance of the Commission that

> '[t]he fact that immunity or reduction in respect of fines is granted cannot protect an undertaking from the civil law consequences of its participation in an infringement of [Article 101]'.[170]

An example of how the leniency programme works is the Fine Art Auction Houses cartel case,[171] wherein Christie's applied for leniency and was granted the same, resulting in hundred per cent reduction of fine.

Civil litigation for damages: Private enforcement

An interesting development in the EU anti-cartel enforcement measures has been the debate on private enforcement of competition rules. On April 2, 2008, the European Competition Commission adopted the *'WHITE PAPER on damages actions for breach of the EC antitrust rules'*.[172] Through this paper, the Commission emphasized the need to have effective measures that

> 'would ensure...that all victims of infringements of EC competition law have access to effective redress mechanisms so that they can be fully compensated for the harm they suffered'.[173]

This in effect is aimed at helping private parties take action for damages, for the harm they may have suffered due to the infringement of the EU competition rules.[174] This attempt of the Commission is evidently aimed at directly involving the consumers with the enforcement of anti-cartel measures. The idea is also to deter cartels from imposing the costs of their anti-competitive behaviour on consumers. Further, private action for damages will strengthen the public enforcement of anti-cartel and other competition rules.[175] There

---

170 *Id.*, point 39.

171 [2005] OJ L 200/92 (n 116).

172 COM(2008) 165 final, http://eur-lex.europa.eu/LexUriServ/LexUriServ.do?uri=COM:2008:0165:FIN:EN:PDF (accessed May 9, 2011).

173 *Id.*, point 1.2.

174 See Denis Waelbroeck, 'Private Enforcement: Current Situation and Methods of Improvement', in *The Reform of EC Competition Law- New Challenges*, ed. IoannisLianos and IoannisKokkoris, (2010, Kluwer Law International), 17–32.

175 See COMP/2006/A3/012, 'Making antitrust damages actions more effective in the EU: Welfare impact and potential scenarios', A report prepared for the EU Competition

are however potential problems of introducing private enforcement/ civil litigation for damages, viz., the question of standing, i.e., who can claim damages, more so when the victim is an indirect purchaser; the question of quantification of damages; access to evidence; the question of fault and the defence of passing on.[176] There is also the issue of balancing the leniency programme with that of the private enforcement measures. Resolving these tensions effectively therefore holds the key to the success of the EU anti-cartel measure.[177] The Commission itself has come up with a number of suggestions for overcoming the obstacles.[178] One will have to wait and see as to what form the private enforcement will eventually materialize in the EU cartel law.

Settlement by cartelists

Finally, in order to further encourage cartel members to break away from cartels, the EU Competition Commission adopted a settlement procedure in cartel cases, whereby, the undertakings, who are implicated by the Commission, for cartel behaviour, are given the option of acknowledging their role and liability in the cartel. If the undertaking agrees to so cooperate with the Commission, the Commission will reward such cooperation by reducing the fines imposed to the extent of ten per cent.[179] The settlement procedure thus concerns only the undertaking's involvement and has nothing to do with the requirement of revealing the names of other cartel members. For this reason, it is different

Commission, http://ec.europa.eu/competition/antitrust/actionsdamages/files_white_paper/impact_study.pdf#page=441 (accessed 9 May 2011).

176 For a detailed discussion on these points, see Andrea Heinemann, 'Private Enforcement in Europe', in *The Development of Competition Law- Global Perspectives,* ed. Roger Zach, Andreas Heinemann and Andrea Kellerhals, (2010, Edward Elgar Publishers), 300–318. See also COM (2008) 165, Final,Commission staff working paper accompanying the White paper on damages actions for breach of the EC antitrust rules, http://eur-lex.europa.eu/LexUriServ/LexUriServ.do?uri=CELEX:52008SC0404:EN:NOT (accessed 9 May 2011).

177 See generally, Christian Kersting, 'Perspectives for Private Enforcement in European Antitrust Law', http://papers.ssrn.com/sol3/papers.cfm?abstract_id=1161254 (accessed 9 May 2011).

178 *Id.*

179 See [2008] OJ C 167/1, Commission notice on the conduct of settlement procedures in view of the adoption of decisions pursuant to Article 7 and Article 23 of Council Regulation (EC) No 1/2003 in cartel cases, http://eur-lex.europa.eu/LexUriServ/LexUriServ.do?uri=CELEX:52008XC0702(01):EN:NOT (accessed May 9, 2011). See also [2008] OJ L 171/3, Commission Regulation (EC) No 622/2008 of June 30, 2008 amending Regulation (EC) No 773/2004, regarding the conduct of settlement procedures in cartel cases, http://eur-lex.europa.eu/LexUriServ/LexUriServ.do?uri=CELEX:32008R0622:EN:NOT (accessed 9 May 2011).

from the leniency notices. The settlement procedure adds up to the efforts of the EU Competition Commission to create an effective anti-cartel regime that not only deters the formation of cartels but also makes it easier for the Commission to detect cartels. Importantly though, the settlement procedure furthers the pro-consumer agenda of the EU Competition Commission. As on October 19, 2011, the EU Competition Commission has settled four cases.[180]

Looking forward

The review of the EU's response to cartels brings out the fact that Article 101, clause 1 renders all cartels *per se void.* This is so because the *object* of cartels is regarded as anti-competitive. Consequently, under the EU law, there is no need to establish the *effect* of the cartels. Technically though, a cartel can still escape the consequence of infringing Article 101, clause 1 if the cartel is able to satisfy cumulatively the conditions prescribed under Article 101, clause 3. Nonetheless, the case law has established that a cartel may find it next to impossible to satisfy the conditions prescribed in Article 101, clause 3. One of the reasons for this is that Article 101, clause 3 requires that the anti-competitive conduct should pass on a fair share of the benefit to the consumers. For a cartel, this will inevitably mean a failure to satisfy the pro-competitive defence as required by Article 101, clause 3. Further,

---

[180] These four cases are: (1) IP/11/1214 (This case involved a settlement of fines with four producers of cathode ray tube glass used in television and computer screens. The cartel members were involved in price coordination and exchange of sensitive and confidential market information, http://europa.eu/rapid/pressReleasesAction.do?reference=IP/11/1214&format=HTML&aged=0&language=EN&guiLanguage=en#footnote-1 (accessed 27 October 2011); (2) IP/11/473 (This case involved settlement of fines with Procter & Gamble and Unilever, who along with Henkel were operating a cartel concerning household powder detergents. The cartel members fixed the prices of their product.), http://europa.eu/rapid/pressReleasesAction.do?reference=IP/11/473&format=HTML&aged=0&language=EN&guiLanguage=en (accessed 27 October 2011); (3) IP/10/985 (This case involved settlement of fines with the producers of animal feed phosphates. Animal feed phosphates are chemical compounds used in the feed of animals such as cattle, fish, poultry, pigs and pets. The cartel indulged in market sharing and price fixing of the animal feed phosphates.), http://europa.eu/rapid/pressReleasesAction.do?reference=IP/10/985&format=HTML&aged=0&language=EN&guiLanguage=en (accessed 27 October 2011); (4) IP/10/586 (This was the first case involving settlement of fines with ten producers of memory chips of DRAMS used in computers and servers. The cartel members indulged in fixing of prices and quotas.), http://europa.eu/rapid/pressReleasesAction.do?reference=IP/10/586&format=HTML&aged=0&language=EN&guiLanguage=en (accessed 9 May 2011).

the EU law takes into account a wide spectrum of consumer interests when framing its anti-cartel response. This is evident from the definition of a 'consumer' used by the Commission, which includes both intermediaries as well as end consumers ensuring a middle-of-the-road approach, taking into account the various interest groups affected by the cartel conduct. The pro-consumer approach of the EU law is further established by its declared policy of zero-tolerance towards crisis cartels. Under the EU law, Article 101, clause 3 may allow the Commission to grant block exemptions to certain kinds of horizontal cooperative arrangements. However, apart from such exemptions based on policy considerations, a crisis cartel will be treated like any other cartel. This is evident from the fact that the EU Courts have constantly rejected the argument of ruinous competition or crisis, given to justify the creation of a cartel. Further, the Commission has also shifted the burden of proof on to the cartelists, who want to benefit from Article 101, clause 3, to establish the pro-competitive aspect of the cartel. Finally, the effectiveness of the *per se void* approach is enhanced by the Commission's fining policy, leniency programme, the incorporation of private enforcement measures and the settlement of fine procedures. These four enforcement tactics are used by the EU Competition Commission to effectively utilize its resources against cartels. In view of these conclusions, it is time to analyse the Indian response towards cartels.

5 India, Cartels and Consumer Interests: The MRTP Phase

Context

The discussion on cartels in India has to begin with the analyses of the Monopolies and Restrictive Trade Practices Act, 1969 (hereinafter called the MRTP). More specifically, the treatment of cartels under the MRTP will be analysed to understand India's initial response to cartels. The first step will be to analyse the socio-political context in which the MRTP was enacted. Reference to the Monopolies Inquiry Commission report will further help in establishing the context of the MRTP. The next step would be to analyse the MRTP to understand the substantive law on cartels. Finally, the efficacy of the MRTP will be better understood by evaluating the extent to which cartelization continues to be a reality in India. The questions that get addressed in the process are: (a) how effective was the anti-cartel provision in the MRTP Act in deterring cartels? and (b) how far did consumer interests govern the enactment and enforcement of the anti-cartel provision of the MRTP?

MRTP and anti-cartel measures: Poles apart?

The response of the government of India to the cartel problem was not specific—rather the attempt was to tackle certain anti-competitive issues afflicting the Indian economy at that time. It was for this reason that the government of India enacted the MRTP. The genesis of the MRTP was a concern for the growing income inequalities, with the economic wealth accumulating in the hands of a few large enterprises.[1] The government

---

1 See Amit Kapur, Manas Kumar Chaudhuri and Mansoor Ali Shoket, 'Competition Regulation: History, Insights and Issues for the Way Forward', http://articles.manupatra.com/PopOpenArticle.aspx?ID=ebaae57cb2aa43b7af9fac02df0a35b2&txtsearch= (accessed 23 May 2011)

of India, at the time, followed a command and control regime wherein it determined the manner in which the economic actors functioned.[2] The government controlled, at least to some extent, the allocation of raw material and production, as well as the distribution and pricing of the finished products.[3] The predominant economic philosophy that underlined such a government controlled system was the curbing of monopoly.[4] In real terms, it meant that legislative devices had to be used to prevent dominance of large industrial houses and prevent them from maximizing their profits at the cost of small enterprises and the public sector.[5]

The Industries (Development and Regulation) Act, 1951 (hereinafter called IDRA), for example, was enacted by the government of India for regulating private investment through the licencing procedure.[6] The government of India set the criteria for issuing the industrial licences, thereby ensuring absolute control over the pattern of private investment.[7] Industrial licence therefore was required for

> 'the establishment of a new industrial undertaking, manufacturing of a new item by an existing undertaking, change of location of an industry, substantial expansion of existing capacity and for all other purposes'. [8]

---

2 See Pradeep S. Mehta, 'Competition Law Regime in India: Evolution, Experience and Challenges, Horizons', *Concurrences* N° 1 (2006), 150–156, http://www.cuts-ccier.org/pdf/PDF-AR1.pdf (accessed 23 May 2011).

3 See SVS Raghavan Committee Report (n 26 of Chapter 1) para 2.2.3.

4 See Anurag K Agarwal, 'Competition Law in India: Need to go Slow and Steady', http://www.iimahd.ernet.in/publications/data/2005-10-05anurag.pdf (accessed 25 May 2011).

5 See generally (Dr.) N.K. Sengupta, *The Monopolies and Restrictive Practices Act, 1969,* (Eastern Law House, 1977), 8–10.

6 See 'Legal Aspects, Industrial Acts and Legislations: Industries (Development and Regulation) Act 1951', http://business.gov.in/legal_aspects/industries_act.php (accessed 25 May 2011).

7 See 'Report of the Working Group on Competition Policy' (commissioned by the Planning Commission, Government of India, 2007. The Working Group was headed by VinodDhall, then a member of the Competition Commission of India), http://planningcommission.nic.in/aboutus/committee/wrkgrp11/wg11_cpolicy.pdf (accessed 25 May 2011).

8 See Legal Aspects, Industrial Acts (n 6) ['The new industrial policy has liberalised this and exempted many industries from obtaining industrial licence. In today's scenario, only 6 categories of industries require industrial licencing under the Industries (Development and Regulation) Act, 1951 (IDRA). Such industries file an Industrial Entrepreneur Memoranda (IEM) with the Secretariat of Industrial Assistance (SIA), Department of Industrial Policy and Promotion to obtain an acknowledgement'.] See also Gurcharan Das, 'India Unbound', *The American Spectator*, 30 (July 2001), 34:6. Explaining the deleterious effect of the IDRA, Das notes that 'Large business houses set up parallel bureaucracies in Delhi to follow up on their files, organize bribes, and win licenses. If the entrepreneur did

The MRTP was enacted to further strengthen these measures of the government of India. This furthered the command and control model of running the economy. Consequently, controlling or eliminating cartels were not in the horizon of the Indian policy makers. In addition, the enactment of the MRTP was preceded by events that set the tone of the MRTP.[9]

Socio-political context of MRTP

As mentioned before, the government of India had from the beginning decided to take a cautionary approach to the role of private enterprise in the Indian economy. This is evident from the IDRA and the first five year plan, wherein the intention to bring the private enterprise within the control and supervision of the central government was clearly outlined.[10] The Industrial Policy Resolution of 1956 reiterated this approach of the government of India.[11] Accordingly, in the 1956 policy, the government clearly demarcated sectors wherein industries could be set up only by the public sector or state, with the private sector having only a secondary role.[12] This command and

finally make a success of his enterprise, he was again in trouble. It was illegal to manufacture beyond the licensed capacity. We became the only country in the non-communist world where the production of goods sorely needed by people was punishable by law. In many cases the basic entrepreneurial decisions, such as the choice of technology and the size and location of plants, were taken away from risk-taking businessmen and made by bureaucrats. We, thus, killed at birth any hope for an industrial revolution'.

9 See generally Shiju Varghese Mazhuvanchery, 'The Indian Competition Act: A Historical and Developmental Perspective', *The Law and Development Review*, 240–270 (2010) 3: 2, http://www.bepress.com/ldr/vol3/iss2/art8 (accessed May 25, 2011). Varghese notes that 'An understanding of the political undercurrents is highly useful in the analysis of the competition law that emerged'.

10 See Francine R. Frankel, *India's Political Economy: 1947–2004,* 2nd ed., (OUP, 2005), 94. See also the First Five Year Plan, 'Industrial Development and Policy-Chapter 29', http://planningcommission.nic.in/plans/planrel/fiveyr/default.html (accessed 31 October 2011).

11 See 'The Industrial Policy Resolution, 1956', http://eaindustry.nic.in/handbk/chap001.pdf (accessed 26 May 2011) para 5, page 2.

12 The 1956 policy classified industries into three categories. Industries in the first category were listed as Schedule A industries. The responsibility to develop these industries was exclusively entrusted to the State. Industries in the second category were listed as Schedule B industries. In these industries, the State will have a predominant role though the private enterprise was expected to 'supplement the efforts of the State'. The third category comprised the remaining industries wherein the private sector was expected to take the initiative. It was however made clear that the 'Industrial undertakings in the private sector have necessarily to fit into the framework of the social and economic policy of the State and will be subject to control and regulation in terms of the Industries (Development and Regulation) Act and other relevant legislation'.

control regime was however severely tested during the 1960s, when India got stuck in a severe financial crisis accompanied by political uncertainties. As Guha notes

> '[t]o the historian, the late 1960s are reminiscent of the late 1940s, likewise a time of crisis and conflict, of resentment along lines of class, religion, ethnicity and region, of a centre that seemed barely to hold'.[13]

In the face of these twin crises, the then Prime Minister Indira Gandhi adopted a pro-poor stance wherein the public sector continued to have a dominant role.[14] She made her aversion to big businesses clear by agreeing to appoint a monopolies commission and deciding to ban the entry of big businesses into the consumer goods industries.[15] This was the background against which the MRTP was introduced and the conditions which laid the foundation for India's competition law in general and anti-cartel law in particular.

The twin crisis were the result of successive monsoon failures, depleting foreign exchange reserves, shrinking foreign aid, famine like situations and high inflation rates, forcing the government of India to search for solutions. One of the solutions that the then Prime Minister Indira Gandhi came up with was the passing of the MRTP in 1969.[16] The provisions of the MRTP were based on the recommendations of several committees appointed by the government of India to look into the issue of concentration of economic power in the Indian market. The reports which acted as the foundation for MRTP were the *Mahalanobis Committee Report on Distribution of Income and Levels of Living, 1964, The Monopolies Inquiry Commission Report, 1965, The Hazari Committee Report on Industrial Licensing Procedure, 1966* and the *Industrial Licensing Policy Inquiry Committee Report, 1969.*[17] The thrust of these reports was on the effective way of controlling the growth of monopolist undertakings and the solution suggested was the creation of a Monopolies Commission.[18] Understandably, the 1965 report on monopolies was to become the main reference point for the purpose of determining the

---

13 See generally RamachandraGuha, *India after Gandhi* (Picador, 2007) 433.

14 *Id.*, 436.

15 *Id.*, 418.

16 See generally Bipan Chandra, Mridula Mukherjee and Aditya Mukherjee, *India After Independence:1947–2000,* Fifth Impression (Penguin Books India, 2002), 351–353.

17 See Abir Roy and Jayant Kumar, *Competition Law in India* (Eastern Law House, 2008), 32–35.

18 See Virendra Kumar, *Committees and Commissions of India:1947–73,* vol. 8:1967 (Concept Publishing Company, 1979), 115.

scope of the MRTP.[19] One thing that is clear from this discussion though is that cartels were not to be the primary concern of the MRTP.

The inquiry commission and cartels: Lack of focus?

The Monopolies Inquiry Commission was appointed in 1964, with the mandate to

> 'inquire into the extent and effect of concentration of economic power in private hands and the prevalence of monopolistic and restrictive practices in important sectors of economic activity…'.[20]

In this respect, the Monopolies Inquiry Committee was the first of its kind and the only Committee constituted by the government of India to study the concentration of economic power and monopoly and restrictive trade practices in reference to industries.[21] The Committee accordingly prepared its report giving details of the concentration in the various sectors, though excluding the public sector. This was in keeping with the command and control regime existing at the time. The Committee noted that the concentration of economic power manifests itself when one or more industrial unit acquires a dominant position by which it can 'control the market by regulating prices or output or eliminating competition'.[22] This statement of the Committee reflects the belief that free competition among industrial units or enterprises was a must to avoid concentration of economic power and monopoly. Further, looking into the terms of reference of the Committee, it can be said that the Committee was mandated to look into all anti-competitive issues, viz., monopoly, abuse of dominance and restrictive trade practices. The mandate to study restrictive trade practices also implied that the Committee had to look into both vertical restraints as well as horizontal restraints. This leads one

---

[19] See Amitabh Kumar, 'The Evolution of Competition Law in India', in *Competition Law Today-Concepts, Issues, and the Law in Practice,* VinodDhall, ed. (OUP, 2007) (n 5 of Chapter 1) 479–486.

[20] See Government of India, *Report of the Monopolies Inquiry Commission* (Manager of Publications, 1965) 438, i.

[21] The other committees mentioned herein, viz., the Mahalanobis Committee, the Hazari Committee and the Industrial Licensing Policy Committee, were required to look into the various aspects that were responsible for economic concentration in the Indian economy in general. On the other hand, the focal point of the Monopolies Commission was the study of economic concentration, monopoly and restrictive trade practices, as a question of fact. Further, the Monopolies Commission was also required to suggest legislative measures to curb concentration of economic power and monopolies and restrictive trade practices with reference to industries.

[22] Government of India (n 20) 1.

to safely argue that the study of horizontal restraints would have inevitably required the Committee to review the existence of cartel agreements within the Indian economy.

Nonetheless, as mentioned above, the Committee was more concerned with the dominance of certain undertakings and the abuse of this dominant position than cartels. Accordingly, the report of the Committee was divided into part 1 and part 2—the former dealt with economic concentration and the latter dealt with monopolistic and restrictive trade practices. On the aspect of economic concentration within industries, the Committee noted that they will look into industry-wise or product-wise concentration and country-wise concentration.[23] On the other hand, the Committee included cartel conduct within e examples of 'restrictive practices'.[24] This establishes that the Committee recognized the possibility of cartels causing harm. It needs to be noted however that the 1965 Committee never defined cartels. Nonetheless, the identified restrictive practices are nothing but cartel conduct. The fact that there was a possibility of the existence of horizontal price-fixing agreements or cartels, in India, at that point of time, is acknowledged by the Committee when it declared that

> '[s]everal instances were brought to our notice of the practice of fixation of prices by agreement between competitors'.[25]

The Committee, for example, found instances of price-fixing arrangements between: manufacturers of tyres and tubes, manufacturers of cables and winding wares, producers of rolled glass and manufacturers of electric lamp.[26]

---

23 *Id.*, 2 [The Committee explained the categorization thus 'Two main kinds of concentration of economic power may be said to prevail in industries. The first is where in respect of the production and distribution of any particular commodity or service the controlling power whether by reason of ownership of capital or otherwise is in a single concern or comparatively limited number of concerns or though in a fairly large number of concerns these concerns themselves are controlled by only a single family or a few families or business houses; this may be called product-wise concentration. Where the industry is engaged in the production of one product, it may be called also 'industry-wise' concentration. Again, where a large number of concerns engaged in the production or distribution of different commodities are in the controlling hands of one individual or family or group of persons, whether incorporated or not, connected closely by financial or other business interests, concentration of economic power will also be clearly considered to exist. For lack of proper terms we shall call this kind of concentration 'country-wise' concentration'.]

24 *Id.,* 126 [According to the Committee, 'As instances of restrictive practices...we may mention the following: (i) horizontal fixation of prices... (iii) allocation of markets between producers;...(v) boycott'.]

25 *Id.,* 132.

26 *Id.*

It also came across evidence of price-fixing arrangements between alkali manufacturers association.[27] Similarly, the Committee received submissions regarding formation of association by producers of ferromanganese, for the purpose of controlling sales.[28] The evidence of market sharing arrangements between competing producers was found in the arrangement between oil distributing companies.[29] The justification given for such arrangements was 'to achieve economic distribution, to avoid cross haulage and ensure continuity of supplies…'.[30] There were hardly any instances of horizontal arrangements to restrict output. The sole evidence of such arrangements was provided by one producer of steel tubes who admitted to the existence of output restriction arrangements among producers of steel tubes in Western India.[31]

However, these instances of cartel behaviour were used by the Committee to strengthen the argument that big was bad. Further, the concern showed was less for the end consumer and more for the small and medium enterprises. The Committee thus argued that

> 'It is well to remember that… the small business concerns are a good training ground for business talent and managerial skill of which we have not a surfeit in the country. The elimination of small men in industries, in so far as it dries up the source of managerial and entrepreneurial ability is therefore bad for industry as a whole. Not less important is the fact that elimination of small men in business increases the imbalance in the distribution of national wealth and income. Even where such elimination by big business results in an increase in the national wealth and income, the income of a few already wealthy men increases at a faster rate than that of the many poor'.[32]

The danger that big businesses posed to small businesses thus formed the core of the findings and the recommendations of the Committee. This concern for all and not just the end consumer is similar to the current approach of the EU Competition Commission. Therefore, one can see that there was a potential for developing a law that accommodated a wider spectrum of interests. However, as monopoly and dominance was the focal point of the Committee's report, the consequent legal response too was likely to focus less on the harm arising out of cartel conduct. It is not surprising therefore that

27 *Id.*
28 *Id.*, 133.
29 Government of India (n 20) 134.
30 *Id.*
31 *Id.*
32 *Id.*, 138.

the Committee recommended the setting up of a permanent body for the purpose of

> 'taking action to protect the country against the dangers [resulting from] excessive concentration of economic power…and also…from monopolistic and restrictive practices'.[33]

The dangers being referred to are the ones discussed above, viz., the ill effects of big businesses on small businesses.

Consumer interests and cartel conduct: Analysing the recommendations of the committee

Though the Committee ignored the harmful effects of economic concentration, monopolistic and restrictive practices on end consumers, in its suggestions, it recognized the role that organized consumer societies could play to counter anti-competitive practices (like cartel conduct). The Committee expressed confidence that

> 'consumer societies…with proper encouragement gather sufficient strength in course of time to be able to fight back against practices of [big] industrialists – whether manufacturer, or trader – which tend to injure consumer's interests'.[34]

The Committee then went on to explain the manner in which consumer societies can fulfil their role of guardian against economic concentration, monopoly and restrictive practices. As an interim measure, the Committee suggested that individual consumers could, till the formation of organized societies, file complaints with the permanent body.[35] Sadly, these recommendations were part of the Committee's non-legislative suggestions. This point is significant because it reflects the lack of thought process to integrate the wide spectrum of consumer interests, viz., both intermediary as well as end consumers, in any proposed competition legislation. This would also affect the anti-cartel law, which will equally be bereft of any pro-consumer intent.

Accordingly, the recommendation of the Committee on the proposed legislative measures reflected this lack of a pro-consumer intent. To begin, the Committee emphasized that the objective of the proposed competition legislation was not to attack concentration of economic power except 'when

---

33 *Id.* 139–140.

34 *Id.*

35 *Id.,* 146.

it becomes a menace to the best production…or to fair distribution'.[36] Further, the proposed legislation can discourage monopolistic conditions, however, the same has to be done 'without injury to the interests of the general public'.[37] Finally, the proposed legislation can curb monopolistic and restrictive practices 'except when they conduce to the common good'.[38] The Committee clearly accepted the importance of the big business houses in the economic development of the country. Accordingly, it observed

> 'what is directed to be guarded against is not concentration of economic power per se but such concentration as may be to the common detriment'.[39]

Therefore, the focus was on the abuse of dominant positions and not on dominance itself. As a result, the suggested objective of the proposed legislative response does away with all concerns for end consumer interests. Further, terms like 'common good' and 'interest of general public' are too ambiguous to help the cause of the intermediary consumers. Finally, ignoring end consumer interests and usage of ambiguous terms reflected a lack of seriousness vis-à-vis anti-cartel measures.

To substantiate, the Committee suggested that all restrictive practices should be compulsorily registered with the Commission. The purpose of such registration though would not mean either its approval or condemnation.[40] Such registration would, among other things,

> 'facilitate the work of investigation of complaints from consumers and other members of the public, against restrictive practices'.[41]

If the Commission came to a decision that the complaint was true and restrictive practices of the sort complained of was indeed being carried out to the common detriment, the maximum that the Commission could do was issue an order to discontinue the practice. The disobedience of such a cease and desist order was to entail a fine.[42] For a cartel, therefore, things were as easy as before, even if India got its first competition legislation. The maximum cost that the cartel would entail would be a fine for disobeying

---

36 *Id.*, 159.

37 *Id.*

38 Government of India (n 20) 159

39 *Id.*, 160.

40 *Id.*, 160.

41 *Id.*

42 *Id.*, 161.

the cease and desist order.[43] Importantly, the Committee regarded a resale price maintenance agreement, hoarding, cornering and profiteering as more serious restrictive practices requiring the *per se void* approach.[44] This meant that any cartel which was involved in hoarding, cornering and profiteering was likely to face severe penalty. The Committee suggested that where traders (who either on their own or in association with other traders) hoard, corner or profiteer by raising prices, their licence to carry on the trade or industry should be cancelled or suspended.[45]

This was thought to be a severe punishment since in those days one could not trade or have an industry without a licence. Apart from these practices, no other cartel practice like market sharing, collective boycott or fixing prices without hoarding was considered in terms of its severity. These suggestions clearly were not enough in terms of efforts taken to curb cartels. The Committee then went on to suggest the manner in which the Commission needed to deal with monopolies. It was suggested by the Committee that practices like mergers and amalgamations which give rise to monopoly should not be treated as *per se* bad.[46] The same suggestion was given with regard to other monopolistic practices like monopoly pricing. The Commission was thus required to apply the test of reasonableness in assessing the harmful effects of monopolistic practices. Similarly, other restrictions were suggested by the Committee to check the abuse of dominant position by the big industries. The Committee concluded its legislative recommendation by outlining the constitution of the proposed Commission as well as proposing a draft bill. The bill was titled the Monopolies and Restrictive Trade Practices Bill, 1965.[47]

---

[43] The reason is that the Committee never decided the proposed quantum of fine which would be large enough to deter cartels. Further, theoretically, a cartel could pay the fine and continue its activity. But most importantly there was nothing in the recommendation that talked about incentives for registering cartel conduct. One has to remember that a cartel is difficult to detect; hence registration and fines could not possibly have had any effect.

[44] The reason for the special treatment was that the Committee found abundant examples of dominant undertakings incorporating price maintenance clauses which forced the distributors not to sell below the price list. According to the Committee, this forces the end consumers to pay higher prices and monopolies to dictate prices to the distributors. This was clearly a case of abuse of dominance as per the Committee and hence regarded reprehensible. One would argue that with regard to cartels, as the Committee could not find strong evidence of widespread cartel conduct, it was not convinced about its harm on the consumers.

[45] Government of India (n 20) 163.

[46] *Id.*

[47] *Id.*, 166.

The 1965 bill, anti-cartel measures and consumer interests: An analysis

The 1969 Act was largely inspired by the 1965 draft bill with all the three elements, viz., concentration of economic power, monopolistic trade practices and restrictive trade practices being dealt with under separate chapters.[48] There was also a chapter devoted to the constitution, powers and functioning of the Monopolies and Restrictive Trade Practices Commission (hereinafter called the MRTP Commission). Any cartel activity would thus have to be dealt with under the chapter on restrictive trade practices. A restrictive practice was defined by the bill as a trade practice which either has or may have

> 'the effect of preventing, distorting or restricting competition in any manner and, in particular, if it tends to obstruct the flow of capital or resources into the stream of production or to the manipulation of prices, conditions of delivery or the flow of supplies in the market relating to specified goods or services in such a manner as to impose on consumers unjustified costs or restrictions'.[49]

The definition on the face of it would cover price-fixing cartels as well as quota restriction cartels. This is so because the definition included practices like manipulation of prices and flow of supplies into the market. Further, collective boycotts by cartels, raising entry barriers into the market would also be covered as the definition refers to practices that restrict the flow of capital or resources into the stream of production. Accordingly, a manufacturer's cartel indulging in collective boycotts, thereby preventing new players from entering the particular stream of production would be a restrictive practice within the meaning of this definition.

As discussed above, the Monopolies Inquiry Committee had proposed that all agreements relating to restrictive trade practices needed to be registered with the Monopolies and Restrictive Trade Practices Commission. Accordingly, the 1965 bill listed the agreements which will be regarded as agreements relating to restrictive trade practices requiring mandatory registration. The list covered both horizontal as well as vertical agreements relating to restrictive trade practices. Hence

48 For a critical analyses comparing the MRTP bill that was introduced by the government of India in the parliament and which eventually got passed (with changes) as the MRTP Act of 1969 and the 1965 bill proposed by the Monopolies Inquiry Commission, see A N Oza, 'Monopolies and Restrictive Practices Bill', *Annual Number, EPW*, (1969) January, 91–102.

49 Government of India (n 20) 174 [Section 20 of the draft MRTP bill 1965].

> 'any agreement between producers or wholesalers… to limit, restrict or withhold the output or supply of any goods or allocate any area or market for the disposal of any goods'[50]

was an example of a horizontal agreement to divide the market and impose quota restrictions. Such agreements would necessarily be enforced by a cartel. On the other hand,

> 'any agreement to sell goods on condition that the prices to be charged on resale by the purchaser shall be the prices stipulated by the seller…'[51]

was an example of a resale price maintenance agreement and thus a vertical agreement. Furthermore, the bill provided for a Registrar of Restrictive Trade Agreements, to be appointed by the central government, who would be subject to the control of the MRTP Commission.[52] The date from which registration of agreements relating to the restrictive trade practices would become necessary was to be notified by the central government.[53] The draft bill vested the power of investigations and the power to pass orders, on the MRTP Commission.[54]

In addition, in the case of restrictive trade practices like price fixing, market sharing, quota restriction, bid rigging etc. (which are cartel conducts), the MRTP Commission could order that

> 'the practice shall be discontinued or shall not be repeated or the agreement relating thereto, if any, shall be void in respect of such restrictive trade practice or shall stand modified in respect thereof in such manner as may be specified in the order'.[55]

However, the MRTP Commission could, in certain cases, decide not to make any of the above quoted orders if it was 'satisfied that…necessary steps [had] been taken' to ensure that the 'trade practice [was] no longer contrary to public interest'.[56] Restrictive agreements were therefore not *per se void.* They would have been declared void or acted against only if they infringed public interest. For this reason, a cartel under the 1965 bill was *per se valid.* The bill explained that to determine if a restrictive trade practice was contrary to public interest, the effect of such a practice had to be looked into. It listed

---

50 *Id.,* [Section 21(i) of the draft MRTP bill, 1965].

51 *Id.,* 174 [Section 21(h) of the draft MRTP bill 1965].

52 *Id.*, 175 [Section 22 of the draft MRTP bill, 1965].

53 *Id.* [Section 23 of the draft MRTP bill, 1965].

54 *Id.*, 177 [Section 26 of the draft MRTP bill, 1965].

55 *Id.* [Section 26(a), (b) of the draft MRTP bill 1965].

56 Government of India (n 20) [Section 26(2) of the draft MRTP bill 1965].

the effects, the result of which would render the restrictive trade practice contrary to public interest.[57] This incorporation of a public interest-based exemption was inspired by the Restrictive Trade Practices Act, 1956 of the United Kingdom (hereinafter called the UK).[58] The bill also identified those cases of restrictive trade practices wherein the MRTP Commission need not pass any order.[59] This meant that under the bill specific exemption were created for goods bought for consumption only. The bill also empowered the MRTP Commission to direct the Director of Investigations to inquire into complaints against restrictive trade practices.[60] Further, in addition to the power to pass a cease and desist order, the MRTP Commission, under the bill, was also empowered to impose a fine on the cartelists in case they disregarded the cease and desist order.[61]

On the whole though, the chapter on restrictive trade practices in the draft bill of 1965 did not help the cause of cartel enforcement. This is so because a cartel being a practice in secret among competitors would have rarely been registered. Further, even if it would have been registered there was always a possibility of escaping action on the ground of public interest. These were also the fallout of the UK Act wherein the public interest-based exemption or the gateway clauses proved ineffective while dealing with cartels.[62] Further the absence of any specific measures to ensure effective detection would have left most cartel activities beyond the purview of the

[57] Thus according to Section 27 of the MRTP bill of 1965, the following effect of a restrictive trade practice would render the said practice contrary to public interest: '(a) to increase unreasonably the cost relating to the production, supply or distribution of goods or the performance of any service; (b) to increase unreasonably the prices at which goods are sold or the profits derived from the production, supply or distribution of the goods or from the performance of any service; (c) to reduce or limit unreasonably competition in the production, supply or distribution of any goods (including their sale or purchase), or in the provision of any service; (d) to limit or prevent the supply of goods to consumers'.

[58] See generally James P. Cairns, 'Benefits from Restrictive Agreements: The British Experience', *The Canadian Journal of Economics and Political Science*, 228–240 (1964) 30:2.

[59] *Id.*, 177 [Section 26(3) of the draft MRTP bill, 1965].

[60] The Director of Investigation was an officer of the MRTP Commission, appointed by the Commission for the purpose of making investigations. See *Id.* [Section 9 of the draft MRTP bill, 1965]. See also Section 33 of the draft MRTP bill 1965.

[61] *Id.*, 182 [Section 47 of the MRTP bill 1965. The amount of the fine was rupees five thousand. However for a continuing offence, an additional fine of rupees five hundred was imposed.].

[62] Andrew Scott, 'The Evolution of Competition Law and Policy in the United Kingdom', *LSE Law, Society and Economy Working Papers,* (2009): 9/2009, www.lse.ac.uk/collections/law/wps/wps.htm (accessed October 7, 2013). According to Scott, the ambiguity of the gateway clauses ensured that cartelists 'learned not to expose themselves by registering their activities, but rather preferred to "go underground" by masking the existence of agreements'.

MRTP Commission. As seen in the case of the US and the EU, specific measures relating to leniency enables effective enforcement of cartels. Further, with the absence of any organized consumer movement in the country, the possibility of having provisions relating to private action for damages had to be ruled out. The bill though enabled the MRTP Commission to take cognizance of complaints from 'any trade or consumers' association or from any seven or more individual consumers'.[63] The adoption of a *rule of reason* approach towards all restrictive trade practices therefore meant that cartels, even if detected, were valid. Further, to determine whether a restrictive trade practice was against the public interest, what would be looked into was the *effect* of such a trade practice. In the case of cartels, therefore, the MRTP Commission would look into the *effect* and not the *object* of the cartel agreements. This approach accompanied by mild penalties meant that cartels were not taken seriously. Additionally, the requirement of registration itself underlined the fact that cartels and other restrictive trade practices were not to be considered *per se* bad or void or illegal.[64]

The MRTP Act, 1969, cartels and consumer interests: Analysing the provisions and case law

One would therefore expect a more refined approach when the MRTP Act of 1969 finally got enacted. That however was not to be as will be evident from the analyses of the provisions on restrictive trade practices. In the 1969 Act, a restrictive trade practice was defined as

> 'a trade practice which has, or may have, the effect of preventing, distorting or restricting competition in any manner and in particular (i) which tends to obstruct the flow of capital or resources into the stream of production, or (ii) which tends to bring about manipulation of prices, or conditions of delivery or to affect the flow of supplies in the market relating to goods or services in such manner as to impose on the consumers unjustified costs or restrictions'.[65]

This definition therefore is the same as the one in the 1965 draft bill. Accordingly, a cartel conduct will be covered by this definition since its

---

[63] Government of India (n 20) at page 179 [Section 32 of the draft MRTP bill, 1965].

[64] See CUTS International and National Law University, Jodhpur, 'Study of Cartel Case Laws in Select Jurisdictions– Learnings for the Competition Commission of India', (April 25, 2008) submitted to the Competition Commission of India, http://www.cci.gov.in/images/media/completed/cartel_report1_20080812115152.pdf (accessed 4 June 2011).

[65] Section 2(o) of the MRTP Act, 1969.

purpose is to either manipulate prices or affect the conditions of supply of goods or services at the cost of consumers. Similarly, the examples of restrictive trade practices enumerated in the 1969 Act were worded in a manner to cover cartel conduct. For example, clause (g) of section 33 of the MRTP Act illustrates a typical cartel conduct of restricting output and dividing markets.[66]

Similarly, clause (a) of section 33 of the MRTP Act, 1969 covers collective boycott, again a typical cartel conduct.[67] Further, under the 1969 Act also the maximum that the MRTP Commission could do was to pass a cease and desist order[68] or order that the

> 'agreement relating [to the concerned restrictive trade practice] shall be void in respect of such restrictive trade practice or shall stand modified in respect thereof in such manner as may be specified in the order'.[69]

These orders are again to be passed only if the said restrictive trade practice is against public interest. Therefore, like the draft bill of 1965, the MRTP Act too adopted the *rule of reason approach* vis-à-vis all kinds of restrictive trade practices including cartels. In other words, all restrictive trade practices were *per se valid* unless they infringed public interest. This is evident from the language of the various clauses of section 38. Importantly, section 38 of the MRTP Act had been completely overhauled as against the proposed section 27 of the draft bill, which also dealt with the norms determining public interest. The re-drafted section 38 of the MRTP Act created a rebuttable presumption that every agreement relating to restrictive trade practices is against public interest.[70] This presumption could be rebutted by the parties

---

66 Section 33 (g)- '[A]ny agreement to limit, restrict or with hold the output or supply of any goods or allocate any area or market for the disposal of the goods'

67 Section 33 (a)- '[A]ny agreement which restricts or is likely to restrict, by any method the persons or classes of persons to whom goods are sold or from whom goods are bought'.

68 See section 37 (1) (a) of the MRTP Act, 1969.

69 See section 37 (1) (b) of the MRTP Act, 1969.

70 According to Section 38 of the MRTP Act, 1969-'(1) For the purposes of any proceedings before the Commission... restrictive trade practices shall be deemed to be prejudicial to the public interest unless the Commission is satisfied of any one or more of the following circumstances, that is to say- (a) that the restriction is reasonably necessary, having regard to the character of the goods to which it applies, to protect the public against injury (whether to persons or to premises) in connection with the consumption, installation or use of those goods; (b) that the removal of the restriction would deny to the public as purchasers, consumers or users of any goods, other specific and substantial benefits or advantages enjoyed or likely to be enjoyed by them as such, whether by virtue of the restriction itself or of any arrangements or operations resulting there from; (c) that the restriction is reasonably necessary to counteract measures taken by any one person not party to the agreement with a view to preventing or

to the agreement if they could prove to the contrary by bringing their case within the ambit of any one or more of the clauses of section 38. The change that had been brought about by the 1969 Act as against the 1965 draft bill, was that in the latter, the burden of proof that the restrictive trade practice was against public interest was on the applicant or complainant, whereas in the former the burden would be on the parties or undertaking indulging in the restrictive trade practice. Further, the undertaking would also have to prove that

> 'the restriction is not unreasonable having regard to the balance between those circumstances and any detriment to the public or to persons not parties to the agreement (being purchasers, consumers or users of goods produced or sold by such parties, or persons engaged or seeking to become engaged in the trade or business of selling such goods or of producing or selling similar goods) resulting or likely to result from the operation of the restriction'.[71]

The underlying test incorporated in section 38 of the MRTP Act was therefore that of *reasonableness.*

Take, for example, clause (a) of section 38, which states that the presumption of the restrictive trade practice being against public interest

restricting competition in or in relation to the trade or business in which the persons party thereto are engaged; (d) that the restriction is reasonably necessary to enable the persons party to the agreement to negotiate fair terms for the supply of goods to, or the acquisition of goods from, any one person not party thereto who controls a preponderant part of the trade or business of acquiring or supplying such goods, or for the supply of goods to any person not party to the agreement and not carrying on such trade or business who, either alone or in combination with any other such persons, controls a preponderant part of the market for such goods; (e) that, having regard to the conditions actually obtaining or reasonably foreseen at the time of the application, the removal of the restriction would be likely to have serious and persistent adverse effect on the general level of unemployment in an area, or in areas taken together, in which a substantial proportion of the trade, or industry to which the agreement relates is situated; (f) that,having regard to the conditions actually obtaining or reasonably foreseen at the time of the application, the removal of the restriction would be likely to cause a reduction in the volume or earnings of the export business which is substantial either in relation to the whole export business of India or in relation to the whole business (including export business) of the said trade or industry; (g) that the restriction is reasonably required for purposes in connection with the maintenance of any other restriction accepted by the parties, whether under the same agreement or under any other agreement between them, being a restriction which is found by the Commission not to be contrary to the public interest upon grounds other than those specified in this paragraph, or has been so found in previous proceedings before the Commission; (h) that the restriction does not directly or indirectly restrict or discourage competition to any material degree in any relevant trade or industry and is not likely to do so…'.

71 See section 38 of the MRTP Act, 1969.

can be rebutted by showing that 'the restriction is reasonably necessary… to protect the public against injury…'.[72] This test of *reasonableness* or *the rule of reason* flows through all the clauses of section 38 including the final paragraph, quoted above. Applying this to a cartel scenario it would work as follows: an applicant, say consumer or consumers' association brings to the notice of the MRTP Commission the existence of a price-fixing cartel. It needs to be mentioned here that like the draft proposal of 1965, in the MRTP Act of 1969 too, the MRTP Commission was empowered to take cognizance of complaints about restrictive trade practices from any

> 'trade or consumer's association having a membership of not less than 25 persons or from 25 or more consumers…'[73].

The MRTP Commission accordingly will conduct inquiry, according to section 37, to determine whether the cartel practice is against the public interest or not. For this purpose, during the inquiry, as per the regulations framed by the MRTP Commission, the onus will be on the cartel to prove that the agreement is reasonable in consonance with the requirement of section 38. Therefore, notwithstanding the fact that according to section 38, the cartel will be presumed to be restrictive in nature, it can still save the day and the impugned cartel practice by showing the reasonability of the cartel agreement, balancing the necessity of the agreement against the detriment caused to the larger public.

The anti-cartel law under the MRTP Act, like the proposed draft bill of 1965 and the recommendations of the Monopolies Inquiry Commission, was premised on the *rule of reason* test. As seen in the case of the US and the EU as well as the discussion on cartels elsewhere in this book, no reasonableness could justify a cartel. In the case of EU, even crisis cartels have been prohibited—theonly justification being the rectification of structural over-capacity. Further, the *rule of reason* test also creates uncertainty so far as consumers are concerned since they are not sure of the outcome, viz., whether a cartel agreement is or is not against public interest. In 1984, section 33 of the MRTP Act was amended to render all agreements enumerated under

---

72 See section 38 of the MRTP Act, 1969.

73 See section 10 (a) (i) of the MRTP Act, 1969. This clause was amended in the year 1987 by the MRTP (Amendment) Act, 1986, w.e.f. June 1, 1987. The amended section 10 (a) (i) of the MRTP Act, 1969 reads as: 'The Commission may inquire into (a) any restrictive trade practice- (i) upon receiving a complaint of facts which constitute such practice from any trade association or from any consumer or a registered consumer's association, whether such consumer is a member of that consumer's association or not'.

section 33 as *per se* restrictive in nature.[74] Further, the categories of agreement relating to restrictive trade practice which were compulsorily to be registered were also increased. One of the new categories that were added by the 1984 amendment concerned bid rigging, and thus was an improvement upon the 1965 draft bill.[75] Another improvement over the draft bill of 1965 that the 1969 Act had brought in was the fact that in the case of restrictive trade practices, the MRTP Commission could *suo moto* start an inquiry.[76] This feature was unique as unlike the powers of the MRTP Commission with respect to monopolistic trade practices, here there were follow up provisions for *suo moto* inquiry in the chapter on restrictive trade practices.[77]

Nonetheless, these improvements did not in any way change the fact that anti-cartel law was excessively weak under the 1969 Act. The *per se* restrictiveness of section 33 agreements hardly affects the requirement to test reasonability when passing orders against cartels.[78] In terms of effective implementation of the law, such *rule of reason* tests, in case of cartels has the potential to cause more failures than success for the MRTP Commission.[79] A review of the cartel decisions under the MRTP Act, 1969 would give a clearer picture as to the effectiveness of the anti-cartel provision under the Act. Importantly, it would reveal the success rate of the MRTP Commission in effectively acting against cartels. Nevertheless, as is clear from the above discussions on the anti-cartel law in the US and the EU, the effectiveness of any such law depends upon the interpretation given to it by the enforcers. The interpretation given by the MRTP Commission, to the provisions relating to the restrictive trade practices, came under the scrutiny of the Supreme Court of India.[80] In *Tata Engineering & Locomotive Co. Ltd., Bombay v.*

[74] After the amendment, section 33 (1) reads: 'Every agreement falling within one or more categories shall be deemed, for the purposes of this Act, to be an agreement relating to restrictive trade practices…'.

[75] See section 33 (1) (jb): 'any agreement as to bids which any of the parties thereto may offer at an auction for the sale of goods or any agreement whereby any party thereto agrees to abstain from bidding at any auction for the sale of goods'.

[76] See section 10 (a) (iv) of the MRTP Act, 1969.

[77] See section 37.

[78] CUTS International (n 64) 59–72.

[79] See Udai S Mehta and Sanjay Pandey, 'Cartels and other Anticompetitive Agreements' (March 14–15, 2007) presentation at the Competition Commission Workshop, http://www.cci.gov.in/images/workshop/14_15march07/14udai.pdf?phpMyAdmin=NMPFRahGKYeum5F74Ppstn7Rf00 (accessed 3 June 2011)

[80] According to section 55 of the MRTP Act 1969, 'Any person aggrieved by [any decision on any question referred to…] or any order made by the Central Government…or the Commission …may within sixty days from the date of the order, prefer an appeal to the Supreme Court…'.

The Registrar of the Restrictive Trade Agreement, New Delhi[81], the Supreme Court had to review the decision of the MRTP Commission, by which the agreement between the appellant and its dealers was declared as an agreement relating to restrictive trade practice.

The determination of restrictive trade practice by the MRTP Commission was challenged before the Supreme Court. The Registrar of Restrictive Trade Agreements alleged that the appellants had entered into agreement with its dealers for: allocating markets, enforcing re-sale price maintenance and exclusive dealership.[82] The appellant argued that none of the alleged practices amounted to restrictive trade practices within the meaning of the MRTP Act, 1969. Further, the appellant argued that even if it amounted to restrictive trade practices, it complied with the test of reasonableness as provided under section 38 of the MRTP Act, 1969. The MRTP Commission emphasized that all agreements falling within any one or more of the clauses under section 33 'must be regarded as a restrictive trade practice'.[83] In giving this interpretation, the MRTP Commission disregarded the definition of restrictive trade practice given in section 2 (o) of the MRTP Act, 1969. Further, it was dealing with the pre-1984 section 33 which contained nothing in the language to support this interpretation. Nonetheless, the MRTP Commission stuck with this line of interpretation and declared that the alleged practices were restrictive trade practices according to the MRTP Act, 1969. It then went on to assess the validity of the restrictive trade practices under the provisions of section 37 and section 38.

The MRTP Commission accordingly determined that with regard to the clause on resale price maintenance, the appellant having assured that for future dealings, the dealers were free to sell below the minimum price it did not need to pass any order. This was in accordance with section 37 (2) of the MRTP Act, 1969. Similarly, with regard to the exclusive dealership clause, the MRTP Commission found that the same was in compliance with section 38 (1) (a), (b) and (h) as well as the last paragraph of section 38 (1).[84] The Commission though did not find any public interest justification in the clauses relating to division of territory or market and declared them to be void and thereby restrained the appellant from continuing with the practice. The appellant in its arguments before the MRTP Commission stated that

---

81 1977 SCR (2) 685; AIR 1977 SC 973; (1977) 2 SCC 55 http://indiankanoon.org/doc/1075616/ (accessed June 4, 2011).

82 1977 SCR (2) 685 (n 81) 690.

83 *Id.*, 692.

84 *Id.*, 692.

the Registrar had failed to establish through sufficient factual evidence, the existence of the alleged restrictive trade practice.[85] This argument, though rejected by the MRTP Commission, was accepted by the Supreme Court. The justification for this acceptance can be easily seen in the way section 33 (1) was worded prior to the 1984 amendment. According to that section, 'any agreement relating to a restrictive trade practice falling within one or more of the following categories...' need to be mandatorily registered. Accordingly, before an agreement can be mandated to be registered it needs to be (a) an agreement relating to restrictive trade practice as per section 2 (o) and (b) fall into one or more categories of restrictive trade practices enumerated under section 33 (1) clauses (a) to (l).

This meant that the Registrar while making an application to the MRTP Commission for inquiry and passing of appropriate orders under section 10 (a) (iii) of the MRTP Act, 1969, need to state

> 'facts which, in the Registrar's opinion, constitute a restrictive trade practice and, if it is in relation to any agreement, set out, such portions of the agreement as may be necessary to bring out the facts complained of'.[86]

In the case at hand, the Supreme Court declared that no such facts were mentioned by the Registrar which could establish the allegation of restrictive trade practice. Finally, the Supreme Court, based on the pre-1984 structure of the MRTP Act, held that the determination of whether a trade practice is restrictive or not has to be based on the *rule of reason* test and not on the *per se* basis.[87] It then went on to lay down the factors which need to be accounted for before arriving at a conclusion as to whether, as per section 2 (o), the trade practice was restrictive or not. These are:

> 'First, what facts are peculiar to the business to which the restraint is applied Second, what was the condition before and after the restraint is imposed. Third what is the nature of the restraint and what is its actual and probable effect'.[88]

It is only after determination of all these criteria, that the next step comes, i.e., the registration of an agreement relating to restrictive trade practice. According to the Supreme Court, only those agreements which satisfy section

85 *Id.*

86 *Id.*

87 See A N Oza, 'Putting Teeth into the Monopolies Act', *EPW, Special Number*, (July 1971): 1703–1708.

88 1977 SCR (2) 685 (n 81) 693.

2 (o) and are included in the section 33 (1) list can be registered by the Registrar. In other words, section 2 (o) describes the genus of a restrictive trade practice and the section 33 (1) list enumerates those species of restrictive trade practices which needs to be registered. This meant that for the purpose of establishing a practice or agreement as a restrictive trade practice, the criteria laid down in section 2 (o) has to be satisfied. An agreement or practice which fails to satisfy section 2 (o) will not be a restrictive trade practice, just because it is covered by one of the species mentioned in the section 33 (1) list.[89] This analysis of the Supreme Court thus overruled the interpretation given by the MRTP Commission.

Further, the Supreme Court declared that it is only those agreements which fall within the definition of restrictive trade practices as under section 2 (o), that can be investigated against under section 37. Finally, the determination of public interest is relevant only in the case of agreements which are established as restrictive trade practices, irrespective of the fact that they have been registered or not. In essence, therefore, it is section 2 (o) which, in the pre-1984 MRTP Act, 1969, was relevant for the determination of a restrictive trade practice.[90] Having thus explained the manner in which the provisions of the chapter on restrictive trade practices under the pre-1984 MRTP Act, 1969 ought to be interpreted and applied, the Supreme Court went on to uphold the validity of the clauses relating to the division of the territory or market between the dealers. In effect, according to the Supreme Court, the impugned clause was not a restrictive trade practice under section 2 (o).[91] The Supreme Court declared that territorial restriction ensured 'equitable distribution of' the Telco vehicles.[92] This was done by ensuring that there is no over-booking in one zone, causing deprivation of the consumers in other zones. In essence, by restricting the territories within which a dealer could accept bookings and sell, the customers in all the territories were provided a chance to buy the vehicles. In the absence of such a clause, the dealer would have been free to take bookings from any area thereby selling off all the vehicles, before the local customers could get a chance to buy. Further in the absence of dedicated customers, the dealers would not have any incentive to invest and thus provide efficient after-sales service. This would again be detrimental to the consumer.[93] Importantly, the Supreme Court noted that

---

89 *Id.*, 693–694.

90 1977 SCR (2) 685 (n 81) 693–694

91 *Id.*, 701.

92 *Id.*, 697–698.

93 *Id.*

the exclusive dealership

> 'do not impede competition but promote it. Such dealings lead to specialisation and improvement in after-sales-service… The customer has the choice of buying any make he likes. It is by specialising in each make of vehicle and providing the best possible service that the competition between the various makes is enhanced'.[94]

The ruling of the Supreme Court, though given in a case of vertical agreement between the manufacturer and dealer, is helpful in understanding how cartel cases would be dealt with under the MRTP Act, 1969. In a cartel case, the Registrar will have to state the specific facts which will establish the restrictive nature of the cartel agreement. In other words, the onus would be on the Registrar to prove that the cartel agreement was an agreement relating to restrictive trade practices according to section 2 (o).[95] It is on the basis of such factual statements and references to portions in the agreement, alleging the restrictive trade practice, that the MRTP Commission in the pre-1984 scenario will be required to apply *rule of reason* while conducting its inquiry. The MRTP Commission will have to verify whether the Registrar has been able to conclusively establish the restrictive nature of the cartel conduct, as per section 2 (o). The *rule of reason analysis* also meant that the MRTP Commission has to assess not the *object* but the restrictive *effects* of a cartel agreement. The onus therefore was on the complainant filing a complaint under section 10 (a), to adduce evidence regarding the existence of restrictive trade practices by a cartel. The same would have to be further enquired upon by the MRTP Commission as provided under section 11 of the MRTP Act, 1969 to determine its compliance with section 2(o). Thereafter any decision on cartels has to be arrived at on the basis of the *rule of reason* test laid down by the Supreme Court.[96]

Post-1984 and anti-cartel provisions: Old wine in new bottle

As discussed above, post-1984, the burden on the applicant and the

---

94 *Id.*, 698–699

95 See also *State of Uttar Pradesh and Ors.v.Gir Prasad and Ors*, MANU/SC/0165/2004; AIR2004SC1756.

96 The same test was reiterated by the Supreme Court in *Mahindra & Mahindra Limited v. Union of India &Anr*, AIR 1979 SC 798 http://indiankanoon.org/doc/1000517/ (accessed 4 June 2011); *Rajasthan Housing Board v. Smt. Parvati Devi*, (2000) 6 SCC 104 http://indiankanoon.org/doc/793235/ (accessed 4 June 2011) and *Principal Apeejay School v. The M.R.T.P Commission & Another* (2001) 8 SCC 702 http://www.indiankanoon.org/doc/252432/ (accessed 4 June 2011)

investigating body may have eased in so far as the agreements under section 33 (1) was rendered *per se* restrictive. However, it still did not do away with the requirement of satisfying the public interest, as per section 38. This ambiguous criterion of public interest harmed any effort to proceed against alleged cartels. In the *Director-General of Investigation and Registration v. Cement Manufacturers Association and Ors.*[97] case, the Monopolies and Restrictive Trade Practices Commission refused to grant temporary injunction against an alleged cartel of cement manufacturers because the Commission was bound by the niceties of the language of section 12 A (1).[98] The Director-General adduced circumstantial evidence to show the existence of a concerted price rise, but the Commission was not satisfied since it reiterated that the circumstantial evidence proved only price parallelism[99] without showing any strong proof of collusion. Importantly, even if collusion leading to price rise would have been proved, it had to satisfy the criteria of '*prejudicial to public interest*' as per section 12 A (1).[100] Arguably, since the Commission had to issue temporary injunction it needed *prima facie* proof.

The council for the Director-General however was right in stating that the cartel behaviour was difficult to prove through direct evidence hence circumstantial evidence like letters, meetings, exchange of information etc. had to be used to prove the existence of collusion. One can see this approach in the manner the investigations are carried on in the EU and the US. Price parallelism on its own may not be conclusive, but a reading of the case indicates

---

97 1991 71 CompCas 46 NULL available at http://www.indiankanoon.org/doc/382510/ (accessed 4 June 2011).

98 Section 12 A (1) reads: 'Where, during an inquiry before the Commission, it is proved, whether by the complainant , Director-General, any trader or class of traders or any other person, by affidavit or otherwise, that any undertaking or any person is carrying on, or is about to carry on, any monopolistic or any restrictive or unfair, trade practice and such monopolistic or restrictive, or unfair, trade practice, is likely to affect prejudicially the public interest or the interest of any trader, class of traders or traders generally or of any consumer or consumers generally, the Commission may, for the purposes of staying or preventing the undertaking or, as the case may be, such person from causing such prejudicial effect, by order, grant a temporary injunction restraining such undertaking or person from carrying on any monopolistic or restrictive, or unfair, trade practice until the conclusion of such inquiry or until further orders'.

99 Price parallelism means similarity in pricing of cement, in this case, by various producers without there being proof of collusion leading to pricing decisions. In essence, price parallelism does not discount independent decisions of individual producers.

100 See *Haridas Exports v. All India Float Glass Manufacturers Assn.*, (2002) 111 Comp Cas 617 (SC) available at http://www.indiankanoon.org/doc/838587/ (accessed 4 June 2011). Here the Supreme Court emphasized that granting of temporary injunction has to be subject to the satisfaction of the public interest criteria.

that the Director-General indeed had adduced other supporting evidence.[101] Importantly, as the Supreme Court in *M/s Haridas Exports*[102] had clarified, an agreement falling under section 2 (o) or section 33 (1) (a) to (l) need not be in writing; it is enough if there is an arrangement or understanding among the alleged cartelists.[103] Further, the interpretation of the word '*public interest*' by the MRTP Commission itself has been subject to numerous criticisms. In the *Haridas Exports* case, for example, the public interest identified was that of the industry or association members. The Supreme Court rejected this interpretation and stated that public interest should include interest of the general body of the consumers. This was contrary to what the MRTP Commission had said.[104] Similarly, in *Director-General Investigations and Registration v. Reliance Industries Ltd. and Anr.*[105], the Director-General failed to adduce enough evidence to prove collusion resulting in price rise. This case involved Reliance and Tamil Nadu Petro Product Ltd (TPPL), who were manufacturers of LAB (linear alkaline bezene), a basic raw material required for the manufacture of synthetic detergent.

The Commission held that while there was evidence of price parallelism, there was absence of concrete evidence to lead to a positive conclusion as to the existence of a cartel. While the Director-General did produce documents in the form of complaints from small-scale industries and traders association, it did not have the facts and the figures that would have helped establish cartelization positively. It was thus not able to establish any agreement or collusion. According to the MRTP Commission, circumstantial evidence should 'clearly and conclusively indicate the establishment of a cartel'[106]. Here too the Commission emphasized that though both the manufacturers have been frequently increasing prices, which adversely affected the consumers, the same cannot be shown to be unreasonable as to be prejudicial to the public interest. The Commission, in the absence of any conclusive evidence of cartelization, decided to close the enquiry.[107] This again highlights the

[101] The Director-General adduced a letter written by the alleged cement cartel members which indicated that they intended to fix and monitor cement prices.

[102] *Haridas Exports* (n 100) 20.

[103] See section 2 (a) of the MRTP Act, 1969: 'agreement includes any arrangement or understanding, whether or not it is intended that such agreement shall be enforceable (apart from any provision of this Act), by legal proceedings'.

[104] See Aditya Bhattacherjes, 'India's Competition Policy- An Assessment' http://papers.ssrn.com/sol3/papers.cfm?abstract_id=440080 (accessed 4 June 2011).

[105] 1 (2003) CPJ 80 MRTP http://www.indiankanoon.org/doc/450187/ (accessed 4 June 2011).

[106] *Id.*, 3.

[107] *Id.*, 4.

ambiguity of the word 'public interest' since the affect of price increase on consumers was not taken as affecting public interest. One is therefore clueless as to what is public interest for the purpose of determining the effect of cartels under the MRTP Act, 1969.

The above discussion also reveals an inherent dichotomy in the understanding of the concept of 'public interest' between the Supreme Court and the MRTP Commission.[108] As evident from the *Haridas Export* case, the enumeration of public interest in section 38 of the MRTP Act did nothing to clarify the uncertainty on the scope of the term 'public interest'. This adds to the weakening of any effective implementation of the anti-cartel law in the country, from a consumer perspective. Similarly, there were other reasons contributing to the ineffectiveness of the anti-cartel law under the MRTP Act, 1969. For example, after the introduction of the section on unfair trade practices[109], the workload of the MRTP Commission was dominated by cases involving complaints of individual consumers regarding defective products and deficiency of services.[110] As a consequence, anti-cartel inquiries took a severe hit affecting the effectiveness of the enforcement measures. As the MRTP Commission got increasingly involved in these matters, it failed to develop the expertise required to deal with issues involved in cartel cases. Understandably so, because a case of unfair trade practice had nothing to do with the issues involved in cartels or any other anti-competitive conduct. The unfair trade practices cases involved matters like misleading advertisements, misleading prize schemes etc. which did not involve any anti-competitive conduct.[111] For example, in the *Shri Sarabjit S. Mokha* case[112], a complaint of price hike by the cement manufacturers cartel was filed in 2001, decision on which was given by the Commission in 2008. The intervening period was not spent by the Commission in conducting inquiry through its Director-General for collecting hard evidence. The maximum the Commission did was perusing the records submitted to it by the complainant, who were members of the Builders' Association of India. The Commission was convinced that there was indeed evidence of collusion by the cement manufacturers to raise

[108] See Aditya Bhattacharjea, 'Protection and the "Public Interest"', *EPW*, 4327–4336 (December 2–8, 2000), 35:49. In the *Haridas*case, the MRTP Commission read public interest as the interest of the industry whereas the Supreme Court regarded the same as interest of the consumer.

[109] See Part B, Chapter V, of the MRTP Act, 1969.

[110] See section 36 A (1) (i) and (ii) of the MRTP Act 1969.

[111] See Aditya Bhattacharjea, 'Competition Policy: India and the WTO', *EPW* 4710–4713 (22 December 2001) 36:51.

[112] *Shri Sarabjit S. Mokha and another v. M/s. Cement Manufacturers Association and others*, RTPE 21/2001(decision on 29 February 2008).

the prices and accordingly it passed a cease and desist order. There is no evidence of any follow up inquiry nor is there any explanation as to the basis on which this price rise was considered anti-competitive. Further, the cease and desist order did not result in the disbanding of the so-called cartel—it only prohibited the cartel from fixing the selling price of cement.

A report prepared by CUTS International and the National Law University, Jodhpur,[113] reviewed ninety cases involving various types of cartel activity like bid rigging, collective boycott and price fixing. The report concluded that: in many cases, the Director-General could not prove much beyond price parallelism, due to lack of hard direct or indirect evidence. Further, the report noted that in the absence of any power to impose penalty, merely passing cease and desist order did not have any deterrent effect on cartels. The report also found that the exemption clauses of section 38 of the MRTP Act proved beneficial to cartels that were able to bring their case within the ambit of one or more exemptions.[114] It further concluded that non-cooperation of the accused during inquiry by the Director-General proved to be a major impediment in proving the case against cartels.[115] The report also found that in cases where there was proof of the existence of a cartel, the written assurance by the cartel members that they will not continue with the cartel activity was good enough for the Commission not to proceed with the inquiry as the assurance was considered as good as a cease and desist order.[116]

This approach is reflective of the way the MRTP provision, viz., section 37 (2), was read and implemented by the Commission, so far as anti-cartel enforcement was concerned. A plain reading of section 37 (2) nowhere gives an indication that the Commission need to complete its inquiry. According to section 37 (1) and (2), the MRTP Commission has two options. Under section 37 (1) (a) and (b), the Commission can pass a cease and desist order or declare the agreement as void or order an amendment of the agreement. Under section 37 (2) however, the Commission can stop inquiries against the cartel, if the cartel members give an undertaking that they will discontinue the practice which was prejudicial to the public interest. In this manner, another provision of the MRTP Act, 1969 proves beneficial for the cartel.[117] Finally,

---

[113] CUTS International (n 64) 62.

[114] *Id.*, 71–72.

[115] *Id.*, 73.

[116] *Id.*, 90. It needs to be mentioned here that the CUTS report was largely based on the unpublished M.Phil Book of Oindrila De (2005), submitted to the Department of Economics, University of Delhi. Ms. De is presently a faculty at IIM Indore.

[117] On the manner in which the provision of restrictive trade practices were implemented along with the use of the gateway clause, see generally P. V. Krishna Rao and K. P. Sastry,

the CUTS report notes that the lack of power of the MRTP Commission to impose stringent penalties or fines demeaned the effectiveness of any anti-cartel measures.[118] It should be noted that under section 50 (2) of the MRTP Act, 1969, the infringement of the cease and desist order was made punishable with both imprisonment and a fine. This therefore meant that no fines would be imposed for engaging in cartel conduct. Accordingly, cartel conduct *per se* was only to be met with a cease and desist order. Other structural problems highlighted by the CUTS report include vacancies in the Commission which resulted in inertia in the disposal of cases.[119]

Cartelization in India and MRTP: Comfortable Co-existence

The discussion so far outlines the fault lines that contributed to the inefficiencies of the MRTP Act. Consequently, the presence of cartels in the domestic sphere continues comfortably. Cartel affects a large number of sectors in India. One of the first examples of cartel in India is the Indian Sugar Syndicate, established in 1932. The syndicate was primarily formed to fix sugar prices and it ensured compulsory membership for all manufacturers.[120] Another industry which got cartelized during the 1930s was the automotive tyre industry. There was complete lack of price competition between the players in that sector, at that point of time, viz., Dunlop, Good Year and India Tyre, Rubber Co (ITR) and Firestone.[121] Their incentive to collude and cartelize was the fact that these companies could match each other at price wars, because of their immense financial resources. As a result, they decided to avoid a price competition and rather chose to expand their individual market share through other means. Consequently, these companies relied on quality and after-sales service as a tool to expand their market share. Since there were organizational arrangements between Dunlop, Goodyear and ITR, to use the same manufacturing facility, there was not much variety that these companies could offer on quality and after-sale services. The best option for these companies therefore was to protect their existing markets by entering

'Restrictive Trade Practices Policy in India', *The Journal of Industrial Economics*, 427–435 (June 1989) 37:4.

118 CUTS International (n 64) 61.

119 *Id.*, 62.

120 See SanjayaBaru, 'Cartels and Competition', *Business Standard* (December 6, 2010), http://www.business-standard.com/india/news/sanjaya-baru-cartelscompetition/417211/ (accessed 12 May 2011).

121 See Sunil Mani, 'Concentration and Market Power in Indian Automotive Tyre Industry', *EPW*, M 53–64 (1985) Vol. 20:21.

into agreements on price fixation and output restriction.[122] The growth of cartels in the post-Independent era continued unabated. For example, the tyre manufacturers re-cartelized in the year 1968 to fix prices and restrict output quota. This re-cartelization happened despite the intervention on the part of the Union government, in the 1950s to break down the excessive concentration in the automotive tyre industry, by facilitating the entry of new manufacturers.[123]

What follows is a sectoral review, for establishing the fact that cartelization exists within the Indian economy, at the expense of the consumer.

Cartelization in India: Road, rail, air, port, pesticide, cement, paint and tyre

To begin in the road goods transportation industry (RGTI), studies have revealed the existence of cartelization, especially in the market of local transportation, viz., within the city limits or periphery of the city.[124] The report referred to cartels being formed by truckers who fixed prices or formed association that restricted the entry of outsiders.[125] The report also notes the existence of bid rigging by a collusion of large fleet operators.[126] Similarly, the Competition Commission of India commissioned studies in the paint and tyre industry, to understand the state of competition in these sectors.[127] The conclusions drawn by the study indicates possible price-fixing arrangements in the tyre industry, whereas in the paint industry the existence of cartels could

---

122 For details on the cartelization of the automotive tyre industry see Sunil Mani and P.K. Michael Tharakan, 'Competitiveness in the Indian Tyre Industry: 1936–1984', Working Paper No. 203, http://cds.edu/download_files/wp-1971-95/wp203.pdf (accessed 12 May 2011).

123 *Id.*, 9–10.

124 See for example, the study conducted at the instance of the Competition Commission of India into the competition issues in the road goods transport industry in India with special reference to the Mumbai Metropolitan Region. http://www.cci.gov.in/images/media/completed/1Road-goodstrans_20080508111358.pdf (accessed 12 May 2011). The study was commissioned to the University of Mumbai to examine and understand the nature of competition and competitiveness in this industry.

125 *Id.*, at 81–84.

126 Competition Issues in the Road Goods Transport Industry (n 679) 90–93, 97.

127 See Prof. Manoj Pant, 'Assessing the State of Competition in Indian Manufacturing Sector: Paint and Tyre Industry', Field researcher was Rabi Ranjan, Centre for International Trade and Development, School of International Studies, Jawaharlal Nehru University, New Delhi http://cci.gov.in/images/media/presentations/1_20june08/5assessing_paint_tyre.pdf?phpMyAdmin=NMPFRahGKYeum5F74Ppstn7Rf00 (accessed 13 May 2011). The study was commissioned by the Competition Commission of India.

not be proven conclusively. Another study commissioned by the Competition Commission of India relates to the pesticides and cement industries.[128] The report found evidence of price-fixing and market sharing cartels in the cement industry, while no such evidence was found in the pesticide industry.[129] A report published by CUTS (Consumer Unity and Trust Society) also indicates the existence of price-fixing cartels in the cement industry.[130]

Evidence of cartelization has been found in the Indian Railways procurement system, by various studies.[131] Indian Railways need to store items for various purposes, viz., 'track materials, fuel and construction, manufacture of rolling stock, operations, repairs and maintenance'.[132] Store procurement forms a substantial part of the Indian Railways expenditure. According to the estimate given by a TERI report, during 2006–2007, the total procurement of store items by the Indian Railways was estimated at Rs. 18,651 crore. [133] Unfortunately though, the procurement system is exploited by vendors who collude amongst themselves and enter into agreements for bid rigging, sharing markets, barring entry into the market of new players and collective boycotts.[134] The report gives specific examples where vendors formed cartels to abuse the procurement system. For example, it explains how the bidding for

> 'CASNUB high speed cast steel bogies required for manufacture of wagons in railway workshops' was rigged.[135]

---

[128] See Prof. Manoj Pant, 'Assessing the State of Competition in Indian Manufacturing Sector: Pesticides and Cement Industries', Field researchers were C. G Hariprasad and Rabi Ranjan, Centre for International Trade and Development, School of International Studies, Jawaharlal Nehru University, New Delhi. The report was commissioned by the Competition Commission of India. http://www.cci.gov.in/images/media/completed/3pesticide_20080508111242.pdf (accessed 13 May 2011).

[129] *Id.*, para 6.1 and 6.5.

[130] Pradeep S Mehta and Nitya Nanda, 'Competition Issues in the Indian Cement Industry', in *Towards a Functional Competition Policy for India- An Overview,* ed. Pradeep S Mehta (CUTS International, 2005), 155–162.

[131] See T E R I. 2008, 'Competition Issues in Regulated Industries: Case of the Indian Transport Sector', New Delhi: The Energy and Resources Institute, [Project Report No. 2007CP21], http://www.cci.gov.in/images/media/completed/transport_20090723115524.pdf (accessed May 16, 2011). The report was commissioned by the Competition Commission of India in 2009 and covered two industries, viz., railways and ports.

[132] *Id.*, para 1.5.1.

[133] *Id.*, para 1.5.1.

[134] *Id.*, para 1.5.2.

[135] *Id.*, para 2.4.2.2 [CASNUB, according to the TERI report is cast steel bogies with friction damping arrangements (CAst steel SNUBer equipped)].

The TERI report based its conclusions on the 2006 report prepared by the Comptroller and Auditor General of India. In the 2006 report, seven out of the nine firms, who participated in the bidding process, had formed a cartel and rigged the bid. They had all quoted similar rates in their bids, forcing the railway board to negotiate with a member of the cartel. The audit report noted that accepting the bid of the firms belonging to the cartel caused the railways to suffer excess expenses to the tune of Rs.2.32 crore.[136] The TERI report also found the existence of cartels in the shipping liner industry, in the form of price-fixing arrangements, known as conferences.[137] A conference is

> 'a route specific agreement between carriers to charge common freight rates, pool revenue and costs, pool profits and engage in capacity management. These agreements also establish the sailing schedules, ports of call and minimum service levels. The aim of conferences is to limit competition between members with a view to stabilising market freight rates. Conferences monitor members to ensure compliance. Discipline can be enforced by fines for non-compliance or by expulsion'.[138]

As evident, a conference therefore is a pure price-fixing arrangement and so is nothing but a cartel of shipping liners.

The TERI report also noted the possibility of collusive bidding or bid rigging in the port industry, by cartels.[139] Another sector in which studies have indicated the possibility of cartelization is the air transport sector.[140] The report commissioned by the Competition Commission of India noted that the structure of the air transport sector is such that it is prone to cartelization.[141] The report identified the factors which is likely to make cartelization attractive in the sector. The factors were: increasing prices of air traffic fuel (ATF) and increase in surcharges and taxes, which adds to the operational cost and increases the cumulative losses. For example, for the year 2008, the report estimated that the cumulative loss suffered by the domestic air transport industry was to the tune of Rs. 700 billion.[142] The report used the Jet and Kingfisher alliance as an example of the possible ways in which

---

136 *Id.*

137 *Id.*, para 3.8.1.

138 *Id.*, para 3.8.1.1.

139 *Id.*, para 3.9.1.1.2.

140 See Administrative Staff College of India, Hyderabad, 'Competition Issues in the Air Transport Sector in India', http://www.cci.gov.in/images/media/completed/transport_20090421133744.pdf (accessed 16 May, 2011). The Competition Commission of India commissioned the report.

141 *Id.*, 92.

142 *Id.*

cartelization can happen in the air transport sector.[143] The report identified specific features of the proposed alliance which were indicative of cartelization. For example, one of the objectives of the proposed alliance was 'joint network rationalization and synergies'[144] which in other words meant 'agreement to limit production and supply and agreement to allocate markets'.[145] This is a typical feature of a cartel and would have clearly determined the choices available to the consumers.[146]

Cartelization in India: Onion, steel, sugar, public works, local transport and public procurement

Another report commissioned by the Competition Commission of India, found evidence of cartelization in the steel industry.[147] The report conducted a product-wise survey to ascertain the existence and extent of cartelization within the steel industry. For example, in the product market of HR coils[148], the report noted that the pricing behaviour of the major manufacturers 'clearly exhibits a pattern reflected in the timing of the pricing decisions and the quantum of price changes each undertakes'.[149] The report further notes that

> 'There is open acceptance, even by the government, of the fact that till recently the HRC producers adjusted their prices to the landed costs of import or there is a desire for them to do so. Landed costs of import

---

143 The Jet and Kingfisher proposed an alliance in August 2008, which however did not materialize due to various reasons. The alliance was formed to cut their operational costs. See for example 'Jet, Kingfisher form alliance to cut costs', *Reuters* (14 October 2008), http://in.reuters.com/article/2008/10/14/idINIndia-35946620081014 (accessed 16 May 2011).

144 Administrative Staff College of India (n 140) 93.

145 Administrative Staff College of India (n 140) 93

146 *Id.* [The report notes that 'As regards the reciprocity of the frequent flier programmes, one aim of such schemes and programmes is to influence the behaviour of travellers in such a way that they become more inclined to seek a specific airline's products and services. Therefore, they can be potentially serious obstacles to effective competition. Any alliance between players in an oligopolistic market should come under the purview of the Competition Authority'.]

147 See Indicus Analytics, '*Public Enterprises, Government Policy and Impact on Competition-Indian Steel Industry*' (2009) New Delhi, http://www.cci.gov.in/images/media/completed/Indicussteel_20090420151842.pdf (accessed 18 May 2011).

148 The product is called hot rolled coils.

149 Indicus Analytics (n 147) 19.

> mean the fully duty paid cost of the imported material. They still wish to do that but for the government's informal arm twisting that the industry is forced to cut prices below such levels. This is precisely the reason why the government also has in most of time and overwhelmingly resorted to import duty cut to bring prices down in the home market'.[150]

The report notes that there was evidence of the HR coil producers creating a scenario of artificial shortage in the domestic market, thereby maintaining higher prices.[151] It also notes certain factors which indicate cartel-like behaviour by the major manufacturers though the report admits the lack of substantive evidence to support the allegation.[152] Further, the report observes similar lack of conclusive evidence to prove or disprove the allegation of market sharing agreements among the steel producers.[153]

Overall though, within the Indian steel industry, cartelization remains an area of concern for the Competition Commission of India.[154] In the recent past, the rising inflation rate has led the government of India to look into the possibility of cartelization in the agricultural produce market.[155] Similar concerns of cartelization continue to be raised against the sugar industry.[156] Another sector where cartelization has been alleged as a cause for rising prices is the onion trading sector.[157] There are also reports of cartels operating at the local level rather than the national level. For example, reports have indicated that the school bus and van operators in Lucknow have formed a cartel for fixing the rates and dividing the routes for the purpose of plying the buses or

---

150 *Id.*

151 *Id.*, 21

152 *Id.*, 22. [The report states that 'there has been a lot of talk about cartelization in the steel industry especially involving large HRC producers, which cannot be easily substantiated'.]

153 *Id.*, 23.[The report notes that 'The market sharing arrangements can come up to collectively raise average revenue by calibrating sales to maximize prices in the regional markets. But little hard evidence of the same exists. Only some undocumented and circumstantial evidence is available, that is not good enough to establish or disprove the allegation.']

154 *Id.*, 24 and 31.

155 See 'Agri Trade Cartels under Review to Check Inflation', *Press Trust of India* (21 March 2011), http://profit.ndtv.com/news/show/agri-trade-cartels-under-review-to-check-inflation-145621 (accessed 18 May 2011).

156 See Ajay Modi, 'CCI Probes Alleged Sugar Cartel', *Business Standard* (8 February 2011),,http://www.business-standard.com/india/news/cci-probes-allegedsugar-cartel/424361/ (accessed 18 May 2011).

157 See Sandip Das and K. G. Narendranath, 'CCI to Investigate Onion Cartel', *The Financial Express* (January 7, 2011), http://www.financialexpress.com/news/cci-to-investigate-onion-cartel/734432/ (accessed 18 May 2011)

vans.[158] Another instance of cartelization was reported in Chennai where the newspapers reported the existence of road contractor's cartels who indulged in bid rigging for the purpose of procuring road work contracts.[159] Another example of cartelization was noted by the Comptroller Auditor General (CAG), in its 2010 report, in the procurement system of ordinance factories. The CAG audit report found glaring instances of collusion where firms with the same address, fax number, mobile number and telephone number were being given supply orders, by the ordinance factories, thereby completely ignoring the issue of cartelization.[160]

There evidently exists a real issue of cartelization within the Indian economy. As the above review establishes, almost all the sectors of the economy are equally susceptible to cartel formation. The proof of the same may be non-conclusive in some industries, but the allegation of cartelization continues to persist.

Looking Forward

The discussion has established that cartelization is a reality in the Indian domestic market. It afflicts almost all the sectors and causes harm to consumers. The response of the Indian law has however not been specific to cartels. In fact, the existing socio-political situation ensured that the law passed by the Parliament dealt primarily with dominance and abuse of dominance. The other concern which got reflected in the MRTP Act of 1969 was agreement relating to resale price maintenance. The reason why cartels were considered less serious was the lack of evidence which established the harm caused to the consumers. On the other hand, the effect of large dominant undertakings on small enterprises was clearly mapped out by the committees established to study the reasons for economic stagnation. Similarly, the effect of resale price

---

[158] See TNN, 'Bus Mishap: It's a Cartel Thriving on Parents' Helplessness', *The Times of India* (26 April 2009), http://articles.timesofindia.indiatimes.com/2009-04-26/lucknow/28017663_1_cartel-school-bus-bus-mishap (accessed 18 May 2011)

[159] See Julie Mariappan, 'Cartels Kill Purpose of Road Work Bidding', *The Times of India* (February 17, 2011), http://articles.timesofindia.indiatimes.com/2011-02-17/chennai/28554542_1_contractors-road-works-tender-process (accessed 18 May 2011). See also TNN, 'Corporation Commissioner Responds to TOI Report', *The Times of India* (February 17, 2011),,http://articles.timesofindia.indiatimes.com/2011-02-17/chennai/28554311_1_bus-route-roads-corporation-commissioner-quality (accessed 18 May 2011).

[160] See GautamGuha, Director-General of Audit, CAG, 'Collusion in Procurement' December 8, 2010 http://cci.gov.in/images/media/presentations/Guha241210.pdf (accessed 19 May 2011)

on distributors and consumers was equally documented. The MRTP Act, 1969 therefore confined its anti-cartel response to the chapter on restrictive trade practices. Further highlighting the lax approach towards cartels, the MRTP Act, 1969 employed the *rule of reason* analysis to gauge the effect of cartels on public interest. Thus even if cartels are treated as *per se* restrictive, they could still get away with the public interest argument. The only problem was that neither the Supreme Court nor the MRTP Commission could come to a consensus on what amounts to public interest. Add to this substantive weakness was the structural problem in the way MRTP functioned. Apart from the added burden of dealing with unfair trade practices, the Commission often was not fully staffed to hear matters. The lack of expertise in detecting cartels, adducing insufficient proof to show collusion or agreement added to the woes of the MRTP Commission. Further, the MRTP Commission also lacked powers to deter cartelists. The maximum punishment that a cartelist could be met with was a cease and desist order. Only if the cease and desist order was infringed would the cartelist face the prospect of imprisonment and fines. In all these problems, the biggest sufferers were the consumers (both intermediaries and end). Hence it was time for India to look beyond the MRTP Act, 1969. The next chapter analyses the post-MRTP phase.

6 Cartels, Consumer Interests and India Post-MRTP Phase

Context

From the review of the MRTP Act, 1969 in the previous chapter, it is evident that cartels have been a low priority area of concern in India's first competition law. The preamble of the MRTP Act states that the object of enacting the MRTP Act is to ensure

> 'that the operation of the economic system does not result in the concentration of economic power to the common detriment, for the control of monopolies, for the prohibition of monopolistic and restrictive trade practices and for matters connected therewith or incidental thereto'.[1]

The concern of the times was definitely not consumer interests, nor was there *per se* prohibition of cartels. The incorporation of exemption clauses under section 38 substantiates this line of argument. It was admittedly the idea that cartels *per se* were not void and would be considered bad only when they fail to justify their conduct through the *rule of reason* analysis involving the determination of the question, viz., whether the conduct is prejudicial to public interest. The ambiguous term 'public interest' failed to explain whether it includes consumer interest or only interest of the industry. In the absence of expertise and resources, the Commission was accused of failing to effectively enforce the anti-cartel provisions. Growing criticism of the Commission was accompanied by change in the economic policies of the country which consequently led the government of India to re-look into the MRTP Act. The outcome was the enactment of the Competition Act 2002. The following is an analyses of the anti-cartel provision of the Act. The discussion however begins with the context which shaped the anti-cartel provisions of the Act. Thereafter, specific provisions will be analysed to

---

1 See the Preamble of the MRTP Act, 1969.

understand the changes in approach adopted towards cartels under the Act. Finally the implementation and interpretation of the anti-cartel provisions will be analysed. In the process, the following questions will be answered : (a) Does the Act accommodate the consumer interests in devising its response towards cartels?; b) What approach has been adopted towards cartels, viz., *rule of reason* or *per se*; (c) Has the Act distinguished between hard core restraints and ancillary restraints and (d) Will the anti-cartel provisions in the Act have a deterrent effect on cartels?

Contextualizing the Competition Act, 2002: The background

In the light of the above discussed drawbacks in the MRTP Act, 1969 and the changed economic policies, the government of India constituted a high powered committee to evaluate the adequacy of the MRTP Act, 1969.[2] The year 1991 was a watershed year for India because it witnessed a serious economic crisis that year. The country was on the verge of going bankrupt thus discrediting the virtues of the command and control system of running the economy.[3] To meet this situation, the then government of India, headed by Prime Minister P.V. Narasimha Rao, decided to liberalize the Indian economy and introduce reforms.[4] It was as part of this reform measure that the MRTP Act was amended in 1991, wherein, as mentioned above, major sections in the chapter on concentration of economic power, were omitted. This was done primarily to decontrol the procedural requirements for expansion, mergers and amalgamations and setting up of new industrial undertakings. The new economic environment did not do away with the reality of old abuses like abuse of dominance, cartels and other anti-competitive behaviour. The need to re-look into the whole gamut of anti-competitive issues therefore arose in the context of the many failures of the MRTP Act, 1969.[5]

Further, there was also the international context, viz., the WTO negotiations on issues like trade and investment, competition policy, transparency in government procurement and trade facilitation. Consequently, the government of India needed to understand the implications of the linking multilateral trade

---

2 S. Chakravarthy, 'Evolution of Competition Policy and Law in India', in *Towards A Functional Competition Policy For India-An Overview,* ed.Pradeep S Mehta(CUTS International, 2005), 43–51.

3 See JagdishBhagwati, 'The Design of Indian Development', in, *India's Economic Reforms and Development: Essays for Manmohan Singh* (OUP, 2001), 23–39.

4 See M Narasimham, *Economic Reforms: Development and Finance* (UBSPD, 2002), 108–117.

5 Amitabh Kumar (n 19 of Chapter 5) 494.

negotiations with the competition policy. Accordingly, an expert group was set up which suggested the enactment of a new competition law.[6] The then Finance Minister Yashwant Sinha in his budget speech noted that

> 'The Monopolies and Restrictive Trade Practices Act has become obsolete in certain areas in the light of international economic developments relating to competition laws. We need to shift our focus from curbing monopolies to promoting competition. The Government has decided to appoint a commission to examine this range of issues and propose a modern competition law suitable for our conditions'.[7]

Soon thereafter the government of India in October 1999 under the chairmanship of Mr S.V.S Raghavan set up a High Level Committee on Competition Policy and Law.[8] The committee comprised nine members[9] entrusted with the task of recommending a suitable legislative and administrative framework for the competition law.[10] The Finance Minister's speech set the agenda of the Committee, viz., to suggest measures to promote competition.

Cartels and consumers: Analysing the recommendation of the committee

Accordingly, the Committee began its report by defining competition, thus setting out the first change from the Monopolies Inquiry Commission. This was natural as in the terms of the reference of the latter, competition issues were not in focus, whereas the former was required to formulate

> 'a suitable legislative framework, in the light of international developments and the need to promote competition, relating to competition law…'.[11]

---

6 Report of the Working Group (n 7 of Chapter 5) 15, para 3.1.9.

7 Report of the Working Group (n 7 of Chapter 5) 15, para 3.1.10.

8 Interestingly, Raghavan had been an erstwhile chairman of two state monopolies, viz., the State Trading Corporation of India and the Minerals and Metals Trading Corporation of India. See Speaking Notes for Research Symposium, 'Political Economy Constraints in Regulatory Regimes in Developing Countries' (March 22–24, 2007) Journey of India's new competition law through a practitioner's eye http://www.circ.in/pdf/INDNewCompetitionLaw.pdf (accessed 7 June 2011).

9 *Id.*, 4.

10 See P.M Narielvala, 'Competition Law for the New Millennium', The Hindu (June 22, 2000) http://www.hinduonnet.com/thehindu/2000/06/22/stories/0622000d.htm (accessed 7 June 2011)

11 Amitabh Kumar (n 19) 494.

The Committee mapped out the pros and cons of an unregulated free market economy and notes that

> 'in most parts of the world, free competition is supported by relevant rules and regulations to ensure free trade and absence of unfair practices'.[12]

The Committee identified that the

> '[t]he ultimate raison d'être of competition is the interest of the consumer. The consumer's right to free and fair competition cannot be denied by any other consideration'.[13]

This was another significant departure from the philosophy of the Monopolies Inquiry Committee, which never so declared the need to protect consumer interest. It did refer to public interest but, as seen, the term lacked any definite contours and was fraught with vagueness. The Committee however was concerned only with the interests of the end consumer and not the intermediary consumers.

One important reason for this change in focus was the fact that by the late 1990s, the consumer movement in India had strengthened to an extent that it could influence government policies. The gain of strength was largely assisted by the enactment of the Consumer Protection Act, 1986. This Act was aimed at providing a dispute redressal forum for individual consumers, at the district, state and central level. The Act ensured speedy relief and adequate compensation for aggrieved consumers. Armed with this legislative enactment, consumer groups in India ensured that their voices are heard by the policy makers when re-looking competition issues.[14] This background, which was missing in the late 1960s, ensured that the Raghavan Committee took a pro-consumer approach. The Committee accordingly re-emphasized that 'Competition policy should thus have the positive objective of promoting consumer welfare'.[15] It then went on to review and suggest changes to the existing laws that according to it will create a competitive environment and promote competition.[16] The Committee thus satisfactorily noted that the reforms in the industrial policy with the virtual abolition of industrial licensing requirement, promoted competition in the domestic market. Similarly, as per the Committee the trade policy reforms ensured foreign imports and better quality inputs and technology for domestic producers. These reforms, the

---

12 S.V.S. Raghavan Committee Report (n 26 of Chapter 1) para 1.1.7.

13 *Id.*, para 1.1.9.

14 Speaking Notes (n 8) 1–2.

15 S.V.S. Raghavan Committee Report (n 26 of Chapter 1) para 1.2.0.

16 *Id.*, para 2.5.9.

Committee noted will enable '[getting prices right], achieving efficiency in resource use and maximising consumer welfare'.[17]

In the Committee's view, the other reforms that were needed to promote competition was: (a) doing away with the protection offered to small-scale industries; (b) removing quota restrictions in consumer goods; (c) disinvestment of public sector undertakings; (d) deregulation of prices of petroleum products, fertilizers, sugar cane, power and transport; (e) further opening up of sectors like power, transport and communications to private players and setting up of independent regulatory agencies.[18] After explaining the rationale of these recommendations, the Committee outlined the mandate that any new competition law for India ought to have viz. dealing with cartelization, price-fixing and other abuses of market power and regulation of mergers.[19] In the recommendations of the Raghavan Committee, cartels were specifically identified and acknowledged as a serious problem to be specifically dealt with. This was another departure from the approach of the Monopolies Inquiry Commission, which clubbed all anti-competitive agreements as restrictive trade practices.

The Raghavan Committee's approach also reflects the influence of the international thought process, which as noted in the case of the US and the EU, was completely against cartels. The recommendation of the Raghavan Committee on cartels however also indicates a difference of opinion among the Committee members on the approach that ought to be taken towards anti-cartel enforcement.[20] The difference was on the fundamental issue of choosing between a *per se void* approach and a *rule of reason* approach while dealing with cartels. In the context of the present discussion, this difference of opinion will be re-visited and investigated further to understand the reasons for the same. Moving on, the Committee then makes a recommendation with regard to other anti-competitive practices like vertical agreements[21], abuse of dominance,[22] predatory pricing[23], exclusionary practices[24] and mergers.[25] For the Committee, all vertical restraints, including the resale price maintenance agreement are to be tested against the *rule of reason* principle. With regard to

---

17 *Id.*, para 2.8.
18 S.V.S. Raghavan Committee Report (n 26 of Chapter 1) para 2.8.1.
19 *Id.*, para 2.9.7.
20 *Id.*, para 4.3.8.
21 *Id.*, para 4.3.9-4.4.1.
22 *Id.*, para 4.4.3–4.5.0.
23 *Id.*, para 4.5.1–4.5.7.
24 *Id.*, para 4.5.8–4.6.0.
25 *Id.*, para 4.6.1–4.8.3.

abuse of dominance also, the Committee recommended the application of *rule of reason* principle. The Committee thus insisted that

> 'law should ensure that only when dominance is clearly established, can abuse of dominance be alleged'.[26]

Accordingly apart from market shares what need to be looked at would be the entry barriers that exist because of the dominant undertaking. The Committee was clear that large efficient firms should not be endangered.[27]

On predatory pricing, the Committee felt that it will be best left to the proposed Competition Law Tribunal to draw regulations on predatory pricing and revise it from time to time based upon its experience.[28] Further, the Committee recommended a *rule of reason* approach, requiring thereby that

> 'predatory pricing [will be regarded as] an abuse, only if it is unambiguously established and indulged in by a dominant undertaking'.[29]

In the case of exclusionary practices like tie-in-sales, exclusive or selective distribution etc. being indulged in by a dominant undertaking, the Committee recommended the application of the *rule of reason* test.[30] With respect to mergers too, the Committee took a *rule of reason* approach, viz., mergers need to be challenged only if they 'reduce or harm competition and adversely affect welfare'.[31] The Committee also recommended that '[t]he Competition Law should have extra-territorial reach'.[32] This recommendation was meant to remove the ambiguity that existed under section 14 of the MRTP Act, 1969.[33] As the *Haridas Exports* case[34] showed, there was confusion as to

26 *Id.*, para 4.4.6.

27 *Id.*

28 *Id.*, para 4.5.3.

29 *Id.*, para 4.5.7.

30 *Id.*, para 4.5.9.[The Committee thus recommended that in all cases of exclusionary practices, 'it needs to be established whether the restraints create a barrier to new entry or force existing competitors out of the market'.]

31 *Id.*, para 4.6.3.

32 *Id.*, para 5.4.1.

33 According to section 14 of the MRTP Act, 1969: 'Orders where party concerned does not carry on business in India.- Where any practice substantially falls within monopolistic, restrictive, or unfair, trade practice, relating to the production, storage, supply, distribution or control of goods of any description or the provision of any services and any party to such practice does not carry on business in India, an order may be made under this Act with respect to that part of the practice which is carried on in India'.

34 *Haridas Exports* (n 100 of Chapter 5). Herein the Supreme Court declared that the MRTP does not have extra-territorial jurisdiction, as orders can be passed only with respect to that portion of the restrictive trade practices which is carried within India.

whether the MRTP Commission had extra-territorial jurisdiction or not. The decision of the Supreme Court therein brought out the inherent conflict in the interpretation of section 14 between the Commission and the Court.

Committee's critique of the MRTP Act, 1969:- Setting the stage for the Competition Act, 2002

Having thus made specific recommendations, which according to the Committee would ensure an effective competition law in India, it addressed the crucial issue of the best way to implement these recommendations. The Committee thus reviewed the efficacy of the MRTP Act against the backdrop of its recommendations. It felt that the MRTP Act does not squarely address competition concerns and thus is not adequate for

> 'fostering competition in the market and trade and for reducing, if not eliminating, anti-competitive practices in the country's domestic and international trade'.[35]

The Committee noted that the MRTP Act lacked specific provisions defining anti-competitive practices like abuse of dominance; cartels, collusion and price fixing; bid rigging; boycotts and refusal to deal and predatory pricing.[36] This the Committee felt led to variance in the way the law was applied, as there was a possibility of different interpretations by different forums.[37] According to the Committee, it would require extensive amendments to the MRTP Act to accommodate all its recommendations. It was therefore desirable that a new Competition law be enacted on the lines of the Committee's recommendations.

Importantly, it was pointed out by the Committee that the chapter on unfair trade practices, ought not to have any place under a standard competition law because that was clearly covered by the Consumer Protection Act, 1986. It was further noted by the Committee that the provisions on mergers, which were repealed by the 1991 Amendment, from the MRTP Act, ought to be brought in afresh, in line with their recommendation. Finally, the Committee noted the changed economic scenario from that of command and control to the liberalized set-up, leading to different challenges that needed a new competition law.[38] Accordingly, the Committee recommended the repealing of the MRTP Act, 1969 and the winding up of the MRTP

---

[35] S.V.S. Raghavan Committee Report (n 26 of Chapter 1) para 7.1.3.

[36] *Id.*, para 7.1.9.

[37] *Id.*, 7.2.1.

[38] *Id.*, para 7.2.0–7.2.3.

Commission. The Committee further recommended that the pending cases relating to unfair trade practices be transferred to the Consumer Courts set up under the Consumer Protection Act, 1986.[39] So far as the cases related to monopolistic trade practices and the restrictive trade practices were concerned, it was recommended that be taken over by the proposed new Competition Commission of India.[40]

The Competition Commission of India and the proposed legislative framework: Recommending a new set-up

In order to ensure proper implementation of its recommendation and effectiveness of a new competition law, the Committee proposed the establishment of a 'Specialised Court or Tribunal which can be christened 'Competition Commission of India'' (hereinafter referred to as CCI).[41] It was recommended that such a commission would both hear competition cases as well as conduct competition advocacy.[42] Similar to the recommendation of the Monopolies Inquiry Committee, this Committee too emphasized the need for independence and impartiality of the CCI.[43] It was envisaged that the new Commission would have powers to investigate, prosecute and adjudicate on all competition-related issues. The Committee however insisted on the separation of these powers.[44] Further, the new Commission was perceived as one having *suo moto* power to initiate investigations in all competition-related matters.[45] The Committee recommended that the prosecutorial and the investigative wings need to be headed by one official designated as the Director-General (Investigation and Prosecution).[46] As noted above, both the wings were to be segregated from each other and discharge their responsibilities independently without any overlap. The adjudication power was to be discharged by the CCI.[47]

In order to have an effective discharge of the powers, viz., investigative, prosecutorial and adjudicative, the Committee recommended the creation of multiple benches of the CCI with the corresponding appointment of

---

39 *Id.*, para 7.4.1.

40 *Id.*, para 7.4.0–7.4.1.

41 *Id.*, para 6.1.4.

42 *Id.*

43 *Id.*, para 6.1.5.

44 *Id.*, para 6.1.5 (c).

45 *Id.*, para 6.1.6.

46 *Id.*, para 6.1.8.

47 *Id.*, para 6.2.2.

Deputy Director-Generals, in various cities.[48] The Committee felt that in order to review mergers from the perspective of competition, there needs to be a Merger Commission, which will be part of the CCI, though there will be a separate bench to handle pre-merger scrutiny cases.[49] The Committee detailed out the modalities pertaining to the appointment, pay and perks and the removal from office of the members of the CCI. The Committee emphasized that

> 'it should not be mandatory that the Chairperson should be only from the judiciary. As the Chairperson should be one who has considerable exposure and knowledge in international trade, commerce and complicated issues relating to trade, the net needs to be cast very wide in order that an appropriate person is selected for this post'.[50]

As will be seen later, the composition of the CCI became a controversial issue as soon as the new competition law was enacted. Nonetheless, as far as the recommendations were concerned, the Committee provided details as to how the CCI ought to function, what should be its power et al. In this connection, the Committee recommended that

> 'The trial before the CCI should be summary in nature. All evidence should be by way of affidavits unless, in exceptional cases, the CCI would like cross examination of the witnesses by the other side or would like to seek clarifications from those who have sworn the affidavits. By and large, the Code of Civil Procedure, 1908 should not be made applicable and the procedure to be followed may be made by the CCI itself through Regulations. CCI should have the power to co-opt experts, where it deems fit'.[51]

This recommendation ousting the application of the Code of Civil Procedure was probably done to cut down on the delays that may entail due to procedural formalities. This was in contrast to the position under section 12 of the MRTP Act, 1969.[52] Another interesting recommendation was with regard to the power of CCI vis-à-vis other regulatory bodies. The Committee recommended that the CCI should be empowered to review the orders of other regulatory bodies on the 'touchstone of competition'.[53] This

[48] *Id.*, para 6.2.0, 6.2.4 and 6.2.5.

[49] S.V.S. Raghavan Committee Report (n 26 of Chapter 1) para 6.2.7.

[50] *Id.*, para 6.3.5.

[51] *Id.*, para 6.4.3.

[52] According to section 12 of the MRTP Act, 1969, the MRTP Commission was to have the same powers as a Civil Court under the Code of Civil Procedure, 1908.

[53] S.V.S. Raghavan Committee Report (n 26 of Chapter 1) para 6.4.5.

again was a potential area of controversy so far as inter-regulatory jurisdiction is concerned.[54] The Raghavan Committee thus thought that it had provided India the blue print of a robust and effective competition law. It is then required to review the second competition law, one that ultimately superseded the MRTP Act, 1969. It will also be required, from the perspective of the present discussion, to analyse in detail the anti-cartel provisions of the law. Importantly, the analyses need to factor in the internal differences of the Raghavan Committee members on the cartel provisions.

The internal dissensions of the Committee; Different voices, same concern?

The recommendations of the Committee laid the foundation for a new competition law, which came into force in January 2003.[55] The recommendations though were criticized on the grounds of being evasive and for overlooking the potential problem arising from big businesses.[56] Further, the lack of norms defining the approach to be taken towards predatory pricing was also criticized.[57] This criticism was due to the fact that the Committee failed to define predatory pricing. There were also reservations expressed on the recommendations relating to mergers.[58] In addition to all these criticisms, there was also the fact that the report contained two supplementary notes and two notes of dissent. This in effect meant that four of the nine Committee members had differences of opinion on fundamental issues relating to competition. Hence any one reading the document was faced with

---

[54] In light of India's commitment under GATS (General Agreement on Trade in Services), the Committee devoted a chapter to study the issues relating to competition in the context of professional services. See S.V.S. Raghavan Committee Report (n 26) chapter VIII: Competition Policy and Professional Services. For details on the extent of India's commitment under GATS, visit http://commerce.nic.in/trade/international_trade_tis_gaitis.asp (accessed 9 June 2011).

[55] See VinodDhall, Key Note Address at the Seminar on 'Competition Policy and its Impact on Industry' (September 20, 2004) Ahmedabad, http://cci.gov.in/images/media/speeches/5policyandimpact_20080411101736.pdf (accessed 10 June 2011).

[56] See RuddarDutt, 'Competition Law Report: An Evasive Document', *Business Line* (August 1, 2000) http://www.thehindubusinessline.in/businessline/2000/08/ 01/stories/040120ru.htm (accessed 10 June 2011).

[57] *Id.*

[58] See *Business Line*, 'Competition Policy: Need for an Intentional Approach' (July 6, 2000), http://www.hindu.com/businessline/2000/07/06/stories/040654ma.htm (accessed 10 June 2011).

multiple voices on the issue of defining a competition law/policy for India.[59] Dr S. Chakravarthy, a member of the Committee, in his supplementary note, emphasized the need for a phased introduction of any proposed competition law or policy. His reasons were that the domestic industry needed to be given time to

> 'get educated and exposed to competition and thereby address themselves towards enhanced efficiency, economies of scale and subserving of the consumer interest (in the broadest sense of the term)...'.[60]

Accordingly, he suggested a transition period during which the proposed competition law or policy should be slowly introduced and strengthened. Further, he insisted that any proposed competition law or policy ought to be flexible enough to accommodate the needs of the Indian economy. He suggested that the reservations for small-scale industries be continued for a transition period of seven to ten years. The idea was that this much time was needed to make the small-scale undertaking efficient enough to face the outside competition. The thrust of his recommendation was to provide a level playing field for the domestic industry vis-à-vis the global competitors.[61] Dr Rakesh Mohan, another member of the Committee, also suggested going slow on the implementation of any proposed competition law or policy. His concern however was the lack of expertise in the adjudication of anti-competitive issues, through the application of the *rule of reason*. He felt that any authority that is vested with such enormous discretionary powers through the *rule of reason* approach is likely to commit mistakes that would come 'in the way of Indian entrepreneurship rather than promoting competition'.[62]Accordingly, he suggested that there should be an exhaustive public debate on the Committee's recommendations. This would, according to Dr Mohan

> 'help in improving and sharpening the recommendations made in this report. It would also familiarise all stakeholders with the dimensions of what a modern competition policy look like and then make it easier to draft a law that has wide acceptability and understanding. Second, it would provide more time to digest the experience in other countries, particularly in developing countries where such laws are relatively new'.[63]

---

59 See T.T. Ram Mohan, 'Competition Policy Dilemmas', *EPW*, 2499–2502 (July 15, 2000) 35:28&29.

60 S.V.S. Raghavan Committee Report (n 26 of Chapter 1), para 84.

61 *Id.*, para 85.

62 *Id.*, para 86.

63 *Id.*, para 87.

Finally, it was suggested by Dr Mohan that the proposed CCI should at the initial stages—for three to five years—be entrusted with only advocacy role. The intervening time period should be devoted in developing an effective law, based on public discussion. In addition, the CCI should also use the advocacy time period for training personnel. This would help to acquire the necessary expertise required to effectively enforce the *rule of reason* approach.[64]

Of the two dissenting notes, the one by Sudhir Mulji reflected an extreme position, wherein he denounced the proposed competition law. His reasons were that economic forces should not be subject to the control of a statute law. Mulji argued that the need was to promote the freedom of the markets to such an extent that even excesses can be tolerated.[65] It was thus an opinion to the extreme right of the mainstream approach of the Committee's recommendations.[66] The other dissenting voice was that of P.M. Narielvala, who emphasized the need to do away with the pre-merger notifications. His reasons were that for the domestic industry to compete globally, there was a need to encourage mergers and amalgamation. He further argued that dominance *per se* was not bad, its abuse was. When a merger is about to occur, it is difficult to decide whether the same will lead to abuse of dominance or not. Further, post-merger challenges can always be made on the grounds of abuse of dominance.[67] Of all the four opinions of the Committee members reviewed above, it is evident that, philosophically, Dr Mohan's opinion was the closest to the mainstream opinion of the Committee. The only point where he differed was the staggered time frame within which the proposed competition law was to be fully implemented. The Committee's recommendation suggested giving immediate statutory effect to all measures contained in the report, incorporating both *rule of reason* as well as *per se* rule. Dr Mohan, on the other hand, wanted that the implementation of the statute incorporating the *rule of reason* measure be slightly delayed. There is however unanimity as far as the philosophy governing such law is concerned. This was evident from the fact that Dr Mohan's reason for delayed enforcement of law was the lack of necessary expertise in dealing with anti-competitive issues. There was no fundamental difference of opinion on the need of such a law or policy.

In contrast, Dr Chakravarthy wanted a staggered implementation of the competition law, with exemptions and protection for the domestic industry,

---

64 *Id.*, para 87.

65 *Id.*, para 90.

66 T.T. Ram Mohan (n 59) 2499.

67 S.V.S. Raghavan Committee Report (n 26 of Chapter 1) para 92.

wherever required. In this respect, he took a philosophically divergent position to that of the mainstream recommendation. As is evident, the Committee was clear on fast tracking the implementation of a new competition law or policy regime. This fast tracking was recommended to be done without any of the baggage of a planned economy. The recommendations of the Committee with respect to the industrial policy or labour policy are proof of this intent. On the other hand, Dr Chakravarthy had fundamental issues with the pace of liberalization and the opening of the Indian economy to global competitors. He was afraid that in the name of competition, we might end up destroying our domestic industry. This philosophy was more towards the left of the mainstream recommendation of the Committee. Indeed, there was an attempt at bringing about a harmony between industrial policy and competition concerns. He suggested exemptions being created in sectors like defence to safeguard the interest of the country. In the context of the present discussion, this becomes an important issue which needs to be dealt with in more detail—and will be done so while discussing the need to promote consumer interest within the anti-cartel law framework. As far as the new competition law was concerned, it had to bear the burden of these criticisms and philosophical differences, right from the day of its enforcement in 2003.

The Competition Act, 2002: Teething problems and abundance of amendments

The Competition Act, 2002 (hereinafter called the Act) faced its first challenge in the form of a writ petition, soon after it was notified on 14 January 2003. According to section 1 (3) of the Act, different provisions may be brought into force on different dates.[68] Accordingly, some sections were notified in March 2003 and some sections were notified in June 2003. Of the sections notified, there were provisions with regard to the constitution of the CCI. The relevant provisions empowered the central government to prescribe rules for the selection of the chairperson and other members of the CCI. On April 4, 2003, the central government notified the relevant rules, whereby a Committee was constituted to select the chairperson and other members of the CCI.[69] According to the prescribed rules, the

[68] The Act, section 1(3) proviso.

[69] The rule was notified by the central government in exercise of its powers under clause (a) of sub-section (2) of section 63 read with section 9 of the Act, available at http://www.cci.gov.in/images/media/rules/gsr_303.pdf?phpMyAdmin=NMPFRahGKYeum5F74Ppstn7Rf00 (accessed 13 May 2011).

Committee shall comprise persons from varied backgrounds, viz,. a retired judge of the Supreme Court or High Court or a Chairperson of a Tribunal or a distinguished jurist or a Senior Advocate. In addition, a person with special knowledge and professional experience of twenty-five years or more in international trade, economics, business, commerce or industry was also to be appointed as a member of the Committee. Finally, a person with special knowledge and professional experience of twenty-five years or more in accountancy, management, finance, public affairs or administration, was to be nominated as member of the Committee by the central government. The writ petition challenged the legitimacy of the Committee so envisaged by these rules, on the ground that the rules violated the 'doctrine of separation of powers recognized by the Indian Constitution'.[70] The petitioner argued that, since the CCI was to be like a judicial body, the chairperson of the CCI has to mandatorily be a retired Chief Justice or Judge of the Supreme Court or High Court. Moreover, such a chairperson had to be necessarily nominated by the 'Chief Justice of India or by a Committee presided over by the Chief Justice of India'.[71]

The central government agreed to make necessary amendments to the Act and in the impugned rules, ensuring that the chairperson and the members of the CCI are selected by a Committee headed by the Chief Justice of India or his nominee.[72] The government insisted that the chairperson had to be an expert and 'not necessarily a Judge or a retired Judge of the High Court or the Supreme Court'.[73] In the light of these submissions by the central government, the Supreme Court, decided to dispose of the writ petition, without addressing the questions raised. The Court suggested that if the CCI is intended to be an expert body, then there should ideally be another body, i.e., an appellate body that will be in accordance with the doctrine of separation of power.[74] The Act was accordingly amended once in 2007 and again in 2009, with the 2007 amendments leading to the establishment of a Competition Appellate Tribunal (hereinafter called CompAT) for hearing appeals against the orders passed by the CCI.[75] The 2007 amendment also caused the repeal of the MRTP Act, though it provided for the continuation of the MRTP Commission for a period of two years, from the date of the

[70] See *BrahmDutt v. Union of India*, (2005) 2 SCC 431, 434, para 3.

[71] *Id.*

[72] *Id.*, 435, para 4.

[73] *Id.*

[74] *Id.*, 435–436, para 5–7.

[75] The Act (n 68) Chapter VIII A, sections 53A–53U.

commencement of the Act.[76] Notwithstanding the 2007 amendment, not all the provisions of the Act were notified.[77]

Section 66 of the Act, for example, was not brought into force in 2007, and consequently, the MRTP Commission was as good as non-functional. This greatly jeopardized the disposal process of the pending cases during the transition period, viz., during the time when the CCI was taking over from the MRTP Commission. Despite the fact that in 2009, all the sections including section 66 were notified, it did not help matters. Accordingly, with the Parliament not in session, the President of India on 14 October 2009 promulgated an Ordinance called the Competition (Amendment) Ordinance, 2009. Consequently, section 66 of the Act was once again amended whereby the MRTP Commission was dissolved with immediate effect and the pending cases were transferred to the CompAT.[78] Subsequently, both the Houses of Parliament passed the Competition (Amendment) Bill, in December 2009, by which the Ordinance was repealed and section 66 of the Act was amended, with changes. The cases involving unfair trade practices which were earlier transferred to the National Commission, by the Ordinance, were

---

[76] The Act (n 68) at section 66 (1), as amended in 2007['The Monopolies and Restrictive Trade Practices Act, 1969 (54 of 1969) is hereby repealed and the Monopolies and Restrictive Trade Practices Commission established under sub-section(1) of section 5 of the said Act (hereinafter referred to as the repealed Act) shall stand dissolved: Provided that, notwithstanding anything contained in this sub-section, the Monopolies and Restrictive Trade Practices Commission established under sub section(1) of section 5 of the repealed Act, may continue to exercise jurisdiction and power under the repealed Act for a period of two years from the date of the commencement of this Act in respect of all cases or proceedings (including complaints received by it or references or applications made to it) filed before the commencement of this Act as if the Monopolies and Restrictive Trade Practices Act, 1969 (54 of 1969) had not been repealed and all the provisions of the said Act so repealed shall mutatis mutandis apply to such cases or proceedings or complaints or references or applications and to all other matters'.]

[77] On October 12, 2007, the government notified the enforcement of section 2, sections 6–9, sections 11 and 12, sections 17 and 18, section 27, 29, 30 and 32 and section 40–49 of the Act. On December 20, 2007, the government brought into force sections 53C–53M of the Act by gazette notification,. The rest of the sections including the establishment of CompAT were brought into effect in the year 2009. The details of the notifications are available at
http://www.cci.gov.in/index.php?option=com_content&task=view&id=21 (accessed June 14, 2011).

[78] See the Statement and Objects of the Competition (Amendment) Bill, 2009, at http://www.prsindia.org/uploads/media/Competition/Competition%20Amendment%20Bill.pdf (accessed June 14, 2011). All the cases relating to unfair trade practices were transferred to the National Commission established under the Consumer Protection Act, 1986.

re-transferred to the CompAT in accordance with the 2009 bill.[79] The MRTP Commission however stood dissolved with immediate effect.[80]

The Act, cartels and consumer interests: Interpreting the provisions against cartels

It has to be understood, though, that the substantive provisions relating to anti-competitive practices did not undergo any amendments either in 2007 or in 2009. The delayed enforcement did not therefore change the content of the provisions relating to cartels. The Act defines cartels under section 2 (c) as

> '"cartel" includes an association of producers, sellers, distributors, traders or service providers who, by agreement amongst themselves, limit, control or attempt to control the production, distribution, sale or price of, or, trade in goods or provision of services'.[81]

The definition is thus inclusive and may be extended through interpretation to include any anti-competitive agreements that has the affect of fixing prices, quotas, sharing markets etc. This is possible as the usage of the words '*include*' in a definition makes it *prima facie* extensive.[82] For example, in the *Reynolds v. John*[83] case, the Court of Appeal (Queen's Bench) was required to interpret the definition of 'loudspeaker'. Section 115 of the Glamorgan County Council Act, 1952 had defined the term 'loudspeaker' in section 115 (5) as follows: 'In this section the expression "loudspeaker" includes an amplifier...'.[84] Ashworth, J. held that

> 'the word "includes" in s.115 (5), was inserted for the purpose of enlarging rather than restricting the meaning which might arise from the use of the word "loudspeaker" simpliciter'.[85]

In this context, Ashworth, J. quoted from the Privy Council decision in *Dilworth's* case[86] wherein it was held that

---

79 See The Competition (Amendment) Bill 2009, section 66 (1), (3), (4), (5) and (7) http://www.bareactsonline.com/pdfs/2010/THE%20COMPETITION%20(AMENDMENT).pdf (accessed June 14, 2011).

80 *Id.* Accordingly in section 66 (1), the proviso and the explanation stands omitted.

81 The Act (n 68) section 2(c).

82 See Guru Prasanna Singh, *Principles of Statutory Interpretation,* 12th ed., (Lexis NexisButterwothsWadhwa, 2010) 180.

83 [1956] 1 All E.R. 306.

84 *Id.*, 308.

85 *Id.*, 309.

86 See *Dilworth v. Stamps Comrs., Dilworth v. Land & Income Tax Comrs.*, [1899] A.C. 99, as given in *Id.*, 306

> 'the word "include" is very generally used in interpretation clauses in order to enlarge the meaning of words or phrases occurring in the body of the statute; and when it is so used these words or phrases must be construed as comprehending, not only such things as they signify according to their natural import, but also those things which the interpretation clause declares that they shall include.'[87]

Similarly, the Supreme Court of India in the *Shree Gollaleshawr Dev* case held that the usage of the word 'includes' in the definition enlarged the meaning of the concerned word, viz., 'person having interest'.[88] The inclusive definition of cartels also means that other definitions of cartels can be looked at to determine whether a particular behaviour is covered by section 2 (c) or not. The definition of hard core cartels given by OECD thus can be referred to, to understand the meaning of cartels within the Act.[89] This approach would help enforce the pro-consumer objective of the Act as stated in the long title of the Act viz. 'An Act… to protect the interests of consumers…'.[90] This approach can be further substantiated by referring to section 3 (3) of the Act. Section 3 of the Act deals with all types of anti-competitive agreements including cartels, while section 3 (3) of the Act spells out an exhaustive list of activities that are to be treated as cartel activities. This list covers bid rigging or collusive bidding as a cartel activity. As shown above, section 2 (c) does not refer to collusive bidding while defining cartels. However, reading the

---

87 Dilworth (n 86) 309.

88 See *Shree GollaleshwarDev and others v. GangawaKomShantayya Math and others*, (1985) 4 SCC 393,401. Herein the Supreme Court was required to answer the question with regard to the precise meaning of the words '*persons having interest*' under section 2 (10) of the Bombay Public Trusts Act, 1950. By the Bombay Public Trusts (Amendment) Act, 1953, section 2 (10) was amended whereby the word 'includes' was substituted for the word 'means'. The Supreme Court categorically declared that this amendment 'set at rest all doubts and difficulties as to the meaning of these words, which were intended and meant to be used in a generic sense so as to include not only the trustees but also the beneficiaries and other persons interested in the trust'.

89 According to the OECD Council recommendation concerning effective action against hard core cartels, hard core cartels are defined as 'an anticompetitive agreement, anticompetitive concerted practice, or anticompetitive arrangement by competitors to fix prices, make rigged bids (collusive tenders), establish output restrictions or quotas, or share or divide markets by allocating customers, suppliers, territories, or lines of commerce'. The recommendation is available at http://acts.oecd.org/Instruments/ShowInstrumentView.aspx?InstrumentID=193&InstrumentPID=189&Lang=en&Book=False (accessed 15 June 2011).

90 The Act (n 68) the Preamble.

inclusive definition with section 3 (3) establishes the fact that the Act treats collusive bidding or bid rigging as a cartel activity.[91]

The Act thus goes a step ahead of the EU Article 101, clause 1, as it specifically includes collusive bidding as cartel activity. Going along with the spirit of the Raghavan Committee report, section 3 (3) renders all cartel activities as void. These activities are listed in the said sub-section to be read along with section 2 (c) of the Act. This can be gathered if one reads the sub-sections (1), (2) and (3) of section 3 together. To begin with, under section 3 (3) of the Act, all cartel activities are 'presumed to have an appreciable adverse effect on competition'.[92] Further, under section 3 (2) of the Act, any agreement which under section 3 (1) of the Act causes an '*appreciable adverse effect on competition*' is void. This also means that all cartel agreements are *per se void* as they are presumed to have *appreciable adverse effect on competition.* On the face of it this approach is in keeping with the US and the EU decisions, where cartels are *per se* void. Further as noted in the discussion on the MRTP Act, 1969 as well as the EU anti-cartel law, a *per se void* approach to cartels exemplifies a pro-consumer measure.

This is so because under the *per se* void approach, cartels are not provided any escape routes in the garb of reasonableness or any other test. The approach also ensures that consumers have no doubt that cartels will be disbanded and deterred. Finally, this also means that there is less discretion on the part of enforcing authorities as they do not have to determine the efficiency aspect or pro-competitive aspect of cartels through complex economic analysis.[93] The exhaustive list of section 3, sub-section 3 in the Act however creates a problem in terms of the fact that it will preclude the inclusion of other anti-competitive practices indulged in by cartels which may not necessarily

---

[91] *Id.* Section 3 (3) states that 'Any agreement entered into between enterprises or associations of enterprises or persons or associations of persons or between any person and enterprise or practice carried on, or decision taken by, any association of enterprises or association of persons, including cartels, engaged in identical or similar trade of goods or provision of services, which— (a) directly or indirectly determines purchase or sale prices; (b) limits or controls production, supply, markets, technical development, investment or provision of services; (c) shares the market or source of production or provision of services by way of allocation of geographical area of market, or type of goods or services, or number of customers in the market or any other similar way; (d) directly or indirectly results in bid rigging or collusive bidding, shall be presumed to have an appreciable adverse effect on competition'.

[92] *Id.* Section 3 (3).

[93] VinodDhall, 'The Indian Competition Act, 2002', in VinodDhall, ed. (n 5 of Chapter 1) 505.

fall within the enumerated list. For example, if a cartel decides to boycott its competitor, then it has to be shown that the decision to collectively boycott the competitor was done to raise prices or restrict supply etc. Further when suing a cartel, not only does the existence of the cartel have to be proven but the nature of the acts that the cartel is indulging in has to be proven. Finally, the acts complained of have to be covered by the enumerated list of section 3 (3) of the Act.

The Act, anti-cartel provisions and consumer interests: Analysing the defences and exemptions

One could say that section 3 (3), read along with section 3 (1) and 3 (2), was thus an improvement on the MRTP Act, 1969. As mentioned above, while the post-1984 amendment rendered all agreements under section 33 (1) as *per se* restrictive, it did not render them *per se* void. The Act, on the other hand, renders all anti-competitive agreements under section 3 (3) as *per se* void. This does away with the ambiguity that was attached to the MRTP provisions on agreements relating to restrictive trade practices. Unfortunately, however a closer reading of the Act reveals that all is not well for the Indian consumer, as far as the anti-cartel law is concerned. To begin with, while section 3 (3) raises a *presumption of* appreciable adverse effect on competition, the same is a case of *rebuttable presumption.*[94] This is so because the usage of the word *'shall presume'* contains a rule of rebuttable presumption. The Indian Evidence Act, 1872, in section 4 defines *'shall presume'* as:

---

[94] The burden of proof is shifted on to the other party, which in the case of a cartel agreement would be the alleged cartelists. In other words, the cartel agreement will be presumed to be anti-competitive according to section 3 (1) and (2) of the Act, unless the parties to the agreement prove to the contrary and thus rebut the presumption. For a discussion on rebuttable and irrebuttable presumption refer to the judgment of J. Gajendragadkar in the *Izhar Ahmed v. Union of India*, AIR 1962 SC 1052. Further in the *Sodhi Transport CO. v. State of U.P*, AIR 1986 SC 1099; (1986) 2 SCC 486 case, it is stated by the Supreme Court that 'A presumption is not itself evidence but only makes a prima facie case for party in whose favour it exists. It is a rule concerning evidence. It indicates the person on whom the burden of proof lies. When presumption is conclusive, it obviates the production of any other evidence to dislodge the conclusion to be drawn on proof of certain facts. But when it is rebuttable it only points out the party on whom lies the duty of going forward with evidence on the fact presumed, and when that party has produced evidence fairly and reasonably tending to show that the real fact is not as presumed the purpose of presumption is over. Then the evidence will determine the true nature of the fact to be established. The rules of presumption are deduced from enlightened human knowledge and experience and are drawn from the connection, relation and coincidence of facts, and circumstances' [para 14 of (1986) 2 SCC 486].

> 'Whenever it is directed by this Act that the Court shall presume (emphasis added) a fact, it shall regard such fact as proved, unless and until it is disproved.'

This lays down the rule of *rebuttable presumption* and the same has been so understood by the courts in India. In the *Sodhi Transport CO*[95] case, the Supreme Court highlighted this point by stating that

> '[t]he words 'shall presume' require the court to draw a presumption... unless the fact is disproved. They contain a rule of rebuttable presumption. These words i.e. 'shall presume' are being used in Indian judicial lore for over a century to convey that they lay down a rebuttable presumption in respect of matters with reference to which they are used...'.[96]

This discussion leaves no doubt that a cartel under section 3 (3) read with section 2 (c) of the Act is treated in the same manner as under the MRTP Act, 1969. The statement may appear contradictory to the previous assertion but it is not so. As stated previously, under the Act, a cartel is definitely *per se* void, in contra-distinction to the MRTP Act, 1969. The *rebuttable presumption* however mandates that the cartelists will have to be given a chance to disprove the *presumption* of *appreciable adverse effect* on competition. Consequently, the CCI will have to take into account factors which may go on to disprove its *presumption.* This is in contrast to the *per se* approach that was developed by the US Supreme Court vis-à-vis cartels. In the *Socony-Vacuum Oil Co.*[97] case, for example, Justice Douglas of the US Supreme Court declared that

> '...this Court has consistently and without deviation adhered to the principle that price-fixing agreements are unlawful per se (emphasis applied) under the Sherman Act and that no showing of so-called competitive abuses or evils which those agreements were designed to eliminate or alleviate may be interposed as a defense'.[98]

The Indian law however has no option but to provide a list of justification or defences which the cartels could use to escape section 3 (2). Section 19 (3) of the Act provides the so-called defence list. A perusal of this list may cause *déjà vu* as one may be reminded of the section 38 (1) gateway clauses or public interest defences, under the MRTP Act, 1969. The only difference being that the section 19 (3) defences are worded more specifically, identifying the specific pro-competitive concerns that have to be established by a cartel.

---

95 *Id.*

96 *Id.*, 495, para 12.

97 310 US 150 (n 94 of Chapter 3).

98 *Id.*, 218.

According to section 19 (3), the defences available to a cartel are the following: (a) that the cartel agreement does not create barriers to new entrants in the market; (b) that the cartel agreement does not drive existing competitors out of the market; (c) that the cartel agreement does not foreclose competition by hindering entry into the market; (d) that the cartel agreement accrues benefits to the consumers; (e) that the cartel agreement leads to improvements in production or distribution of goods or provision of services; (f) that the cartel agreement leads to promotion of technical, scientific and economic development by means of production or distribution of goods or provision of services.[99] The import of the said sub-section is that the CCI

> 'shall, while determining whether an agreement has an appreciable adverse effect on competition under section 3, have due regard to all or any'[100]

of the stated defences. This defence provision of the Act on the face of it may be compared to the EU Article 101, clause 3. As discussed, Article 101, clause 3 dispenses with the applicability of Article 101, clause 1 if a cartel is able to prove that it contributes in improving production or distribution of goods; promotes technical or economic progress, while allowing the consumer a fair share of the resulting benefits and does not impose on the undertakings concerned restrictions which are not indispensable to the attainment of the stated pro-competitive objectives and does not afford such undertakings the possibility of eliminating competition in respect to a substantial part of the products in question.[101] Further, as already discussed, all the conditions viz. both positive assertions and negative assertions, will have to be satisfied before a cartel can get the benefit of Article 101, clause 3. This makes it next to impossible for a cartel to get away with any defence.[102]

The defence provision of the Act, viz., section 19 (3) however is less stringent on the issue of burden of proof. It provides a convenient escape route for the cartel as it does not mandate the CCI to take into account all the defenses cumulatively. The cartel can thus prove any one of the stated criteria in its defense and expect to be let off by the CCI. [103] Since the word used

---

[99] The Act (n 68) section 19 (3).

[100] *Id.*, section 19 (3).

[101] 101 clause 3 (n 79 of Chapter 4).

[102] As a cartel will fail on the ground of proving fair share to consumers.

[103] See Aditya Bhattacharjea, 'India's Competition Policy: An Assessment', *EPW*, 3561–3574 (August 23, 2003) 38:34. The author notes that the 'It is…not clear whether they [the 19 (3) defenses] can override section 3 [of the Act] according to which certain "hard-core" cartel agreements are presumed to have an adverse effect on competition, which would

in sub-section 3 of section 19 is 'regard to all *or* any', the intent conveyed is that of a choice to be made by CCI. This is so because the usage of the word *or* is normally read as disjunctive unless the legislative intent is to the contrary. The reference to the legislative intent is an important tool for the purpose of interpreting a statute. This is because the intention of the statute maker will help clarify the true meaning or the legal meaning of the words, which are capable of more than one meaning. It is essentially a fiction created by judges so as to interpret the statue in accordance with its letter and spirit. One of the best ways to determine this fictional intent is to refer to the words used in the statute concerned. Thereafter, the next best option is to refer to the objective and purpose of the statute. If one looks at the long title of the Act, it reads as

> 'An Act to provide, keeping in view of the economic development of the country, for the establishment of a Commission to prevent practices having adverse effect on competition, to promote and sustain competition in markets, to protect the interests of consumers and to ensure freedom of trade carried on by other participants in markets, in India, and for matters connected therewith or incidental thereto'.[104]

This indicates the objective and reasons for which the Act was passed, i.e., to promote competition, to protect consumer interests and to ensure that all anti-competitive practices are prevented. Moving further, section 3 (1) clearly prohibits the formation of any agreement *'which causes or is likely to cause an appreciable adverse effect'* on competition within India. The legislative intent that one can thus derive by reading the long title and section 3 (1) is that all agreements that have appreciable adverse effect on competition are to be prohibited.

On the other hand, the list that section 19 (3) provides has both negative and positive defences. Of the six defences available, the first three would require a cartel to prove that (a) no entry barrier has been created for new entrants in the market; (b) that existing competitors are not driven out and (c) there is no foreclosure of competition by hindering entry into the market.[105] Each of these three defences has a bearing on consumer interests

make such agreements illegal per se. In short, the door has once again been kept wide open to subjective case-by-case interpretations'. [3566–3567] The author alludes to the practice prevailing under MRTP, as discussed above. This case-by-case assessment, according to the author is similar to the rule of reason analyses of cartel agreements, as practiced under the MRTP Act, 1969.

[104] The Act (n 68), the Preamble/long title.

[105] These three are thus the negative defences or outcome which has to be ruled out by the cartel in order to rebut the presumption of appreciable adverse effect.

and the competition process. The usage of *or* means that the CCI will not be required to take a holistic approach and could end up ignoring more than one crucial indicator for assessing the cartels' effect on competition and consumer interest. Similarly, looking into the positive defences[106] that the cartel will have to prove, one can safely conclude that here too there is the danger of missing out on a holistic approach, which will harm consumer interest.[107]If one goes through the Raghavan Committee report, it can be seen that the emphasis is on the fact that competition is needed to protect consumer interest. Even if one argues that a competition law is also to ensure free trade in the market and should have many other objectives, it still does not explain how the CCI can assess appreciable effect on competition by ignoring all but the one criteria mentioned in section 19 (3). As the Act especially mentions protection of consumer interests as one of its objectives, it is pertinent that cartels are not allowed any gateways. According to section 18 of the Act, the CCI is duty bound

> 'to eliminate practices having adverse effect on competition, promote and sustain competition, protect the interests of consumers and ensure freedom of trade carried on by other participants, in markets in India…'.[108]

The protection of consumer interests as one of the primary goals of the Act forms an integral part of both its long title as well as its provisions. The usage of the word *or* in section 19 (3) will however defeat both the letter and the spirit of the Act and make the anti-cartel provisions ineffective. Adding to this interpretational problem is the ambiguity of the words *'appreciable adverse effect on competition'*. If one revisits section 3 (1) and (3), it says that a cartel *presumed to have appreciable adverse effect on competition* is void. Further, as noted in section 19 (3), CCI has to determine the existence of *appreciable*

---

[106] The positive criteria that a cartel has to prove are: (d) accrual of benefits to consumers; (e) improvements in production or distribution of goods or provision of services; (f) promotion of technical, scientific and economic development by means of production or distribution of goods or provision of services.

[107] See for example, Subhadip Ghosh and Thomas W Ross, 'The Competition (Amendment) Bill 2007: A Review and Critique', *EPW*, 35-40. (December 20, 2008) 43:51 Commenting on the section 19, sub-section 3 defences, the authors note that 'It is certainly not obvious to us how this…provision might apply to what would otherwise be (nearly) per se prohibitions in Section 3 (3). …[I]t seems the cartels may only have to show some efficiency, not that the efficiency gains must be 'greater than' the anti-competitive costs of say, price fixing. It would of course be unfortunate if small efficiencies (even if genuine) were allowed to exempt an agreement with large anti-competitive effects'. [on page 38]

[108] The Act (n 68) section 18.

adverse effect on competition by taking into account the criteria mentioned therein. The reading of section 3 (3) and section 19 (3) together raises the question as to what amounts to an *appreciable adverse effect on competition.* This is so because under the Act, to sue a cartel, one has not only to prove the existence of an agreement[109] but also that the same involves a conduct which is *presumed to have an appreciable adverse effect* on competition. As discussed above, the mere *presumption* of appreciable adverse effect may help CCI to treat the matter as a *prima facie* case of anti-competitive practice but to penalize the cartel and disband it, CCI would need to counter the section 19 sub-section 3 defences. CCI can do so only when it is able to establish *appreciable adverse effect on competition.*

One may refer to the EU competition law where this term, viz., '*appreciable adverse effect on competition*' has been subject to interpretation. The European Court of Justice held that

> 'an agreement falls outside the prohibition in [Article 101 clause 1] when it has only an insignificant effect on the markets, taking into account the weak position which the persons concerned have on the market of the product in question'.[110]

This came to be known as the *de minimis* doctrine and has led the EU Competition Commission to issue *de minimis* notices, the latest being of 2001. In this notice, the EU Competition Commission quantified, with the help of market share thresholds, what is not an appreciable restriction of competition under Article 101, clause 1 of the EU Competition law.[111] It draws a distinction between horizontal agreements and vertical agreements. Accordingly, for horizontal agreements/agreements between competitors, the threshold requirement is ten per cent of the relevant market. For vertical

---

[109] *Id.*, section 2 (b) defines agreement as one which 'includes any arrangement or understanding or action in concert,— (i) whether or not, such arrangement, understanding or action is formal or in writing; or (ii) whether or not such arrangement, understanding or action is intended to be enforceable by legal proceedings'.

[110] See Case 5/69, *Franz Volk v. S.P.R.L. Ets J. Vervaecke* [1969] ECR 295. It is important to note that Article 101, clause 1 does not, in the text, require that the effect on competition should be appreciable. This is in contrast to the Act which prescribes determination of appreciable adverse effect on competition as the main criteria.

[111] See [2001] OJ C368/13, 'Commission Notice on agreements of minor importance which do not appreciably restrict competition under [Article 101 clause (1)] of the Treaty establishing the European Community (deminimis)', http://eurlex.europa.eu/LexUriServ/LexUriServ.do?uri=OJ:C:2001:368:0013:0015:EN:PDF (accessed 18 June 2011). This can help in understanding how the CCI/Competition Appellate Tribunal or the Supreme Court should read the term '*appreciable adverse effect*'.

agreements/agreements between non-competitors, the threshold is fifteen per cent of the relevant market.[112] Thus, horizontal agreements or agreements between competitors are treated more stringently. This is substantiated by the fact that hard core restraints like cartels are not exempted from the applicability of Article 101, clause 1 by the *de minimis* notice.[113]

This non-inclusion of cartels is also related to the fact that cartels are regarded as those anti-competitive agreements which have as their *object* the restriction of competition. The need to determine the *effect* of a cartel agreement is therefore not present under the EU Competition law. On the other hand, under the Act, since the anti-cartel law is *effect* based, the CCI will have to come up with specific guidelines regarding the threshold limit or any other criteria that will be the reference point to determine *appreciable adverse effect on competition*. One important factor that the guidelines will have to take note of will be the concept of a relevant market. In the Act, section 2 (r) defines a relevant market and section 2 (s) and section 2 (t) define the relevant geographic market and relevant product market, respectively. It essentially explains the method of identifying the product or the area which would be affected by cartelization. This entails detailed economic analyses with the purpose of identifying the product or services which

> 'are such close substitutes for one another that they operate as a competitive constraint on the behaviour of the suppliers or those respective products and services.'[114]

In other words, the test of relevant product market or geographical market has been developed in order to determine the extent to which consumers will be deprived of choices if the relevant market is cartelized.

For example, the Act defines relevant product market as

> 'a market comprising all those products or services which are regarded as interchangeable or substitutable by the consumer, by reason of characteristics of the products or services, their prices and intended use'[115].

---

112 *Id.*, para 7.

113 [2001] OJ C368/13 (n 111) para 11 clause 1 which lays down that the deminimis notice will not apply 'as regards agreements between competitors as defined in point 7, restrictions which, directly or indirectly, in isolation or in combination with other factors under the control of the parties, have as their object (a) the fixing of prices when selling the products to third parties; (b) the limitation of output or sales; (c) the allocation of markets or customers'.

114 Alison Jones and Brenda Sufrin (n 42) 63.

115 The Act (n 68) section 2 (t).

This definition is similar to the one adopted by the European Competition Commission, as evident from its notice on the definition of relevant market.[116] The definition of the relevant geographic market given in the Act is also similar to the one given in the EU notice.[117] Accordingly, like the EU notice, the Act too appears to focus on the demand-side substitution, i.e., the substitutability of the concerned product or availability of alternate suppliers of the concerned product from the perspective of consumers.[118]

This determination of demand-side substitutability is measured by a test called the small but significant non-transitory increase in price test (hereinafter called the SSNIP test). As Whish explains

> 'suppose that a producer of a product—for example a widget—were to introduce a Small but Significant Non-transitory Increase in Price. In those circumstances, would enough customers be inclined to switch

[116] See [1997] OJ C372/5, 'Commission Notice on the definition of relevant market for the purposes of Community competition law', http://eur-lex.europa.eu/LexUriServ/LexUriServ.do?uri=CELEX:31997Y1209(01):EN:HTML (accessed 20 June 2011). The relevant product market has been defined therein as 'A relevant product market comprises all those products and/or services which are regarded as interchangeable or substitutable by the consumer, by reason of the products' characteristics, their prices and their intended use'.

[117] The Act (n 68) section 2 (s) defines relevant geographic market as 'a market comprising the area in which the conditions of competition for supply of goods or provision of services or demand of goods or services are distinctly homogenous and can be distinguished from the conditions prevailing in the neighbouring areas'. The definition of relevant geographical market given in the EU Competition Commission notice is 'The relevant geographic market comprises the area in which the undertakings concerned are involved in the supply and demand of products or services, in which the conditions of competition are sufficiently homogeneous and which can be distinguished from neighbouring areas because the conditions of competition are appreciably different in those area'. See [1997] OJ C372/5 (n 116) para. 8

[118] *Id.*, para 13 wherein it is stated by the EU Competition Commission that 'Firms are subject to three main sources or competitive constraints: demand substitutability, supply substitutability and potential competition. From an economic point of view, for the definition of the relevant market, demand substitution constitutes the most immediate and effective disciplinary force on the suppliers of a given product, in particular in relation to their pricing decisions. A firm or a group of firms cannot have a significant impact on the prevailing conditions of sale, such as prices, if its customers are in a position to switch easily to available substitute products or to suppliers located elsewhere. Basically, the exercise of market definition consists in identifying the effective alternative sources of supply for the customers of the undertakings involved, in terms both of products/services and of geographic location of suppliers'.

> their purchases to other makes of widgets, or indeed even to blodgets, to make the price rise unprofitable? If the answer is yes, this would suggest that the market is at least as wide as widgets generally and includes blodgets as well. The same test can be applied to the delineation of the geographic market: if the price of widgets were to be raised in France by a small but significant amount, would customers switch to suppliers in Germany? If a firm could raise its price by a significant amount and retain its customers, this would mean that the market would be worth monopolizing: price could be raised profitably, since there would be no competitive constraint'.[119]

However, as the EU notice mentions, in certain situations, the supply-side substitutability need to be taken as criteria for defining the relevant market.[120] The Act in section 19 (6) and section 19 (7) lays down the factors which need to be taken into account for defining the relevant market.[121] The listed factors indicate a combined approach that takes into account both the demand-side substitution and the supply-side substitution. The difference in the definition of relevant product market under section 2 (t) and the factors prescribed under section 19 (7) creates an ambiguity as to when the supply-side substitutability should be taken into account.[122] This ambiguity in the context of anti-cartel measures can lead to a problem when framing guidelines to determine the question of *appreciable adverse effect on competition.*

---

119 Richard Whish (n 4 of Chapter 1) 30.

120 [1997] OJ C372/5 (n 116) para. 20. The EU Competition Commission notes that 'Supply-side substitutability may also be taken into account when defining markets in those situations in which its effects are equivalent to those of demand substitution in terms of effectiveness and immediacy. This means that suppliers are able to switch production to the relevant products and market them in the short term (4) without incurring significant additional costs or risks in response to small and permanent changes in relative prices. When these conditions are met, the additional production that is put on the market will have a disciplinary effect on the competitive behaviour of the companies involved. Such an impact in terms of effectiveness and immediacy is equivalent to the demand substitution effect.'

121 The Act (n 68) [section 19 (6) 'The Commission shall, while determining the "relevant geographic market", have due regard to all or any of the following factors, namely:—(a) regulatory trade barriers;(b) local specification requirements;(c) national procurement policies;(d) adequate distribution facilities;(e) transport costs;(f) language;(g) consumer preferences;(h) need for secure or regular supplies or rapid after-sales services'. Section 19 (7) 'The Commission shall, while determining the "relevant product market", have due regard to all or any of the following factors, namely:—(a) physical characteristics or end-use of goods;(b) price of goods or service;(c) consumer preferences;(d) exclusion of in-house production;(e) existence of specialised producers;(f) classification of industrial products'.].

122 Shiju Varghese Mazhuvanchery (n 9 of Chapter 5) 257–258.

As the Act insists on an *effect*-based approach to cartel, the concept of *appreciable adverse effect on competition* has to be clarified. Going by the EU example, market threshold analysis is one method of identifying adverse effect. The definition of relevant market has to be unambiguous. Jones and Sufrin argue that where market share thresholds are used to determine the *effect* on competition, exclusion of supply-side substitution would lead to a narrow construction of the relevant market. This in turn will lead to an incorrect *effect*-based analysis, as the producers or parties to an agreement may be considered to have too large a share of a narrower market. In contrast, the inclusion of supply-side substitution will enable the enlargement of the relevant market and help exclude non-cartel or non anti-competitive agreements.[123] It is important for the CCI to have a proper assessment of all the issues requisite for a positive determination of cartel and subsequent actions. Otherwise like the MRTP Commission, CCI too will draw flak from the Supreme Court, as was seen in the *Haridas case*.[124]

Another glaring problem that will harm consumer interest and help cartels is the lack of exemptions for small-scale industries. According to the Raghavan Committee report, there should be few exemptions. However, it was also emphasized that any exemptions within the Competition law should be pre-decided on the basis of proper policy considerations.[125] Unfortunately, the Act misses out on creating the important exemptions that would be needed, apart from everything else, to ensure benefits to the consumer. The lack of exemptions to agreements entered into by small enterprises or industries also means that the CCI will have to evaluate all agreements on a case-by-case basis, keeping in mind the section 19 (3) criteria.[126] As discussed above, proving those criteria, along with rebutting the *per se void* presumption of section 3 (3) would require extensive legal and economic analysis. A small-scale enterprise will be comparatively at a disadvantageous position vis-à-vis a large enterprise on providing effective defence. Consequently, agreements which in the long run would benefit consumers are in danger of being regarded as anti-competitive. In contrast, cartels, entered into by big business, may escape the prohibition of the Act through means of effective defence. This possibility is more likely to occur at the initial stages where both the small-scale enterprises and the CCI are taking baby steps towards working and interpreting the Act.

[123] Alison Jones and Brenda Sufrin (n 42 of Chapter 4) 77.

[124] *Haridas Exports* (n 100 of Chapter 5).

[125] S.V.S. Raghavan Committee Report (n 26 of Chapter 1) 30, para 4.1.6.

[126] Aditya Bhattacharjea (n 103) 3570 [herein Aditya Bhattacharjea noted the problem of lack of exemption for small-scale industries]. See Shiju Varghese Mazhuvanchery (n 9 of Chapter 5) 256–257.

It is interesting to note that even those exemptions which were part of the old Act, viz., the MRTP Act, 1969[127] has been done away with. The best example of this is the lack of trade union exemption and exemptions for other types of collective bargaining agreements.[128] Furthermore, exempting the 'efficiency' increasing joint ventures from the applicability of section 3 (3) is problematic. Such narrow categorization ignores other types of business arrangements which could be equally beneficial to consumers. It may also be noted that while there may be an argument supporting the tendency for fewer exemptions in the new competition law regimes[129], the same does not apply to India. Khemani, for example, argues that the tendency to have fewer exemptions in the new competition law regimes

> 'could be reflective of the fact that in many of the less developed countries, effective implementation of competition law has yet to take place. And various businesses are likely to be still unaware of the potential impact competition law can have on their economic activities, and lobbying for exclusions from the application of competition law may yet take place'.[130]

In the case of India, this argument is discounted by the fact that India had the MRTP Act, 1969. From 1970 onwards, therefore, India experienced a competition law regime irrespective of the fact that the political philosophy governing the same was different from the Act. This is in contradistinction with many regimes who are experimenting with competition law for the first time or are still contemplating experimenting with one in the future.[131] Hence it is but natural to expect that the 2002 Act would have been a more evolved response to specific concerns having a bearing on consumer interest.

---

[127] See Section 3 of the MRTP Act, 1969.

[128] This is a problematic area as well, though it is beyond the scope of the present discussion. For an understanding of the lack of labour exemption and consequential problems under the Competition Act, 2002, see generally, PraachiMisra and M.P. Ram Mohan, 'Competition Law and Policy, The Changing Market Structure and the Consequences for the Labour Force: A Perspective from India', http://www.competition-regulation.org.uk/conferences/southafrica04/misra.pdf (accessed 22 May 2011).

[129] See for example R. ShyamKhemani (n 5 of Chapter 1) 155–165.

[130] *Id.,* at 155.

[131] See for example Mark Williams, *Competition Policy and Law in China, Hong Kong and Taiwan,* (Cambridge, 2005), 153–221 and 271–300. The author discusses the dilemma that China and Hong Kong are going through in the process of adopting a new competition law for their jurisdiction. While China had its own version of a competition law since 1993, Hong Kong continues to dither on adoption of a competition law for itself, though it has introduced sector-specific regulations relating to anti-competitive practices.

The approach of the Act also ignores the fact that there was a representation from the small industries to the Raghavan Committee identifying the need for exemptions from the application of the competition law.[132]

The lack of specific exemption is also contrary to the argument of Dr S. Chakravarthy who in his supplementary note had argued for accommodation of the needs of the Indian economy—one recommendation made for enabling this accommodation was providing exemption to the small industries for a limited period of time.[133] As noted above, similar accommodations with regard to business arrangements, apart from joint ventures, was needed for the benefit of both the Indian economy and Indian consumers. An example of such accommodation can be found in both the US and the EU competition law. While in the US, the judiciary has contributed to the creation of the anti-trust or competition law exemption[134] in the EU it is the EU Competition Commission which issues notices and guidelines to block exemptions of

---

[132] S.V.S Raghavan Committee Report (n 26 of Chapter 1) 93–96 ['Letter from Federation Of Associations Of Small Industries Of India', addressed to Mr Raghavan by Mr V.S. Narasimhan, President Federation of Associations of Small Industries of India. The letter pointed out that 'small scale industries are entrepreneur oriented and hence fiercely competitive. Thus they can never indulge in cartelization. Further since they operate on the basis of product quality and reasonable price, hence they have no incentive to cartelize or indulge in any other anti-competitive practices. Further since the owners are primarily self-employed hence the survival instinct dictates their competitive spirit. This ensures that they have no incentive to cooperate or cartelize. These were the arguments proffered for promoting small scale industries and continuing with their reservations'.]

[133] *Id.*, 84.

[134] Take for example the Sports Broadcasting Act, US Code Title 15, Chapter 32 (15 USC. 32, which was passed by the US Congress on the demand of the NFL (National Football League), whose attempt at collective selling of the sports broadcasting rights were nullified by the US courts as being anti-competitive. To quote from Section 1291of the Sports Broadcasting Act, 'The antitrust laws, as defined in section 1 of the Act of October 15,1914, as amended (38 Stat. 730) [15 USC. 12], or in the Federal Trade Commission Act, as amended (38 Stat. 717) (IS USG. 41 et esq.,) shall not apply to any joint agreement by or among persons engaging in or conducting the organized professional team sports of football, baseball, basketball, or hockey, by which any league of clubs participating in professional football, baseball, basketball, or hockey contests sells or otherwise transfers all or any part of the rights of such league's member clubs in the sponsored telecasting of the games of football, baseball, basketball, or hockey, as the case may be, engaged in or conducted by such clubs. In addition, such laws shall not apply to a joint agreement by which the member clubs of two or more professional football leagues, which are exempt from income tax under section 501(c)(6) of the Internal Revenue Code of 1986 {26 USC. 501 (c)(6)J, combine their operations in expanded single league so exempt from income tax, if such agreement increases rather than decreases the number of professional football clubs so operating, and the provisions of which are directly relevant thereto'. See also R. Shyam Khemani (n 13 of Chapter 2).

certain types of horizontal cooperative agreements, that are not cartels.[135] Thus the EU Competition Commission has issued revised guidelines on the applicability of Article 101 to horizontal cooperation agreements on January 14, 2011.[136] The purpose of these guidelines, as stated in its purpose and scope is

> 'to provide an analytical framework for the most common types of horizontal co-operation agreements; they deal with research and development agreements, production agreements including subcontracting and specialisation agreements, purchasing agreements, commercialisation agreements, standardisation agreements including standard contracts, and information exchange'.[137]

Thus joint ventures for the purpose of research and development are not the only types of agreements that can benefit the consumer.

Finally, reference to section 54[138] of the Act does not help the problem relating to lack of specific exemptions. The section has laid down a narrow sphere within which the central government may decide to exempt the application of the Act. The criteria for granting exemption have been stated as: public interest or security of the state; obligations under international treaty (both multilateral like WTO and bilateral) and enterprise performing sovereign functions. This leaves no scope for creating exemptions for small-scale industries or horizontal cooperation agreements which are beneficial for consumers. The central government can grant exemption to small-scale industries by invoking the public interest grounds.[139] However, as seen in the

---

135 Alison Jones and Brenda Sufrin (n 42 of Chapter 4) 983.

136 [2011] OJ C11/1 (n 12 of Chapter 2) These guidelines replaced [2001] OJ C3/2 guidelines.

137 *Id.*, para 5.

138 The Act (n 68) section 54 which states that 'The Central Government may, by notification, exempt from the application of this Act, or any provision thereof, and for such period as it may specify in such notification—(a) any class of enterprises if such exemption is necessary in the interest of security of the State or public interest;(b) any practice or agreement arising out of and in accordance with any obligation assumed by India under any treaty, agreement or convention with any other country or countries;(c) any enterprise which performs a sovereign function on behalf of the Central Government or a State Government: Provided that in case an enterprise is engaged in any activity including the activity relatable to the sovereign functions of the Government, the Central Government may grant exemption only in respect of activity relatable to the sovereign functions'.

139 This is so because only enterprises can be granted exemption on the basis of public interest/ security of the state. Hence cooperation agreements, whether vertical or horizontal, are ruled out. This is clear from section 2 (h) of the Act which defines enterprise. As is evident,

MRTP cases, the concept of public interest itself is ambiguous. Interestingly, the central government will be forced to exempt a horizontal cooperation agreement under its international obligations. It cannot however do so in view of its domestic compulsion. With all the drawbacks that the Act has vis-à-vis the anti-cartel provisions, it remains to be seen how the CCI has been interpreting these provisions. An assessment of CCI's approach may be helpful in understanding its pro-consumer concerns. Admittedly, as the enforcer of the Act, CCI's role in promoting consumer interest while enforcing anti-cartel provisions will be crucial. In this regard, it has also to be seen how the procedural requirements of the Act have improved upon the MRTP Act, 1969 enabling smoother operations. In addition, the penal provisions or the cost imposed on cartels are equally crucial for the Act to have a deterrent effect. As seen in the case of the MRTP Act, 1969, cease and desist orders hardly made any impression on potential cartelists. In other words, effective procedural and penal provisions might help CCI and the other forums to override the glaring lacuna of the substantive provisions. A review of these procedural provisions will help in understanding the effectiveness of CCI in dealing with cartels and other issues.

CCI: Hierarchy

As discussed before, the CCI became fully operational from the year 2009, making rules and regulations concerning its operations.[140] The CCI comprises

---

the definition does not include agreements between enterprises. For a critical analyses of the anti-cartel provision under the Act, see Aditya Bhattacharjea, 'India's New Competition Law: A Comparative Assessment', *J. Competition L. & Econ.* 609 (September 2008) 4: 628–629.

[140] The CCI is empowered under Section 64 of the Act to make regulations for the purpose of performing its duties under the Act. The regulation so made however will have to be approved by the Parliament, and any alteration or annulment made to such a regulation by the Parliament shall have effect prospectively. The Act (n 68) section 64 states that 'Power to make regulations- (1) The Commission may, by notification, make regulations consistent with this Actand the rules made thereunder to carry out the purposes of this Act. (2) In particular, and without prejudice to the generality of the foregoing provisions,such regulations may provide for all or any of the following matters, namely:—(a) the cost of production to be determined under clause (b) of the Explanation to section 4;(b) the form of notice as may be specified and the fee which may be determined under sub-section (2) of section 6;(c) the form in which details of the acquisition shall be filed under subsection (5) of Section 6;(d) the procedures to be followed for engaging the experts and professionals under sub-section (3) of section 17;(e) the fee which may be determined under clause (a) of sub-section (1) of section 19;(f) the rules of procedure in regard to the transaction of

a chairperson and a maximum of six members.[141] The appointment of the chairperson and the members are made by the central government, on the recommendation of a Selection Committee.[142] The Selection Committee comprises the Chief Justice of India or his nominee along with four other members. Of the four members, two are central government nominees, viz., Secretary, Ministry of Corporate Affairs and Secretary, Ministry of Law and Justice. The other two have to be professional experts in the field of commercial law, international trade and economics or competition law and policy. The chairperson and the members are also required to have professional experience and special knowledge in the field of competition law and advocacy or commercial law, international trade and economics.[143] They are appointed for a period of five years, with the provision of

---

business at the meetings of the Commission under sub-section (1) of section 22;(g) the manner in which penalty shall be recovered under sub-section (1) of section 39;(h) any other matter in respect of which provision is to be, or may be, made by regulations.(3) Every regulation made under this Act shall be laid, as soon as may be after it is made, before each House of Parliament, while it is in session, for a total period of thirty days which may be comprised in one session or in two or more successive sessions, and if, before the expiry of the session immediately following the session or the successive sessions aforesaid, both Houses agree in making any modification in the regulation, or both Houses agree that the regulation should not be made, the regulation shall thereafter have effect only in such modified form or be of no effect, as the case may be; so, however, that any such modification or annulment shall be without prejudice to the validity of anything previously done under that regulation'.

141 The Act (n 68) section 8 (1) states that 'The Commission shall consist of a Chairperson and not less than two and not more than six other Members to be appointed by the Central Government'.

142 *Id.,* section 9 (1): 'The Chairperson and other Members of the Commission shall be appointed by the Central Government from a panel of names recommended by a Selection Committee consisting of–a) the Chief Justice of India or his nominee ---- Chairperson; b) the Secretary in the Ministry of Corporate Affairs ---- Member; c) the Secretary in the Ministry of Law and Justice ---- Member; d) two experts of repute who have special knowledge ---- Members. of, and professional experience in international trade, economics, business, commerce, law, finance, accountancy, management, industry, public affairs or competition matters including competition law and policy'.

143 *Id.* section 8 (2): 'The Chairperson and every other Member shall be a person of ability, integrity and standing and who has special knowledge of, and such professional experience of not less than fifteen years in, international trade, economics, business, commerce, law, finance, accountancy, management, industry, public affairs or competition matters, including competition law and policy, which in the opinion of the Central Government, may be useful to the Commission'.

re-appointment.[144] In order to safeguard the integrity of the CCI, the chairperson and the members are barred from taking up employment in any company/enterprise that has been party to any anti-competitive proceedings before the CCI. This bar is to remain in force for a period of two years from the date the chairperson or the members cease to be in office.[145] The Act also provides for the appointment of a Director-General to assist the CCI in conducting inquiries and other functions.[146] The Act also makes provision for the appointment of Additional, Joint, Deputy or Assistant Director-General, who will be subject to the control, supervision and direction of the Director-General.[147] From the preceding discussion, it is evident that the Act has ignored the recommendation of the Raghavan Committee for having multiple benches of the CCI. The provisions in the Act are made for just one centrally headquartered multi-member CCI.[148]

The Act also empowers the CCI to engage experts and professionals to assist it in effective implementation of the Act. Accordingly, the CCI issued regulations describing the modalities for engaging professional and experts.[149] The person has to have knowledge in economics, law, business

[144] *Id.* section 10 (1): 'The Chairperson and every other Member shall hold office as such for a term of five years from the date on which he enters upon his office and shall be eligible for re-appointment: [Provided that the Chairperson or other Members shall not hold office as such after he has attained the age of sixty-five years]'.

[145] *Id.* section 12 states that 'The Chairperson and other Members shall not, for a period of 2 [two years] from the date on which they cease to hold office, accept any employment in, or connected with the management or administration of, any enterprise which has been a party to a proceeding before the Commission under this Act: Provided that nothing contained in this section shall apply to any employment under the Central Government or a State Government or local authority or in any statutory authority or any corporation established by or under any Central, State or Provincial Act or a Government company as defined in section 617 of the Companies Act, 1956 (1 of 1956)'.

[146] *Id.,* section 16 (1) states: 'The Central Government may, by notification, appoint a Director General for the purposes of assisting the Commission in conducting inquiry into contravention of any of the provisions of this Act and for performing such other functions as are, or may be provided by or under this Act'.

[147] *Id.,* section 16 (1A) states: 'The number of other Additional, Joint, Deputy or Assistant Directors General or such officers or other employees in the office of Director General and the manner of appointment of such Additional, Joint, Deputy or Assistant Directors General or such officers or other employees shall be such as may be prescribed'. Further section 16, sub-section 2 states: 'Every Additional, Joint, Deputy and Assistant Directors General or such officers or other employees, shall exercise his powers, and discharge his functions, subject to the general control, supervision and direction of the Director General'.

[148] S.V.S. Raghavan Committee Report (n 26 of Chapter 1) 6.2.4, 6.2.5 and 6.2.6.

[149] See the Competition Commission of India (Procedure for Engagement of Experts and Professionals) Regulations, 2009,

or any other area related to competition.[150] Apart from this, the Act makes provision for inter-regulatory coordination, i.e., coordination between the CCI and other sectoral regulators.[151] Both the CCI and the other sectoral regulators can decide to refer such questions which require the determination of questions specific to their area of regulation. For example, if the CCI in the course of its proceedings comes across an issue that involves matter pertaining to telecommunication, the same question or issue may be referred to the Telecom Regulatory Authority of India (TRAI) for determination.[152]

---

http://www.cci.gov.in/images/media/Regulations/engagement.pdf?phpMyAdmin=NMPFRahGKYeum5F74Ppstn7Rf00 (accessed June 23, 2011).

[150] The Act (n 68) section 17 (3) states: 'The Commission may engage, in accordance with the procedure specified by regulations, such number of experts and professionals of integrity and outstanding ability, who have special knowledge of, and experience in, economics, law, business or such other disciplines related to competition, as it deems necessary to assist the Commission in the discharge of its functions under this Act'.

[151] *Id.,* section 21 states: 'Reference by statutory authority- (1) Where in the course of a proceeding before any statutory authority an issue israised by any party that any decision which such statutory authority has taken orproposes to take is or would be, contrary to any of the provisions of this Act, thensuch statutory authority may make a reference in respect of such issue to theCommission:Provided that any statutory authority, may, suomotu, make such a reference to the Commission. (2) On receipt of a reference under sub-section (1), the Commission shall give its opinion, within sixty days of receipt of such reference, to such statutory authority which shall consider the opinion of the Commission and thereafter, give its findings recording reasons therefor on the issues referred to in the said opinion'. Further section 21A states that: 'Reference by Commission- (1)Where in the course of a proceeding before the Commission an issue is raised by any party that any decision which, the Commission has taken during such proceeding or proposes to take, is or would be contrary to any provision of this Act whose implementation is entrusted to a statutory authority, then theCommission may make a reference in respect of such issue to the statutory authority:Provided that the Commission, may, suomotu, make such a reference to the statutory authority.(2) On receipt of a reference under sub-section (1), the statutory authority shall give its opinion, within sixty days of receipt of such reference, to the Commission which shall consider the opinion of the statutory authority, and thereafter give its findings recording reasons therefor on the issues referred to in the said opinion'.

[152] However there are problems regarding the issue of interface between CCI and sectoral regulators. See for example, Rahul Singh, 'The Teeter-Totter of Regulation and Competition: Why Indian Competition Authority must Trump Sectoral Regulators', 2007, http://www.cci.gov.in/images/media/completed/interface_sr_ca_20080508112129.pdf (accessed June 23, 2011). See also Amitabh Kumar, 'Relationship between Competition Authority and Sectoral Regulator', 2006, http://www.cci.gov.in/images/media/presentations/11lahore_25_26march06_20080410175442.pdf (accessed 23 June 2011). However a detailed analysis of these problems is beyond the scope of the present discussion.

Further, the Act equips the CCI with extra-territorial jurisdiction.[153] Any international cartel having appreciable adverse effect on competition in the relevant market in India will be subject to the jurisdiction of CCI.[154] The CCI also has the power to conduct advocacy programmes for the purpose of spreading awareness about competition-related issues.[155]

5.7.1 Acting against cartels: Procedural route

As far as cartels are concerned, the Act has empowered the CCI to *suo moto* start inquiry. In addition, inquiry into cartels can be taken up by the CCI on receipt of complaint by an individual consumer or their associations. Apart from this, trade associations or any other person can file a complaint with the CCI about cartel activities. Finally, inquiries into cartels can also be taken up by the CCI on a reference by the central, state or any other statutory body.[156] The provision is similar to section 10 of the MRTP Act, 1969, relating to restrictive trade practices.[157] The only difference being that

---

[153] Not part of the present discussion.

[154] The Act (n 68) Section 32: 'Acts taking place outside India but having an effect on competition in India-The Commission shall, notwithstanding that,—(a) an agreement referred to in section 3 has been entered into outside India; or (b) any party to such agreement is outside India; or (c) any enterprise abusing the dominant position is outside India; or (d) a combination has taken place outside India; or (e) any party to combination is outside India; or (f) any other matter or practice or action arising out of such agreement or dominant position or combination is outside India, have power to inquire in accordance with the provisions contained in sections 19, 20, 26, 29 and 30 of the Act into such agreement or abuse of dominant position or combination if such agreement or dominant position or combination has, or is likely to have, an appreciable adverse effect on competition in the relevant market in India and pass such orders as it may deem fit in accordance with the provisions of this Act'.

[155] *Id.* section 49 (3) states: 'The Commission shall take suitable measures for the promotion of competition advocacy, creating awareness and imparting training about competition issues'.

[156] *Id.* Section 19 (1) states that 'The Commission may inquire into any alleged contravention of the provisions contained in sub-section (1) of section 3 or sub-section (1) of section 4 either on its own motion or on—(a) receipt of any information, in such manner and] accompanied by such fee as may be determined by regulations, from any person, consumer or their association or trade association; or (b) a reference made to it by the Central Government or a State Government or a statutory authority'.

[157] See Section 10 (a) of the MRTP Act, 1969.['The Commission may inquire into-(a) any restrictive trade practice-(i) upon receiving a complaint of facts which constitute such practice from any trade association or from any consumer or a registered consumer's association, whether such consumer is a member of that consumer's association or not, or (ii) upon a reference made to it by the Central Government or a State Government, or (iii) upon an application made to it by the Director General or (iv) upon its own knowledge or information'].

the *suo moto* power of the CCI is across the board, and covers all types of anti-competitive agreements and mergers and amalgamation and abuses.[158] On being convinced that there exists a *prima facie* case of cartel, the CCI will direct the Director-General to investigate the matter.[159] The CCI can accordingly close the matter if it is not convinced of a *prima facie* case.[160] Once the Director-General receives direction to inquire and conduct investigations, it has to submit its report within the time frame prescribed by the CCI.[161] If the report of the Director-General gives a positive assessment supporting the CCI's preliminary opinion about the existence of cartel, the CCI will conduct further inquiries about the existence of the cartel.[162] If the Director-General's report comes up with negative findings as to the existence of a cartel, the CCI will call in for any objections or suggestions from the aggrieved parties.[163]

In this case, it can be the central or state government or private parties including consumers. After considering all the suggestions or recommendations, if the CCI agrees with the negative findings of the Director-General, it will close the matter passing necessary orders.[164] In case the CCI disagrees with the

---

158 This is evident from a perusal of Section 19 and 20 of the Act.

159 The Act (n 68) section 26 (1) states that 'On receipt of a reference from the Central Government or a State Government or a statutory authority or on its own knowledge or information received under section 19, if the Commission is of the opinion that there exists a prima facie case, it shall direct the Director General to cause an investigation to be made into the matter…'.

160 *Id.*, section 26 (2): 'Where on receipt of a reference from the Central Government or a State Government or a statutory authority or information received under section 19, the Commission is of the opinion that there exists no prima facie case, it shall close the matter forthwith and pass such orders as it deems fit and send a copy of its order to the Central Government or the State Government or the statutory authority or the parties concerned, as the case may be'.

161 *Id.*, section 26 (3) states that 'The Director General shall, on receipt of direction under sub-section (1), submit a report on his findings within such period as may be specified by the Commission'.

162 *Id.*, section 26 (8) states: 'If the report of the Director General referred to in sub-section (3) recommends that there is contravention of any of the provisions of this Act, and the Commission is of the opinion that further inquiry is called for, it shall inquire into such contravention in accordance with the provisions of this Act'.

163 *Id.*, section 26 (5) states: 'If the report of the Director General referred to in sub-section (3) recommends that there is no contravention of the provisions of this Act, the Commission shall invite objections or suggestions from the Central Government or the State Government or the statutory authority or the parties concerned, as the case may be, on such report of the Director General'.

164 *Id.*, section 26 (6) states: 'If, after consideration of the objections and suggestions referred to in sub-section (5), if any, the Commission agrees with the recommendation of the

findings of the Director-General, the CCI can require the Director-General to further investigate or inquire into the alleged cartel.[165] On the other hand, the CCI can itself decide to conduct inquiries into the matter without giving any directions to the Director-General.[166] In case of a positive finding as to the existence of cartels, on the completion of the inquiry, the CCI is empowered to pass either a cease and desist order or impose

> 'penalty of up to three times of its profit for each year of the continuance of such agreement or ten per cent of its turnover for each year of the continuance of such agreement, whichever is higher'.[167]

or impose both, viz., penalty and cease and desist order. In addition, contravention of these orders will attract additional fines.[168] Further, the Act confers on the CCI the same powers as that of a Civil Court. Powers like issuing summons, discovery and production of documents, evidence on affidavit et al. are available to the CCI.[169] However, unlike the MRTP

Director General, it shall close the matter forthwith and pass such orders as it deems fit and communicate its order to the Central Government or the State Government or the statutory authority or the parties concerned, as the case may be'.

[165] *Id.*, section 26 (7) states: 'If, after consideration of the objections or suggestions referred to in sub-section (5), if any, the Commission is of the opinion that further investigations is called for, it may direct further investigation in the matter by the Director General or cause further inquiry to be made by in the matter or itself proceed with further inquiry in the matter in accordance with the provisions of this Act'.

[166] *Id., See Competition Commission of India v. Steel Authority of India Ltd. and Anr*, MANU/SC/0690/201. Herein the Supreme Court of India interpreted section 26, section 33 and section 53A sub-section 1 of the Act to determine as to when the orders of the CCI are appealable to the Competition Appellate Tribunal. The Supreme Court held that 'the legislature in its wisdom, made only the order under Section 26(2) and 26(6) appealable under Section 53A of the Act. Thus, it specifically excludes the opinion/decision of the authority under Section 26(1) and even an order passed under Section 26(7) directing further inquiry, from being appealable before the Tribunal'.

[167] *Id.*, section 27 (a) and proviso to section 27 (b).

[168] *Id.*, section 42 (2): 'If any person, without reasonable clause, fails to comply with the orders or directions of the Commission issued under sections 27... of the Act, he shall be punishable with fine which may extend to rupees one lakh for each day during which such non-compliance occurs, subject to a maximum of rupees ten crore, as the Commission may determine'. In addition, the CompAT can also award compensation to a person injured by cartel activity according to section 42 A.

[169] *Id.*, section 36 (2) states: 'The Commission shall have, for the purposes of discharging its functions under this Act, the same powers as are vested in a Civil Court under the Code of Civil Procedure, 1908 (5 of 1908), while trying a suit, in respect of the following matters, namely:-(a) summoning and enforcing the attendance of any person and examining him on oath; (b) requiring the discovery and production of documents; (c) receiving evidence on affidavit; (d) issuing commissions for the examination of witnesses or documents; (e) requisitioning, subject to the provisions of sections 123 and 124 of the Indian Evidence

Commission, the CCI does not have the power of search and seizure. This may hamper the CCI when it is conducting an inquiry into alleged cartel activity under section 26 of the Act.[170] A review of cases decided by the CCI so far will thus reveal how these procedural requirements are met in practice. It needs to be noted that such a review may also help to identify whether the search and seizure power of the Director-General[171] have enabled the CCI to overcome the aforestated lacunae in the Act.

The CCI against cartels: Pursuing a pro-consumer approach?

The first case to be reviewed is *Consumer Online Foundation v. Tata Sky Limited & Ors.*[172] The complaint was filed by a consumer group and thus is important in the context of the present discussion. Fled under section 19 (1) of the Act, the complaint alleged the contravention of sections 3 and 4 of the Act. The allegations did involve reference to cartelization of the

Act, 1872 (1 of 1872), any public record or document or copy of such record or document from any office'.

[170] The Act (n 68) section 12 (5) of the MRTP Act, 1969: 'Where, during any inquiry under this Act, the Commission has any grounds to believe that any books or papers of, or relating to any undertaking in relation to which such inquiry is being made or which the owner of such undertaking may be required to produce in such inquiry, are being, or may be, destroyed, mutilated, altered, falsified or secreted, it may, by a written order, authorize any officer of the Commission to exercise the same powers of entry, search and seizure in relation to the undertaking, or the books or papers, aforesaid as may be exercised by the Director-General while holding a preliminary investigation under section 11'.

[171] *Id.*, section 41 sub-section 3 states: 'Without prejudice to the provisions of sub-section (2), sections 240 and 240A of the Companies Act, 1956 (1 of 1956), so far as may be, shall apply to an investigation made by the Director General or any other person investigating under his authority, as they apply to an inspector appointed under that Act'. Section 240 A of the Companies Act, 1956 confers search and seizure power on the Inspector conducting investigations under the Act. [Section 240 A of the Companies Act: Seizure of documents by inspector.—'(1) Where in the course of investigation under section 235 or section 237 or section 239 or section 247, the inspector has reasonable ground to believe that the books and papers of, or relating to, any company or other body corporate or managing director or manager of such company or other body corporate, may be destroyed, mutilated, altered, falsified or secreted, the inspector may make an application to the Magistrate of the First Class or, as the case may be, the Presidency Magistrate, having jurisdiction for an order for the seizure of such books and papers. (2) After considering the application and hearing the inspector, if necessary, the [5][Magistrate] may by order authorise the inspector— (a) to enter, with such assistance, as may be required, the place or places where such books and papers are kept; (b) to search that place or those places in the manner specified in the order; and (c) to seize books and papers he considers necessary for the purposes of his investigation'].

[172] Case No. 2 of 2009.

direct-to-home (DTH) services market. Specifically, the complainant claimed that the DTH service providers prevented interoperability between hardware and DTH signals provided by different manufacturers and DTH service providers. This was done by ensuring that the consumers did not receive DTH services, unless they purchased the hardware from the DTH service provider (whose services the consumer wanted). The hardware included the dish antennae and the set top box (STB). For example, if a consumer wants to subscribe to the services of Tata Sky (a DTH service provider), he or she will have to mandatorily buy the hardware from Tata Sky. Subsequently, if the same consumer wants to change to Airtel (another DTH service provider), he or she cannot continue to use the existing hardware. The consumer will have to buy a new hardware from Airtel.

Allegation of cartelization was made by pointing out that all DTH service providers were carrying on this practice of restricting interoperability and imposing costs on consumers. This was claimed to be indicative of a tacit understanding between the existing DTH service providers to reduce competition among them. The tacit understanding thus amounted to violation of section 3 (1).[173] Additionally, the complaint also alleged other anti-competitive practices, viz., using restrictive conditions or clauses in consumer contracts to reduce competition, forcing the consumer to enter into tie-in arrangements with the DTH service providers, entering into exclusive dealing arrangements with the hardware manufacturers and abuse of dominance. The CCI accordingly directed the Director-General to conduct an inquiry, having formed an opinion of the existence of a prima facie case.[174] The Director-General submitted its report within a period of three months from the date of being so directed by the CCI.[175] He found that the conduct of all the DTH service providers amounted to infringement of section 3 (3) of the Act. In other words, the Director General did find cartel-like behaviour amongst the DTH service providers. It appeared that all the DTH service providers failed to provide their respective conditional access modules (CAMs) which could be inserted into the common slot of the STB. This would have enabled interoperability among DTH service providers.

---

173 The Act (n 68) Section 3 (1) of the Act: 'No enterprise or association of enterprises or person or association of persons shall enter into any agreement in respect of production, supply, distribution, storage, acquisition or control of goods or provision of services, which causes or is likely to cause an appreciable adverse effect on competition within India'.

174 Section 26 (1) of the Act.

175 The CCI issued its order for investigations on June 30, 2009 and the Director-General submitted the report on 24 September 2009.

In addition, the STB also needs a smart card/viewing card. Inserting a smart card is similar to inserting a subscriber identity module (SIM) card in a mobile hand set. Due to this unavailability of interchangeable smart cards, the STBs cannot decode the signal of any other DTH except for the one to whom it belongs. Further, like a SIM card, the smart card too has to be recharged or else they are de-activated by the DTH service provider. As a consequence of this, even the free to air (FTA) channels are de-activated. The consumer is not informed about the FTAs; later, the FTAs are made part of the pay package. Thus a consumer will have to pay and get the package in order to view the FTAs. This practice of all the DTH for service providers reduced the exit options of customers and hence amounted to *appreciable adverse effect* on consumers. All the DTH operators were given opportunity to raise their objections and give their submissions in view of the Director-General's report. Expectedly, they all denied the allegations of infringement of sections 3 and 4 of the Act. The informant or complainant in its written submissions alleged cartelization on the basis of uncanny similarity of practices by the DTH service providers in the relevant market. It was alleged that there appeared to be a tacit understanding between the DTH service providers '*not to compete with each other*'.[176] This, the complainant argued, limited competition among the DTH service providers. The CCI went through the allegations and came to the conclusion that the lack of interoperability was due to technical constraints and not due to anti-competitive behaviour. Accordingly, the CCI rejected the allegations of cartelization.

Further, the CCI noted that the issue of interoperability among DTH service providers was being looked into by the sector regulator, viz., TRAI. Hence, the CCI felt that it would not be wise for it to interfere, in the absence of any competition angle in the matter.[177] From the consumer perspective, this decision of the CCI was not encouraging—it philosophically orients itself differently from that of the Raghavan Committee's report. The CCI makes it plain and clear that the protection of consumer welfare cannot be the sole purpose of the Act. It stated that

---

[176] Case No. 2 of 2009 (n 172) 73, para 16.3.

[177] The allegation of vertical restraints was also rejected on the ground of technical restraints. Accordingly, the CCI did not find any infringement of section 3 due to lack of appreciable adverse effect. Further, the allegations of abuse of dominance was also rejected by the CCI noting that the 'TV subscription market is very dynamic and competitive where not only are DTH operators vigorously competing with each other but also with the entrenched cable TV providers. Therefore, allegation of dominance cannot be established. In absence of dominance, the question of any abuse, including predatory pricing, does not arise'.

> 'The onus to protect freedom of trade is as much at the heart of competition laws as is consumer welfare and economic development'.[178]

Thus lack of technological development was used as a ground to discount the existence of uniform practice and lack of consumer choice. The CCI insisted that proof of cartel, as alleged by the complainant in the DTH service market, must be concluded through amassment of undisputable evidences. This is indicative of the enormous burden that will be laid on any consumer or consumers who think of acting against cartels. Importantly, the Director-General's report never reflected upon the lack of technological development. On the contrary, the said report did indicate cartel-like behaviour.[179] On the allegations of cartel, the insistence of 'undisputable evidence' is contrary to the wording of section 3 (3), viz., 'presumption of appreciable adverse effect on competition'. The CCI never elaborated on this aspect and how the presumption was rebutted by the DTH service providers.

Further, the CCI nowhere explained what would amount to an appreciable adverse effect on competition. It was bothered about the cost entailed in enforcing interoperability. Here the CCI completely ignored the evidence adduced by the complainant that one of the DTH service providers, Dish TV, had provided four hundred and eighty one CAMs to Kingfisher Airlines.[180] This, the complainant insisted goes to prove that interoperability was possible in India. Further, the CCI ignored the information asymmetry that the consumer had with regard to the STBs. While the consumers had the choice of taking the STBs either on rent or hire purchase or outright purchase, they were not made aware of the same by the DTH service providers. As a result, they ended up buying the STBs from the DTH service provider. The CCI also ignored the fact that an action in concert with each other was regarded as an agreement under section 2 clause (b) of the Act.[181] It did not explain how the uniformity in the practice of the DTH service providers did not amount to *an action in concert*. The CCI sought to confine the meaning of the term '*an action in concert*' by insisting that the same has to be counterpoised on the fulcrum of '*by agreement amongst themselves*'. It did not bother to elaborate upon what amounted to an *action in concert,* and when it be treated as an

---

[178] Case No. 2 of 2009 (n 172) 97, para 18.22.

[179] *Id.*, 26, para 4.5.

[180] *Id.,* 8, R.Prasad, dissenting opinion.

[181] The Act (n 68) section 2 (b): 'agreement' includes any arrangement or understanding or action in concert,— (i) whether or not, such arrangement, understanding or action is formal or in writing; or (ii) whether or not such arrangement, understanding or action is intended to be enforceable by legal proceedings'.

agreement amongst themselves.[182] Another important point which the CCI did not address was the question of '*relevant market*'. Accordingly, the CCI failed to explain how and why DTH services and cable TV are part of the same relevant market. The CCI clearly gave an evasive decision by ignoring all legal points and relying purely on technological arguments.

In this regard it is enlightening to read the dissenting opinion of R. Prasad. Applying the definition of relevant product market to this case, Mr Prasad insisted that it is for the consumer to decide whether a product is substitutable or not. According to him

> '[t]he consumer in India do not regard DTH TV as substitutable or interchangeable with IPTV and Cable T.V.'.[183]

He concluded that DTH services

> 'constitute a separate relevant product market and DTH TV is a satellite T.V., its relevant geographic market is whole of India'.[184]

Mr Prasad also refers to the switching costs involved if a consumer wants to shift from one DTH service provider to the other. He concluded, as did the Director-General's report, that the switching costs are enormous thereby capturing the consumer. This will lead to entry barrier for a new service provider, as the new DTH service provider will find it difficult to get a customer. This analysis was missing in the main decision of the CCI. Mr Prasad concludes that on all the grounds mentioned in section 19 (3), the case of DTH service provider fails. Mr Prasad thus notes that

> '[b]y having high switching costs, as a new entrant in the business of DTH operations would not be able to get customers from the operators who were in the field earlier, a barrier to the new entrants in the market has been created. There is also a foreclosure of competition by hindering entry into the market. Further by having switching costs, there is no accrual of benefits to the consumers. In the long run if someone comes with better technology in the DTH market, because of high switching costs, there would be an impediment to the operator with better technology'.[185]

Mr Prasad then specifically analysed the acts of the DTH service providers under section 3 (3) of the Act. He concluded that each concerned service

---

[182] Case No. 2 of 2009 (n 172) 96.

[183] Case No. 2 of 2009 (n 172)23, R. Prasad dissenting opinion.

[184] *Id.*,24.

[185] *Id.*, 26, R. Prasad, dissenting opinion.

provider, by following the same type of business model of bundling all the services, was contributing to the lack of inter-se competition.

This ensured that each DTH service provider got to keep its customers and share of the market. Further, with the lack of interoperability and high switching costs, the existing DTH service provider had also limited the growth of the hardware market. These effects clearly are covered by section 3, sub-section 3. There is thus a presumption of *appreciable adverse effect.* Further it was noted by Mr Prasad that clauses (c), (a) and (f) of section 19 (3) could be used to establish the case of the complainant under section 3 sub-section 3. Mr Prasad finally noted that the DTH service providers had failed to rebut the presumption of section 3 (3).[186] Unfortunately, this was a dissenting opinion and did not help the case of consumers. It however, indicated the way in which consumer interests can be protected in cartel cases, under the Act. This case also reiterates the misgivings expressed while reviewing the substantive provisions. The CCI had failed to act when it had the chance and further the cause of consumer interests within the Indian competition law. Another set of important cases relating to allegations of cartels that had come before the CCI relates to imposition of pre-payment penalty charges on home loan borrowers by banking and non-banking financial companies.

The first case of this type to be reviewed will be that of *Neeraj Malhotra v Deustche Post Bank Home Finance Limited (Deustche Bank) and others.*[187] The allegation was that the banking and non-banking financial companies were acting in concert and levying pre-payment penalty charges on home loan borrowers. The charges, according to the complainant varied from 1 per cent to 4 per cent of the outstanding principal amount of the loan/interest, for the balance unexpired period of the loan.[188] These charges were levied at the time when the borrower decides to re-finance the home loan by another bank at cheaper interest rates. The whole purpose evidently, according to the complainant, was to discourage customers from switching over from one lender to another, by foreclosing the existing loan. All the banking and non-banking financial institutions thus were cartelizing the home loan market by determining the prices of the services being provided to the consumer and by limiting the supply/provision of services, as the client is unable to opt for other sources of loans.[189] As a consequence, there is *appreciable adverse effect* on competition under section 3 of the Act.

---

[186] *Id.,* 28, para 48–50. R.Prasad dissenting opinion.

[187] Case No. 5/2009.

[188] *Id.,* 13, para 2.

[189] *Id.,* 14, para 6.

The CCI once again got a chance to apply the provisions of the Act and protect consumer interest against cartelization. The Director-General's report confirmed the allegations of the complainant regarding cartelization, through levy of pre-payment penalty/charges on foreclosure of home loan. Further the Director-General's report also found the levying of pre-payment penalty charges as falling foul of section 19 (3) clauses (a) (c) and (d).[190] The CCI however was faced with a dilemma as to the manner in which to balance the issues of financial stability against the interest of the consumer. As the banks/non-banking financial institutions noted, quoting Reserve Bank of India (RBI) regulations, that imposition of pre-payment charges/penalty was essential for the viability of the banking industry. The imposition of the pre-payment charge/penalty enables the bank to manage its risks and protect the interest of its depositors and other customers.[191]

Another problem in this case was that the consumer base itself was fragmented. While the home loan borrowers regarded pre-payment penalty as anti-competitive, the same was found to be necessary for the asset liability management of the banking/non-banking financial institutions. Importantly, this asset liability management was needed to protect the interest, as noted above, of the depositors. Also, as in the previous case, here too the CCI had to factor in the role of the RBI and the relevant statutes bearing on the functioning of banks/non-banking financial institutions. The CCI thus proceeded to evaluate the competition concerns, keeping in mind all these constraints. It first concluded that there lacked a uniform pattern/ practice in the imposition of pre-payment charges/penalty among banks/ non-banking financial institutions. The next query related to the existence of any agreement to levy pre-payment penalty among banking/non-banking financial institutions. To answer the same, the CCI went on to determine the relevant market in this case. Curiously though, the CCI failed to define the relevant market except to explain the concept of supply side and demand side.

It then went on to discuss the concept of agreement and concluded that there was nothing in record to suggest the existence of an agreement according to section 2 (b). The Director-General had relied on the directions of the Indian Bank Association (IBA) issued to its members which allegedly led to large-scale imposition of pre-payment penalty charges. Interestingly though, the replies of several banks like HDFC Ltd. showed that they were not members of IBA, though they were charging pre-penalty charges. Then

---

190 *Id.*, 22.

191 Case No. 5/2009 (n 187) 22–128, replies of the concerned banking and non-banking financial institutions.

there were other banks like Axis which did not charge pre-payment charges. Thus, there was no proof of the existence of collusion or agreement, to bring the practice of charging pre-payment charges within the definition of cartel. The CCI noted that

> 'In the instant case, the Indian Banking Association (IBA) can be said to be an association of banks but there is no evidence on record which leads us to conclude that IBA has adopted the practice or taken a decision in the matter. The practice of charging prepayment penalty cannot be said to be a concerted decision of all the Banks/HFCs as all of them have not started charging prepayment penalty at one point of time. HDFC and LICHF are charging prepayment penalty since 1993 and 1995 respectively. The other Banks/HFCs started charging prepayment penalty after many years. It is noted that all HFCs are not members of IBA, which is an association of banks.'[192]

The CCI for the first time clarified that to prove the existence of an agreement within the meaning of the Act, there has to be 'a conscious and congruous act that has to be associated to a point in time'.[193] Clearly, the Director-General's reliance on the IBA communication could not be treated by the CCI as proof of such an act, for the reasons mentioned above. The CCI accordingly declareds that 'congruence of action, which is an integral part of any agreement, does not get established by the investigation of the DG'.[194] Nonetheless, the CCI went ahead to evaluate the *effect* of the pre-payment penalty on the fulcrum of section 3 (3) read with section 19 (3) of the Act. It went through the data and statistics provided by the banks as well as relied on by the Director-General and came to the conclusion that the pre-payment penalty had no effect on the provision of home loan in the Indian market.

Further, it concluded that the imposition of pre-payment penalty was necessary to maintain business viability. This in turn would end up benefiting the borrowers/consumers as the pre-payment penalty allows the banking and non-banking financial institutions to lower the barriers to providing home loans as a result of better asset liability management. Further, the existence of multiple lenders was regarded by the CCI as beneficial to the borrowers. The benefit accrued to the depositors was also taken note of by the CCI which went on to dismiss the complaint. Interestingly, the switching costs of the borrower was justified as one determined by the market. Determination by

---

[192] *Id.*, 152.
[193] *Id.*, 146.
[194] *Id.*, 153.

the market was meant to be quantification of damages for breach of home loan contract. The CCI accordingly declared that the relevant Act to determine the same was the Indian Contract Act, 1872 and not the Competition Act. It therefore ruled out the role of a regulator in determining whether the quantum of the switching costs was just or not.[195]

This decision of the CCI once again overlooked the detrimental effect on the consumers, evident from the fact that there were two dissenting opinions highlighting the flaws in the arguments for pre-payment charges, approved by the majority. The dissenting opinions were given by Mr P.N. Parashar and Mr R. Prasad. The first point of dissent in Mr Parashar's opinion was on the applicability of the Contract Act. He was of the opinion that since the pre-payment charges/penalty were detrimental to consumers interest, being anti-competitive in nature, they had to be dealt with under the Act. Mr Parashar, in his opinion, emphasized the need to protect consumer interests and argued that the intent of the Act was to protect consumer interest in addition to freedom of trade.[196] He then went along with the conclusion of the Director-General and held that the imposition of pre-payment charges subsequent to the issuance of the IBA circular, was proof of concurrence and consensus amongst the various banking and non-banking financial institutions. This concurrence and consensus can be regarded as an agreement under section 2 clause (b). Further, he noted that

> 'the 'decision' to be covered within the provisions of section 3(3) of the Act need not necessarily be simultaneous or taken at the same point of time by all parties'.[197]

He also noted that this concurrence or commonality of practice can be prevalent even with non-members of the association. The argument given by HDFC Ltd. and other non-IBA members was discounted. Having taken this approach, it is obvious, that Mr Parashar would have held the banks/non-banking financial institutions guilty of cartelization and charging supra-competitive prices by imposing pre-payment charges. This was done by relying on section 3 (3) (a). As section 3 (3) includes the decision taken by any association, it was noted that the IBA being an associations of the banks, would be covered by section 3 (3). Further, this interpretation was extended to section 3 (3) (a). It implied that IBA's concerted decision was to fix the

[195] *Id.,* 164–167.
[196] *Id.,* 4–8, P. N. Parashar dissent.
[197] Case No. 5/2009 (n 187) 31.

price of the penalty for pre-payment of home loans.[198] Applying a similar analysis, it was held by Mr Parashar that

> 'practice by the opposite parties in fixing common and uniform rates for charging [pre-payment charges/penalty] has resulted into limiting and controlling the provision of services in the banking sector particularly in the relevant market of home loans'.[199]

Having argued for the existence of presumption of *appreciable adverse effect* on competition, it was concluded by Mr Parashar that even on counts of section 19 (3), the banks and the non-banking financial institutions have not rebutted the presumption. Importantly, for him the absence of benefit to the consumer was a crucial factor to strengthen the presumption. Accordingly, he noted

> 'I am of considered opinion that the 'agreement' reached amongst the opposite parties is covered within the per se rule contained in section 3 (3) of the Act even on considering the replies of the opposite parties and evidence adduced in rebuttal of this presumption by them, it is concluded that the opposite parties have failed to demolish the presumption contained therein. Rather, the said presumption is strengthened by the detriment which this practice causes to the interest of consumers'.[200]

However, like in the main order, here too Mr Parashar failed to explain the relevant market. However, the relevant market was regarded as the home loan market. The parameters applied to identify the same as the relevant market however is not there. Nonetheless, the broad interpretation given to the term *agreement* in order to cover the impugned act within the ambit of section 3, sub-section 3 gives hope to the consumer of getting a positive verdict at some level.

The dissenting opinion of Mr Prasad concluded that high switching costs would create entry barriers for new competitors. On the other hand, it would allow the existing players to extract supra-competitive rents from the consumer. It also discouraged product innovation.[201] Mr Prasad and Mr Parashar dismissed the argument that pre-payment charges were asset liability management (ALM) tools. According to them, pre-payment of loans enabled the bank to receive the principal money well in advance and thereby, they could go in for fresh investments. This approach thus ruled out the argument that pre-payment charges were necessary to set off other risks like paying

---

[198] *Id.*, 34, P. N. Parashar dissent.

[199] *Id.*, 38.

[200] *Id.*, 40.

[201] *Id.*, 37, R. Prasad dissenting.

the depositors. It also ruled out the concern of the CCI that catering to the concern of borrowers would harm the depositors. It was thus evident that the different classes of consumers cannot be used to justify any anti-competitive practice. He also pointed out the fact that the only ground for imposition of pre-payment charges was the capture of the customer, depriving them of the option to switch/re-finance. This leads to the conclusion that the pre-payment charges are in violation of section 3 (3) (a) and (b). Further Mr Prasad also ruled out the applicability of the Contract Act, when competition concerns are involved. On the whole, Mr Prasad also argued on the same lines as Mr Parashar to establish the existence of agreements having an *appreciable adverse effect* on competition. Further, having also established the case under section 3 (3), the rule of rebuttable presumption was invoked. Here too it was concluded that all the opposite parties have failed to rebut the presumption.[202]

Notwithstanding this progressive opinion, what holds is the main order of the CCI, which has so far not been encouraging for consumer interests. The next case that concerned the same issues, viz., pre-payment charges raising anti-competitive concerns was *Yashoda Hospital and Research Centre Ltd. v. Indiabulls Financial Services Limited (IFSL)*[203] Here too the complainant alleged that by imposing pre-payment charges, the IFSL was indulging in anti-competitive practices. The allegation was both under section 3 and section 4. The Director-General referred to the investigation report of the *Neeraj Malhotra* case and concluded that there was breach of section 3 (3) (b) along with section 19 (3) clauses (a), (c) and (d).[204] The IFSL attacked the DG report on the ground of absence of agreement with other banks/financial institutions. Accordingly, section 3 (3) could not be invoked as there has to be an agreement with another entity. The CCI agreed with this argument and declared that

> 'there is absolutely nothing on record which can show that IFSL has been imposing pre-payment penalty and foreclosure charges in pursuance of some agreement entered into by it with any enterprise engaged in similar trade or business. For an agreement to exist there has to be an act in the nature of an arrangement, understanding or action in concert including existence of an identifiable practice or decision taken by an association of enterprise or persons'.[205]

---

[202] Mr Prasad also regarded the IBA meeting in 2003 and the subsequent circular as proof of agreement. See Case No. 5/2009 (n 187) 62.

[203] Case No. 12/2010.

[204] *Id.*, 3–4.

[205] *Id.*, 5.

Even otherwise, going by its previous decision, the CCI would have dismissed the complaint on the same grounds as in the *Neeraj Malhotra* case. Thus the lack of pro-consumer approach continues to be embedded in the CCI's application of the Act.

In *Vijay Gupta v. M/s. Paper Merchants Association and others*[206], the CCI had to deal with the issue of collective boycott. The complainant alleged that certain terms and conditions in the regulations of the Paper Merchant's Association, Delhi (PMAD), infringed the Act. The Director-General on inquiry found that while there was no infringement of section 4 of the Act, certain rules of the PMAD relating to arbitration and powers of the PMAD's committees appeared to be in violation of section 3 (3) (b). In particular, these rules empowered the PMAD's disciplinary committee (called the Quida committee) to instruct its members to boycott anyone who fails to comply with the PMAD's executive committee's directions. This practice of collective boycotting the defaulter falls within section 3 (3) (b) which refers to limiting or controlling supply of material as anti-competitive.[207] The CCI went along with the findings of the Director-General and held that the rule of collective boycott was in violation of section 3 (3) (b). Importantly, from a consumer welfare perspective, the CCI concluded that such clauses deprive the consumers of the ability to freely negotiate with the PMAD members, who were the sellers. Accordingly, the CCI declared that

> 'Deprivation of such rights is a clear indicator of appreciable adverse effect on competition under section 3, in terms of section 19(3) (d) of the Act.'[208]

This case did not involve complicated issues as in the previous cases such as technological or financial aspects. Further herein the impugned rules were agreed to be amended by the opposite party, i.e., PMAD.[209] The CCI accordingly found it easier to apply a pro-consumer approach. It however needs to be noted that the CCI only passed a cease and desist order along with directions to suitably amend/modify the impugned rules.[210] No penalty was imposed. Hence the cartel-like behaviour was let off lightly. As noted, the cooperation received from the opposite party to abide by the directions of the CCI appeared to be the compelling reason for this decision. The challenge

---

206 Case No. 07/2010.

207 *Id.*, 13–15.

208 *Id.*, 24.

209 *Id.*, 18, para 3.1 clause (v).

210 *Id.*, 32, para 6.4.

though will be the more complicated cases and it has to be seen how CCI furthers consumer interest. At present, however, there does not appear to be any major efforts in furthering the pro-consumer approach by the CCI. The *Surinder Bhakoo v. The HDFC Bank Ltd.*[211] decision substantiates this observation. This case also involved the anti-competitive concerns regarding pre-payment penalty and foreclosure charges. The only difference being that here unlike the *Neeraj Malhotra* case, the borrower had taken a car loan.

Further, as in the IFSL case, here too the complaint was against an individual bank. Thus for the CCI, the choice was clear and it followed its decision in the *Neeraj Malhotra* and *IFSL* case. It accordingly declared that there was no competition issues involved in pre-payment penalty and foreclosure charges. Additionally, the CCI also closed the matter on the ground that since the complaint was against an individual bank there was lack of proof of an agreement between two or more enterprises/persons. There could not be a case of infringement of section 3 of the Act.[212] A similar decision was arrived at by the CCI in *M/s. Metalrod Ltd. v. M/s. Religare Finvest Ltd.*[213] Here too the complaint was against an individual enterprise, a non-banking financial institution. The concern again was regarding imposition of pre-payment penalty and foreclosure charges being anti-competitive in nature. And again the complaint was dismissed on the ground of lack of an agreement. The CCI reiterated its earlier stand and declared that

> 'from the plain reading of the provisions of section 3 sub-section 3 clause (b) it is amply clear that for application of this provision there must be two or more enterprises engaged in identical or similar trade of goods or provision of services whereas in the present matter the impugned practice of imposing foreclosure charges has been imputed to a single enterprise…'.[214]

---

211 Case No. 15 of 2009.

212 *Id.,* 4–6. See also the dissenting opinion of R.Prasad, who divided the car loan market into two, one from where the borrower takes the loan, and hence has the choice of multiple players. The other is the after market or loan recovery market where there is only one player, i.e., there is monopoly of the lending bank.

213 Case No. 28/2010.

214 Case No. 28/2010 (n 213) 7, para 14. Interestingly, in all the cases involving complaints against single entity indulging in anti-competitive behaviour under section 3, sub-section 3, Mr. R. Prasad has dissented claiming that 'There is no doubt it is a case of a single complainant against a particular bank but…the issues involved here are one which is prevalent in the entire banking industry and there the case is one of class action'. This appears to be a relevant argument considering the fact that the same concern has been coming up before the CCI time and again.

Another competition concern regarding the activities of banking and non-banking financial companies relates to the charging of differential interest rates from different sets of home loan borrowers. In *Shri V. Ramachandran Reddy and others v. HDFC Ltd. and Another*,[215] the complainants alleged the practice of the banks in discriminating between new home loan borrowers qua the existing home loan borrowers. It was alleged that where home loans had been taken on a floating rate basis, the benefit of reduced rate of interest was not passed on to the existing customers. The claim was based on cartelization according to section 3 (3) and abuse of dominance. Here the Director-General concluded that there was no contravention of section 3 (3) since the interest rates were dependant upon the prevailing market conditions. The CCI went along with this conclusion ignoring the switching costs and information asymmetry.[216] Allegation of cartelization has also been rejected by the CCI due to lack of proper evidence being adduced by the consumer. While circumstantial evidence can lead to the conclusion about existence of a cartel, lack of the same will negate the complaint.

For example, in the *Neeraj Malhotra v. North Delhi Power Limited and others*,[217] the CCI rejected the allegation of price-fixing cartelization of the electricity supply sector, due to lack of evidence. The complainant had alleged that the electricity supply companies' concerted action and decision of prohibiting the consumer to buy their own meters resulted in appreciable adverse effect on competition. It was noted by the complainant that the meters being installed by the companies were faulty as they were found to be running faster. This increased the electricity bills of the consumers and consequently made the service costlier. All the allegations of the complainant however were based on newspaper reports and were not supported by any data or survey. Further, no proof of any concerted practice or agreement was adduced, circumstantial or otherwise. The same was also pointed out in the report of the Director-General, wherein it was further noted that no such evidence could be found during the course of investigation. The CCI agreed with this conclusion and closed the matter. In this context, it may be reiterated that direct proof of collective boycott or any other cartel-like behaviour had led the CCI to give a pro-consumer decision.

This was evident in the *PMAD* case and was further substantiated by the decision of th CCI in the *FICCI-Multiplex Association of India v. United*

215 Case Ref: Case No. 7/28, 25/28, 8/28, 9/28, 10/28.

216 *Id.*, 23–24, the dissenting opinion of Mr.R.Prasad.

217 Case No. 06/2009.

Producers/Distributors Forum & Ors.[218] Here the dispute was essentially between the multiplex owners and the film producers regarding a revenue-sharing arrangement. The multiplex owners alleged that the Hindi film producer's association was acting like a cartel and dictating the terms under which the multiplex owner can exhibit a film.[219] In particular, the producer's association had issued notices barring the exhibition of films in the multiplexes belonging to the complainant. This notice thus was used as a coercive measure to force the complainant to agree to the terms dictated by the producer's association. The Director-General in its report concluded that the Hindi film producer's association, viz., United Producers/Distributors Forum (hereinafter referred to as UPDF), the Association of Motion Pictures and TV Programme Producers (hereinafter referred to as AMTPP) and the Film and Television Producers Gild of India Ltd. (hereinafter referred to as FTPGI) were acting like a cartel.

It was found by the Director-General that there were meetings and conferences held where the issue of revenue-sharing was discussed. Further, evidence was also there of issuance of letters which contained threat of boycott/suspension. As a consequence of this collective boycott, no films were released resulting in revenue loss to the complainant. The complainant was thus forced to agree to the terms of revenue-sharing laid down by the film producer's association. This increased the cost of exhibiting the film, as a result of which the ticket prices had to be increased, thus indirectly passing the burden of the cartel-behaviour to the film goers who were the end consumers.[220] This case was thus clearly covered by section 3 (3). The CCI was convinced by the findings of the Director-General and concluded that the Hindi film producer's association activities were like that of a cartel. The CCI summarized the acts which, according to the CCI, established the existence of cartels, viz., ability to control release of Hindi films; the pre-meditated and joint stand of the Hindi film producers; intense and regular interaction; policing of the cartel agreement and ability to punish the violators and intimidation through threats of dire consequences.[221]

Interestingly, in view of the overwhelming evidence of cartel-like behaviour, the CCI declared that to establish a cartel-like conduct, relevant market need not be defined.[222] Though as seen in the previous cases, the

---

218 Case No. 01 of 2009.

219 *Id.,* 5–6.

220 *Id.,* at 9–11 and 19.

221 Case No. 01 of 2009 (n 218) 71.

222 *Id.,* 73.

relevant market does become important to establish cartelization. As the Act is *effect* based, the description of the relevant market becomes important within the Indian law. Notwithstanding this observation, the decision of the CCI was primarily governed by the concern of the indirect costs imposed on the consumers. As noted in the *PMAD* case, here too it was easy for the CCI to give a pro-consumer decision. The pro-consumer approach is evident from the fact that even the multiplexes have been regarded as consumers by the CCI under the Act.[223] This is possible because of the wide definition of consumer given in the Act which includes buying or hiring for the purpose of re-sale or any other commercial use.[224] The loss to both the multiplex and the end consumers therefore affected the decision of the CCI. But like the *PMAD* case here too the cartel activities were let off lightly. The CCI passed only a cease and desist order and imposed a fine of one lakh rupees upon each of the infringer. This is a miniscule amount considering the advantage that the cartel members obtained from the new revenue-sharing agreement. The approach of the CCI in these cases cannot be termed as pro-consumer, though these are cases where the consumer's interest had a bearing on its decision.

Subsequent decisions of the CCI do not change these impressions as so far barring blatant infringement of the Act, lack of direct evidence of cartels continue to be detrimental to the consumer cause. For example in *Re:Domestic Airlines,* [225] the CCI took cognizance of the various media reports which alleged price-fixing collusion on the part of domestic airline operators. The DG on investigating the matter noted that increase in price, though a case of price parallelism was the result of competitive pricing.[226] The existence of cartelization or tacit collusion leading to price rise by domestic airlines was thus negated by the DG. The majority opinion of the CCI agreed with these findings, accepting that the ticket pricing in the domestic airline market followed market dynamics of demand and supply. Accordingly, the ticket prices tend to rise during the peak season and lower during lean seasons. One can safely note the emphasis on economic analysis, taking note of market structure and dynamic pricing. This is proof of a more nuanced analysis by

---

223 *Id.*, 93.

224 The Act (n 68) Section 2 (f). See chapter I for discussion on the broad definition of consumer under the Act.

225 RTPE 05/2009 of MRTPC/Suo-Motu Case No.02/2010 (In Re: Domestic Air Lines) [There were two cases with the same facts. One was taken up by the erstwhile MRTP Commission, on the basis of newspaper reports regarding price fixing by airlines and the other was taken up by the CCI, again on the basis of newspaper reports].

226 *Id.*, 5.8.

the CCI to anti-cartel allegations as compared to the earlier cases discussed above. The outcome for the consumer however does not change as the lack of direct evidence negates the finding of cartelization. Accordingly, the majority observed that

> 'in absence of evidence of any organized, express or tacit collusion among the airlines, the Commission feels that it cannot be concluded that the airlines have entered into any anti-competitive agreement in violation of section 3(3) of the Act'[227]

Nonetheless, the suo moto cognizance of the matter indicates a conscious effort on the part of the CCI to actively protect consumer interest. The attempt though leaves a lot to be desired. The finding of price parallelism was completely ignored by both the DG and the majority. R. Prasad who gave the dissenting note, observed that while assessing the demand and supply scenario, the majority ignored the fact that there was information asymmetry on the part of the consumer.[228] Consequently, according to R. Prasad the demand for tickets was vitiated because consumers

> 'are not able to know how many seats are available in respective fare buckets by the airlines and whether consumer has made an optimal choice by purchasing a ticket out of a particular fare bucket'.[229]

For R. Prasad, parallel pricing by itself might not prove cartelization; however, he strongly argued that the same is either a proof of concerted behaviour or leads to a presumption of collusion.[230] In the given scenario, there is proof of parity in pricing practices of the airlines. For R. Prasad, the DG ought to therefore have investigated the manner in which airlines exchanged price information. The same would have established the extent of collusion among the airlines for the purpose of increasing the prices of the tickets. Coupled with information asymmetry, consumers are put in a highly disadvantageous position.[231] Importantly, R. Prasad insisted that the Act widens the concept of agreement, as the word agreement also includes practice. Consequently, according to R. Prasad

> 'In this particular case the parallel behavior over a long period of time by the different airlines amounts to practice carried out by them'.[232]

---

227 *Id.*, 6.25.

228 *Id.*, 41, in the dissenting opinion of Mr R. Prasad.

229 *Id.*, 41, in the dissenting opinion of Mr R. Prasad.

230 *Id.*, 56.

231 RTPE 05/2009 of MRTPC/Suo-Motu Case No.02/2010 (n 225) 57–60.

232 *Id.*, 68.

This line of analyses reflects the lacunae that persist in most of the decisions of CCI analysed so far. As explained earlier, the CCI will have to regard alternative analysis to find cartelization, as direct evidence is hard to come by.[233] Interestingly, in the *Jet Airways* case[234] while the DG report found price parallelism as leading to price collusion[235], the majority rejected this finding. The case involved challenging the validity of the strategic alliance between Jet Airways and Kingfisher Airlines Ltd. on the grounds that it amounted to limiting supply and allocating the market of passenger air transport services in the domestic market.[236] The DG concluded that due to the dominant position held by both the parties, their alliance was likely to have *appreciable adverse effect on competition.*[237] The post alliance increase in the market share of both the parties was further noted by the DG. As discussed above, the presumption of *appreciable adverse effect* being rebuttable, the DG tested the findings under section 19(3). It concluded that on all counts, the agreement had the *effect* of distorting competition and reducing the choices of consumers.[238] The majority ignored these findings, justifying the alliance on the ground that it was necessitated by market recession.[239] In effect, the CCI appeared to be upholding the rationalization agreement on the ground of financial crisis. This approach will inevitably lead to overriding consumer interest. Furthermore, the CCI rejected the DG findings on the ground that the publicly announced alliance had not been fully implemented. Consequently, the anti-competitive effects were not evident. Interestingly, the majority observed

> 'Had all the elements of publicly announced alliance were given affect to and coordination between the Opposite Parties had extended to the fullest extent then that might have given rise to competition concern in view of the combined market share of Jet Airways and Kingfisher Airlines'[240]

The CCI further concluded in favour of the arrangement on the ground that it was common industry practice. One therefore finds an unwillingness

[233] The approach of the CCI to domestic airline's ticket pricing remains unchanged as they continue to hold that the behaviour of the airlines though indicative of price parallelism, is not enough proof of cartelization. See Reference Case No. 01/2012.

[234] Case No. 04/2009.

[235] *Id.*, 5.5.9.

[236] *Id.*, 3.5.

[237] *Id.*, 5.5.12, 5.5.14.

[238] *Id.*, 5.5.13.

[239] *Id.*, 8.5.

[240] *Id.*, 8.8.

on the part of the majority to conduct an in-depth analysis of the potential cartelization of the domestic airline industry. There also appears to be an inherent contradiction in the majority's analysis, as on the one hand, CCI acknowledges potentiality of anti-competitive outcome and on the other hand, ignores such outcome on the basis of industry practice and economic crisis. The dissent by R. Prasad rightly observed that the

> 'opposite parties could have resorted to measures independent of each other to reduce costs and improve efficiency. Coordinating with the immediate competitor for these purposes will not only impact the ordinary market dynamics but also enable them to distort the market in their favor.'[241]

The majority failed to investigate whether there were better alternatives to the one that the parties had adopted to enhance their efficiency. Hence this appears to be another case of missed opportunity by the CCI to evolve a pro-consumer approach in anti-cartel regulation.

As discussed earlier in the context of the *PMAD* case and the *FICCI-Multiplex Association of India,* in cases of direct evidence, CCI finds it easier to give pro-cosumer decisions. This is evident from the case of *Puja Enterprises*[242]. In this case, the Director-General of Supplies and Disposals of the Ministry of Commerce and Industry alleged collusive and restrictive bidding and cartel formation by bidders with respect to the procurement of 'polyester blended duck ankle boots rubber sole'.[243] The DG investigations focused on the nature of the industry to determine the scope of collusion among the various bidders.[244] This helped the DG to find both direct as well as indirect proof of collusion among the bidders. Importantly, it was evident that although there were differences among the bidders in terms of cost factors like installed capacities and sources of raw material procurement, their bid quotations were almost same.[245] Furthermore, the bidders made inter se arrangement with respect to the quantity each bidder will bid for. There was thus, according to the DG, an

> '*inter se* agreement/arrangement of parties, made with a view to limit and control the supply of the product and to share the market by way of mutual allocation'.[246]

---

[241] *Id.* , 7.18, in the dissenting opinion of Mr. R. Prasad.

[242] Ref. Case No. 01 of 2012.

[243] Ref. Case No. 01 of 2012 (n 242) 2.

[244] *Id.*, 6.

[245] *Id.*

[246] *Id., 6 (iii).*

These conducts were proof of bid rigging according to section 3(1), read with section 3(3) (b), (c) and (d) clauses. The CCI accepted these findings, and with the overwhelming evidence of collusion, safely referred to the wide definition of agreement within the Act. Interestingly, the CCI noted that in cases of cartels, direct evidence was a rarity.[247] However one needs to observe that the present case was straightforward, as the bidders could not rebut the allegation of collusion. Furthermore, the obviousness in the conduct of the bidders with respect to pricing and quota restrictions did not leave much to the imagination. What is of significance from a pro-consumer perspective is that the CCI not only issued cease and desist order but also imposed a penalty of 5 per cent on the average turnover of each enterprise involved in the bid rigging.[248] This imposition of increased penalty became an important feature of the anti-cartel regulation by CCI. It also underlines the current trend of CCI which in view of clear proof of cartelization has been imposing severe penalties. One can argue that in such cases, CCI wants to give a clear and deterring message to all potential cartelists.

The case that arguably has been the most discussed and debated case in recent times[249] has been the *Cement Cartel* case.[250] The case involved allegations by a builder's association against twelve cement manufacturers of cartelizing the domestic market by fixing the prices of cement. The informant adduced circumstantial evidence and statistics to prove that the cement manufacturers in the garb of an association of cement manufacturers had indulged in reducing production of cement so as to artificially raise the prices.[251] It was alleged that notwithstanding government stimulus packages, the prices of cement had remained high.[252] It was also alleged that the pricing pattern remained uniform across the country notwithstanding that demand was not same across all the regions.[253] The increase in the price per cement bag was uniform across the board irrespective of the fact that the manufacturers were different.[254] The DG investigated the allegations and

---

[247] *Id.*, 42.

[248] *Id.*, 49.

[249] See for example Suzanne Rab, *Indian Cement Cartel Order- An International Comparative Analysis; Supplement to Indian Competition Law-An International perspective,* (CCH-a Wolters Kluwer business, 2012)

[250] Builders Association of India v Cement Manufacturer's Association and Others. Case No. 29/2010.

[251] *Id.*, 2.4.

[252] *Id.*, 2.13.4.

[253] *Id.*, 2.13.16–2.13.17

[254] *Id.*, 2.13.24.

found the existence of price parallelism which was indicative of collusion.[255] There was also a deliberate attempt on the part of all manufacturers to reduce supply and increase prices.[256]

There was according to the DG, production parallelism indicating collusive behaviour. Further the price rise was triggered by the bigger players.[257] This was also indicative of collusive behaviour. Further, exchange of price information was also another evidence to prove collusion and concerted behaviour on the part of all the cement manufacturers.[258] The DG thus held the conduct of the cement manufacturers as in violation of section 3(1), section 3(3) (a) and (b). Finally the DG conducted section 19(3) analyses and affirmed the allegations of the informant. On a detailed analysis, the CCI explicitly laid down that circumstantial evidence can be used to prove agreement and direct evidence was not needed.[259] This was an important observation considering that in some of the earlier cases like the domestic airline case, circumstantial evidence was ignored. The CCI also declared that price and production parallelism can be used as circumstantial evidence to establish cartels.[260] This was an important observation as this showed that the CCI was developing a more sophisticated approach to analysing evidence vis-à-vis cartels.[261] This case thus clearly establishes the value of circumstantial evidence within the cartel jurisprudence of this country. The fact that there was proof of exchange of sensitive information among the cement manufacturers through the medium of the association was also important for the CCI in deciding the case against the cement manufacturers.[262]

Another jurisprudence developed by the CCI in this case was the declaration that analysis under section 3(1) read with section 3(3) and section 19(3) does not require identification of relevant market. This is again important because the Act does not make such a distinction. The CCI distinguished between the term market and relevant market, as used in section 3 and section 4, respectively.[263] This is an interesting analysis as it emphasized the fact that cartelization itself is prohibited and it does not matter which market is affected. However, the relevant market analyses will be needed

---

255 *Id.*, 4.2.28.

256 *Id.*, 4.2.36.

257 *Id.*, 4.2.38, 4.2.40, 4.2.41, 4.2.42.

258 *Id.*, 4.2.45, 4.2.46.

259 *Id.*, 6.5.3.

260 Case No. 29/2010 (n 250) 6.5.4.

261 *Id.*, 6.5.7 and 6.5.8.

262 *Id.*, 6.5.23–6.5.24.

263 *Id.*, 6.5.44.

when identifying the existence of cartelization in many cases. It would be therefore advisable to limit these observations to such type of cases where the anti-competitive act was pan India in nature. The CCI conducted section 19(3) analyses and found it against the cement companies.[264] Finally, the case is also important for the huge penalty that the CCI imposed on the cement companies which was to the tune of Rs. 6,307 crores. The CCI imposed a penalty of 0.5 times of the net profit for 2009–2010 and 2010–2011 in case of each cement manufacturer.[265]

Since then till date, the CCI has issued many orders on cartels, wherein the penalty provisions against cartels as given under the proviso to section 27 clause (b) has been used.[266] While in the multiplex case, the imposition of fine was not done on the basis provided in the Act, the cement cartel case had shifted the balance to the other extreme wherein there appears to be no rational basis as to how the limit laid down within the Act was being overshot. If the penalty provision has to have its desired result than the basis for calculating it has to be clear. Understandably, in the cement cartel case, the ComPAT had granted stay with respect to the penalties imposed by CCI.[267] The CCI can take ideas from both the EU and the US on this.[268] The Act also has leniency measures incorporated for inducing members of cartel to break ranks. Section 46 of the Act empowers the CCI to impose lesser penalty on cartel members breaking the ranks and providing vital information.[269] The

[264] *Id.*, 6.10.11.

[265] *Id.*, 7.5.

[266] *Id.*, section 27 of the Act: 'Where after inquiry the Commission finds that any agreement referred to in section 3 or action of an enterprise in a dominant position, is in contravention of section 3 or section 4, as the case may be, it may pass all or any of the following orders…. (b) Provided that in case any agreement referred to in section 3 has been entered into by a cartel, the Commission may impose upon each producer, seller, distributor, trader or service provider included in that cartel, a penalty of up to three times of its profit for each year of the continuance of such agreement or ten per cent of its turnover for each year of the continuance of such agreement, whichever is higher'.

[267] See ComPAT Orders of 17 May, 2013.

[268] See Aditya Bhattacharjea and Oindrila De, 'Cartels and the Competition Commission', *EPW* (2012), , Vol. XLVII, No 35.

[269] *Id.* section 46 of the Act: 'The Commission may, if it is satisfied that any producer, seller, distributor, trader or service provider included in any cartel, which is alleged to have violated section 3, has made a full and true disclosure in respect of the alleged violations and such disclosure is vital, impose upon such producer, seller, distributor, trader or service provider a lesser penalty as it may deem fit, than leviable under this Act or the rules or the regulations:[Provided that lesser penalty shall not be imposed by the Commission in cases where the report of investigation directed under section 26 has been received before making of such disclosure.] Provided further that lesser penalty shall be imposed by the Commission only in respect of a producer, seller, distributor, trader or service

CCI accordingly came out with lesser penalty regulations in the year 2009 wherein reduction of penalty up to one hundred per cent has been provided for.[270] The regulations make provision for graded reduction with the first applicant getting the maximum and the third applicant, being the last in the priority order, getting thirty per cent reduction.[271] The regulations are comparable to those of the US and the EU. They however have yet to be put into practice as no case has come up so far involving implementation of the leniency scheme. Again the procurement of evidence through this scheme may help the consumers as the CCI then may have more conclusive evidence. As seen in the *PMAD* and the *multiplex* case and the *Puja Enterprises* case, the more clearer the proof of cartel the easier it is for the consumer. Finally, the role of the Supreme Court and the CompAT in interpreting and applying the Act will determine the future of the consumer welfare vis-à-vis cartels.[272]

Looking Forward

The above discussion brings out the dilemma of enacting a competition law within the Indian framework. The internal dissensions of the Raghavan Committee members highlight the socio-political realities that need to be accommodated in drafting the competition law. The Act is testimony of this accommodation. The preamble/long title of the Act makes consumer interest one of its objective. The definition of consumer given in the Act is wide to include both the end consumer as well as intermediaries like small=scale industries. Hence when reading the anti-cartel provision, it will not be against the legislative intent to take a pro-consumer approach. The

---

provider included in the cartel, who [has] made the full, true and vital disclosures under this section. Provided also that lesser penalty shall not be imposed by the Commission if the person making the disclosure does not continue to cooperate with the Commission till the completion of the proceedings before the Commission.] Provided also that the Commission may, if it is satisfied that such producer, seller, distributor, trader or service provider included in the cartel had in the course of proceedings,—(a) not complied with the condition on which the lesser penalty was imposed by the Commission; or (b) had given false evidence; or (c) the disclosure made is not vital, and thereupon such producer, seller, distributor, trader or service provider may be tried for the offence with respect to which the lesser penalty was imposed and shall also be liable to the imposition of penalty to which such person has been liable, had lesser penalty not been imposed'.

270 See 'The Competition Commission of India (Lesser Penalty) Regulations, 2009' http://www.cci.gov.in/images/media/Regulations/regu_lesser.pdf?phpMyAdmin=NMPFRahGKYeum5F74Ppstn7Rf00 (accessed on 29 June 2011).

271 *Id.*, Point 4.

272 See Chapter VIIIA of the Act for provisions on the CompAT. Section 53T provides for appeal to the Supreme Court from the decision of the CompAT.

substantive law has a lot of loopholes for the cartels to slip through. Though the gateway clauses of the MRTP Act, 1969 have been done away with, the Act still provides for pro-competitive justifications. This dilutes the *per se void approach* towards cartels which are presumed to have *appreciable adverse effect.* In other words, though cartels are regarded as hard core restraint, they still are allowed to give justifications. Hence a cartel with the help of efficient lawyers and economists can rebut the presumption of anti-competitive effect. This is more so possible because the defences are not cumulatively to be proven. It is enough if a cartel manages to prove any one of the defences. Procedural provisions place the CCI in a better position than the MRTP Commission. The CCI is empowered to initiate inquiry, pass cease and desist orders and importantly impose stringent penalties. Further it has the power to reduce penalties and thus grant leniency to the cartelist. However, the law in practice has not so far given positive vibes. The cases decided by CCI show that in highly complex matters, the CCI fumbles and has failed to define important concepts like *appreciable adverse effect.* Further, though it has started accepting circumstantial evidence, the practice is not consistent and hence there appears to be uncertainty as to when direct evidence will be insisted upon by the CCI. The CCI has also not defined relevant market in the case involving cartels. This failure is grave as the Act is *effect* based. The insistence on ignoring determination of relevant market in cartel cases will further complicate the matters in so far as proving cartelization. The concern for consumers has also not been factored in by CCI despite proof of harm and cost on consumers being imposed by cartel conduct. Finally, the penalty imposed has not been in accordance with the requirement of the Act. It has either been too low or too high resulting in an ambiguous scenario as to the method of calculating the same. Consequently, the effectiveness of the leniency programme will also be in jeopardy. This is so as leniency works only if the cartelists fear the eventual punishment which will surely be upheld by ComPAT and the Supreme Court.

Conclusion

The discussion in Chapter 2 revealed that cartels fall within the spectrum of horizontal cooperation. However, cartels are formed to avoid the cost of competition and not for any other purpose. The idea of such a cooperative arrangement is always to benefit the producer or the cartelists. The loss inevitably has to be borne by the consumer. Irrespective of all socio-political justifications for promoting cartels, it has hardly ever been benevolent to the consumer. Cartels essentially feed on the weaker bargaining power of the consumer. Therefore, in dealing with cartels, a pro-consumer approach is justified. This is more so in the context of India where the law itself recognizes a broader definition of consumers, the focal point of the competition law. From the Indian perspective, both the intermediaries as well as the end consumers are included within the concept of a consumer. The common link between these wide spectra of consumers is the lack of bargaining power vis-à-vis the corporate bodies that form the cartels. As cartels resemble contracts, they are equally susceptible to the contractual doctrine of restraint of trade. The doctrine of restraint of trade was developed essentially with the idea of preventing oppressive contracts.

Accordingly, all contracts which imposed naked restraints without any just cause were declared to be void. Under the common law, the only criterion to assess the justness of the restraint is the test of reasonableness. The courts in England therefore assess whether the restraint is necessary to protect the interest of the party in whose favour it was given and whether the restraint interferes with public interest. Be that as it may, under the Indian law, the doctrine renders all clauses in restraint of trade as *per se void.* Therefore, analysis on the basis of ancillary or naked restraint is not permitted under Indian law. This difference though does not affect the utility of the doctrine in dealing with cartel cases. Theoretically, the doctrine can be used by a party to a cartel agreement to challenge the validity of the agreement. But as cartels are prohibited under the Competition Act, 2002, any person challenging the cartel agreement on the ground of restraint of trade will be faced with the challenge of *in pari delicto.* Consequently, the party may be denied any relief unless the party is able to show inequality of bargaining power.

Similarly, a third party like a consumer affected by the conduct of a cartel cannot use the doctrine as the challenged conduct will be defeated on the ground of lack of privity. The doctrine of privity lays down that only the party to the contract can sue or be sued on a contract. Therefore, the consumer being a stranger to the cartel contract cannot use the doctrine against the cartel conduct. The only option thus left for dealing with cartels is within the competition law framework. A review of the US and the EU jurisdictional response to cartels reveals that price-fixing cartels are bad and need to be treated as *per se illegal.* Secondly, horizontal ancillary restraint is regarded as outside the ambit of *per se void* approach. Thirdly, the identification of the ancillary from the hard core continues to be problematic. Fourthly, horizontal agreements to divide markets, customers, bid rigging, price fixing etc. are regarded as those agreements whose *object* is to restrict competition. Accordingly, there is no need to establish the *effect* of the cartels. Fifthly, a *per se void* approach is regarded as best suited to advance a pro-consumer approach. But there are situations where the cartel-like arrangement may end up benefitting the consumers. Hence a blanket ban on cartels has been conditioned by specific exemptions.

The exemptions are based on policy considerations and are an attempt to nuance the approach towards cartels. The response of the Indian law has however not been specific to cartels. In fact, the existing socio-political situation ensured that the law passed by the Parliament dealt primarily with dominance and abuse of dominance. The other concern which got reflected in the MRTP Act of 1969 was agreement relating to resale price maintenance. The reason why cartels were considered less serious was the lack of evidence which established the harm caused to the consumers. On the other hand, the effect of large dominant undertakings on small enterprises was clearly mapped out by the committees established to study the reasons for economic stagnation. Similarly, the effect of resale price on distributors and consumers was equally documented. The MRTP Act therefore confined its anti-cartel response to the chapter on restrictive trade practices. Further, highlighting the lax approach towards cartels, the MRTP Act employed the *rule of reason* analysis to gauge the effect of cartels on public interest. Thus, even if cartels are treated as *per se* restrictive they still could get away with the public interest argument. The only problem was that neither the Supreme Court nor the MRTP Commission could come to a consensus on what amounted to public interest. Further, there was no inbuilt mechanism enabling effective detection of cartels. The reliance on mandatory registration of cartels was entirely based on voluntary disclosures. This was expecting too much from entities whose purpose was to collude to harm consumers. Added to this substantive weakness was the structural problem in the way the MRTP Commission functioned. Apart from the added burden of dealing with unfair trade practices, the Commission often was not fully staffed to hear the matters.

The lack of expertise in detecting cartels, adducing insufficient proof to show collusion or agreement, added to the woes of the MRTP Commission. Further, the MRTP Commission also lacked any power to deter cartelists. The maximum punishment that could be enforced on a cartelist was the cease and desist order. Only if the cease and desist order was infringed would the cartelist face the prospect of imprisonment and fines. In all these problems, the biggest sufferers were the consumers—intermediaries as well as end consumers. The dilemma of enacting a competition law within the Indian framework was underlined with the setting up of a high-powered committee to suggest an alternative to the MRTP Act, 1969. The internal dissensions of the Raghavan Committee members, though, highlights the socio-political realities that need to be accommodated while drafting the competition law. The Competition Act, 2002 is testimony of this accommodation. The preamble or the long title of the Act makes consumer interest as one of its objectives. The definition of consumer given in the Act is wide enough to include both the end consumer as well as the intermediaries like small-scale industries. Accordingly, when reading the anti-cartel provision it will not be against the legislative intent to take a pro-consumer approach. The substantive law though has a lot of loopholes for cartels to slip through.

Although the gateway clauses of the MRTP Act, 1969 have been done away with, the 2002 Act provides for pro-competitive justifications. This dilutes the *per se void approach* towards cartels which are presumed to have an *appreciable adverse effect.* In other words, though cartels are regarded as hard core restraint they are still allowed to give justifications. Hence, a cartel with the help of efficient lawyers and economists can rebut the presumption of anti-competitive effect. This is possible because the defences need not be cumulatively proven. It is enough if a cartel manages to prove any one of the defences. Procedural provisions place the CCI in a better position than the MRTP Commission. The CCI is empowered to initiate inquiry, pass cease and desist orders and importantly impose stringent penalties. Further, it has the power to reduce penalties and thus grant leniency to a cartelist. Nevertheless, the law in practice has not so far given positive vibes. The cases decided by the CCI show that in highly complex matters, it has fumbled and failed to define important concepts like *appreciable adverse effect.* Further, though it has started accepting circumstantial evidence, the practice is not consistent and hence there appears to be uncertainty as to when direct evidence will be insisted upon by the CCI. The CCI has also not defined relevant market in cases involving cartels. This failure is grave as the Act is *effect* based. The insistence on ignoring determination of relevant market in cartel cases will further complicate matters in so far as proving cartelization. The concern for the consumer has also not been factored into by the CCI despite proof of harm and cost on consumer being imposed by the cartel conduct. Finally, the penalty imposed has not been in accordance with the requirement of the Act. It has either been too low or too high resulting in an ambiguous scenario as to the method of calculating the same. Consequently, the effectiveness of the leniency programme will also be in jeopardy. This is so as leniency works only if the cartelists fear the eventual punishment which will be sure of being upheld by ComPAT and the Supreme Court and not be overturned.

In the light of the above discussions and conclusions, the following suggestions are made to ensure a pro-consumer approach in the anti-cartel provisions of the Act:

1. The effect–based approach of the Act towards cartels means that the CCI should make the task of rebutting presumption harder by choosing to consider all the defences cumulatively. This is theoretically possible as under section 19 (3), the CCI has the discretion to consider all the norms for coming to a conclusion on whether the pro-competitive benefits of the cartel agreement outweighs the anti-competitive effects.

2. To further ensure certainty in the approach to be adopted when assessing cartels, the CCI can make regulations in accordance with the power vested under section 64 (1) read with clause h of section 64 (2). According to section 18 of the Act, CCI is duty bound to eliminate cartels that are presumed to have an *appreciable adverse effect* on competition. Accordingly, the CCI needs to clarify, in the regulation, that any agreement, which is presumed to have an *appreciable adverse effect* on competition under section 3, will be able to rebut the presumption by cumulatively satisfying all the conditions of section 19 (3). In case any one of the defences is not

satisfied, the presumption of *appreciable adverse effect* is established. The CCI can accordingly pass an adverse order along with the imposition of necessary penalties.

3. Admitting the fact that *appreciable adverse effect* requires that the effects have to be established, it is also important for the CCI to come up with an analytical framework as to what would not amount to an appreciable adverse effect or de minimis guidelines. The CCI can, apart from the aggregate market share threshold criteria, as used in the EU de minimis notice, also take into account the fact that the agreement is between enterprises which are neither actual nor potential competitors of each other. It needs, however to be clarified by the CCI that notwithstanding the de minimis guidelines, a cartel, according to section 3 (3) will always be presumed to have an *appreciable adverse effect* on competition. This will ensure that in the case of cartels, the only thing to be proven by the complainant will be the existence of a cartel agreement. There is no need to prove the *effect* of the cartel. This is evident from the difference in the language of section 3 (3) and section 4. It is only in case of section 4 agreements that the complainant has to prove *effect*.
4. Specific exemptions to 'class of enterprises' should be given by the central government, for example addressing unequal bargaining or economic concerns [such as cooperative societies]. This can be done under section 54 (a), under which the central government can exempt 'class of enterprises' from the purview of the Competition Act, 2002 as required by public interest. Further, the word enterprise has been defined under section 2 (h) of the Act to include a 'person'. Furthermore under section 2 (l), the word person includes cooperative societies and firms. Accordingly, a class of enterprises can include a class of cooperative societies or small and medium-size firms, which can be exempted on the ground of unequal bargaining power or weak economic power.
5. Finally, non-price horizontal agreements between enterprises need to be selectively exempted by the central government on the grounds of public policy concerns. This is possible under section 55 (1) which makes the CCI bound by the policy decisions of the central government.

In view of the conclusions that I have drawn, if the suggestions givn above are taken into account by the Central Government and the CCI, the Competition Act, 2002 will serve the consumers better. The adoption of the suggestions will ensure that the intention of the law makers are given effect. Further, it will assure consumers that cartels will not be allowed to get away easily. It will also ensure that parties to non-price horizontal agreements will not worry about the legality of their agreements. Finally, small and medium enterprises as well as other small traders will be provided with a forum where they can take on the economic might of cartelists.

Appendix 1

CASE NAME AND NO.	THE DISPUTE	SECTION INVOLVED	ORDER ISSUED	QUORUM
In re: Raaj Kamal Film International v. M/s Tamil Nadu Theater Owners Association, Case No. 01 of 2013	Refusal by association of Tamil Nadu Theater Owners to release the film '*Vishwaroopam*' as the informant decided to release the film a day prior to the theatrical release through DTH technology, to be made available to consumers paying movies subscription charges	Violation of section 3(1) read with section 3(3)(b)	*Prima facie* case found and directions issued under section 26 (1) to the DG to investigate and report within 60 days	Unanimous
Indian Glycols Limited v Indian Oil Corporation and others, Case No. 14/2012	Allegation of cartelization against oil marketing companies as well as members of the Indian Sugar Mills Association leading to price	Violation of section 3(3) (a) (b) and (c)	As per majority: No *Prima facie* case exists and the case ordered to be closed as per section 26(2) As per dissent,	Not unanimous

	fixation of ethanol		a *prima facie* case exists of violation of section 3(3)	
Association of Third Party Administrators v General Insurers (Public Sector) Association of India (GISPA), Case No. 49/2010	Allegation by the informant against opposite parties of cartelization in the field of health insurance services through the formation of an association	Violation of section 3(3)	As per the majority: No *Prima facie* case exists and the case ordered to be closed as per section 26(2) As per dissent, a *prima facie* case exists of violation of section 3(3)	Not unanimous
In re: Charging of differential rate of interest by banks, MRTP Case No. DGIR/2007/ IP/104-RTPE Case No. 33/2007	Allegation against banks of cartelization through the means of charging differential rate of interest	Violation of section 3(3)	As per the majority: No *Prima facie* case exists and the case ordered to be closed as per section 26(2) As per dissent: a *prima facie* case exists of violation of section 3(3)	Not unanimous
In re: All India Tyre Dealers' Federation v Tyre Manufacturers, MRTP Case: RTPE No. 20 of 2008	Allegation against tyre manufacturers of cartelization through the means of price manipulation and restriction of production and supplies	Violation of section 3(3)	As per majority: Not enough proof to establish the existence of cartel As per dissent: There is conclusive proof of cartelization	Not unanimous

			by the tyre manufacturers and infringement of section 3(3)(a) and (b) read with 3(1)	
Film & Television Producers Guild of India v Multiplex Association of India (MAI), Case No. 37/2011	Allegation against the multiplex association of cartelization by imposing terms, fixing prices of their services and by collectively boycotting the producers not agreeing to their terms	Violation of section (3) (1) read with section (3) (3) (a) and (b)	As per the majority: No sufficient evidence to establish existence of cartel by fixing prices for exhibition of films or limiting supply of films As per dissent: The group of multiplex owners acted in concert by limiting the supply of films and fixing the prices of their services, thus violating section (3) (3) (a) and (b)	Not unanimous
In re: Rise in onion prices, suo moto Case No. 01/2011	Allegation of cartelization leading to rise in onion prices	Violation of section 3(3)	As per majority: No evidence of collusion or cartelization leading to rise in prices of onion	Not unanimous

			As per dissent: The DG investigation was flawed as it failed to take note of peculiarities of agriculture markets that is inherently anti-competitive and conducive to cartelization	
In Re: Domestic airlines, Reference Case No. 01/2011	Allegation of cartelization against the domestic airlines by charging exorbitant fares for the ticket	Violation of section 3(3)	As per majority: No proof of cartelization among the domestic airlines As per the dissent: There is price parallelism and price fixing as well as concerted behaviour leading to price parallelism, thus proving cartelization	Not unanimous
In re: Domestic airlines, RTPE 05/2009 of MRTPC/Suo-Motu Case No.02/2010	Allegation of price fixing collusion on the part of the domestic airline operators	Violation of section 3(3)	As per majority: No proof of cartelization among the domestic airlines	Not unanimous

			As per dissent: Proof of concerted behaviour leading to price parallelism and proving cartelization	
In re: Sugar Mills, Suo Motu Case No.1 of 2010	Cartelization of sugar industry leading to fixing of sugar prices by the sugar producers	Violation of section 3(3)(a) and (b)	As per majority: No case of violation of section 3(3) (a) and (b) is established As per dissent: The facts clearly establish violation of section (3) (3) (a) though not section (3) (3) (b)	Not unanimous
Shri Govind Aggarwal & Ors v M/s ICICI Bank Ltd. & Ors, Case No. 15/28,6/28,13/28, 12/28,2/28	Allegation of cartelization against banks through imposition of differential interest rates and pre-payment penalty on loans	Violation of section (3)(3)	As per majority: No case of violation of section 3(3) As per dissent: The facts clearly establish violation of section (3) (3)	Not unanimous

Consumer Online Foundation v. Tata Sky Limited & Ors, Case No. 2 of 2009	The allegations involved reference to cartelization of the direct-to-home (DTH) services market.	Violation of section (3)(3)	As per majority: No case of violation of section 3(3) As per dissent: The facts clearly establish violation of section (3) (3)	Not unanimous
Neeraj Malhotra v Deustche Post Bank Home Finance Limited (Deustche Bank) and others, Case No. 5/2009	Allegation was that the banking and non-banking financial companies were acting in concert and levying pre-payment penalty charges on home loan borrowers	Violation of section (3)(3)	As per majority: No case of violation of section 3(3) As per dissent: The facts clearly establish violation of section (3) (3)	Not unanimous
Yashoda Hospital and Research Centre Ltd. v Indiabulls Financial Services Limited (IFSL), Case No. 12/2010	Complainant alleged that by imposing pre-payment charges the IFSL was indulging in anti-competitive practices akin to cartel conduct	Violation of section (3)(3)	As per majority: No case of violation of section 3(3) As per dissent: The facts clearly establish violation of section (3) (3) (b)	Not unanimous

The Surinder Bhakoo v. The HDFC Bank Ltd., Case No. 15 of 2009	This case involved the anti-competitive concerns regarding pre-payment penalty and foreclosure charges leading to cartelization	Violation of section (3)(3)	As per majority: No case of violation of section 3(3) As per dissent: The facts clearly establish violation of section (3) (3) (b)	Not unanimous
M/s. Metalrod Ltd. v. M/s. Religare Finvest Ltd, Case No. 28/2010	The concern was regarding imposition of pre-payment penalty and foreclosure charges being anti-competitive in nature leading to cartelization	Violation of section (3)(3)	As per majority: No case of violation of section 3(3) As per dissent: The facts clearly establish violation of section (3) (3) (b)	Not unanimous
Shri V. Ramachandran Reddy and others v. HDFC Ltd. and another, Case Ref: Case No. 7/28, 25/28, 8/28, 9/28, 10/28	The complainants alleged the practice of the banks in discriminating between new home loan borrowers qua the existing home loan borrowers, indicating cartelization	Violation of section (3)(3)	As per majority: No case of violation of section 3(3) As per dissent: The facts clearly establish violation of section (3) (3)	Not unanimous

Neeraj Malhotra v. North Delhi Power Limited and others, Case No. 06/2009	The allegation was of price fixing cartelization of the electricity supply sector	Violation of section (3)(3)	As per majority and dissenting: No case of violation of section 3(3). The dissent was on violation of abuse of dominant position	Unanimous
M/s Reliance Big Entertainment Private Limited v Tamil Nadu Film Exhibitors Association, Case No. 78 of 2011	Allegation of anti-competitive behaviour against opposite parties who were indulging in collective boycott of the informant	Violation of section 3(3)	Violation of section 3(3) (b) read with section (3) (3)(1) is established. Penalty under section 27 imposed	Unanimous
DGS & D, M/o Commerce, Govt. of India vs M/s Puja Enterprises & Ors, Ref. Case No. 01/2012	The Director General of Supplies and Disposals of Ministry of Commerce and Industry, alleged collusive and restrictive bidding and cartel formation by bidders with respect to procurement of 'polyester blended duck ankle boots rubber sole'	Violation of section 3(3)	Violation of section (3)(3) (b),(c) and (d) is established and penalty under section 27 imposed	Unanimous

M/s Santuka Associates Pvt. Ltd v All India Organization of Chemists and Druggists and Ors, Case No. 20/2011	Allegation of cartel-like behaviour against the opposite party	Violation of section 3(3)	As per majority: Violation of section 3(3)(b) As per dissent: No violation of section 3(3) is established. Penalty under section 27 imposed.	Non unanimous
Vijay Gupta v. M/s. Paper Merchants Association and others, Case No. 07/2010	The complainant alleged that certain terms and conditions in the regulations of the Paper Merchant's Association, Delhi (PMAD) amounted to collective boycott	Violation of section 3(3)	Violation of section (3)(3)(b) established. Cease and desist order passed under section 27	Unanimous
M/s Cinergy Independent Film Services Pvt. Ltd. v Telangana Telugu Film Distributors Association and Ors, Case No. 56 of 2011	Allegation against association of film producers, distributors and exhibitors, of cartel activity in the form of collective boycott	Violation of section 3(3)	Violation of section (3)(3) (b) established read with section 3(1). Cease and desist order and penalty passed under section 27	Unanimous
Vedant Bio Sciences v Chemists and Druggists Association of Baroda, In Re: MRTP Case No. C-87/2009/DGIR	Allegation against chemists and druggists association of indulging in anti-competitive practices, akin to cartel conduct	Violation of section 3(3)	As per majority: Violation of section (3)(3)(a) and (b) read with section (3)(1) established. As per dissent: No	Not unanimous

			application of section (3)(3). Cease and desist order and penalty imposed under section 27	
Mr. Sajjan Khaitan v Eastern India Motion Picture Association and ors, Case No. 16/2011	Allegation of cartelization against the Eastern India Motion Picture Association, by indulging in collective boycott	Violation of section 3(3)	As per majority: Violation of section (3)(3) (b) read with section (3)(1) As per dissent: No violation of section 3. Cease and desist order passed under section 27	Not unanimous
In re: Alleged cartelization by cement manufacturers, Case No. RTPE 52 of 2006	Allegation of cartelization by cement manufacturers by fixing prices	Violation of section 3(3)	Violation of section (3)(3) (a) and (b) established read with section (3)(1). Penalty under section 27 imposed.	Unanimous
Varca Druggists & Chemist & others v Chemists & Druggists Association, Goa, In Re: MRTP Case No. C-127/2009/ DGIR(4/28)	Allegation against chemists and druggists association for indulging in anti-competitive practices, akin to cartel conduct	Violation of section (3)(3)	As per majority: Violation of section (3)(3) (a) and (b) established read with section (3)(1). As per dissent: No violation of section 3.	Not unanimous

			Penalty under section 27 imposed.	
In re:-Aluminum phosphide tablets manufacturers, suo-motu Case No. 02/2011	Allegations against aluminum phosphide tablets manufacturers of collective boycott through cartelization	Violation of section (3)(3)	Violation of section (3)(3) (a), (b) and (d) established. Penalty imposed under section 27	Unanimous
Sunshine Pictures Private Limited & Eros International Media Limited vs Central Circuit Cine Association, Indore & Ors., Case No. 52 of 2010 and Case No. 56 of 2010	Allegation against film bodies/ association of cartelization by indulging in collective boycott and other coercive and collusive activities	Violation of section (3)(3)	As per majority: Violation of section (3)(3) (b) read along with section (3)(1) As per dissent: Section (3) not applicable. Penalty imposed under section 27	Not unanimous
Builders Association of India v Cement Manufacturer's Association and Others. Case No. 29/2010	Allegations by the builder association against twelve cement manufacturers of cartelizing the domestic market by fixing the prices of cement.	Violation of section (3)(3)	Violation of section(3) (3)(a) and (b) read with section (3)(1)	Unanimous

FICCI-Multiplex Association of India v. United Producers/ Distributors Forum & Ors, Case No.01 of 2009	Multiplex owners alleged that the Hindi film producer's association was acting like a cartel and dictating the terms on which the multiplex owner can exhibit a film.	Violation of section (3)(3)	Violation of section (3)(3) established. Cease and desist order and penalty was imposed under section 27	Unanimous

Appendix 2

THE COMPETITION ACT, 2002[1]

No. 12 OF 2003

[13th January, 2003.]

An Act to provide, keeping in view of the economic development of the country, for the establishment of a Commission to prevent practices having adverse effect on competition, to promote and sustain competition in markets, to protect the interests of consumers and to ensure freedom of trade carried on by other participants in markets, in India, and for matters connected therewith or incidental thereto.

BE it enacted by Parliament in the Fifty-third Year of the Republic of India as follows:—

Chapter I
Preliminary

Short title, extent and commencement

1. (*1*) This Act may be called the Competition Act, 2002.

(*2*) It extends to the whole of India except the State of Jammu and Kashmir.

(*3*) It shall come into force on such date as the Central Government may, by notification in the Official Gazette, appoint:

Provided that different dates may be appointed for different provisions of this Act and any reference in any such provision to the

[1] The following Act of Parliament received the assent of the President on the 13th January, 2003

commencement of this Act shall be construed as a reference to the coming into force of that provision.

Definitions

2. In this Act, unless the context otherwise requires,—

(a) "acquisition" means, directly or indirectly, acquiring or agreeing to acquire—

(i) shares, voting rights or assets of any enterprise; or

(ii) control over management or control over assets of any enterprise;

(b) "agreement" includes any arrangement or understanding or action in concert,—

(i) whether or not, such arrangement, understanding or action is formal or in writing; or

(ii) whether or not such arrangement, understanding or action is intended to be enforceable by legal proceedings;

[2][(ba)"Appellate Tribunal" means the Competition Appellate Tribunal established under sub-section (*1*) of Section 53A"]

(c) "cartel" includes an association of producers, sellers, distributors, traders or service providers who, by agreement amongst themselves, limit, control or attempt to control the production, distribution, sale or price of, or, trade in goods or provision of services;

(d) "Chairperson" means the Chairperson of the Commission appointed under sub-section (*1*) of section 8;

(e) "Commission" means the Competition Commission of India established under sub-section(*1*) of section 7;

(f) "consumer" means any person who—

(i) buys any goods for a consideration which has been paid or promised or partly paid and partly promised, or under any system of deferred payment and includes any user of such goods other than the person who buys such goods for consideration paid or promised or partly paid or partly promised, or under any system of deferred payment when such use is made with the approval of such person, whether such purchase of goods is for resale or for any commercial purpose or for personal use;

(ii) hires or avails of any services for a consideration which has been paid or promised or partly paid and partly promised, or under

[2] Ins. by Competition (Amendment) Act, 2007

any system of deferred payment and includes any beneficiary of such services other than the person who hires or avails of the services for consideration paid or promised, or partly paid and partly promised, or under any system of deferred payment, when such services are availed of with the approval of the first-mentioned person whether such hiring or availing of services is for any commercial purpose or for personal use;

(g) "Director General" means the Director General appointed under subsection (*1*) of section 16 and includes any Additional, Joint, Deputy or Assistant Directors General appointed under that section;

(h) "enterprise" means a person or a department of the Government, who or which is, or has been, engaged in any activity, relating to the production, storage, supply, distribution, acquisition or control of articles or goods, or the provision of services, of any kind, or in investment, or in the business of acquiring, holding, underwriting or dealing with shares, debentures or other securities of any other body corporate, either directly or through one or more of its units or divisions or subsidiaries, whether such unit or division or subsidiary is located at the same place where the enterprise is located or at a different place or at different places, but does not include any activity of the Government relatable to the sovereign functions of the Government including all activities carried on by the departments of the Central Government dealing with atomic energy, currency, defence and space.

Explanation.—For the purposes of this clause,—

(a) "activity" includes profession or occupation;

(b) "article" includes a new article and "service" includes a new service;

(c) "unit" or "division", in relation to an enterprise, includes—

(i) a plant or factory established for the production, storage, supply, distribution, acquisition or control of any article or goods;

(ii) any branch or office established for the provision of any service;

(i) "goods" means goods as defined in the Sale of Goods Act, 1930 (3 of 1930) and includes—

(A) products manufactured, processed or mined;

(B) debentures, stocks and shares after allotment;

(C) in relation to goods supplied, distributed or controlled in India, goods imported into India;

(j) "Member" means a Member of the Commission appointed under subsection (*l*) of section8 and includes the Chairperson;

(k) "notification" means a notification published in the Official Gazette;

(l) "person" includes—

(i) an individual;

(ii) a Hindu undivided family;

(iii) a company;

(iv) a firm;

(v) an association of persons or a body of individuals, whether incorporated or not, in India or outside India;

(vi) any corporation established by or under any Central, State or Provincial Act or a Government company as defined in section 617 of the Companies Act, 1956 (1 of 1956);

(vii) any body corporate incorporated by or under the laws of a country outside India;

(viii) a co-operative society registered under any law relating to cooperative societies;

(ix) a local authority;

(x) every artificial juridical person, not falling within any of the preceding sub-clauses;

(m) "practice" includes any practice relating to the carrying on of any trade by a person or an enterprise;

(n) "prescribed" means prescribed by rules made under this Act;

(o) "price", in relation to the sale of any goods or to the performance of any services, includes every valuable consideration, whether direct or indirect, or deferred, and includes any consideration which in effect relates to the sale of any goods or to the performance of any services although ostensibly relating to any other matter or thing;

(p) "public financial institution" means a public financial institution specified under section 4A of the Companies Act, 1956 (1 of 1956) and includes a State Financial, Industrial or Investment Corporation;

(q) "regulations" means the regulations made by the Commission under section 64;

(r) "relevant market" means the market which may be determined by the Commission with reference to the relevant product market or the relevant geographic market or with reference to both the markets;

(s) "relevant geographic market" means a market comprising the area in which the conditions of competition for supply of goods or provision of services or demand of goods or services are distinctly homogenous and can be distinguished from the conditions prevailing in the neighbouring areas;

(t) "relevant product market" means a market comprising all those products or services which are regarded as interchangeable or substitutable by the consumer, by reason of characteristics of the products or services, their prices and intended use;

(u) "service" means service of any description which is made available to potential users and includes the provision of services in connection with business of any industrial or commercial matters such as banking, communication, education, financing, insurance, chit funds, real estate, transport, storage, material treatment, processing, supply of electrical or other energy, boarding, lodging, entertainment, amusement, construction, repair, conveying of news or information and advertising;

(v) "shares" means shares in the share capital of a company carrying voting rights and includes—

  (i) any security which entitles the holder to receive shares with voting rights;

  (ii) stock except where a distinction between stock and share is expressed or implied;

(w) "statutory authority" means any authority, board, corporation, council, institute, university or any other body corporate, established by or under any Central, State or Provincial Act for the purposes of regulating production or supply of goods or provision of any services or markets therefor or any matter connected therewith or incidental thereto;

(x) "trade" means any trade, business, industry, profession or occupation relating to the production, supply, distribution, storage or control of goods and includes the provision of any services;

(y) "turnover" includes value of sale of goods or services;

(z) words and expressions used but not defined in this Act and defined in the Companies Act, 1956 (1 of 1956) shall have the same meanings respectively assigned to them in that Act.

CHAPTER II

PROHIBITION OF CERTAIN AGREEMENTS, ABUSE OF DOMINANT POSITION AND REGULATION OF COMBINATIONS

Prohibition of agreements

Anti-competitive agreements

3. (*1*) No enterprise or association of enterprises or person or association of persons shall enter into any agreement in respect of production, supply, distribution, storage, acquisition or control of goods or provision of services, which causes or is likely to cause an appreciable adverse effect on competition within India.

(*2*) Any agreement entered into in contravention of the provisions contained in subsection (1) shall be void.

(*3*) Any agreement entered into between enterprises or associations of enterprises or persons or associations of persons or between any person and enterprise or practice carried on, or decision taken by, any association of enterprises or association of persons, including cartels, engaged in identical or similar trade of goods or provision of services, which—

(a) directly or indirectly determines purchase or sale prices;

(b) limits or controls production, supply, markets, technical development, investment or provision of services;

(c) shares the market or source of production or provision of services by way of allocation of geographical area of market, or type of goods or services, or number of customers in the market or any other similar way;

(d) directly or indirectly results in bid rigging or collusive bidding,

shall be presumed to have an appreciable adverse effect on competition:

Provided that nothing contained in this sub-section shall apply to any agreement entered into by way of joint ventures if such agreement increases efficiency in production, supply, distribution, storage, acquisition or control of goods or provision of services.

Explanation.—For the purposes of this sub-section, "bid rigging" means any agreement, between enterprises or persons referred to in sub-section (3) engaged in identical or similar production or trading of goods or provision of services, which has the effect of eliminating or reducing competition for bids or adversely affecting or manipulating the process for bidding

(*4*) Any agreement amongst enterprises or persons at different stages or levels of the production chain in different markets, in respect of production, supply, distribution, storage, sale or price of, or trade in goods or provision of services, including—

(a) tie-in arrangement;
(b) exclusive supply agreement;
(c) exclusive distribution agreement;
(d) refusal to deal;
(e) resale price maintenance,

shall be an agreement in contravention of sub-section (*1*) if such agreement causes or is likely to cause an appreciable adverse effect on competition in India.

Explanation.—For the purposes of this sub-section,—

(a) "tie-in arrangement" includes any agreement requiring a purchaser of goods, as a condition of such purchase, to purchase some other goods;
(b) "exclusive supply agreement" includes any agreement restricting in any manner the purchaser in the course of his trade from acquiring or otherwise dealing in any goods other than those of the seller or any other person;
(c) "exclusive distribution agreement" includes any agreement to limit, restrict or withhold the output or supply of any goods or allocate any area or market for the disposal or sale of the goods;
(d) "refusal to deal" includes any agreement which restricts, or is likely to restrict, by any method the persons or classes of persons to whom goods are sold or from whom goods are bought;
(e) "resale price maintenance" includes any agreement to sell goods on condition that the prices to be charged on the resale by the purchaser shall be the prices stipulated by the seller unless it is clearly stated that prices lower than those prices may be charged.

(*5*) Nothing contained in this section shall restrict—

(i) the right of any person to restrain any infringement of, or to impose reasonable conditions, as may be necessary for protecting any of his rights which have been or may be conferred upon him under—

(a) the Copyright Act, 1957 (14 of 1957);

(b) the Patents Act, 1970 (39 of 1970);

(c) the Trade and Merchandise Marks Act, 1958 (43 of 1958) or the Trade Marks Act, 1999 (47 of 1999);

(d) the Geographical Indications of Goods (Registration and Protection) Act, 1999 (48 of 1999);

(e) the Designs Act, 2000 (16 of 2000);

(f) the Semi-conductor Integrated Circuits Layout-Design Act, 2000 (37 of 2000);

(ii) the right of any person to export goods from India to the extent to which the agreement relates exclusively to the production, supply, distribution or control of goods or provision of services for such export.

Prohibition of abuse of dominant position

Abuse of dominant position

4. [3][(*1*)No enterprise or group] shall abuse its dominant position.]

(*2*) There shall be an abuse of dominant position [4][under sub-section (*1*), if an enterprise or a group].—-

(a) directly or indirectly, imposes unfair or discriminatory—

(i) condition in purchase or sale of goods or service; or

(ii) price in purchase or sale (including predatory price) of goods or service.

Explanation.— For the purposes of this clause, the unfair or discriminatory condition in purchase or sale of goods or service referred to in sub-clause (i) and unfair or discriminatory price in purchase or sale of goods (including predatory price) or service referred to in sub-clause (ii) shall not include such discriminatory condition or price which may be adopted to meet the competition; or

---

3 Subs. by Competition (Amendment) Act, 2007 for "No enterprise shall abuse its dominant position."

4 Subs. by Competition (Amendment) Act, 2007 for "under sub-section (1), if an enterprise"

(b) limits or restricts—
  (i) production of goods or provision of services or market therefor; or
  (ii) technical or scientific development relating to goods or services to the prejudice of consumers; or

(c) indulges in practice or practices resulting in denial of market access [5][in any manner]; or

(d) makes conclusion of contracts subject to acceptance by other parties of supplementary obligations which, by their nature or according to commercial usage, have no connection with the subject of such contracts; or

(e) uses its dominant position in one relevant market to enter into, or protect, other relevant market.

Explanation.—For the purposes of this section, the expression—

(a) "dominant position" means a position of strength, enjoyed by an enterprise, in the relevant market, in India, which enables it to—
  (i) operate independently of competitive forces prevailing in the relevant market; or
  (ii) affect its competitors or consumers or the relevant market in its favour.

(b) "predatory price" means the sale of goods or provision of services, at a. price which is below the cost, as may be determined by regulations, of production of the goods or provision of services, with a view to reduce competition or eliminate the competitors.

[6][(c)"group" shall have the same meaning as assigned to it in clause (b) of the Explanation to section 5.]

Regulation of combinations

Combination

5. The acquisition of one or more enterprises by one or more persons or merger or amalgamation of enterprises shall be a combination of such enterprises and persons or enterprises, if—

(a) any acquisition where—
  (i) the parties to the acquisition, being the acquirer and the enterprise, whose control, shares, voting rights or assets have been acquired or are being acquired jointly have,—

---

[5] Ins. by Competition (Amendment) Act, 2007

[6] Ins. by Competition (Amendment) Act, 2007

(A) either, in India, the assets of the value of more than rupees one thousand crores or turnover more than rupees three thousand crores; or

(B) [7][in India or outside India, in aggregate, the assets of the value of more than five hundred million US dollars, including at least rupees five hundred crores in India, or turnover more than fifteen hundred million US dollars, including at least rupees fifteen hundred crores in India; or]

(ii) the group, to which the enterprise whose control, shares, assets or voting rights have been acquired or are being acquired, would belong after the acquisition, jointly have or would jointly have,—

(A) either in India, the assets of the value of more than rupees four thousand crores or turnover more than rupees twelve thousand crores; or

(B) [8][in India or outside India, in aggregate, the assets of the value of more than two billion US dollars, including at least rupees five hundred crores in India, or turnover more than six billion US dollars, including at least rupees fifteen hundred crores in India; or]

(b) acquiring of control by a person over an enterprise when such person has already direct or indirect control over another enterprise engaged in production, distribution or trading of a similar or identical or substitutable goods or provision of a similar or identical or substitutable service, if—

(i) the enterprise over which control has been acquired along with the enterprise over which the acquirer already has direct or indirect control jointly have,—

(A) either in India, the assets of the value of more than rupees one thousand crores or turnover more than rupees three thousand crores; or

---

[7] Subs. by Competition (Amendment) Act, 2007 for:
"in India or outside India, in aggregate, the assets of the value of more than five hundred million US dollars or turnover more than fifteen hundred million US dollars; or"

[8] Subs. by Competition (Amendment) Act, 2007 for:
"in India or outside India, in aggregate, the assets of the value of more than two billion US dollars or turnover more than six billion US dollars; or"

(B) [9][in India or outside India, in aggregate, the assets of the value of more than five hundred million US dollars, including at least rupees five hundred crores in India, or turnover more than fifteen hundred million US dollars, including at least rupees fifteen hundred crores in India; or]

(ii) the group, to which enterprise whose control has been acquired, or is being acquired, would belong after the acquisition, jointly have or would jointly have,—

(A) either in India, the assets of the value of more than rupees four thousand crores or turnover more than rupees twelve thousand crores; or

(B) [10][in India or outside India, in aggregate, the assets of the value of more than two billion US dollars, including at least rupees five hundred crores in India, or turnover more than six billion US dollars, including at least rupees fifteen hundred crores in India; or]

(c) any merger or amalgamation in which—

(i) the enterprise remaining after merger or the enterprise created as a result of the amalgamation, as the case may be, have,—

(A) either in India, the assets of the value of more than rupees one thousand crores or turnover more than rupees three thousand crores; or

(B) [11][in India or outside India, in aggregate, the assets of the value of more than five hundred million US dollars, including at least rupees five hundred crores in India, or turnover more than fifteen hundred million US dollars, including at least rupees fifteen hundred crores in India; or]

(ii) the group, to which the enterprise remaining after the merger or the enterprise created as a result of the amalgamation, would

---

9 Subs. by Competition (Amendment) Act, 2007 for
"in India or outside India, in aggregate, the assets of the value of more than five hundred million US dollars or turnover more than fifteen hundred million US dollars; or"

10 Subs. by Competition (Amendment) Act, 2007 for
"in India or outside India, in aggregate, the assets of the value of more than two billion US dollars or turnover more than six billion US dollars; or"

11 Subs. by Competition (Amendment) Act, 2007 for
"in India or outside India, in aggregate, the assets of the value of more than five hundred million US dollars or turnover more than fifteen hundred million US dollars; or"

belong after the merger or the amalgamation, as the case may be, have or would have,—

(A) either in India, the assets of the value of more than rupees four-thousand crores or turnover more than rupees twelve thousand crores; or

(B) [12][in India or outside India, in aggregate, the assets of the value of more than two billion US dollars, including at least rupees five hundred crores in India, or turnover more than six billion US dollars, including at least rupees fifteen hundred crores in India;]

Explanation.— For the purposes of this section,—

(a) "control" includes controlling the affairs or management by—
  (i) one or more enterprises, either jointly or singly, over another enterprise or group;
  (ii) one or more groups, either jointly or singly, over another group or enterprise;

(b) "group" means two or more enterprises which, directly or indirectly, are in a position to —
  (i) exercise twenty-six per cent. or more of the voting rights in the other enterprise; or
  (ii) appoint more than fifty per cent. of the members of the board of directors in the other enterprise; or
  (iii) control the management or affairs of the other enterprise;

(c) the value of assets shall be determined by taking the book value of the assets as shown, in the audited books of account of the enterprise, in the financial year immediately preceding the financial year in which the date of proposed merger falls, as reduced by any depreciation, and the value of assets shall include the brand value, value of goodwill, or value of copyright, patent, permitted use, collective mark, registered proprietor, registered trade mark, registered user, homonymous geographical indication, geographical indications, design or layout-design or similar other commercial rights, if any, referred to in sub-section (5) of section 3.

---

12 Subs. by Competition (Amendment) Act, 2007 for:
"in India or outside India, the assets of the value of more than two billion US dollars or turnover more than six billion US dollars.

Regulation of combinations

6. (*1*) No person or enterprise shall enter into a combination which causes or is likely to cause an appreciable adverse effect on competition within the relevant market in India and such a combination shall be void.

(*2*) Subject to the provisions contained in sub-section (*1*), any person or enterprise, who or which proposes to enter into a combination, [13][shall] give notice to the Commission, in the form as may be specified, and the fee which may be determined, by regulations, disclosing the details of the proposed combination, within [14][thirty days] of—

(a) approval of the proposal relating to merger or amalgamation, referred to in clause (c) of section 5, by the board of directors of the enterprises concerned with such merger or amalgamation, as the case may be;

(b) execution of any agreement or other document for acquisition referred to in clause (a) of section 5 or acquiring of control referred to in clause (b) of that section.

[15][(2A)No combination shall come into effect until two hundred and ten days have passed from the day on which the notice has been given to the Commission under sub-section(*2*) or the Commission has passed orders under section 31, whichever is earlier.]

(*3*) The Commission shall, after receipt of notice under sub-section (*2*), deal with such notice in accordance with the provisions contained in sections 29, 30 and 31.

(*4*) The provisions of this section shall not apply to share subscription or financing facility or any acquisition, by a public financial institution, foreign institutional investor, bank or venture capital fund, pursuant to any covenant of a loan agreement or investment agreement.

(*5*) The public financial institution, foreign institutional investor, bank or venture capital fund, referred to in sub-section (4), shall, within seven days from the date of the acquisition, file, in the form as may be specified by regulations, with the Commission the details of the acquisition including the details of control, the circumstances for

---

13 Subs. by Competition (Amendment) Act, 2007 for "may, at his or its option"

14 Subs. by Competition (Amendment) Act, 2007 for "seven days"

15 Ins. by Competition (Amendment) Act, 2007

exercise of such control and the consequences of default arising out of such loan agreement or investment agreement, as the case may be.

Explanation.—For the purposes of this section, the expression—

(a) "foreign institutional investor" has the same meaning as assigned to it in clause (a) of the Explanation to section 115AD of the Income-tax Act, 1961(43 of 1961);

(b) "venture capital fund" has the same meaning as assigned to it in clause (b) of the Explanation to clause (23 FB) of section 10 of the Income-tax Act, 1961(43 of 1961);.

CHAPTER III

COMPETITION COMMISSION OF INDIA

Establishment of Commission

7. (*1*) With effect from such date as the Central Government may, by notification, appoint, there shall be established, for the purposes of this Act, a Commission to be called the "Competition Commission of India".

(*2*) The Commission shall be a body corporate by the name aforesaid having perpetual succession and a common seal with power, subject to the provisions of this Act, to acquire, hold and dispose of property, both movable and immovable, and to contract and shall, by the said name, sue or be sued.

(*3*) The head office of the Commission shall be at such place as the Central Government may decide from time to time.

(*4*) The Commission may establish offices at other places in India.

Composition of Commission

[16][**8.**(*1*) The Commission shall consist of a Chairperson and not less than two and not more than six other Members to be appointed by the Central Government.

(*2*) The Chairperson and every other Member shall be a person of ability, integrity and standing and who has special knowledge of, and such professional experience of not less than fifteen years in, international trade, economics, business, commerce, law, finance, accountancy, management, industry, public affairs or competition

---

16 Subs. by Competition (Amendment) Act, 2007 for;

(*1*) The Commission shall consist of a Chairperson and not less than two and not more than ten other Members to be appointed by the Central Government:
Provided that the Central Government shall appoint the Chairperson and a Member during the first year of the establishment of the Commission.

(*2*) The Chairperson and every other Member shall be a person of ability, integrity and standing and who has been, or is qualified to be a judge of a High Court, or, has special knowledge of, and professional experience of not less than fifteen years in international trade, economics, business, commerce, law, finance, accountancy, management, industry, public affairs, administration or in any other matter which, in the opinion of the Central Government may be useful to the Commission.

(*3*) The Chairperson and other Members shall be whole-time Members."

matters, including competition law and policy, which in the opinion of the Central Government, may be useful to the Commission.

(*3*) The Chairperson and other Members shall be whole-time Members.]

[17][**Selection Committee for Chairperson and Members of Commission**]

[18][**9.** (*1*) The Chairperson and other Members of the Commission shall be appointed by the Central Government from a panel of names recommended by a Selection Committee consisting of –

(a) the Chief Justice of India or his nominee — Chairperson;

(b) the Secretary in the Ministry of Corporate Affairs — Member;

(c) the Secretary in the Ministry of Law and Justice — Member;

(d) two experts of repute who have special knowledge of, and professional experience in international trade, economics, business, commerce, law, finance, accountancy, management, industry, public affairs or competition matters including competition law and policy — Members.

(2) The term of the Selection Committee and the manner of selection of panel of names shall be such as may be prescribed.]

Term of office of Chairperson and other Members

10.(*1*) The Chairperson and every other Member shall hold office as such for a term of five years from the date on which he enters upon his office and shall be eligible for re-appointment:

[19][Provided that the Chairperson or other Members shall not hold office as such after he has attained the age of sixty-five years]

(*2*) A vacancy caused by the resignation or removal of the Chairperson or any other Member under section 11 or by death or otherwise shall be filled by fresh appointment in accordance with the provisions of sections 8 and 9.

---

17 Subs. by Competition (Amendment) Act, 2007 for "Selection of Chairperson and other Members"

18 Subs. by Competition (Amendment) Act, 2007 for:
"The Chairperson and other Members shall be selected in the manner as may be prescribed."

19 Subs. by Competition (Amendment) Act, 2007 for:
"Provided that no Chairperson or other Member shall hold office as such after he has attained-
(a) in the case of the Chairperson, the age of sixty-seven years;
(b) in the case of any other Member, the age of sixty-five years."

(*3*) The Chairperson and every other Member shall, before entering upon his office, make and subscribe to an oath of office and of secrecy in such form, manner and before such authority, as may be prescribed.

(*4*) In the event of the occurrence of a vacancy in the office of the Chairperson by reason of his death, resignation or otherwise, the senior-most Member shall act as the Chairperson, until the date on which a new Chairperson, appointed in accordance with the provisions of this Act to fill such vacancy, enters upon his office.

(*5*) When the Chairperson is unable to discharge his functions owing to absence, illness or any other cause, the senior-most Member shall discharge the functions of the Chairperson until the date on which the Chairperson resumes the charge of his functions.

Resignation, removal and suspension of Chairperson and other members

11.(*1*) The Chairperson or any other Member may, by notice in writing under his hand addressed to the Central Government, resign his office:

Provided that the Chairperson or a Member shall, unless he is permitted by the Central Government to relinquish his office sooner, continue to hold office until the expiry of three months from the date of receipt of such notice or until a person duly appointed as his successor enters upon his office or until the expiry of his term of office, whichever is the earliest.

(*2*) Notwithstanding anything contained in sub-section (*1*), the Central Government may, by order, remove the Chairperson or any other Member from his office if such Chairperson or Member, as the case may be,—

(a) is, or at any time has been, adjudged as an insolvent; or

(b) has engaged at any time, during his term of office, in any paid employment; or

(c) has been convicted of an offence which, in the opinion of the Central Government, involves moral turpitude; or

(d) has acquired such financial or other interest as is likely to affect prejudicially his functions as a Member; or

(e) has so abused his position as to render his continuance in office prejudicial to the public interest; or

(f) has become physically or mentally incapable of acting as a Member.

(*3*) Notwithstanding anything contained in sub-section (2), no Member shall be removed from his office on the ground specified in clause (d) or clause (e) of that subsection unless the Supreme Court, on a reference being made to it in this behalf by the Central Government, has, on an inquiry, held by it in accordance with such procedure as may be prescribed in this behalf by the Supreme Court, reported that the Member, ought on such ground or grounds to be removed.

Restriction on employment of Chairperson and other Members in certain cases

12. The Chairperson and other Members shall not, for a period of [20][two years] from the date on which they cease to hold office, accept any employment in, or connected with the management or administration of, any enterprise which has been a party to a proceeding before the Commission under this Act:

Provided that nothing contained in this section shall apply to any employment under the Central Government or a State Government or local authority or in any statutory authority or any corporation established by or under any Central, State or Provincial Act or a Government company as defined in section 617 of the Companies Act, 1956 (1 of 1956).

[21]**[Administrative powers of Chairperson]**

[22][**13.** The Chairperson shall have the powers of general superintendence, direction and control in respect of all administrative matters of the Commission:

[20] Subs. by Competition (Amendment) Act, 2007 for "one year"

[21] Subs. by Competition (Amendment) Act, 2007 for "Financial and administrative powers of Member Administration"

[22] Subs. by Competition (Amendment) Act, 2007 for:
"The Central Government shall designate any Member as Member Administration who shall exercise such financial and administrative powers as may be vested in him under the rules made by the Central Government:
Provided that the Member Administration shall have authority to delegate such of his financial and administrative powers as he may think fit to any other officer of the Commission subject to the condition that such officer shall, while exercising such delegated powers continue to act under the direction, superintendence and control of the Member Administration."

Provided that the Chairperson may delegate such of his powers relating to administrative matters of the Commission, as he may think fit, to any other Member or officer of the Commission."]

Salary and allowances and other terms and conditions of service of Chairperson and other Members

14.(*1*) The salary, and the other terms and conditions of service, of the Chairperson and other Members, including travelling expenses, house rent allowance and conveyance facilities, sumptuary allowance and medical facilities shall be such as may be prescribed.

(*2*) The salary, allowances and other terms and conditions of service of the Chairperson or a Member shall not be varied to his disadvantage after appointment.

Vacancy, etc. not to invalidate proceedings of Commission

15. No act or proceeding of the Commission shall be invalid merely by reason of—

(a) any vacancy in, or any defect in the constitution of, the Commission; or

(b) any defect in the appointment of a person acting as a Chairperson or as a Member; or

(c) any irregularity in the procedure of the Commission not affecting the merits of the case.

Appointment of Director General, etc.

16.[23][(*1*)The Central Government may, by notification, appoint a Director General for the purposes of assisting the Commission in conducting inquiry into contravention of any of the provisions of this Act and for performing such other functions as are, or may be, provided by or under this Act.

---

[23] Subs. by Competition (Amendment) Act, 2007 for:
"The Central Government may, by notification, appoint a Director General and as many Additional, Joint, Deputy or Assistant Directors General or such other advisers, consultants or officers, as it may think fit, for the purposes of assisting the Commission in conducting inquiry into contravention of any of the provisions of this Act and for the conduct of cases before the Commission and for performing such other functions as are, or may be, provided by or under this Act"

(*1A*) The number of other Additional, Joint, Deputy or Assistant Directors General or such officers or other employees in the office of Director General and the manner of appointment of such Additional, Joint, Deputy or Assistant Directors General or such officers or other employees shall be such as may be prescribed."]

(*2*) Every Additional, Joint, Deputy and Assistant Directors General or [24][such officers or other employees,] shall exercise his powers, and discharge his functions, subject to the general control, supervision and direction of the Director General.

(*3*) The salary, allowances and other terms and conditions of service of the Director General and Additional, Joint, Deputy and Assistant Directors General or, [25][such officers or other employees,] shall be such as may be prescribed.

(*4*) The Director General and Additional, Joint, Deputy and Assistant Directors General or [26][such officers or other employees,] shall be appointed from amongst persons of integrity and outstanding ability and who have experience in investigation, and knowledge of accountancy, management, business, public administration, international trade, law or economics and such other qualifications as may be prescribed.

[27][Appointment of Secretary, experts, professionals and officers and other employees of Commission]

[28][**17.**(*1*) The Commission may appoint a Secretary and such officers and other employees as it considers necessary for the efficient performance of its functions under this Act.

(*2*) The salaries and allowances payable to and other terms and conditions

---

[24] Subs. by Competition (Amendment) Act, 2007 for "such other advisers, consultants and officers,"

[25] Subs. by Competition (Amendment) Act, 2007 for "such other advisers, consultants and officers,"

[26] Subs. by Competition (Amendment) Act, 2007 for "such other advisers, consultants and officers,"

[27] Subs. by Competition (Amendment) Act, 2007 for "Registrar and officers and other employees of Commission"

[28] Subs. by Competition (Amendment) Act, 2007 for:

"(1) The Commission may appoint a Registrar and such officers and other employees as it considers necessary for the efficient performance of its functions under this Act

(2) The salaries and allowances payable to and other terms and conditions of service of the Registrar and officers and other employees of the Commission and the number of such officers and other employees shall be such as may be prescribed."

of service of the Secretary and officers and other employees of the Commission and the number of such officers and other employees shall be such as may be prescribed.

(*3*) The Commission may engage, in accordance with the procedure specified by regulations, such number of experts and professionals of integrity and outstanding ability, who have special knowledge of, and experience in, economics, law, business or such other disciplines related to competition, as it deems necessary to assist the Commission in the discharge of its functions under this Act.]

CHAPTER IV

DUTIES, POWERS AND FUNCTIONS OF COMMISSION

Duties of Commission

18. Subject to the provisions of this Act, it shall be the duty of the Commission to eliminate practices having adverse effect on competition, promote and sustain competition, protect the interests of consumers and ensure freedom of trade carried on by other participants, in markets in India:

Provided that the Commission may, for the purpose of discharging its duties or performing its functions under this Act, enter into any memorandum or arrangement with the prior approval of the Central Government, with any agency of any foreign country.

Inquiry into certain agreements and dominant position of enterprise

19. (*1*) The Commission may inquire into any alleged contravention of the provisions contained in subsection (1) of section 3 or sub-section (1) of section 4 either on its own motion or on—

(a) [29][receipt of any information, in such manner and] accompanied by such fee as may be determined by regulations, from any person, consumer or their association or trade association; or

(b) a reference made to it by the Central Government or a State Government or a statutory authority.

(*2*) Without prejudice to the provisions contained in sub-section (*1*), the powers and functions of the Commission shall include the powers and functions specified in sub-sections (*3*) to (*7*).

(*3*) The Commission shall, while determining whether an agreement has an appreciable adverse effect on competition under section 3, have due regard to all or any of the following factors, namely:—

(a) creation of barriers to new entrants in the market;

(b) driving existing competitors out of the market;

(c) foreclosure of competition by hindering entry into the market;

(d) accrual of benefits to consumers;

(e) improvements in production or distribution of goods or provision of services;

---

[29] Subs. by Competition (Amendment) Act, 2007 for "receipt of a complaint,"

(f) promotion of technical, scientific and economic development by means of production or distribution of goods or provision of services.

(*4*) The Commission shall, while inquiring whether an enterprise enjoys a dominant position or not under section 4, have due regard to all or any of the following factors, namely:—

(a) market share of the enterprise;
(b) size and resources of the enterprise;
(c) size and importance of the competitors;
(d) economic power of the enterprise including commercial advantages over competitors;
(e) vertical integration of the enterprises or sale or service network of such enterprises;
(f) dependence of consumers on the enterprise;
(g) monopoly or dominant position whether acquired as a result of any statute or by virtue of being a Government company or a public sector undertaking or otherwise;
(h) entry barriers including barriers such as regulatory barriers, financial risk, high capital cost of entry, marketing entry barriers, technical entry barriers, economies of scale, high cost of substitutable goods or service for consumers;
(i) countervailing buying power;
(j) market structure and size of market;
(k) social obligations and social costs;
(l) relative advantage, by way of the contribution to the economic development, by the enterprise enjoying a dominant position having or likely to have an appreciable adverse effect on competition;
(m) any other factor which the Commission may consider relevant for the inquiry.

(*5*) For determining whether a market constitutes a "relevant market" for the purposes of this Act, the Commission shall have due regard to the "relevant geographic market" and "relevant product market".

(*6*) The Commission shall, while determining the "relevant geographic market", have due regard to all or any of the following factors, namely:—

(a) regulatory trade barriers;
(b) local specification requirements;

(c) national procurement policies;
(d) adequate distribution facilities;
(e) transport costs;
(f) language;
(g) consumer preferences;
(h) need for secure or regular supplies or rapid after-sales services.

(7) The Commission shall, while determining the "relevant product market", have due regard to all or any of the following factors, namely:—
(a) physical characteristics or end-use of goods;
(b) price of goods or service;
(c) consumer preferences;
(d) exclusion of in-house production;
(e) existence of specialised producers;
(f) classification of industrial products.

Inquiry into combination by Commission

20. (*1*) The Commission may, upon its own knowledge or information relating to acquisition referred to in clause (a) of section 5 or acquiring of control referred to in clause (b) of section 5 or merger or amalgamation referred to in clause (c) of that section, inquire into whether such a combination has caused or is likely to cause an appreciable adverse effect on competition in India:

Provided that the Commission shall not initiate any inquiry under this sub-section after the expiry of one year from the date on which such combination has taken effect.

(*2*) The Commission shall, on receipt of a notice under sub-section (2) of section 6 [30][***], inquire whether a combination referred to in that notice or reference has caused or is likely to cause an appreciable adverse effect on competition in India.

(*3*) Notwithstanding anything contained in section 5, the Central Government shall, on the expiry of a period of two years from the date of commencement of this Act and thereafter every two years, in consultation with the Commission, by notification, enhance or

[30] The words "or upon receipt of a reference under sub-section (*1*) of section 21" omitted by Competition (Amendment) Act, 2007

reduce, on the basis of the wholesale price index or fluctuations in exchange rate of rupee or foreign currencies, the value of assets or the value of turnover, for the purposes of that section.

(*4*) For the purposes of determining whether a combination would have the effect of or is likely to have an appreciable adverse effect on competition in the relevant market, the Commission shall have due regard to all or any of the following factors, namely:—

(a) actual and potential level of competition through imports in the market;
(b) extent of barriers to entry into the market;
(c) level of combination in the market;
(d) degree of countervailing power in the market;
(e) likelihood that the combination would result in the parties to the combination being able to significantly and sustainably increase prices or profit margins;
(f) extent of effective competition likely to sustain in a market;
(g) extent to which substitutes are available or arc likely to be available in the market;
(h) market share, in the relevant market, of the persons or enterprise in a combination, individually and as a combination;
(i) likelihood that the combination would result in the removal of a vigorous and effective competitor or competitors in the market;
(j) nature and extent of vertical integration in the market;
(k) possibility of a failing business;
(l) nature and extent of innovation;
(m) relative advantage, by way of the contribution to the economic development, by any combination having or likely to have appreciable adverse effect on competition;
(n) whether the benefits of the combination outweigh the adverse impact of the combination, if any.

Reference by statutory authority

21.(*1*) Where in the course of a proceeding before any statutory authority an issue is raised by any party that any decision which such statutory authority has taken or proposes to take is or would be, contrary to any of the provisions of this Act, then such statutory authority may make a reference in respect of such issue to the Commission:

[31][Provided that any statutory authority, may, suo motu, make such a reference to the Commission.]

[32][(*2*)On receipt of a reference under sub-section (*1*), the Commission shall give its opinion, within sixty days of receipt of such reference, to such statutory authority which shall consider the opinion of the Commission and thereafter, give its findings recording reasons therefor on the issues referred to in the said opinion.]

[33][Reference by Commission]

[34][**21A.**(*1*)Where in the course of a proceeding before the Commission an issue is raised by any party that any decision which, the Commission has taken during such proceeding or proposes to take, is or would be contrary to any provision of this Act whose implementation is entrusted to a statutory authority, then the Commission may make a reference in respect of such issue to the statutory authority:

Provided that the Commission, may, suo motu, make such a reference to the statutory authority.

(*2*) On receipt of a reference under sub-section (*1*), the statutory authority shall give its opinion, within sixty days of receipt of such reference, to the Commission which shall consider the opinion of the statutory authority, and thereafter give its findings recording reasons therefor on the issues referred to in the said opinion.]

[35][Meetings of Commission]

---

31 Ins. by Competition (Amendment) Act, 2007

32 Subs. by Competition (Amendment) Act, 2007 for:
"On receipt of a reference under sub-section (*1*), the Commission shall, after hearing the parties to the proceedings, give its opinion to such statutory authority which shall thereafter pass such order on the issues referred to in that sub-section as it deems fit: Provided that the Commission shall give its opinion under this section within sixty days of receipt of such reference."

33 Ins. by Competition (Amendment) Act, 2007

34 Ins. by Competition (Amendment) Act, 2007

35 Subs. by Competition (Amendment) Act, 2007 for "Benches of Commission"

[36][**22.**(*1*)The Commission shall meet at such times and places, and shall observe such rules and procedure in regard to the transaction of business at its meetings as may be provided by regulations.

(*2*) The Chairperson, if for any reason, is unable to attend a meeting of the Commission, the senior-most Member present at the meeting, shall preside at the meeting.

(*3*) All questions which come up before any meeting of the Commission shall be decided by a majority of the Members present and voting, and in the event of an equality of votes, the Chairperson or in his absence, the Member presiding, shall have a second or/casting vote:

Provided that the quorum for such meeting shall be three Members.]

[37]**23.** [Omitted by the Competition (Amendment) Act, 2007]

---

36 Subs. by Competition (Amendment) Act, 2007 for:

"(1) The jurisdiction, powers and authority of the Commission may be exercised by Benches thereof.

(2) The Benches shall be constituted by the Chairperson and each Bench shall consist of not less than two Members.

(3) Every Bench shall consist of at least one Judicial Member.

Explanation.—For the purposes of this sub-section, "Judicial Member" means a Member who is, or has been, or is qualified to be, a Judge of a High Court.

(4) The Bench over which the Chairperson presides shall be the Principal Bench and the other Benches shall be known as the Additional Benches.

(5) There shall be constituted by the Chairperson one or more Benches to be called the Mergers Bench or Mergers Benches, as the case may be, exclusively to deal with matters referred to in sections 5 and 6.

(6) The places at which the Principal Bench, other Additional Bench or Mergers Bench shall ordinarily sit, shall be such as the Central Government may, by notification, specify."

37 Prior to omission, Section 23 read as under:-

"Distribution of business of Commission amongst Benches

(1) Where any Benches are constituted, the Chairperson may, from time to time, by order, make provisions as to the distribution of the business of the Commission amongst the Benches and specify the matters, which may be dealt with by each Bench.

(2) If any question arises as to whether any matter falls within the purview of the business allocated to a Bench, the decision of the Chairperson thereon shall be final.

(3) The Chairperson may

(i) transfer a Member from one Bench to another Bench, or

(ii) authorize the Members of one Bench to discharge also the functions of the Members of other Bench:

Provided that the Chairperson shall transfer, with the prior approval of the Central Government, a Member from one Bench situated in one city to another Bench situated in another city.

[38]**24.** [Omitted by the Competition (Amendment) Act, 2007]

[39]**25.** [Omitted by the Competition (Amendment) Act, 2007]

[40][Procedure for inquiry under section 19]

[41][**26.**(*1*)On receipt of a reference from the Central Government or a State

(4) The Chairperson may, for the purpose of securing that any case or matter which, having regard to the nature of the questions involved, requires or is required in his opinion or under the rules made by the Central Government in this behalf, to be decided by a Bench composed of more than two Members, issue such general or special orders as he may deem fit."

38 Prior to omission Section 24 read as under:
"Procedure for deciding a case where Members of a Bench differ in opinion
If the Members of a Bench differ in opinion on any point, they shall state the point or points on which they differ, and make a reference to the Chairperson who shall either hear the point or points himself or refer the case for hearing on such point or points by one or more of the other Members and such point or points shall be decided according to the opinion of the majority of the Members who have heard the case, including those who first heard it."

39 Prior to omission, Section 25 read as under:
"Jurisdiction of Bench
An inquiry shall be initiated or a complaint be instituted or a reference be made under this Act before a Bench within the local limits of whose jurisdiction—
(a) the respondent, or each of the respondents, where there are more than one, at the time of the initiation of inquiry or institution of the complaint or making of reference, as the case may be, actually and voluntarily resides, or carries on business, or personally works for gain; or
(b) any of the respondents, where there are more than one, at the time of the initiation of the inquiry or institution of complaint or making of reference, as the case may be, actually and voluntarily resides or carries on business or personally works for gain provided that in such case either the leave of the Bench is given, or the respondents who do not reside, or carry on business, or personally work for gain, as aforesaid, acquiesce in such institution; or
(c) the cause of action, wholly or in part, arises.
Explanation.—A respondent, being a person referred to in sub-clause (iii) or sub-clause (vi) or sub-clause (vii) or sub-clause (viii) of clause
(l) of section 2, shall be deemed to carry on business at its sole or principal place of business in India or at its registered office in India or where it has also a subordinate office at such place."

40 Subs. by Competition (Amendment) Act, 2007 for "Procedure for inquiry on complaints under section 19"

41 Subs. by Competition (Amendment) Act, 2007 for:
"Procedure for inquiry on complaints under Section 19
(1) On receipt of a complaint or a reference from the Central Government or a State Government or a statutory authority or on its own knowledge or information, under

Government or a statutory authority or on its own knowledge or information received under section 19, if the Commission is of the opinion that there exists a prima facie case, it shall direct the Director General to cause an investigation to be made into the matter:

Provided that if the subject matter of an information received is, in the opinion of the Commission, substantially the same as or has been covered by any previous information received, then the new information may be clubbed with the previous information.

(*2*) Where on receipt of a reference from the Central Government or a State Government or a statutory authority or information received under section 19, the Commission is of the opinion that there exists no prima facie case, it shall close the matter forthwith and pass such orders as it deems fit and send a copy of its order to the Central

---

section 19, if the Commission is of the opinion that there exists a prima facie case, it shall direct the Director General to cause an investigation to be made into the matter.

(2) The Director General shall, on receipt of direction under sub-section (1), submit a report on his findings within such period as may be specified by the Commission.

(3) Where on receipt of a complaint under clause (a) of sub-section (1) of section 19, the Commission is of the opinion that there exists no prima facie case, it shall dismiss the complaint and may pass such orders as it deems fit, including imposition of costs, if necessary.

(4) The Commission shall forward a copy of the report referred to in sub-section (2) to the parties concerned or to the Central Government or the State Government or the statutory authority, as the case may be.

(5) If the report of the Director General relates on a complaint and such report recommends that there is no contravention of any of the provisions of this Act, the complainant shall be given an opportunity to rebut the findings of the Director General.

(6) If, after hearing the complainant, the Commission agrees with the recommendation of the Director General, it shall dismiss the complaint.

(7) If, after hearing the complainant, the Commission is of the opinion that further inquiry is called for, it shall direct the complainant to proceed with the complaint.

(8) If the report of the Director General relates on a reference made under sub-section (*l*) and such report recommends that there is no contravention of the pro visions of this Act, the Commission shall invite comments of the Central Government or the State Government or the statutory authority, as the case may be, on such report and on receipt of such comments, the Commission shall return the reference if there is no prima facie case or proceed with the reference as a complaint if there is a prima facie case.

(9) If the report of the Director General referred to in sub-section (2) recommends that there is contravention of any of the provisions of this Act, and the Commission is of the opinion that further inquiry is called for, it shall inquire into such contravention in accordance with the provisions of this Act."

Government or the State Government or the statutory authority or the parties concerned, as the case may be.

(*3*) The Director General shall, on receipt of direction under sub-section (*1*), submit a report on his findings within such period as may be specified by the Commission.

(*4*) The Commission may forward a copy of the report referred to in sub section (*3*) to the parties concerned:

Provided that in case the investigation is caused to be made based on reference received from the Central Government or the State Government or the statutory authority, the Commission shall forward a copy of the report referred to in subsection (*3*) to the Central Government or the State Government or the statutory authority, as the case may be.

(*5*) If the report of the Director General referred to in sub-section (*3*) recommends that there is no contravention of the provisions of this Act, the Commission shall invite objections or suggestions from the Central Government or the State Government or the statutory authority or the parties concerned, as the case may be, on such report of the Director General.

(*6*) If, after consideration of the objections and suggestions referred to in sub section (*5*), if any, the Commission agrees with the recommendation of the Director General, it shall close the matter forthwith and pass such orders as it deems fit and communicate its order to the Central Government or the State Government or the statutory authority or the parties concerned, as the case may be.

(*7*) If, after consideration of the objections or suggestions referred to in sub section (*5*), if any, the Commission is of the opinion that further investigations is called for, it may direct further investigation in the matter by the Director General or cause further inquiriy to be made by in the matter or itself proceed with further inquiry in the matter in accordance with the provisions of this Act.

(*8*) If the report of the Director General referred to in sub-section (3) recommends that there is contravention of any of the provisions of this Act, and the Commission is of the opinion that further inquiry is called for, it shall inquire into such contravention in accordance with the provisions of this Act.]

Orders by Commission after inquiry into agreements or abuse of dominant position

27. Where after inquiry the Commission finds that any agreement referred to in section 3 or action of an enterprise in a dominant position, is in contravention of section 3 or section 4, as the case may be, it may pass all or any of the following orders, namely:—

(a) direct any enterprise or association of enterprises or person or association of persons, as the case may be, involved in such agreement, or abuse of dominant position, to discontinue and not to re-enter such agreement or discontinue such abuse of dominant position, as the case may be;

(b) impose such penalty, as it may deem fit which shall be not more than ten per cent. of the average of the turnover for the last three preceding financial years, upon each of such person or enterprises which are parties to such agreements or abuse:

[42][Provided that in case any agreement referred to in section 3 has been entered into by a cartel, the Commission may impose upon each producer, seller, distributor, trader or service provider included in that cartel, a penalty of up to three times of its profit for each year of the continuance of such agreement or ten per cent. of its turnover for each year of the continuance of such agreement, whichever is higher.]

[43](c) [Omitted by Competition (Amendment) Act, 2007]

(d) direct that the agreements shall stand modified to the extent and in the manner as may be specified in the order by the Commission;

(e) direct the enterprises concerned to abide by such other orders as the Commission may pass and comply with the directions, including payment of costs, if any:;

---

42 Subs. by Competition (Amendment) Act, 2007 for:
"Provided that in case any agreement referred to in section 3 has been entered into by any cartel, the Commission shall impose upon each producer, seller, distributor, trader or service provider included in that cartel, a penalty equivalent to three times of the amount of profits made out of such agreement by the cartel or ten per cent. of the average of the turnover of the cartel for the last preceding three financial years, whichever is higher;"

43 Prior to omission, Clause (c) of Section 27 read as under:-
"award compensation to parties in accordance with the provisions contained in section 34;"

[44](f) [Omitted by Competition (Amendment) Act, 2007]

(g) pass such other [45][order or issue such directions] as it may deem fit.

[46][Provided that while passing orders under this section, if the Commission comes to a finding, that an enterprise in contravention to section 3 or section 4 of the Act is a member of a group as defined in clause(b) of the Explanation to section 5 of the Act, and other members of such a group are also responsible for, or have contributed to, such a contravention, then it may pass orders, under this section, against such members of the group.]

Division of enterprise enjoying dominant position

28 (*1*) The [47][Commission] may, notwithstanding anything contained in any other law for the time being in force, by order in writing, direct division of an enterprise enjoying dominant position to ensure that such enterprise does not abuse its dominant position.

(*2*) In particular, and without prejudice to the generality of the foregoing powers, the order referred to in sub-section (*1*) may provide for all or any of the following matters, namely:—

(a) the transfer or vesting of property, rights, liabilities or obligations;

(b) the adjustment of contracts either by discharge or reduction of any liability or obligation or otherwise;

(c) the creation, allotment, surrender or cancellation of any shares, stocks or securities;

[48](d) [Omitted by Competition (Amendment) Act, 2007]

(e) the formation or winding up of an enterprise or the amendment of the memorandum of association or articles of association or any other instruments regulating the business of any enterprise;

---

44 Prior to omission, Clause (c) of Section 27 read as under:-
"recommend to the Central Government for the division of an enterprise enjoying dominant position;"

45 Subs. by Competition (Amendment) Act, 2007 for "order"

46 Ins. by Competition (Amendment) Act, 2007

47 Subs. by Competition (Amendment) Act, 2007 for "Central Government, on recommendation under clause(f) of section 27"

48 Prior to omission, clause (d) of sub-section(2) of section 28 read as under:-
"the payment of compensation to any person who suffered any loss due to dominant position of such enterprise;"

(f) the extent to which, and the circumstances in which, provisions of the order affecting an enterprise may be altered by the enterprise and the registration thereof;

(g) any other matter which may be necessary to give effect to the division of the enterprise.

(3) Notwithstanding anything contained in any other law for the time being in force or in any contract or in any memorandum or articles of association, an officer of a company who ceases to hold office as such in consequence of the division of an enterprise shall not be entitled to claim any compensation for such cesser.

Procedure for investigation of combination

29.(*1*) Where the Commission is of the [49][prima facie] opinion that a combination is likely to cause, or has caused an appreciable adverse effect on competition within the relevant market in India, it shall issue a notice to show cause to the parties to combination calling upon them to respond within thirty days of the receipt of the notice, as to why investigation in respect of such combination should not be conducted.

[50][*1(A)* After receipt of the response of the parties to the combination under subsection (1), the Commission may call for a report from the Director General and such report shall be submitted by the Director General within such time as the Commission may direct.]

(*2*) The Commission, if it is prima facie of the opinion that the combination has, or is likely to have, an appreciable adverse effect on competition, it shall, within seven working days from the date of receipt of the response of the parties to the combination, [51][or the receipt of the report from Director General called under sub section (*1A*), whichever is later] direct the parties to the said combination to publish details of the combination within ten working days of such direction, in such manner, as it thinks appropriate, for bringing the combination to the knowledge or information of the public and persons affected or likely to be affected by such combination.

---

49 Ins. by Competition (Amendment) Act, 2007

50 Ins. by Competition (Amendment) Act, 2007

51 Ins. by Competition (Amendment) Act, 2007

(*3*) The Commission may invite any person or member of the public, affected or likely to be affected by the said combination, to file his written objections, if any, before the Commission within fifteen working days from the date on which the details of the combination were published under sub-section (2).

(*4*) The Commission may, within fifteen working days from the expiry of the period specified in sub-section (3), call for such additional or other information as it may deem fit from the parties to the said combination.

(*5*) The additional or other information called for by the Commission shall be furnished by the parties referred to in sub-section (4) within fifteen days from the expiry of the period specified in sub-section (4).

(*6*) After receipt of all information and within a period of forty-five working days from the expiry of the period specified in sub-section (5), the Commission shall proceed to deal with the case in accordance with the provisions contained in section 31.

[52][Procedure in case of notice under sub-section (2) of section 6]

[53]**[30.** Where any person or enterprises has given a notice under sub-section (*2*) of section 6, the Commission shall examine such notice and form its prima facie opinion as provided in sub-section (*1*) of section 29 and proceed as per provisions contained in that section.]

Orders of Commission on certain combinations

31.(1) Where the Commission is of the opinion that any combination does not, or is not likely to, have an appreciable adverse effect on competition, it shall, by order, approve that combination including the combination in respect of which a notice has been given under sub-section (2) of section 6.

---

52 Subs. by Competition (Amendment) Act, 2007 for "Inquiry into disclosure under sub-section(2) of section 6"

53 Subs. by Competition (Amendment) Act, 2007 for:
"Where any person or enterprise has given a notice under sub-section (2) of section 6. The Commission shall inquire—
(a) whether the disclosure made in the notice is correct;
(b) whether the combination has, or is likely to have, an appreciable adverse effect on competition."

(2) Where the Commission is of the opinion that the combination has, or is likely to have, an appreciable adverse effect on competition, it shall direct that the combination shall not take effect.

(3) Where the Commission is of the opinion that the combination has, or is likely to have, an appreciable adverse effect on competition but such adverse effect can be eliminated by suitable modification to such combination, it may propose appropriate modification to the combination, to the parties to such combination.

(4) The parties, who accept the modification proposed by the Commission under subsection (3), shall carry out such modification within the period specified by the Commission.

(5) If the parties to the combination, who have accepted the modification under subsection (4), fail to carry out the modification within the period specified by the Commission, such combination shall be deemed to have an appreciable adverse effect on competition and the Commission shall deal with such combination in accordance with the provisions of this Act.

(6) If the parties to the combination do not accept the modification proposed by the Commission under sub-section (3), such parties may, within thirty working days of the modification proposed by the Commission, submit amendment to the modification proposed by the Commission under that sub-section.

(7) If the Commission agrees with the amendment submitted by the parties under subsection (6), it shall, by order, approve the combination.

(8) If the Commission does not accept the amendment submitted under sub-section (6), then, the parties shall be allowed a further period of thirty working days within which such parties shall accept the modification proposed by the Commission under sub-section (3).

(9) If the parties fail to accept the modification proposed by the Commission within thirty working days referred to in sub-section (6) or within a further period of thirty working days referred to in sub-section (8), the combination shall be deemed to have an appreciable adverse effect on competition and be dealt with in accordance with the provisions of this Act.

(10) Where the Commission has directed under sub-section (2) that the combination shall not take effect or the combination is deemed to

have an appreciable adverse effect on competition under sub-section (9), then, without prejudice to any penalty which may be imposed or any prosecution which may be initiated under this Act, the Commission may order that—

(a) the acquisition referred to in clause (a) of section 5; or
(b) the acquiring of control referred to in clause (b) of section 5; or
(c) the merger or amalgamation referred to in clause (c) of section 5, shall not be given effect to:

Provided that the Commission may, if it considers appropriate, frame a scheme to implement its order under this sub-section.

(11) If the Commission does not, on the expiry of a period of [54][two hundred and ten days from the date of notice given to the Commission under sub-section (2) of section 6], pass an order or issue direction in accordance with the provisions of sub-section (1) or sub-section (2) or sub-section (7), the combination shall be deemed to have been approved by the Commission.

Explanation.—For the purposes of determining the period of [55][two hundred and ten] days specified in this subsection, the period of thirty working days specified in sub-section (6) and a further period of thirty working days specified in subsection (8) shall be excluded.

(12) Where any extension of time is sought by the parties to the combination, the period of ninety working days shall be reckoned after deducting the extended time granted at the request of the parties.

(13) Where the Commission has ordered a combination to be void, the acquisition or acquiring of control or merger or amalgamation referred to in section 5, shall be dealt with by the authorities under any other law for the time being in force as if such acquisition or acquiring of control or merger or amalgamation had not taken place and the parties to the combination shall be dealt with accordingly.

(14) Nothing contained in this Chapter shall affect any proceeding initiated or which may be initiated under any other law for the time being in force.

---

54 Subs. by Competition (Amendment) Act, 2007 for:
"ninety working days from the date of publication referred to in sub-section(2) of section 29"

55 Subs. by Competition (Amendment) Act, 2007 for "ninety days"

Acts taking place outside India but having an effect on competition in India

32. The Commission shall, notwithstanding that,—

(a) an agreement referred to in section 3 has been entered into outside India; or

(b) any party to such agreement is outside India; or

(c) any enterprise abusing the dominant position is outside India; or

(d) a combination has taken place outside India; or

(e) any party to combination is outside India; or

(f) any other matter or practice or action arising out of such agreement or dominant position or combination is outside India, have power to inquire [56][in accordance with the provisions contained in sections 19, 20, 26, 29 and 30 of the Act] into such agreement or abuse of dominant position or combination if such agreement or dominant position or combination has, or is likely to have, an appreciable adverse effect on competition in the relevant market in India [57][and pass such orders as it may deem fit in accordance with the provisions of this Act.]

[58][Power to issue interim orders]

[59][**33.** Where during an inquiry, the Commission is satisfied that an act

---

[56] Ins. by Competition (Amendment) Act, 2007

[57] Ins. by Competition (Amendment) Act, 2007

[58] Subs. by Competition (Amendment) Act, 2007 for "Power to grant interim relief"

[59] Subs. by Competition (Amendment) Act, 2007 for:

"(1) Where during an inquiry before the Commission, it is proved to the satisfaction of the Commission, by affidavit or otherwise, that an act in contravention of sub-section (1) of section 3 or sub-section (1) of section 4 or section 6 has been committed and continues to be committed or that such act is about to be committed, the Commission may, by order, grant a temporary injunction restraining any party from carrying on such act until the conclusion of such inquiry or until further orders, without giving notice to the opposite party, where it deems it necessary.

(2) Where during the inquiry before the Commission it is proved to the satisfaction of the Commission by affidavit or otherwise that import of any goods is likely to contravene sub-section (1) of section 3 or subsection (1) of section 4 or section 6, it may, by order, grant a temporary injunction restraining any party from importing such goods until the conclusion of such inquiry or until further orders, without giving notice to the opposite party, where it deems it necessary and a copy of such order granting temporary injunction shall be sent to the concerned authorities.

(3) The provisions of rules 2A to 5 (both inclusive) of Order XXXIX of the First Schedule to the Code of Civil Procedure, 1908 (5 of 1908) shall, as far as may be, apply to a

in contravention of sub-section (1) of section 3 or sub-section (1) of section 4 or section 6 has been committed and continues to be committed or that such act is about to be committed, the Commission may, by order, temporarily restrain any party from carrying on such act until the conclusion of such inquiry or until further orders, without giving notice to such party, where it deems it necessary.]

[60]**34.** [Omitted by Competition (Amendment) Act, 2007]

Appearance before Commission

35. A [61][person or an enterprise] or the Director General may either appear in person or authorise one or more chartered accountants or company secretaries or cost accountants or legal practitioners or any of his or its officers to present his or its case before the Commission.

Explanation.—For the purposes of this section,—

(a) "chartered accountant" means a chartered accountant as defined in clause (b) of sub-section (1) of section 2 of the Chartered Accountants Act, 1949 (38 of 1949) and who has obtained

---

temporary injunction issued by the Commission under this Act, as they apply to a temporary injunction issued by a civil court, and any reference in any such rule to a suit shall be construed as a reference to any inquiry before the Commission."

60 Prior to omission, section 34 read as under:-

" Power to award compensation

(1) Without prejudice to any other provisions contained in this Act, any person may make an application to the Commission for an order for the recovery of compensation from any enterprise for any loss or damage shown to have been suffered, by such person as a result of any contravention of the provisions of Chapter II, having been committed by such enterprise.

(2) The Commission may, after an inquiry made into the allegations mentioned in the application made under sub-section (1), pass an order directing the enterprise to make payment to the applicant, of the amount determined by it as realisable from the enterprise as compensation for the loss or damage caused to the applicant as a result of any contravention of the provisions of Chapter II having been committed by such enterprise.

(3) Where any loss or damage referred to in sub-section (1) is caused to numerous persons having the same interest, one or more of such persons may, with the permission of the Commission, make an application under that sub-section for and on behalf of, or for the benefit of, the persons so interested, and thereupon, the provisions of rule 8 of Order 1 of the First Schedule to the Code of Civil Procedure, 1908 (5 of 1908), shall apply subject to the modification that every reference therein to a suit or decree shall be construed as a reference to the application before the Commission and the order of the Commission thereon."

61 Subs. by Competition (Amendment) Act, 2007 for "complainant or defendant"

a certificate of practice under sub-section (1) of section 6 of that Act;

(b) "company secretary" means a company secretary as defined in clause (c) of sub-section (1) of section 2 of the Company Secretaries Act, 1980 (56 of 1980) and who has obtained a certificate of practice under sub-section (1) of section 6 of that Act;

(c) "cost accountant" means a cost accountant as defined in clause (b) of sub-section (1) of section 2 of the Cost and Works Accountants Act, 1959 (23 of 1959) and who has obtained a certificate of practice under subsection (1) of section 6 of that Act;

(d) "legal practitioner" means an advocate, vakil or an attorney of any High Court, and includes a pleader in practice.

Power of Commission to regulate its own procedure

[62][**36.**(1)In the discharge of its functions, the Commission shall be guided by

---

[62] Subs. by Competition (Amendment) Act, 2007 for:

"(1) The Commission shall not be bound by the procedure laid down by the Code of Civil Procedure,1908 (5 of 1908), but shall be guided by the principles of natural justice and, subject to the other provisions of this Act and of any rules made by the Central Government, the Commission shall have powers to regulate its own procedure including the places at which they shall have their sittings, duration of oral hearings when granted, and times of its inquiry.

(2) The Commission shall have, for the purposes of discharging its functions umder this Act, the same powers as are vested in a civil court under the Code of Civil Procedure, 1908(5 of 1908), while trying a suit, in respect of the following matters, namely:—

(a) summoning and enforcing the attendance of any person and examining him on oath;

(b) requiring the discovery and production of documents;

(c) receiving evidence on affidavits;

(d) issuing commissions for the examination of witnesses or documents;

(e) subject to the provisions of sections 123 and 124 of the Indian Evidence Act, 1872 (1 of 1872), requisitioning any public record or document or copy of such record or document from any office;

(f) dismissing an application in default or deciding it ex parte;

(g) any other matter which may be prescribed.

(3) Every proceeding before the Commission shall be deemed to be a judicial proceeding within the meaning of sections 193 and 228 and for the purposes of section 196 of the Indian Penal Code (45 of 1860) and the Commission shall be deemed to be a civil court for the purposes of section 195 (2 of 1974) and Chapter XXVI of the Code of Criminal Procedure, 1973.

(4) The Commission may call upon such experts, from the fields of economics, commerce, accountancy, international trade or from any other discipline as it deems necessary, to assist the Commission in the conduct of any inquiry or proceeding before it.

the principles of natural justice and, subject to the other provisions of this Act and of any rules made by the Central Government, the Commission shall have the powers to regulate its own procedure.

(2) The Commission shall have, for the purposes of discharging its functions under this Act, the same powers as are vested in a Civil Court under the Code of Civil Procedure, 1908 (5 of 1908), while trying a suit, in respect of the following matters, namely:-

(3) The Commission may call upon such experts, from the field of economics, commerce, accountancy, international trade or from any other discipline as it deems necessary to assist the Commission in the conduct of any inquiry by it.

(4) The Commission may direct any person:
   (a) to produce before the Director General or the Secretary or an officer authorized by it, such books, or other documents in the custody or under the control of such person so directed as may be specified or described in the direction, being documents relating to any trade, the examination of which may be required for the purposes of this Act;
   (b) to furnish to the Director General or the Secretary or any other officer authorized by it, as respects the trade or such other information as may be in his possession in relation to the trade carried on by such person, as may be required for the purposes of this Act.]

---

(5) The Commission may direct any person—
   (a) to produce before the Director General or the Registrar or an officer authorised by it, such books, accounts or other documents in the custody or under the control of such person so directed as may be specified or described in the direction, being documents relating to any trade, the examination of which may be required for the purposes of this Act;
   (b) to furnish to the Director General or the Registrar or any officer authorised by it, as respects the trade or such other information as may be in his possession in relation to the trade carried on by such person, as may be required for the purposes of this Act.

(6) If the Commission is of the opinion that any agreement referred to in section 3 or "abuse of dominant position referred to in section 4 or the combination referred to in section 5 has caused or is likely to cause an appreciable adverse effect on competition in the relevant market in India and it is necessary to protect, without further delay, the interests of consumers and other market participants in India, it may conduct an inquiry or adjudicate upon any matter under this Act after giving a reasonable oral hearing to the parties concerned."

[63]**37.** [Omitted by Competition (Amendment) Act, 2007]

Rectification of orders

38.(1) With a view to rectifying any mistake apparent from the record, the Commission may amend any order passed by it under the provisions of this Act.

(2) Subject to the other provisions of this Act, the Commission may make—

(a) an amendment under sub-section (1) of its own motion;

(b) an amendment for rectifying any such mistake which has been brought to its notice by any party to the order.

Explanation.— For the removal of doubts, it is hereby declared that the Commission shall not, while rectifying any mistake apparent from record, amend substantive part of its order passed under the provisions of this Act.

[64][Execution of orders of Commission imposing monetary penalty]

[65] [**39.**(1)If a person fails to pay any monetary penalty imposed on him under

---

63 Prior to omission, section 37 read as under:-
"Review of orders of Commission
Any person aggrieved by an order of the Commission from which an appeal is allowed by this Act but no appeal has been preferred, may, within thirty days from the date of the order, apply to the Commission for review of its order and the Commission may make such order thereon as it thinks fit:
Provided that the Commission may entertain a review application after the expiry of the said period of thirty days, if it is satisfied that the applicant was prevented by sufficient cause from preferring the application in time:
Provided further that no order shall be modified or set aside without giving an opportunity of being heard to the person in whose favour the order is given and the Director General where he was a party to the proceedings."

64 Subs. by Competition (Amendment) Act, 2007 for "Execution of orders of Commission"

65 Subs. by Competition (Amendment) Act, 2007 for:
"Every order passed by the Commission under this Act shall be enforced by the Commission in the same manner as if it were a decree or order made by a High Court or the principal civil court in a suit pending therein and it shall be lawful for the Commission to send, in the event of its inability to execute it, such order to the High Court or the principal civil court, as the case may be, within the local limits of whose jurisdiction,—
(a) in the case of an order against a person referred to in sub-clause (iii) or sub-clause (vi) or subclause (vii) of clause (l) of section 2, the registered office or the sole or principal

this Act, the Commission shall proceed to recover such penalty, in such manner as may be specified by the regulations.

(2) In a case where the Commission is of the opinion that it would be expedient to recover the penalty imposed under this Act in accordance with the provisions of the Income-tax Act, 1961 (43 of 1961), it may make a reference to this effect to the concerned income-tax authority under that Act for recovery of the penalty as tax due under the said Act.

(3) Where a reference has been made by the Commission under sub-section (2) for recovery of penalty, the person upon whom the penalty has been imposed shall be deemed to be the assessee in default under the Income Tax Act, 1961 (43 of 1961) and the provisions contained in sections 221 to 227, 228A, 229, 231 and 232 of the said Act and the Second Schedule to that Act and any rules made there under shall, in so far as may be, apply as if the said provisions were the provisions of this Act and referred to sums by way of penalty imposed under this Act instead of to income-tax and sums imposed by way of penalty, fine, and interest under the Income–tax Act, 1961 (43 of 1961) and to the Commission instead of the Assessing Officer.

Explanation 1 – Any reference to sub-section (2) or sub-section (6) of section 220 of the income-tax Act, 1961 (43 of 1961), in the said provisions of that Act or the rules made thereunder shall be construed as references to sections 43 to 45 of this Act.

Explanation 2 – The Tax Recovery Commissioner and the Tax Recovery Officer referred to in the Income-tax Act, 1961 (43 of 1961) shall be deemed to be the Tax Recovery Commissioner and the Tax Recovery Officer for the purposes of recovery of sums imposed by way of penalty under this Act and reference made by the Commission under sub-section (2) would amount to drawing of a certificate by the Tax Recovery Officer as far as demand relating to penalty under this Act.

---

place of business of the person in India or where the person has also a subordinate office, that subordinate office, is situated;

(b) in the case of an order against any other person, the place, where the person concerned voluntarily resides or carries on business or personally works for gain, is situated, and thereupon the court to which the order is so sent shall execute the order as if it were a decree or order sent to it for execution."

Explanation 3– Any reference to appeal in Chapter XVIID and the Second Schedule to the Income-tax Act, 1961 (43 of 1961), shall be construed as a reference to appeal before the Competition Appellate Tribunal under section 53B of this Act.]

[66]**40.** [Omitted by Competition (Amendment) Act, 2007]

[66] Prior to omission, section 40 read as under:-
"Any person aggrieved by any decision or order of the Commission may file an appeal to the Supreme Court within sixty days from the date of communication of the decision or order of the Commission to him on one or more of the grounds specified in section 100 of the Code of Civil Procedure, 1908 (5 of 1908): Provided that the Supreme Court may, if it is satisfied that the appellant was prevented by sufficient cause from filing the appeal within the said period, allow it to be filed within a further period not exceeding sixty days: Provided further that no appeal shall lie against any decision or order of the Commission made with the consent of the parties."

CHAPTER V

DUTIES OF DIRECTOR GENERAL

Director General to investigate contravention

41.(*1*) The Director General shall, when so directed by the Commission, assist the Commission in investigating into any contravention of the provisions of this Act or any rules or regulations made thereunder.

(*2*) The Director General shall have all the powers as are conferred upon the Commission under subsection (2) of section 36.

(*3*) Without prejudice to the provisions of sub-section (2), sections 240 and 240A of the Companies Act, 1956 (1 of 1956), so far as may be, shall apply to an investigation made by the Director General or any other person investigating under his authority, as they apply to an inspector appointed under that Act.

[67][Explanation.—For the purposes of this section, --

(a) the words "the Central Government" under section 240 of the Companies Act, 1956 (1 of 1956) shall be construed as "the Commission";

(b) the word "Magistrate" under section 240A of the Companies Act, 1956 (1 of 1956) shall be construed as "the Chief Metropolitan Magistrate, Delhi".]

---

67 Ins. by Competition (Amendment) Act, 2007

CHAPTER VI

PENALTIES

Contravention of orders of Commission

[68][**42.**(*1*)The Commission may cause an inquiry to be made into compliance of its orders or directions made in exercise of its powers under the Act.

(*2*) If any person, without reasonable clause, fails to comply with the orders or directions of the Commission issued under sections 27, 28, 31, 32, 33, 42A and 43A of the Act, he shall be punishable with fine which may extend to rupees one lakh for each day during which such non-compliance occurs, subject to a maximum of rupees ten crore, as the Commission may determine.

(*3*) If any person does not comply with the orders or directions issued, or fails to pay the fine imposed under sub-section (2), he shall, without prejudice to any proceeding under section 39, be punishable with imprisonment for a term which may extend to three years, or with fine which may extend to rupees twenty-five crore, or with both, as the Chief Metropolitan Magistrate, Delhi may deem fit:

Provided that the Chief Metropolitan Magistrate, Delhi shall not take cognizance of any offence under this section save on a complaint filed by the Commission or any of its officers authorized by it.]

---

[68] Subs. by Competition (Amendment) Act, 2007 for:

"(1) Without prejudice to the provisions of this Act, if any person contravenes, without any reasonable ground, any order of the Commission, or any condition or restriction subject to which any approval, sanction, direction or exemption in relation to any matter has been accorded, given, made or granted under this Act or fails to pay the penalty imposed under this Act, he shall be liable to be detained in civil prison for a term which may extend to one year, unless in the meantime the Commission directs his release and he shall also be liable to a penalty not exceeding rupees ten lakhs.

(2) The Commission may, while making an order under this Act, issue such directions to any person or authority, not inconsistent with this Act, as it thinks necessary or desirable, for the proper implementation or execution of the order, and any person who commits breach of. or fails to comply with, any obligation imposed on him under such direction, may be ordered by the Commission to be detained in civil prison for a term not exceeding one year unless in the meantime the Commission directs his release and he shall also be liable to a penalty not exceeding rupees ten lakhs."

[69][Compensation in case of contravention of orders of Commission]

[70][**42 A.** Without prejudice to the provisions of this Act, any person may make an application to the Appellate Tribunal for an order for the recovery of compensation from any enterprise for any loss or damage shown to have been suffered, by such person as a result of the said enterprise violating directions issued by the Commission or contravening, without any reasonable ground, any decision or order of the Commission issued under sections 27, 28, 31, 32 and 33 or any condition or restriction subject to which any approval, sanction, direction or exemption in relation to any matter has been accorded, given, made or granted under this Act or delaying in carrying out such orders or directions of the Commission.]

Penalty for failure to comply with directions of Commission and Director General

[71][**43.** If any person fails to comply, without reasonable cause, with a direction given

by—

(a) the Commission under sub-sections (2) and (4) of section 36; or

(b) the Director General while exercising powers referred to in sub-section (2) of section 41,

such person shall be punishable with fine which may extend to rupees one lakh for each day during which such failure continues subject to a maximum of rupees one crore, as may be determined by the Commission]

---

69 Ins. by Competition (Amendment) Act, 2007

70 Ins. by Competition (Amendment) Act, 2007

71 Subs. by Competition (Amendment) Act, 2007 for:
"If any person fails to comply with a direction given by—
(a) the Commission under sub-section (5) of section 36; or
(b) the Director General while exercising powers referred to in sub-section (2) of section 41, the Commission shall impose on such person a penalty of rupees one lakh for each day during which such failure continues."

[72][Power to impose penalty for non-furnishing of information on combinations]

[73][**43 A.** If any person or enterprise who fails to give notice to the Commission under subsection(2) of section 6, the Commission shall impose on such person or enterprise a penalty which may extend to one per cent. of the total turnover or the assets, whichever is higher, of such a combination.]

Penalty for making false statement or omission to furnish material information

44. If any person, being a party to a combination,—

(a) makes a statement which is false in any material particular, or knowing it to be false; or

(b) omits to state any material particular knowing it to be material,

such person shall be liable to a penalty which shall not be less than rupees fifty lakhs but which may extend to rupees one crore, as may be determined by the Commission.

Penalty for offences in relation to furnishing of information

[74][*45.*(1)Without prejudice to the provisions of section 44, if a person, who furnishes or is required to furnish under this Act any particulars, documents or any information,—

(a) makes any statement or furnishes any document which he knows or has reason to believe to be false in any material particular; or

(b) omits to state any material fact knowing it to be material; or

(c) wilfully alters, suppresses or destroys any document which is required to be furnished as aforesaid,

---

72 Ins. by Competition (Amendment) Act, 2007

73 Ins. by Competition (Amendment) Act, 2007

74 Subs. by Competition (Amendment) Act, 2007 for:

"(1)Without prejudice to the provisions of section 44, if any person, who furnishes or is required to furnish under this Act any particulars, documents or any information,—

(a) makes any statement or furnishes any document which he knows or has reason to believe to be false in any material particular; or

(b) omits to state any material fact knowing it to be material; or

(c) wilfully alters, suppresses or destroys any document which is required to be furnished as aforesaid, the Commission shall impose on such person a penalty which may extend to rupees ten lakhs."

such person shall be punishable with fine which may extend to rupees one crore as may be determined by the Commission.]

(2) Without prejudice to the provisions of sub-section(1), the Commission may also pass such other order as it deems fit.

Power to impose lesser penalty

46. The Commission may, if it is satisfied that any producer, seller, distributor, trader or service provider included in any cartel, which is alleged to have violated section 3, has made a full and true disclosure in respect of the alleged violations and such disclosure is vital, impose upon such producer, seller, distributor, trader or service provider a lesser penalty as it may deem fit, than leviable under this Act or the rules or the regulations:

[75][Provided that lesser penalty shall not be imposed by the Commission in cases where the report of investigation directed under section 26 has been received before making of such disclosure.]

Provided further that lesser penalty shall be imposed by the Commission only in respect of a producer, seller, distributor, trader or service provider included in the cartel, who [76][has] made the full, true and vital disclosures under this section.

[77][Provided also that lesser penalty shall not be imposed by the Commission if the person making the disclosure does not continue to cooperate with the Commission till the completion of the proceedings before the Commission.]

Provided also that the Commission may, if it is satisfied that such producer, seller, distributor, trader or service provider included in the cartel had in the course of proceedings,—

(a) not complied with the condition on which the lesser penalty was imposed by the Commission; or

(b) had given false evidence; or

(c) the disclosure made is not vital,

---

[75] Subs. by Competition (Amendment) Act, 2007 for:
"Provided that lesser penalty shall not be imposed by the Commission in cases where proceedings for the violation of any of the provisions of this Act or the rules or the regulations have been instituted or any investigation has been directed to be made under section 26 before making of such disclosure:"

[76] Subs. by Competition (Amendment) Act, 2007 for "first"

[77] Ins. by Competition (Amendment) Act, 2007

and thereupon such producer, seller, distributor, trader or service provider may be tried for the offence with respect to which the lesser penalty was imposed and shall also be liable to the imposition of penalty to which such person has been liable, had lesser penalty not been imposed.

Crediting sums realised by way of penalties to Consolidated Fund of India

47. All sums realised by way of penalties under this Act shall be credited to the Consolidated Fund of India.

Contravention by companies

48. (1) Where a person committing contravention of any of the provisions of this Act or of any rule, regulation, order made or direction issued thereunder is a company, every person who, at the time the contravention was committed, was in charge of, and was responsible to the company for the conduct of the business of the company, as well as the company, shall be deemed to be guilty of the contravention and shall be liable to be proceeded against and punished accordingly:

Provided that nothing contained in this sub-section shall render any such person liable to any punishment if he proves that the contravention was committed without his knowledge or that he had exercised all due diligence to prevent the commission of such contravention.

(2) Notwithstanding anything contained in sub-section (1), where a contravention of any of the provisions of this Act or of any rule, regulation, order made or direction issued thereunder has been committed by a company and it is proved that the contravention has taken place with the consent or connivance of, or is attributable to any neglect on the part of, any director, manager, secretary or other officer of the company, such director, manager, secretary or other officer shall also be deemed to be guilty of that contravention and shall be liable to be proceeded against and punished accordingly.

Explanation.—For the purposes of this section,—

(a) "company" means a body corporate and includes a firm or other association of individuals; and

(b) "director", in relation to a firm, means a partner in the firm.

CHAPTER VII

COMPETITION ADVOCACY

Competition advocacy

49.[78][(1)The Central Government may, in formulating a policy on competition (including review of laws related to competition) or any other matter, and a State Government may, in formulating a policy on competition or on any other matter, as the case may be, make a reference to the Commission for its opinion on possible effect of such policy on competition and on the receipt of such a reference, the Commission shall, within sixty days of making such reference, give its opinion to the Central Government, or the State Government, as the case may be, which may thereafter take further action as it deems fit.]

(2) The opinion given by the Commission under sub-section (1) shall not be binding upon the Central Government [79][or the State Government, as the case may be] in formulating such policy.

(3) The Commission shall take suitable measures [80][***] for the promotion of competition advocacy, creating awareness and imparting training about competition issues.

---

[78] Subs. by Competition (Amendment) Act, 2007 for:

"(1) In formulating a policy on competition (including review of laws related to competition), the Central Government may make a reference to the Commission for its opinion on possible effect of such policy on competition and on receipt of such a reference, the Commission shall, within sixty days of making such reference, give its opinion to the Central Government, which may thereafter formulate the policy as it deems fit."

[79] Ins. by Competition (Amendment) Act, 2007

[80] The words "as may be prescribed" omitted by Competition (Amendment) Act, 2007

CHAPTER VIII

FINANCE, ACCOUNTS AND AUDIT

Grants by Central Government

50. The Central Government may, after due appropriation made by Parliament by law in this behalf, make to the Commission grants of such sums of money as the Government may think fit for being utilised for the purposes of this Act.

Constitution of Fund

51.(1) There shall be constituted a fund to be called the "Competition Fund" and there shall be credited thereto—

(a) all Government grants received by the Commission;

[81](b) [Omitted by Competition (Amendment) Act, 2007]

(c) the fees received under this Act;

(d) the interest accrued on the amounts referred to in [82][clauses (a) and (c)].

(2) The Fund shall be applied for meeting—

(a) the salaries and allowances payable to the Chairperson and other Members and the administrative expenses including the salaries, allowances and pension payable to the Director General, Additional, Joint, Deputy or Assistant Directors General, the Registrar and officers and other employees of the Commission;

(b) the other expenses of the Commission in connection with the discharge of its functions and for the purposes of this Act.

(3) The Fund shall be administered by a committee of such Members of the Commission as may be determined by the Chairperson.

(4) The committee appointed under sub-section (3) shall spend monies out of the Fund for carrying out the objects for which the Fund has been constituted.

---

[81] Prior to omission, clause (b) of section 51(1) read as under :-
"the monies received as costs from parties to proceedings before the Commission;"

[82] Subs. by Competition (Amendment) Act, 2007 for "clauses (a) to (c)"

Accounts and Audit

52.(1) The Commission shall maintain proper accounts and other relevant records and prepare an annual statement of accounts in such form as may be prescribed by the Central Government in consultation with the Comptroller and Auditor-General of India.

(2) The accounts of the Commission shall be audited by the Comptroller and Auditor-General of India at such intervals as may be specified by him and any expenditure incurred in connection with such audit shall be payable by the Commission to the Comptroller and Auditor-General of India.

Explanation.—For the removal of doubts, it is hereby declared that the orders of the Commission, being matters appealable to the [83][Appellate Tribunal or the Supreme Court], shall not be subject to audit under this section.

(3) The Comptroller and Auditor-General of India and any other person appointed by him in connection with the audit of the accounts of the Commission shall have the same rights, privileges and authority in connection with such audit as the Comptroller and Auditor-General of India generally has, in connection with the audit of the Government accounts and, in particular, shall have the right to demand the production of books, accounts, connected vouchers and other documents and papers and to inspect any of the offices of the Commission.

(4) The accounts of the Commission as certified by the Comptroller and Auditor-General of India or any other person appointed by him in this behalf together with the audit report thereon shall be forwarded annually to the Central Government and that Government shall cause the same to be laid before each House of Parliament.

Furnishing of returns, etc., to Central Government

53.(*1*) The Commission shall furnish to the Central Government at such time and in such form and manner as may be prescribed or as the Central Government may direct, such returns and statements and such particulars in regard to any proposed or existing measures for the promotion of competition advocacy, creating awareness

[83] Subs. by Competition (Amendment) Act, 2007 for "Supreme Court"

and imparting training about competition issues, as the Central Government may, from time to time, require.

(2) The Commission shall prepare once in every year, in such form and at such time as may be prescribed, an annual report giving a true and full account of its activities during the previous year and copies of the report shall be forwarded to the Central Government.

(3) A copy of the report received under sub-section (2) shall be laid, as soon as may be after it is received, before each House of Parliament.

[84][CHAPTER VIIIA

COMPETITON APPELLATE TRIBUNAL

Establishment of Appellate Tribunal:

53A.(1) The Central Government shall, by notification, establish an Appellate Tribunal to be known as Competition Appellate Tribunal –

(a) to hear and dispose of appeals against any direction issued or decision made or order passed by the Commission under sub-sections (2) and (6) of section 26, section 27, section 28, section 31, section 32, section 33, section 38, section 39, section 43, section 43A, section 44, section 45 or section 46 of the Act;

(b) to adjudicate on claim for compensation that may arise from the findings of the Commission or the orders of the Appellate Tribunal in an appeal against any finding of the Commission or under section 42A or under subsection(2) of section 53Q of this Act, and pass orders for the recovery of compensation under section 53N of this Act.

(2) The Headquarter of the Appellate Tribunal shall be at such place as the Central Government may, by notification, specify.

Appeal to Appellate Tribunal

53B.(1)The Central Government or the State Government or a local authority or enterprise or any person, aggrieved by any direction, decision or order referred to in clause (a) of section 53A may prefer an appeal to the Appellate Tribunal.

(2) Every appeal under sub-section (1) shall be filed within a period of sixty days from the date on which a copy of the direction or decision or order made by the Commission is received by the Central Government or the State Government or a local authority or enterprise or any person referred to in that sub-section and it shall be in such form and be accompanied by such fee as may be prescribed: Provided that the Appellate Tribunal may entertain an appeal after the expiry of the said period of sixty days if it is satisfied that there was sufficient cause for not filing it within that period.

[84] "Chapter VIIIA" Inserted by Competition (Amendment) Act, 2007

(3) On receipt of an appeal under sub-section (1), the Appellate Tribunal may, after giving the parties to the appeal, an opportunity of being heard, pass such orders thereon as it thinks fit, confirming, modifying or setting aside the direction, decision or order appealed against.

(4) The Appellate Tribunal shall send a copy of every order made by it to the Commission and the parties to the appeal.

(5) The appeal filed before the Appellate Tribunal under sub-section (1) shall be dealt with by it as expeditiously as possible and endeavour shall be made by it to dispose of the appeal within six months from the date of receipt of the appeal.

Composition of Appellate Tribunal

53 C. The Appellate Tribunal shall consist of a Chairperson and not more than two other members to be appointed by the Central Government.

Qualifications for appointment of Chairperson and Members of Appellate Tribunal

53 D. (1) The Chairperson of the Appellate Tribunal shall be a person, who is, or has been a Judge of the Supreme Court or the Chief Justice of a High Court.

(2) A member of the Appellate Tribunal shall be a person of ability, integrity and standing having special knowledge of, and professional experience of not less than twenty five years in, competition matters including competition law and policy, international trade, economics, business, commerce, law, finance, accountancy, management, industry, public affairs, administration or in any other matter which in the opinion of the Central Government, may be useful to the Appellate Tribunal.

Selection Committee

53 E. (1)The Chairperson and members of the Appellate Tribunal shall be appointed by the Central Government from a panel of names recommended by a Selection Committee consisting of –

(a) the Chief Justice of India or his nominee .... Chairperson;

(b) the Secretary in the Ministry of Corporate Affairs.... Member;
(c) the Secretary in the Ministry of Law and Justice .... Member.

(2) The terms of the Selection Committee and the manner of selection of panel of names shall be such as may be prescribed.

Term of office of Chairperson and Members of Appellate Tribunal

53 F. The Chairperson or a member of the Appellate Tribunal shall hold office as such for a term of five years from the date on which he enters upon his office, and shall be eligible for re-appointment:

Provided that no Chairperson or other member of the Appellate Tribunal shall hold office as such after he has attained, -

(a) in the case of the Chairperson, the age of sixty-eight years;
(b) in the case of any other member of the Appellate Tribunal, the age of sixty-five years.

Terms and conditions of service of chairperson and Members of Appellate Tribunal

53G(1) The salaries and allowances and other terms and conditions of service of the Chairperson and other members of the Appellate Tribunal shall be such as may be prescribed.

(2) The salaries, allowances and other terms and conditions of service of the Chairperson and other members of the Appellate Tribunal shall not be varied to their disadvantage after their appointment.

Vacancies

53 H. If, for any reason other than temporary absence, any vacancy occurs in the office of the Chairperson or a member of the Appellate Tribunal, the Central Government shall appoint another person in accordance with the provisions of this Act to fill the vacancy and the proceedings may be continued before the Appellate Tribunal from the stage at which the vacancy is filled.

Resignation of Chairperson and Members of Appellate Tribunal

53 I. The Chairperson or a member of the Appellate Tribunal may, by notice in writing under his hand addressed to the Central Government, resign his office:

Provided that the Chairperson or a member of the Appellate Tribunal shall, unless he is permitted by the Central Government to relinquish his office sooner, continue to hold office until the expiry of three months from the date of receipt of such notice or until a person duly appointed as his successor enters upon his office or until the expiry of his term of office, whichever is the earliest.

Member of Appellate Tribunal to act as its Chairperson in certain cases

53 J.(1) In the event of the occurrence of any vacancy in the office of the Chairperson of the Appellate Tribunal by reason of his death or resignation, the senior-most Member of the Appellate Tribunal shall act as the Chairperson of the Appellate Tribunal until the date on which a new Chairperson appointed in accordance with the provisions of this Act to fill such vacancy enters upon his office.

(2) When the Chairperson of the Appellate Tribunal is unable to discharge his functions owing to absence, illness or any other cause, the senior-most member or, as the case may be, such one of the Members of the Appellate Tribunal, as the Central Government may, by notification, authorize in this behalf, shall discharge the functions of the Chairperson until the date on which the Chairperson resumes his duties.

Removal and suspension of Chairperson and Members of Appellate Tribunal

53K.(1) The Central Government may, in consultation with the Chief Justice of India, remove from office the Chairperson or any other member of the Appellate Tribunal, who-

(a) has been adjudged an insolvent; or
(b) has engaged at any time, during his terms of office, in any paid employment; or
(c) has been convicted of an offence which, in the opinion of the Central Government, involves moral turpitude; or
(d) has become physically or mentally incapable of acting as such Chairperson or other Member of the Appellate Tribunal; or
(e) has acquired such financial or other interest as is likely to affect prejudicially his functions as such Chairperson or Member of the Appellate Tribunal; or

(f) has so abused his position as to render his continuance in office prejudicial to the public interest.

(2) Notwithstanding anything contained in sub-section (1), no Chairperson or a Member of the Appellate Tribunal shall be removed from his office on the ground specified in clause (e) or clause (f) of sub-section (1) except by an order made by the Central Government after an inquiry made in this behalf by a Judge of the Supreme Court in which such Chairperson or member had been informed of the charges against him and given a reasonable opportunity of being heard in respect of those charges.

Restriction on employment of Chairperson and other Members of Appellate Tribunal in certain cases

53 L. The Chairperson and other members of the Appellate Tribunal shall not, for a period of two years from the date on which they cease to hold office, accept any employment in, or connected with the management or administration of, any enterprise which has been a party to a proceeding before the Appellate Tribunal under this Act:

Provided that nothing contained in this section shall apply to any employment under the Central Government or a State Government or local authority or in any statutory authority or any corporation established by or under any Central, State or Provincial Act or a Government Company as defined in section 617 of the Companies Act,1956 (1 of 1956).

Staff of Appellate Tribunal

53M.(1) The Central Government shall provide the Appellate Tribunal with such officers and other employees as it may think fit.

(2) The officers and other employees of the Appellate Tribunal shall discharge their functions under the general superintendence and control of the Chairperson of the Appellate Tribunal.

(3) The salaries and allowances and other conditions of service of the officers and other employees of the Appellate Tribunal shall be such as may be prescribed.

Awarding compensation

53N.(1) Without prejudice to any other provisions contained in this Act, the Central Government or a State Government or a local authority or any enterprise or any person may make an application to the Appellate Tribunal to adjudicate on claim for compensation that may arise from the findings of the Commission or the orders of the Appellate Tribunal in an appeal against any findings of the Commission or under section 42A or under sub-section(2) of section 53Q of the Act, and to pass an order for the recovery of compensation from any enterprise for any loss or damage shown to have been suffered, by the Central Government or a State Government or a local authority or any enterprise or any person as a result of any contravention of the provisions of Chapter II, having been committed by enterprise.

(2) Every application made under sub-section (1) shall be accompanied by the findings of the Commission, if any, and also be accompanied with such fees as may be prescribed.

(3) The Appellate Tribunal may, after an inquiry made into the allegations mentioned in the application made under sub-section (1), pass an order directing the enterprise to make payment to the applicant, of the amount determined by it as realisable from the enterprise as compensation for the loss or damage caused to the applicant as a result of any contravention of the provisions of Chapter II having been committed by such enterprise:

Provided that the Appellate Tribunal may obtain the recommendations of the Commission before passing an order of compensation.

(4) Where any loss or damage referred to in sub-section (1) is caused to numerous persons having the same interest, one or more of such persons may, with the permission of the Appellate Tribunal, make an application under that sub-section for and on behalf of, or for the benefit of, the persons so interested, and thereupon, the provisions of rule 8 of Order 1 of the First Schedule to the Code of Civil Procedure, 1908 (5 of 1908), shall apply subject to the modification that every reference therein to a suit or decree shall be construed as a reference to the application before the Appellate Tribunal and the order of the Appellate Tribunal thereon.

Explanation.—For the removal of doubts, it is hereby declared that—

(a) an application may be made for compensation before the Appellate Tribunal only after either the Commission or the Appellate Tribunal on appeal under clause (a) of sub-section(1) of section53A of the Act, has determined in a proceeding before it that violation of the provisions of the Act has taken place, or if provisions of section 42A or sub-section(2) of section 53Q of the Act are attracted.

(b) enquiry to be conducted under sub-section(3) shall be for the purpose of determining the eligibility and quantum of compensation due to a person applying for the same, and not for examining afresh the findings of the Commission or the Appellate Tribunal on whether any violation of the Act has taken place.

Procedures and powers of Appellate Tribunal

53O.(1) The Appellate Tribunal shall not be bound by the procedure laid down in the Code of Civil Procedure, 1908 (5 of 1908), but shall be guided by the principles of natural justice and, subject to the other provisions of this Act and of any rules made by the Central Government, the Appellate Tribunal shall have power to regulate its own procedure including the places at which they shall have their sittings.

(2) The Appellate Tribunal shall have, for the purposes of discharging its functions under this Act, the same powers as are vested in a civil court under the Code of Civil Procedure, 1908 (5 of 1908) while trying a suit in respect of the following matters, namely:-

(a) summoning and enforcing the attendance of any person and examining him on oath;
(b) requiring the discovery and production of documents;
(c) receiving evidence on affidavit;
(d) subject to the provisions of sections 123 and 124 of the Indian Evidence Act, 1872 (1 of 1872), requisitioning any public record or document or copy of such record or document from any office;
(e) issuing commissions for the examination of witnesses or documents;
(f) reviewing its decisions;
(g) dismissing a representation for default or deciding it exparte;

(h) setting aside any order of dismissal of any representation for default or any order passed by it ex parte;

(i) any other matter which may be prescribed.

(3) Every proceedings before the Appellate Tribunal shall be deemed to be judicial proceedings within the meaning of sections 193 and 228, and for the purposes of section 196, of the Indian Penal Code (45 of 1860) and the Appellate Tribunal shall be deemed to be a civil court for the purposes of section 195 (2 of 1974) and Chapter XXVI of the Code or Criminal Procedure, 1973.

Execution of orders of Appellate Tribunal

53P.(1) Every order made by the Appellate Tribunal shall be enforced by it in the same manner as if it were a decree made by a court in a suit pending therein, and it shall be lawful for the Appellate Tribunal to send, in case of its inability to execute such order, to the court within the local limits of whose jurisdiction,-

(a) in the case of an order against a company, the registered office of the company is situated; or

(b) in the case of an order against any other person, place where the person concerned voluntarily resides or carries on business or personally works for gain, is situated.

(2) Notwithstanding anything contained in sub-section (1), the Appellate Tribunal may transmit any order made by it to a civil court having local jurisdiction and such civil court shall execute the order as if it were a decree made by that court.

Contravention of orders of Appellate Tribunal

53Q.(1)Without prejudice to the provisions of this Act, if any person contravenes, without any reasonable ground, any order of the Appellate Tribunal, he shall be liable for a penalty of not exceeding rupees one crore or imprisonment for a term up to three years or with both as the Chief Metropolitan Magistrate, Delhi may deem fit:

Provided that the Chief Metropolitan Magistrate, Delhi shall not take cognizance of any offence punishable under this sub-section, save on a complaint made by an officer authorized by the Appellate Tribubnal.

(2) Without prejudice to the provisions of this Act, any person may make an application to the Appellate Tribunal for an order for the recovery of compensation from any enterprise for any loss or damage shown to have been suffered, by such person as a result of the said enterprise contravening, without any reasonable ground, any order of the Appellate Tribunal or delaying in carrying out such orders of the Appellate Tribunal.

Vacancy in Appellate Tribunal not to invalidate acts or proceedings

53R. No act or proceeding of the Appellate Tribunal shall be questioned or shall be invalid merely on the ground of existence of any vacancy or defect in the constitution of the Appellate Tribunal.

Right to legal representation

53S.(1) A person preferring an appeal to the Appellate Tribunal may either appear in person or authorize one or more chartered accountants or company secretaries or cost accountants or legal practitioners or any of its officers to present his or its case before the Appellate Tribunal.

(2) The Central Government or a State Government or a local authority or any enterprise preferring an appeal to the Appellate Tribunal may authorize one or more chartered accountants or company secretaries or cost accountants or legal practitioners or any of its officers to act as presenting officers and every person so authorized may present the case with respect to any appeal before the Appellate Tribunal.

(3) The Commission may authorize one or more chartered accountants or company secretaries or cost accountants or legal practitioners or any of its officers to act as presenting officers and every person so authorized may present the case with respect to any appeal before the Appellate Tribunal.

Explanation – The expressions "chartered accountant" or "company secretary" or "cost accountant" or "legal practitioner" shall have the meanings respectively assigned to them in the Explanation to section 35.

Appeal to Supreme Court

53T. The Central Government or any State Government or the Commission or any statutory authority or any local authority or any enterprise or any person aggrieved by any decision or order of the Appellate Tribunal may file an appeal to the Supreme Court within sixty days from the date of communication of the decision or order of the Appellate Tribunal to them;

Provided that the Supreme court may, if it is satisfied that the applicant was prevented by sufficient cause from filing the appeal within the said period, allow it to be filed after the expiry of the said period of sixty days.

Power to Punish for contempt

53U. The Appellate Tribunal shall have, and exercise, the same jurisdiction, powers and authority in respect of contempt of itself as a High Court has and may exercise and, for this purpose, the provisions of the Contempt of Courts Act, 1971 (70 of 1971) shall have effect subject to modifications that,–

(a) the reference therein to a High Court shall be construed as including a reference to the Appellate Tribunal;

(b) the references to the Advocate-General in section 15 of the said Act shall be construed as a reference to such Law Officer as the Central Government may, by notification, specify in this behalf.]

CHAPTER IX

MISCELLANEOUS

Power to exempt

54. The Central Government may, by notification, exempt from the application of this Act, or any provision thereof, and for such period as it may specify in such notification—

(a) any class of enterprises if such exemption is necessary in the interest of security of the State or public interest;

(b) any practice or agreement arising out of and in accordance with any obligation assumed by India under any treaty, agreement or convention with any other country or countries;

(c) any enterprise which performs a sovereign function on behalf of the Central Government or a State Government:

Provided that in case an enterprise is engaged in any activity including the activity relatable to the sovereign functions of the Government, the Central Government may grant exemption only in respect of activity relatable to the sovereign functions.

Power of Central Government to issue directions

55.(1) Without prejudice to the foregoing provisions of this Act, the Commission shall, in exercise of its powers or the performance of its functions under this Act, be bound by such directions on questions of policy, other than those relating to technical and administrative matters, as the Central Government may give in writing to it from time to time:

Provided that the Commission shall, as far as practicable, be given an opportunity to express its views before any direction is given under this subsection.

(2) The decision of the Central Government whether a question is one of policy or not shall be final.

Power of Central Government to supersede Commission

56. (1) If at any time the Central Government is of the opinion—

(a) that on account of circumstances beyond the control of the Commission, it is unable to discharge the functions or perform the duties imposed on it by or under the provisions of this Act; or

(b) that the Commission has persistently made default in complying with any direction given by the Central Government under this Act or in the discharge of the functions or performance of the duties imposed on it by or under the provisions of this Act and as a result of such default the financial position of the Commission or the administration of the Commission has suffered; or

(c) that circumstances exist which render it necessary in the public interest so to do,

the Central Government may, by notification and for reasons to be specified therein, supersede the Commission for such period, not exceeding six months, as may be specified in the notification:

Provided that before issuing any such notification, the Central Government shall give a reasonable opportunity to the Commission to make representations against the proposed supersession and shall consider representations, if any, of the Commission.

(2) Upon the publication of a notification under sub-section (1) superseding the Commission,—

(a) the Chairperson and other Members shall as from the date of supersession, vacate their offices as such;

(b) all the powers, functions and duties which may, by or under the provisions of this Act, be exercised or discharged by or on behalf of the Commission shall, until the Commission is reconstituted under sub-section (3), be exercised and discharged by the Central Government or such authority as the Central Government may specify in this behalf;

(c) all properties owned or controlled by the Commission shall, until the Commission is reconstituted under sub-section (3), vest in the Central Government.

(3) On or before the expiration of the period of supersession specified in the notification issued under subsection (1), the Central Government

shall reconstitute the Commission by a fresh appointment of its Chairperson and other Members and in such case any person who had vacated his office under clause (a) of sub-section (2) shall not be deemed to be disqualified for re-appointment.

(4) The Central Government shall cause a notification issued under sub-section (1) and a full report of any action taken under this section and the circumstances leading to such action to be laid before each House of Parliament at the earliest.

Restriction on disclosure of information

57. No information relating to any enterprise, being an information which has been obtained by or on behalf of [85][the Commission or the Appellate Tribunal] for the purposes of this Act, shall, without the previous permission in writing of the enterprise, be disclosed otherwise than in compliance with or for the purposes of this Act or any other law for the time being in force.

[86][Chairperson, Members, Director General, Secretary, officers and other employees, etc., to be public servants]

[87]**[58.** The Chairperson and other Members and the Director General, Additional, Joint, Deputy or Assistant Directors General and Secretary and officers and other employees of the Commission and the Chairperson, Members, officers and other employees of the Appellate Tribunal shall be deemed, while acting or purporting to act in pursuance of any of the provisions of this Act, to be public servants within the meaning of section 21 of the Indian Penal Code (45 of 1860).]

---

85 Subs. by Competition (Amendment) Act, 2007 for "the Commission"

86 Subs. by Competition (Amendment) Act, 2007 for "Members, Director General, Registrar, officers and other employees, etc. of Commission to be public servants"

87 Subs. by Competition (Amendment) Act, 2007 for:
"The Chairperson and other Members and the Director General, Additional, Joint, Deputy or Assistant Directors General and Registrar and officers and other employees of the Commission shall be deemed, while acting or purporting to act in pursuance of any of the provisions of this Act, to be public servants within the meaning of section 21 of the Indian Penal Code (45 of 1860)."

Protection of action taken in good faith

59. No suit, prosecution or other legal proceedings shall lie against the Central Government or Commission or any officer of the Central Government or the Chairperson or any Member or the Director-General, Additional, Joint, Deputy or Assistant Directors General or [88][the Secretary or officers or other employees of the Commission or the Chairperson, Members, officers and other employees of the Appellate Tribunal] for anything which is in good faith done or intended to be done under this Act or the rules or regulations made thereunder.

Act to have overriding effect

60. The provisions of this Act shall have effect notwithstanding anything inconsistent therewith contained in any other law for the time being in force.

Exclusion of jurisdiction of civil courts

61. No civil court shall have jurisdiction to entertain any suit or proceeding in respect of any matter which the [89][Commission or the Appellate Tribunal] is empowered by or under this Act to determine and no injunction shall be granted by any court or other authority in respect of any action taken or to be taken in pursuance of any power conferred by or under this Act.

Application of other laws not barred

62. The provisions of this Act shall be in addition to, and not in derogation of, the provisions of any other law for the time being in force.

Power to make rules

63.(1) The Central Government may, by notification, make rules to carry out the provisions of this Act;

---

[88] Subs. by Competition (Amendment) Act, 2007 for "the Registrar or officers or other employees of the Commission"

[89] Subs. by Competition (Amendment) Act, 2007 for "Commission"

(2) In particular, and without prejudice to the generality of the foregoing power, such rules may provide for all or any of the following matters, namely:—

[90][(a) the term of the Selection Committee and the manner of selection of panel of names under sub-section *(2)* of Section 9;]

(b) the form and manner in which and the authority before whom the oath of office and of secrecy shall be made and subscribed to under sub-section *(3)* of section 10;

[91](c) [Omitted by Competition (Amendment) Act, 2007.]

(d) the salary and the other terms and conditions of service including travelling expenses, house rent allowance and conveyance facilities, sumptuary allowance and medical facilities to be provided to the Chairperson and other Members under sub-section *(1)* of section 14;

[92][(da)the number of Additional, Joint, Deputy or Assistant Directors General or such officers or other employees in the office of Director General and the manner in which such Additional, Joint, Deputy or Assistant Directors General or such officers or other employees may be appointed under subsection *(1A)* of section 16;]

(e) the salary, allowances and other terms and conditions of service of the Director General, Additional, Joint, Deputy or Assistant Directors General or [93][such officers or other employees] under sub-section *(3)* of section 16;

(f) the qualifications for appointment of the Director General, Additional, Joint, Deputy or Assistant Directors General or [94][such officers or other employees] under sub-section *(4)* of section 16;

---

90 Subs. by Competition (Amendment) Act, 2007 for:
"the manner in which the Chairperson and other Members shall be selected under section 9;"

91 Prior to omission, clause (c) of sub-section(2) of section 63 read as under:-
"the financial and administrative powers which may be vested in the Member Administration under section 13;"

92 Ins. by Competition (Amendment) Act, 2007

93 Subs. by Competition (Amendment) Act, 2007 for "such other advisers, consultants or officers"

94 Subs. by Competition (Amendment) Act, 2007 for "such other advisers, consultants or officers"

(g) the salaries and allowances and other terms and conditions of service of the [95][Secretary] and officers and other employees payable, and the number of such officers and employees under sub-section (*2*) of section 17;

[96](h) [Omitted by Competition (Amendment) Act, 2007]

[97](i) [Omitted by Competition (Amendment) Act, 2007]

[98](j) [Omitted by Competition (Amendment) Act, 2007]

(k) the form in which the annual statement of accounts shall be prepared under sub-section (1) of section 52;

(l) the time within which and the form and manner in which the Commission may furnish returns, statements and such particulars as the Central Government may require under sub-section (*1*) of section 53;

(m) the form in which and the time within which the annual report shall be prepared under sub-section (*2*) of section 53;

[99][(ma) the form in which an appeal may be filed before the Appellate Tribunal under sub-section (*2*) of section 53B and the fees payable in respect of such appeal;

(mb) the term of the Selection Committee and the manner of selection of panel of names under sub-section(*2*) of section 53E;

(mc) the salaries and allowances and other terms and conditions of service of the Chairperson and other Members of the Appellate Tribunal under subsection (*1*) of section 53G;

(md) the salaries and allowances and other conditions of service of the officers and other employees of the Appellate Tribunal under sub-section (*3*) of section 53M;

(me) the fee which shall be accompanied with every application made under sub-section (*2*) of section 53N;

---

95 Subs. by Competition (Amendment) Act, 2007 for "Registrar"

96 Prior to omission, clause (h) of sub-section(2) of section 63 read as under:-
"for securing any case or matter which requires to be decided by a Bench composed of more than two Members under sub-section (4) of section 23;"

97 Prior to omission, clause (i) of sub-section(2) of section 63 read as under:-
"any other matter in respect of which the Commission shall have power under clause (g) of sub-section (2) of section 36;"

98 Prior to omission, clause (j) of sub-section(2) of section 63 read as under:-
"the promotion of competition advocacy, creating awareness and imparting training about competition issues under sub-section (3) of section 49;"

99 Ins. by Competition (Amendment) Act, 2007

(mf) the other matters under clause (i) of sub-section(*2*) of section 53O in respect of which the Appellate Tribunal shall have powers under the Code of Civil Procedure, 1908 (5 of 1908) while trying a suit;]

[100][(n)the manner in which the monies transferred to the Competition Commission of India or the Appellate Tribunal shall be dealt with by the Commission or the Appellate Tribunal, as the case may be, under the fourth proviso to sub-section(2) of section 66 ;]

(o) any other matter which is to be, or may be, prescribed, or in respect of which provision is to be, or may be, made by rules.

(3) Every notification issued under sub-section(3) of section 20 and section 54 and every rule made under this Act by the Central Government shall be laid, as soon as may be after it is made, before each House of Parliament, while it is in session, for a total period of thirty days which may be comprised in one session, or in two or more successive sessions, and if, before the expiry of the session immediately following the session or the successive sessions aforesaid, both Houses agree in making any modification in the notification or rule, or both Houses agree that the notification should not be issued or rule should not be made, the notification or rule shall thereafter have effect only in such modified form or be of no effect, as the case may be; so, however, that any such modification or annulment shall be without prejudice to the validity of anything previously done under that notification or rule, as the case may be.

Power to make regulations

64.(1) The Commission may, by notification, make regulations consistent with this Act and the rules made thereunder to carry out the purposes of this Act.

(2) In particular, and without prejudice to the generality of the foregoing provisions, such regulations may provide for all or any of the following matters, namely:—

(a) the cost of production to be determined under clause (b) of the Explanation to section 4;

---

[100] Subs. by Competition (Amendment) Act, 2007 for:
"the manner in which the monies transferred to the Central Government shall be dealt with by that Government under the fourth proviso to sub-section (2) of section 66;"

(b) the form of notice as may be specified and the fee which may be determined under sub-section(*2*) of section 6;

(c) the form in which details of the acquisition shall be filed under subsection(*5*) of Section 6;

[101][(d) the procedures to be followed for engaging the experts and professionals under sub-section(*3*) of section 17;

(e) the fee which may be determined under clause (a) of sub-section(1) of section 19;

(f) the rules of procedure in regard to the transaction of business at the meetings of the Commission under sub-section(*1*) of section 22;

(g) the manner in which penalty shall be recovered under sub-section(*1*) of section 39;

(h) any other matter in respect of which provision is to be, or may be, made by regulations.]

(3) Every regulation made under this Act shall be laid, as soon as may be after it is made, before each House of Parliament, while it is in session, for a total period of thirty days which may be comprised in one session or in two or more successive sessions, and if, before the expiry of the session immediately following the session or the successive sessions aforesaid, both Houses agree in making any modification in the regulation, or both Houses agree that the regulation should not be made, the regulation shall thereafter have effect only in such modified form or be of no effect, as the case may be; so, however, that any such modification or annulment shall be without prejudice to the validity of anything previously done under that regulation.

Power to remove difficulties

65.(1) If any difficulty arises in giving effect to the provisions of this Act, the Central Government may, by order published in the Official Gazette, make such provisions, not inconsistent with the provisions of this Act as may appear to it to be necessary for removing the difficulty:

Provided that no such order shall be made under this section after the expiry of a period of two years from the commencement of this Act.

(2) Every order made under this section shall be laid, as soon as may be after it is made, before each House of Parliament.

---

[101] Subs. by Competition (Amendment) Act, 2007 for:
"(d) the fee which may be determined under clause (a) of sub-section (1) of section 19;
(e) any other matter in respect of which provision is to be, or may be, made by regulations."

Repeal and saving

66. [102][(1)The Monopolies and Restrictive Trade Practices Act, 1969 (54 of 1969) is hereby repealed and the Monopolies and Restrictive Trade Practices Commission established under sub-section(*1*) of section 5 of the said Act (hereinafter referred to as the repealed Act) shall stand dissolved:

Provided that, notwithstanding anything contained in this sub-section, the Monopolies and Restrictive Trade Practices Commission established under sub section(*1*) of section 5 of the repealed Act, may continue to exercise jurisdiction and power under the repealed Act for a period of two years from the date of the commencement of this Act in respect of all cases or proceedings (including complaints received by it or references or applications made to it) filed before the commencement of this Act as if the Monopolies and Restrictive Trade Practices Act, 1969 (54 of 1969) had not been repealed and all the provisions of the said Act so repealed shall mutatis mutandis apply to such cases or proceedings or complaints or references or applications and to all other matters.

Explanation: For the removal of doubts, it is hereby declared that nothing in this proviso shall confer any jurisdiction or power upon the Monopolies and Restrictive Trade Practices Commission to decide or adjudicate any case or proceeding arising under the Monopolies and Restrictive Trade Practices Act, 1969 (54 of 1969) on or after the commencement of this Act.

(1A) The repeal of the Monopolies and Restrictive Trade Practices Act, 1969 (54 of 1969) shall, however, not affect,-

(a) the previous operation of the Act so repealed or anything duly done or suffered thereunder; or

(b) any right, privilege, obligation or liability acquired, accrued or incurred under the Act so repealed; or

(c) any penalty, confiscation or punishment incurred in respect of any contravention under the Act so repealed; or

(d) any proceeding or remedy in respect of any such right, privilege,

[102] Subs. by Competition (Amendment) Act, 2007 for:
"(1)The Monopolies and Restrictive Trade Practices Act, 1969 is hereby repealed and the Monopolies and Restrictive Trade Practices Commission established under sub-section (1) of section 5 of the said Act (hereinafter referred to as the repealed Act) (54 of 1969) shall stand dissolved."

obligation, liability, penalty, confiscation or punishment as aforesaid, and any such proceeding or remedy may be instituted, continued or enforced, and any such penalty, confiscation or punishment may be imposed or made as if that Act had not been repealed.]

(2) On the dissolution of the Monopolies and Restrictive Trade Practices Commission, the person appointed as the Chairman of the Monopolies and Restrictive Trade Practices Commission and every other person appointed as Member and Director General of Investigation and Registration, Additional, Joint, Deputy, or Assistant Directors General of Investigation and Registration and any officer and other employee of that Commission and holding office as such immediately before such dissolution shall vacate their respective offices and such Chairman and other Members shall be entitled to claim compensation not exceeding three months' pay and allowances for the premature termination of term of their office or of any contract of service:

Provided that the Director General of Investigation and Registration, Additional, Joint, Deputy or Assistant Directors General of Investigation and Registration or any officer or other employee who has been, immediately before the dissolution of the Monopolies and Restrictive Trade Practices Commission appointed on deputation basis to the Monopolies and Restrictive Trade Practices Commission, shall, on such dissolution, stand reverted to his parent cadre, Ministry or Department, as the case may be:

[103][Provided further that the Director-General of Investigation and Registration, Additional, Joint, Deputy or Assistant Directors

---

[103] Subs. by Competition (Amendment) Act, 2007 for:
"Provided further that the Director General of Investigation and Registration, Additional, Joint, Deputy or Assistant Directors General of Investigation and Registration or any officer or other employee who has been, immediately before the dissolution of the Monopolies and Restrictive Trade Practices Commission, employed on regular basis by the Monopolies and Restrictive Trade Practices Commission, shall become, on and from such dissolution, the officer and employee, respectively, of the Central Government with the same rights and privileges as to pension, gratuity and other like matters as would have been admissible to him if the rights in relation to such Monopolies and Restrictive Trade Practices Commission had not been transferred to, and vested in, the Central Government and shall continue to do so unless and until his employment in the Central Government is duly terminated or until his remuneration, terms and conditions of employment are duly altered by that Government:"

General of Investigation and Registration or any officer or other employee who has been, immediately before the dissolution of the Monopolies and Restrictive Trade Practices Commission, employed on regular basis by the Monopolies and Restrictive Trade Practices Commission, shall become, on and from such dissolution, the officer and employee, respectively, of the Competition Commission of India or the Appellate Tribunal, in such manner as may be specified by the Central Government, with the same rights and privileges as to pension, gratuity and other like matters as would have been admissible to him if the rights in relation to such Monopolies and Restrictive Trade Practices Commission had not been transferred to, and vested in, the Competition Commission of India or the Appellate Tribunal, as the case may be, and shall continue to do so unless and until his employment in the Competition Commission of India or the Appellate Tribunal, as the case may be, is duly terminated or until his remuneration, terms and conditions of employment are duly altered by the Competition Commission of India or the Appellate Tribunal, as the case may be.]

Provided also that notwithstanding anything contained in the Industrial Disputes Act, 1947(14 of 1947), or in any other law for the time being in force, the transfer of the services of any Director General of Investigation and Registration, Additional, Joint, Deputy or Assistant Directors General of Investigation and Registration or any officer or other employee, employed in the Monopolies and Restrictive Trade Practices Commission, to [104][the Competition Commission of India or the Appellate Tribunal], as the case may be, shall not entitle such Director General of Investigation and Registration, Additional, Joint, Deputy or Assistant Directors General of Investigation and Registration or any officer or other employee any compensation under this Act or any other law for the time being in force and no such claim shall be entertained by any court, tribunal or other authority:

Provided also that where the Monopolies and Restrictive Trade Practices Commission has established a provident fund, superannuation, welfare or other fund for the benefit of the Director General of Investigation and Registration, Additional, Joint, Deputy or Assistant Directors General of Investigation and Registration or

[104] Subs. by Competition (Amendment) Act, 2007 for "the Central Government"

the officers and other employees employed in the Monopolies and Restrictive Trade Practices Commission, the monies relatable to the officers and other employees whose services have been transferred by or under this Act to [105][the Competition Commission of India or the Appellate Tribunal, as the case may be, shall, out of the monies standing] on the dissolution of the Monopolies and Restrictive Trade Practices Commission to the credit of such provident fund, superannuation, welfare or other fund, stand transferred to, and vest in, [106][the Competition Commission of India or the Appellate Tribunal as the case may be, and such monies which stand so transferred shall be dealt with by the said Commission or the Tribunal, as the case may be, in such manner as may be prescribed.]

[107][(3)All cases pertaining to monopolistic trade practices or restrictive trade practices pending (including such cases, in which any unfair trade practice has also been alleged), before the Monopolies and Restrictive Trade Practices Commission shall, after the expiry of two years referred to in the proviso to subsection (*1*) stand transferred to the Appellate Tribunal and shall be adjudicated by the Appellate Tribunal in accordance with the provisions of the repealed Act as if that Act had not been repealed.]

(4) Subject to the provisions of sub-section(*3*), all cases pertaining to unfair trade practices other than those referred to in clause (x) of sub-section(*1*) of section 36A of the Monopolies and Restrictive Trade Practices Act, 1969 (54 of 1969) and pending before the Monopolies and Restrictive Trade Practices Commission [108][on or before the expiry of two years referred to in the proviso to sub-section (*1*)], shall, stand transferred to the National Commission constituted

---

[105] Subs. by Competition (Amendment) Act, 2007 for "the Central Government shall, out of the monies standing"

[106] Subs. by Competition (Amendment) Act, 2007 for:
"the Central Government and such monies which stand so transferred shall be dealt with by the said Government in such manner as may be prescribed."

[107] Subs. by Competition (Amendment) Act, 2007 for:
"All cases pertaining to monopolistic trade practices or restrictive trade practices pending before the Monopolies and Restrictive Trade Practices Commission on or before the commencement of this Act, including such cases, in which any unfair trade practice has also been alleged, shall, on such commencement, stand transferred to the Competition Commission of India and shall be adjudicated by that Commission in accordance with the provisions of the repealed Act as if that Act had not been repealed."

[108] Subs. by Competition (Amendment) Act, 2007 for "on or before the commencement of this Act shall, on such commencement"

under the Consumer Protection Act, 1986 (68 of 1986) and the National Commission shall dispose of such cases as if they were cases filed under that Act:

Provided that the National Commission may, if it considers appropriate, transfer any case transferred to it under this sub-section, to the concerned State Commission established under section 9 of the Consumer Protection Act, 1986 (68 of 1986) and that State Commission shall dispose of such case as if it was filed under that Act.

[109][(5)All cases pertaining to unfair trade practices referred to in clause (x) of subsection(*1*) of section 36A of the Monopolies and Restrictive Trade Practices Act, 1969 and pending before the Monopolies and Restrictive Trade Practices Commission shall, after the expiry of two years referred to in the proviso to subsection(*1*) stand transferred to the Appellate Tribunal and the Appellate Tribunal shall dispose of such cases as if they were cases filed under that Act.]

(6) All investigations or proceedings, other than those relating to unfair trade practices, pending before the Director General of Investigation and Registration on or before the commencement of this Act shall, on such commencement, stand transferred to the Competition Commission of India, and the Competition Commission of India may conduct or order for conduct of such investigation or proceedings in the manner as it deems fit.

(7) All investigations or proceedings, relating to unfair trade practices, other than those referred to in clause (x) of sub-section (1) of section 36A of the Monopolies and Restrictive Trade Practices Act, 1969(54 of 1969) and pending before the Director General of Investigation and Registration on or before the commencement of this Act shall, on such commencement, stand transferred to the National Commission constituted under the Consumer Protection Act, 1986 (68 of 1986) and the National Commission may conduct or order for conduct of such investigation or proceedings in the manner as it deems fit.

---

[109] Subs. by Competition (Amendment) Act, 2007 for:
"All cases pertaining to unfair trade practices referred to in clause (x) of sub-section (1) of section 36A of the Monopolies and Restrictive Trade Practices Act, 1969 (54 of 1969) and pending before the Monopolies and Restrictive Trade Practices Commission on or before the commencement of this Act shall, on such commencement, stand transferred to the Competition Commission of India, and the Competition Commission of India shall dispose of such cases as if they were cases filed under that Act,."

(8) All investigations or proceedings relating to unfair trade practices referred to in clause (x) of subsection (1) of section 36A of the Monopolies and Restrictive Trade Practices Act, 1969(54 of 1969), and pending before the Director General of Investigation and Registration on or before the commencement of this Act shall, on such commencement, stand transferred to the Competition Commission of India and the Competition Commission of India may conduct or order for conduct of such investigation in the manner as it deems fit.

(9) Save as otherwise provided under sub-sections (3) to (8), all cases or proceedings pending before the Monopolies and Restrictive Trade Practices Commission shall abate.

(10) The mention of the particular matters referred to in sub-sections (3) to (8) shall not be held to prejudice or affect the general application of section 6 of the General Clauses Act, 1897 (10 of 1897) with regard to the effect of repeal.

STATEMENT OF OBJECTS AND REASONS

1. The Competition Act was enacted in 2002 keeping in view the economic development that resulted in opening up of the Indian economy, removal of controls and consequent economic liberalization which required that the Indian economy be enabled to allow competition in the market from within the country and outside. The Competition Act, 2002 (hereinafter referred to as the Act) provided for the establishment of a Competition Commission, (the Commission) to prevent practices having adverse effect on competition, to promote and sustain competition in markets, to protect the interests of consumers and to ensure freedom of trade carried on by other participants in markets in India, and for matters connected therewith or incidental thereto.
2. The Competition Commission of India was established on the 14th October, 2003 but could not be made functional due to filing of a writ petition before the Hon'ble Supreme Court. While disposing of the writ petition on the 20th January, 2005, the Hon'ble Supreme Court held that if an expert body is to be created by the Union Government, it might be appropriate for the Government to consider the creation of two separate bodies, one with expertise for advisory and regulatory functions and the other for adjudicatory functions based on the doctrine of separation of powers recognised by the Constitution. Keeping in view the judgment of the Hon'ble Supreme Court, the Competition (Amendment) Bill, 2006 was introduced in Lok Sabha on the 9th March, 2006 and the same was referred for examination and report to the Parliamentary Standing Committee. Taking into account the recommendations of the Committee, the Competition (Amendment) Bill, 2007 is being introduced.
3. The Competition (Amendment) Bill, 2007, *inter alia*, provides for the following:
   (*a*) the Commission shall be an expert body which would function as a market regulator for preventing and regulating anti-competitive practices in the country in accordance with the Act and it would also have advisory and advocacy functions in its role as a regulator;
   (*b*) for mandatory notice of merger or combination by a person or enterprise to the Commission within thirty days and to empower the Commission for imposing a penalty of up to one per cent. of

the total turnover or the assets, whichever is higher, on a person or enterprise which fails to give notice of merger or combination to the Commission;

(*c*) for establishment of the Competition Appellate Tribunal, which shall be a three member *quasi judicial* body headed by a person who is or has been a Judge of the Supreme Court or the Chief Justice of a High Court to hear and dispose of appeals against any direction issued or decision made or order passed by the Commission;

(*d*) for adjudication by the Competition Appellate Tribunal of claims on compensation and passing of orders for the recovery of compensation from any enterprise for any loss or damage suffered as a result of any contravention of the provisions of the Act;

(*e*) for implementation of the orders of the Competition Appellate Tribunal as a decree of a civil court;

(*f*) for filing of appeal against the orders of the Competition Appellate Tribunal to the Supreme Court;

(*g*) for imposition of a penalty by the Commission for contravention of its orders and in certain cases of continued contravention a penalty which may extend to rupees twenty-five crores or imprisonment which may extend to three years or with both as the Chief Metropolitan Magistrate, Delhi may deem fit, may be imposed.

4. The Bill also aims at continuation of the Monopolies and Restrictive Trade Practices Commission (MRTPC) till two years after constitution of Competition Commission, for trying pending cases under the Monopolies and Restrictive Trade Practices Act, 1969 after which it would stand dissolved. The Bill also provides that MRTPC would not entertain any new cases after the Competition Commission is duly constituted. Cases still remaining pending after this two year period, would be transferred to Competition Appellate Tribunal or the National Commission under the Consumer Protection Act, 1986 depending on the nature of cases.

5. The Bill seeks to achieve the above objectives.

NEW DELHI; PREM CHAND GUPTA.
The 9th August, 2007.

PRESIDENT'S RECOMMENDATION UNDER ARTICLE 117 OF THE CONSTITUTION OF INDIA

[Copy of letter No. 5/18/2006-IGC, dated the 20th August, 2007 from Shri Prem Chand Gupta, Minister of Corporate Affairs to the Secretary-General, Lok Sabha]

The President, having been informed of the subject matter of the proposed Competition (Amendment) Bill, 2007, recommends introduction of the Bill under article 117(1) of the Constitution and also recommends the consideration of the Bill under article 117(3) of the Constitution.

Notes on Clauses

Clause 2. —This clause seeks to amend section 2 of the Competition Act, 2002 relating to definitions. It is proposed to define the expression "Appellate Tribunal" used in the Bill.

Clause 3. —This clause seeks to amend section 4 of the Competition Act, 2002 relating to abuse of dominant position. The existing provisions of section 4 applies only to an enterprise and not to the group of enterprises. Clause (*c*) of sub-section (*2*) of section 4 states that there shall be an abuse of dominant position if an enterprise indulges in practice or practices resulting in denial of market access.

It is proposed to amend the provisions of section 4 so as to make it applicable to group of enterprises also. It is also proposed to amend clause (*c*) of sub-section (*2*) of said section so as to insert the words "in any manner". This amendment is clarificatory in nature.

Clause 4. —This clause seeks to amend section 5 of the Competition Act, 2002 relating to combination.

Under the existing provisions of section 5, there is no specific provision regarding local nexus for foreign entities which are parties to combinations.

It is proposed to substitute item (*B*) in sub-clause (*i*) and item (*B*) in sub-clause (*ii*) of clause (*a*) of section 5 to provide for a local nexus for combinations involving foreign entity and an Indian entity. A threshold value of local assets and operations in terms of asset value of at least rupees 500 crores and turnover of atleast rupees 1500 crores, is proposed for operations in India in addition to the existing global asset or turnover limits provided in the Act.

Clause 5. —This clause seeks to amend section 6 of the Competition Act, 2002 relating to regulation of combinations.

Under the existing provisions of section 6, it is voluntary for a person or enterprise to give notice of the formation of combination within seven days to the Commission.

It is proposed to amend sub-section (*2*) of section 6 so as to provide for mandatory notice of combinations to the Commission within thirty days. It is also proposed to add subsection (*2A*) providing that no combination shall come into effect until two hundred and ten days have passed from the day on which the notice has been given to the Commission or the Commission has passed orders under section 31, whichever is earlier.

Clause 6. —This clause seeks to substitute section 8 of the Competition Act, 2002 relating to composition of Competition Commission of India.

The new clause provides that the Commission shall consist of a Chairperson and not less than two and not more than six other Members instead of ten Members as provided for under the existing provisions of section 8, to be appointed by the Central Government. It also proposes to remove from eligibility requirement that the person who has been or is qualified to be a Judge of a High Court, and to omit the special knowledge of, and professional experience of administration or in any other matter from the qualifications for appointment as Chairperson or any other Member.

Clause 7. —This clause seeks to substitute section 9 of the Competition Act, 2002 relating to selection of Chairperson and other Members of the Competition Commission of India.

Under the existing provisions, the Chairperson and other Members shall be selected in the manner as may be prescribed by the rules made by the Central Government. The Competition Commission of India (Selection of Chairperson and other Members of the Commission) Rules, 2003 made under this section provide for selection of the Chairperson and other Members by a Selection Committee consisting of (*a*) a person, who has been a retired judge of the Supreme Court or a High Court or a retired Chairperson of a Tribunal established or constituted under an Act of Parliament or a distinguished jurist or a Senior Advocate for five years or more – as Member, (*b*) a person who has special knowledge of, and professional experience of twenty-five years or more in international trade, economics, business, commerce or industry – as Member, (*c*) a person who has special knowledge of, and professional experience of twenty-five years or more in accountancy, management, finance, public affairs or administration – as Member nominated by the Central Government.

The new clause provides that the Chairperson and other Members of the Competition Commission of India shall be appointed by the Central Government from a panel of names recommended by a Selection Committee consisting of (*a*) the Chief Justice of India or his nominee— as Chairperson, (*b*) the Secretary in the Ministry of Corporate Affairs – as Member, (*c*) the Secretary in the Ministry of Law and Justice—as Member and (*d*) two experts of repute having special knowledge in specified fields – as Member.

It also provides that the term of the Selection Committee and the manner of selection of panel of names shall be such as may be prescribed.

Clause 8.—This clause seeks to amend section 10 of the Competition Act, 2002 relating to term of office of Chairperson and other Members of the Competition Commission of India.

Under the existing provisions contained in section 10, no Chairperson of the Competition Commission of India shall hold office as such after he has attained the age of sixty-seven years and no other Member shall hold office as such after he has attained the age of sixty-five years.

It is proposed to amend the said section 10 to provide that the Chairperson or other Member shall not hold office as such after he has attained the age of sixty-five years.

Clause 9.—This clause seeks to amend section 12 of the Competition Act, 2002 relating to restriction on employment of Chairperson and other Members of the Competition Commission of India in certain cases.

Under the existing provisions contained in the said section, the Chairperson and other Members shall not, for a period of one year from the date on which they cease to hold office, accept any employment in, or connected with the management or administration of, any enterprise which has been a party to a proceeding before the Commission under this Act. However, this provision does not apply to any employment under the Central Government or a State Government or local authority or in any statutory authority or any corporation established by or under any Central, State, or Provincial Act or a Government company as defined in section 617 of the Companies Act, 1956.

It is proposed to amend the said section so as to increase the said period of restriction on employment of Chairperson and other Members of the Competition Commission of India from one year to two years.

Clause 10.—This clause seeks to substitute section 13 of the Competition Act, 2002 relating to financial and administrative powers of Member Administration.

Under the existing provisions contained in the said section, the Central Government is to designate any Member as Member Administration who shall exercise such financial and administrative powers as are vested in him under the rules.

It is proposed to substitute the said section 13 by a new section to provide that the Chairperson shall have the powers of general superintendence, direction and control in respect of all administrative matters of the Commission. However, the Chairperson may delegate such of his powers relating to administrative matters of the Commission, as he may think fit to any other Member or officer of the Commission.

Clause 11.—This clause seeks to amend section 16 of the Competition Act, 2002 relating to appointment of Director General, etc.

Under the existing provisions contained in the said section, the Central Government can appoint a Director General and as many Additional, Joint, Deputy or Assistant Director General or such other advisers, consultants or officers, as it may think fit, for the purposes of assisting the Commission in conducting inquiry into contravention of any of the provisions of the Act and for the conduct of cases before the Commission and for performing such other functions as are, or may be, provided by or under the Act.

It is proposed to amend the said section so as to, *inter alia*, omit the "advisers" and "consultants" from the scope of section 16 and therefore the Central Government would not appoint "advisers" and "consultants" in the Competition Commission of India. The power to engage the "advisers", and "consultants" is proposed to be conferred upon the Competition Commission of India.

Clause 12.—This clause seeks to substitute section 17 of the Competition Act, 2002 relating to Registrar and officers and other employees of the Competition Commission of India by a new section.

Under the existing provisions contained in the said section, the Commission may appoint a Registrar and such officers and other employees as it considers necessary for the efficient performance of its functions under this Act.

It is proposed to substitute said section so as to confer power upon the Commission to appoint a Secretary instead of Registrar in addition to officers and other employees in the discharge of its functions under the said Act and also proposed to confer power on the Commission to engage such experts and professionals of integrity and outstanding ability who have special knowledge of, and experience in, economics, law, business or such other disciplines related to competition, as it deems necessary to assist the Commission.

Clause 13.—This clause seeks to amend section 19 of the Competition Act, 2002 relating to inquiry into certain agreements and dominant position of enterprise.

Under the existing provisions contained in clause (*a*) of sub-section (*1*) of said section, the Commission may inquire into any alleged contravention of the provisions contained in sub-section (*1*) of section 3 or sub-section (*1*) of section 4 either on its own motion or on receipt of a complaint.

It is proposed to amend said section so as to substitute "receipt of a complaint", by the words "receipt of any information, in such manner" to enable the Commission to inquire into any alleged contravention on receipt of any information instead of receipt of a complaint.

Clause 14. —This clause seeks to amend sub-section (*2*) of section 20 of the Competition Act, 2002 relating to inquiry into combination by the Commission.

Under the existing provisions contained in sub-section (*2*) of section 20, the Commission shall, upon receipt of a reference under sub-section (*1*) of section 21, inquire whether the combination referred to in the reference is likely to cause an appreciable adverse effect on competition in India.

It is proposed to amend the said sub-section (*2*) so as to delete the provision of inquiry on a reference from a statutory authority as the reference has been made on an issue, which is under consideration of the statutory authority.

Clause 15.—This clause seeks to amend sub-sections (*1*) and (*2*) of section 21 of the Competition Act, 2002 relating to reference by statutory authority.

Under the existing provisions contained in sub-section (*1*) of said section where in the course of a proceeding before any statutory authority an issue is raised by any party that any decision which such statutory authority has taken or proposes to take, is or would be, contrary to any of the provisions of the Act then such statutory authority may make a reference in respect of such issue to the Commission. Under the existing sub-section (*2*), on receipt of a reference from a statutory authority, the Commission shall, after hearing the parties to the proceedings, give its opinion to such statutory authority which shall thereafter pass such order on the issues referred to in that subsection as it deems fit.

It is proposed to add a proviso to said sub-section (*1*) so as to provide that any statutory authority may *suo motu* make a reference to the Commission. It is also proposed to amend sub-section (*2*) so as to provide that the statutory authority on the opinion of the Commission shall give its findings recording reasons therefor.

Clause 16.—This clause seeks to insert a new section 21A regarding reference by Commission.

This new section provides for making of a reference by the Commission to statutory authorities on an issue raised in any matter before it or *suo motu*. The statutory authority shall be duty bound to give its opinion within sixty days to the Commission and the Commission shall consider the opinion of the statutory authority and give its findings recording reasons therefor.

Clause 17.—This clause seeks to substitute section 22 of the Competition Act, 2002 relating to Benches of the Competition Commission of India.

Under the existing provisions contained in the said section, the jurisdiction, powers and authority of the Commission may be exercised by Benches thereof.

It is proposed to substitute the said section for the meetings of the Competition Commission of India. It, *inter alia*, provides that the Commission shall meet at such times and places, and shall observe such rules of procedure in regard to the transaction of business at its meetings as may be provided by the regulations. It also provides that all questions which come up before any meeting of the Commission shall be decided by a majority of the members present and voting, and in the event of an equality of votes, the Chairperson or in his absence, the Member presiding, shall have a second or casting vote. It also provides that the quorum for such meeting shall be three Members.

Clause 18. — This clause seeks to omit sections 23, 24 and 25 of the Competition Act, 2002 relating to distribution of business of the Competition Commission of India amongst Benches, procedure for deciding a case where Members of a Bench differ in opinion and jurisdiction of Bench.

Clause 19. — This clause seeks to substitute section 26 of the Competition Act, 2002 relating to procedure for enquiry on complaints under section 19.

It is proposed to provide that on receipt of a reference from the Central Government or a State Government or a statutory authority or on its own knowledge or information received under section 19, if the Commission is of the opinion that there exists a *prima facie* case, it shall direct the Director General to cause an investigation to be made into the matter. It also provides that on receipt of reference under the above provision, if the Commission is of the opinion that there exists no *prima facie* case, it shall close the matter forthwith and pass such orders as it deems fit and send a copy of its order to the Central Government or the State Government or the statutory authority or the parties concerned, as the case may be. The Director General on receipt of direction under the above provision shall submit a report on his findings within such period as may be specified by the Commission. The Commission may forward a copy of the report to the parties concerned. It also provides that if the report of the Director General recommends that there is no contravention of the provisions of this Act, the Commission shall invite objections or suggestions from the Central Government or the State Government or the statutory authority or the parties concerned, as the case may be, on such report of the Director General. It provides that if the Commission agrees to the recommendations of the Director General, it shall close the matter and pass such order as it deems fit and communicate its order to the authorities mentioned. It further provides that after consideration of the objections or suggestions referred to above, if any, the Commission is of the opinion that further investigation is called for, it may direct for further investigation. It further provides that if the report of the Director General recommends that there is contravention of any of the provisions of the Act and the Commission is of the opinion that further inquiry is called for, it shall inquire into such contravention in accordance with the provisions of the Act. It is also proposed to provide that if the subject matter of an information received is, in the opinion of the Commission, substantially the same as or has been covered by any previous information received, then the new information may be clubbed with the previous information.

Clause 20. —This clause seeks to amend section 27 of the Competition Act, 2002 relating to orders by Commission after inquiry into agreements or abuse of dominant position.

The existing provisions contained in the said section, *inter alia*, confer power upon the Commission to pass orders awarding compensation to parties in accordance with the provisions contained in section 34.

The power to award compensation is proposed to be conferred upon the Appellate Tribunal by new section 53N proposed to be inserted by clause 43 of the Bill. It is, therefore, proposed to omit clauses (*c*) and (*f*) of section 27 which confer powers on the Commission to pass orders awarding compensation.

It is also proposed to add a proviso to this section providing that if the Commission comes to a finding that an enterprise, in contravention to section 3 or section 4 of the Act, is a member of a group as defined in clause (*b*) of the *Explanation* to section 5 of the Act, and other members of such a group are also responsible for, or have contributed to, such a contravention, then it may pass any orders against such members of the group.

Clause 21. —This clause seeks to amend section 28 of the Competition Act, 2002 relating to division of enterprise enjoying dominant position.

Under the existing provisions contained in the said section the Central Government can, on recommendation of the Commission, order division of enterprise enjoying dominant position.

It is proposed to amend section 28 so as to confer said power upon the Commission to order division of an enterprise instead of the Central Government to order the division.

Clause 22. —This clause seeks to amend section 29 of the Competition Act, 2002 relating to procedure for investigation of combinations.

It is, *inter alia*, proposed to insert a new sub-section (*1A*) to provide that the Commission may, after receipt of the response of the parties to the combination under subsection (*1*), call for a report from the Director General and such report shall be submitted by the Director General within such time as the Commission may direct.

Clause 23. —This clause seeks to substitute section 30 of the Competition Act, 2002 relating to inquiry into disclosures under sub-section (2) of section 6.

Under the existing provisions contained in the said section, where any person or enterprise has given a notice under sub-section (*2*) of section 6, the Commission shall inquire, (*a*) whether the disclosure made in the notice is correct, (*b*) whether the combination has, or is likely to have, an appreciable adverse effect on competition.

It is proposed to substitute section 30 so as to provide that where any person or enterprise has given a notice under sub-section (*2*) of section 6, the Commission shall examine such notice and form its *prima facie* opinion and proceed in accordance with the provisions of section 29.

Clause 24.—This clause seeks to amend sub-section (*11*) of section 31 of the Competition Act, 2002 relating to orders of Commission on certain combinations.

Under the existing provisions contained in the said sub-section (*11*) the combination is deemed to have been approved by the Commission if the Commission does not pass orders on expiry of a period of ninety working days from the date of publication referred to in sub-section (*2*) of section 29.

It is proposed to provide for deemed approval for the combination if the Commission does not pass orders in two hundred and ten days from the date of notice given to the Commission under sub-section (*2*) of section 6. This amendment is consequential in nature.

Clause 25. —This clause seeks to amend section 32 of the Competition Act, 2002 relating to acts taking place outside India but having an effect on competition in India. The proposed amendment is clarificatory in nature.

Clause 26. —This clause seeks to substitute section 33 of the Competition Act, 2002 relating to power to grant interim relief.

The existing provisions of section 33 provides that where during an inquiry before the Commission it is proved to the satisfaction of the Commission that an act in contravention of sections 3, 4 and 6 has been committed, the Commission may by order grant a temporary injunction restraining any party from carrying on such act. It also provides that where during the inquiry before the Commission, if the Commission is satisfied that import of any goods is likely to contravene sections 3, 4 and 6 it may, by order, grant a temporary injunction restraining any party from importing such goods until the conclusion of such inquiry or until further orders, without giving notice to the opposite party, where it deems it necessary and a copy of such order granting temporary injunction shall be sent to the concerned authorities. It further provides that the provisions of rules 2A to 5 (both inclusive) of Order XXXIX of the First Schedule to the Code of Civil Procedure, 1908 shall, as far as may be, apply to a temporary injunction issued by the Commission under this Act, as they apply to temporary injunction issued by a civil court.

The proposed section 33 provides that where during an inquiry, the Commission is satisfied that an act in contravention of sections 3, 4 and 6 has been committed, the Commission may, by order, temporarily restrain any party from carrying on such act until the conclusion of such inquiry or until further orders, without giving notice to such party.

Clause 27. —This clause seeks to omit section 34 of the Competition Act, 2002 relating to power to award compensation.

The power to award compensation is proposed to be conferred upon the Appellate Tribunal by new section 53N proposed to be inserted by clause 43 of the Bill. It is, therefore, proposed to omit aforesaid section 34 conferring power upon the Competition Commission of India to award compensation.

Clause 28. —This clause seeks to amend section 35 of the Competition Act, 2002 relating to appearance before the Competition Commission of India.

Under the existing provisions contained in the said section, a complainant or defendant or the Director General may either appear in person or authorise one or more chartered accountants or company secretaries or cost accountants or legal practitioners or any of his or its officers to present his or its case before the Commission.

It is proposed to amend the said section so as to substitute the words "person or an enterprise", for the words "complainant or defendant" for appearance before the Commission.

Clause 29. —This clause seeks to substitute section 36 of the Competition Act, 2002 relating to power of Commission to regulate its own procedure.

The existing section 36 confer powers upon the Commission, *inter alia*, to dismiss an application in default or deciding it *ex parte* or exercise power in respect of any other matter which may be prescribed. It also provides that every proceeding before the Commission shall be deemed to be a judicial proceeding within the meaning of sections 193 and 228 and for the purpose of section 196 of the Indian Penal Code and the Commission shall be deemed to be a civil court for the purposes of section 195 and Chapter XXVI of the Code of Criminal Procedure, 1973.

It is proposed to substitute the said section so as to provide that the Commission may direct any person to produce before the Director General or Secretary or an officer authorized by it the books or other documents, being documents relating to any trade, in the custody or under the control of such person for the purpose of examination under the Act and also that the Commission may direct any person to furnish to the Director General or Secretary or any officer authorised by it, such other information as may be in his position in relation to the trade carried on by such person as required for the purpose of this Act.

Clause 30. —This clause seeks to omit section 37 of the Competition Act, 2002 relating to review of orders of the Competition Commission of India.

Clause 31. —This clause seeks to substitute section 39 of the Competition Act, 2002 relating to execution of orders of the Competition Commission of India.

The existing section provides that every order passed by the Commission under this Act shall be enforced by the Commission in the same manner as if it were a decree or order made by a High Court or the principal civil court in a suit pending therein and it shall be lawful for the Commission to send, in the event of its inability to execute it, such order to the High Court or the principal civil court, as the case may be.

It is proposed to substitute said section, *inter alia*, to provide that if a person fails to pay any monetary penalty imposed on him under the Act, the Commission shall proceed to recover such penalty, in the manner as may be specified by regulations. Sub-section (*2*) of proposed section provides that in a case where the Commission is of the opinion that it would be expedient to recover the penalty imposed under the Competition Act, 2002 in accordance with the provisions of the Income-tax Act, 1961, it may make a reference to this effect to the concerned income-tax authority under the Income-tax Act, 1961 for recovery of the penalty as tax due under the said Act. It is also proposed to provide that any reference made by the Commission under sub-section (*2*) would amount to drawing of a certificate by the Tax Recovery Officer as far as demand relating to penalty under this Act and any reference to appeal in Chapter XVIID and the Second Schedule of the Income-tax Act, 1961, shall be construed as a reference to appeal before the Competition Appellate Tribunal under section 53B of this Act.

Clause 32. —This clause seeks to omit section 40 of the Competition Act, 2002 relating to appeal.

Under the existing provisions contained in the said section, any person aggrieved by any decision or order of the Commission may file an appeal to the Supreme Court within sixty days from the date of communication of the decision or order of the Commission to him on one or more of the grounds specified in section 100 of the Code of Civil Procedure, 1908.

It is proposed to insert, by clause 43 of the Bill, new sections 53B and 53T to provide filing of appeal from any direction, decision or order referred to in clause (*a*) of new section 53A to the Appellate Tribunal and filing of an appeal to the Supreme Court from any decision or order of the Appellate Tribunal. Omission of section 40 is therefore consequential in nature.

Clause 33.—This clause seeks to amend section 41 of the Competition Act, 2002 relating to Director General to investigate contraventions.

The existing sub-section (*3*) of section 41 provides that, without prejudice to the provisions of sub-section (*2*), sections 240 and 240A of the Companies Act, 1956, so far as may be, shall apply to an investigation made by the Director General or any other person investigating under his authority, as they apply to an inspector appointed under that Act.

It is proposed to add an *Explanation* to sub-section (*3*) of section 41 to provide that the words "the Central Government" under section 240 of the Companies Act, 1956 shall be construed as "the Commission" and the word "Magistrate" under section 240A of the Companies Act, 1956 shall be construed as "the Chief Metropolitan Magistrate, Delhi".

Clause 34.—This clause seeks to substitute section 42 of the Competition Act, 2002 relating to contravention of orders of the Competition Commission of India.

Under the existing provisions contained in the said section if any person contravenes, without any reasonable ground, any order of the Commission, or any condition or restriction subject to which any approval, sanction, direction or exemption in relation to any matter has been accorded, given, made or granted under this Act or fails to pay the penalty imposed under this Act, he shall be liable to be detained in civil prison for a term which may extend to one year, unless in the meantime the Commission directs his release and he shall also be liable to a penalty not exceeding rupees ten lakh.

It is proposed to substitute the said section so as to provide that if any person, without reasonable cause fails to comply with the orders or directions issued under the sections specified therein, he shall be punishable with fine which may extend to rupees one lakh for each day subject to a maximum of rupees ten crore as the Commission may determine. It also provides that if any person does not comply with the orders or directions issued under this section, he shall be punishable with imprisonment for a term which may extend to three years or with fine which may extend to rupees twenty-five crore or with both as the Chief Metropolitan Magistrate, Delhi may deem fit. It further provides that the Chief Metropolitan Magistrate, Delhi may pass such orders as it may deem fit on a complaint filed before it by the Commission for non-compliance of its orders.

Clause 35.—This clause seeks to insert a new section 42A regarding compensation in case of contravention of orders of Commission.

The proposed new section provides that any person may make an application to the Appellate Tribunal for an order for the recovery of compensation from any enterprise for any loss or damage shown to have been suffered, by such person as a result of the said enterprise violating directions issued by the Commission or contravening, without any reasonable ground, any decision or order of the Commission.

Clause 36. —This clause seeks to substitute section 43 of the Competition Act, 2002 relating to penalty for failure to comply with the directions of the Competition Commission of India and Director General of the Commission. The new section seeks to provide that a penalty which may extend to rupees one lakh for each day subject to a maximum of rupees one crore may be imposed on the person who, without reasonable cause, fails to comply with the directions given by the Commission and the Director General issued under the specified sections.

Clause 37.—This clause seeks to insert a new section 43A regarding power to impose penalty for non-furnishing of information on combinations.

The new section seeks to empower the Commission for imposing a penalty on the person or enterprise for not giving the notice to the Commission about the combination under sub-section (*2*) of section 6. This insertion is consequential in nature.

Clause 38.—This clause seeks to substitute sub-section (*1*) of section 45 of the Competition Act, 2002 regarding penalty for offences in relation to furnishing of information.

The existing provision provides for imposition of a penalty on a person, which may extend to rupees ten lakh, for furnishing documents or making statements which he knows and has reasons to believe to be false.

It is proposed to provide for imposition of a fine which may extend to rupees one crore, as the Commission may determine, on a person for furnishing documents or making statements which he knows and has reason to believe to be false.

Clause 39.—This clause seeks to amend section 46 of the Competition Act, 2002 relating to power to impose lesser penalty.

Under the existing provisions of the said section the Competition Commission of India has been conferred power to impose lesser penalty in the circumstances mentioned in that section. The first proviso to said section provides that the Commission shall not impose lesser penalty in cases where proceedings, for the violation of any of the provisions of this Act or the rules or the regulations, have been instituted or any investigation has been directed to be made under section 26 before making of such disclosure.

It is proposed to substitute said first proviso to provide that the Commission shall not impose lesser penalty in cases where the report of investigation directed under section 26 has been received before making of such disclosure. It is also proposed to amend second proviso so as to provide for lesser penalty upon a person who discloses the information about a cartel. It is also proposed to add a third proviso to the said section providing that lesser penalty shall not be imposed by the Commission if the person making the disclosure does not continue to co-operate with the Commission till the completion of the proceedings before the Commission.

Clause 40.—This clause seeks to amend section 49 of the Competition Act, 2002 relating to Competition advocacy.

Under the existing provisions contained in sub-section (*1*) of the said section the Central Government may, in formulating a policy on competition (including review of laws related to competition), make a reference to the Commission for its opinion on possible effect of such policy on competition and on receipt of such a reference, the Commission shall, within sixty days of making such reference, give its opinion to the Central Government, which may thereafter formulate the policy as it deems fit. The existing sub-section (*2*) provides that the opinion given by the Commission shall not be binding upon the Central Government in formulating such policy. The existing subsection (*3*) provides that the Commission shall take suitable measures, for the promotion of competition advocacy, creating awareness and imparting training about competition issues in the manner as may be prescribed by rules.

It is proposed to amend sub-section (*1*) of the said section so as to enable the Central Government to make reference to the Commission on any other matter also apart from the existing proviso of making a reference on policy on competition (including review of laws related to competition) and also to enable the State Government to make a reference to the Commission in formulating a policy on competition or on any other matter. It is also proposed to amend sub-section (*2*) of the said section to provide that the opinion of the Commission shall not be binding on State Government as well as the Central Government. It is further proposed to amend sub-section (*3*) of the said section to provide that the Commission shall take suitable measures for the promotion of competition advocacy, creating awareness and imparting training about competition issues in the manner as may be decided by the Commission and not as may be prescribed by rules.

Clause 41. —This clause seeks to amend section 51 of the Competition Act, 2002 relating to constitution of fund.

The provisions contained in clause (*b*) of sub-section (*1*) of the said section, *inter alia*, provide that the monies received as costs from parties to proceedings before the Commission shall be credited to the "Competition Fund" constituted by that section.

It is proposed to omit said clause (*b*).

Clause 42. —This clause seeks to amend section 52 of the Competition Act, 2002 relating to accounts and audit.

The *Explanation* to the existing sub-section (*2*) of the said section clarified that the orders of the Commission, being matters appealable to the Supreme Court, shall not be subject to audit under this section.

It is proposed to amend the said *Explanation* so as to provide that the orders of the Commission, being matters appealable to the Competition Appellate Tribunal shall also not be subject to audit under this section.

Clause 43. — This clause seeks to insert new Chapter VIIIA to the Competition Act, 2002 relating to establishment of Competition Appellate Tribunal.

The new Chapter VIIIA contains provisions for (a) establishment of Appellate Tribunal, (b) appeal to Appellate Tribunal, (c) composition of Appellate Tribunal, (d) qualifications for appointment of Chairperson and Members of Appellate Tribunal, (e) Selection Committee, (f) term of office of Chairperson and Members of Appellate Tribunal, (g) terms and conditions of service of Chairperson and Members of Appellate Tribunal, (h) vacancies, (i) resignation of Chairperson and Members, (j) Member of Appellate Tribunal to act as Chairperson in certain cases, (k) removal and suspension of chairperson and Members of Appellate Tribunal, (l) restriction on employment of Chairperson and other Members in certain cases, (m) staff of Appellate Tribunal, (n) Procedure for awarding compensation, (o) procedure and powers of Appellate Tribunal, (p) execution of orders of Appellate Tribunal, (q) contravention of orders of Appellate Tribunal, (r) vacancy in Appellate Tribunal not to invalidate acts or proceedings, (s) right to legal representation, (t) appeal to the Supreme Court and (u) power to punish for contempt.

Clause 44. —This clause seeks to amend section 57 of the Competition Act, 2002 relating to restriction on disclosure of information.

It is proposed to bring the Appellate Tribunal also within the scope of section 57 of the Competition Act, 2002 consequent to the proposal to insert a new Chapter VIII-A *vide* clause 43 of the Bill. The proposed amendment is consequential in nature.

Clause 45.—This clause seeks to amend section 58 of the Competition Act, 2002 relating to Members, Director General, Registrar, officers and other employees, etc., of the Competition Commission of India.

Under the existing provisions contained in the said section, the Chairperson and other Members and the Director General, Additional, Joint, Deputy or Assistant Directors General and Registrar and officers and other employees of the Commission shall be deemed, while acting or purporting to act in pursuance of any of the provisions of the Competition Act, 2002, to be public servants within the meaning of section 21 of the Indian Penal Code. Clause 12 of the Bill proposes to confer power upon the Commission to appoint a Secretary instead of Registrar. Clause 43 of the Bill proposes to insert new Chapter VIII-A in the Competition Act, 2002 to establish the Competition Appellate Tribunal. Hence, it is proposed to bring the Secretary, officers and other employees of the Commission and the Chairperson, Members, officers and other employees of the Appellate Tribunal within the scope of section 58 of the Competition Act, 2002. The proposed amendment is consequential in nature.

Clause 46.—This clause seeks to amend section 59 of the Competition Act, 2002 relating to protection of action taken in good faith.

Under the existing provisions contained in the said section, no suit, prosecution or other legal proceedings can lie against the Central Government or Commission or any officer of the Central Government or the Chairperson or any Member or the Director General, Additional, Joint, Deputy or Assistant Directors General or Registrar or officers or other employees of the Commission for anything which is in good faith done or intended to be done under this Act or the rules or regulations made thereunder.

Clause 12 of the Bill proposes to confer power upon the Commission to appoint a Secretary instead of Registrar. Clause 43 of the Bill proposes to insert new Chapter VIIIA in the Competition Act, 2002 proposing to establish the Competition Appellate Tribunal. It is proposed to bring the Secretary, officers and other employees of the Commission and the Chairperson, Members, officers and other employees of the Appellate Tribunal within the scope of the aforesaid section. The proposed amendment is consequential in nature.

Clause 47.—This clause seeks to amend section 61 of the Competition Act, 2002 relating to exclusion of jurisdiction of civil courts.

Under the existing provisions contained in the said section, no civil court shall have jurisdiction to entertain any suit or proceeding in respect of any matter which the Commission is empowered by or under this Act to determine and no injunction shall be granted by any court or other authority in respect of any action taken or to be taken in pursuance of any power conferred by or under this Act.

Clause 43 of the Bill proposes to insert new Chapter VIII-A in the Competition Act, 2002 proposing to establish the Competition Appellate Tribunal. It is proposed to exclude the jurisdiction of civil courts in respect of any matter in which the Commission or Appellate Tribunal is empowered to determine. The proposed amendment is consequential in nature.

Clause 48. —This clause seeks to amend section 63 of the Competition Act, 2002 relating to power to make rules.

It is proposed to amend said section so as to confer powers upon the Central Government to make rules in respect of certain matters specified in that section and to make certain other amendments which are consequential in nature.

Clause 49.—This clause seeks to amend section 64 of the Competition Act, 2002 relating to power to make regulations by the Competition Commission of India.

It is proposed to amend said section 64 so as to confer powers upon the Competition Commission of India to make regulations in respect of certain matters specified in the said section.

Clause 50. —This clause seeks to amend section 66 of the Competition Act, 2002 relating to repeal and saving.

Under the existing provisions, the Monopolies and Restrictive Trade Practices Act, 1969 is proposed to be repealed and upon such repeal, the Monopolies and Restrictive Trade Practices Commission established under sub-section (*1*) of section 5 of the repealed Act shall stand dissolved. Sub-sections (*2*) to (*10*) of the aforesaid section deals with the matters arising out of such repeal.

It is proposed to amend said section 66 so as to provide that the Monopolies and Restrictive Trade Practices Commission may continue to exercise jurisdiction and powers under the Monopolies and Restrictive Trade Practices Act, 1969 for a period of two years from the date of bringing into force of section 66 of the Competition Act, 2002 only in respect of cases or proceedings filed before such commencement. It further provides for the transfer of pending cases after the two years period to the Appellate Tribunal or the National Commission under the Consumer Protection Act, 1986 depending on the nature of cases. It also provides that the staff of the Monopolies and Restrictive Trade Practices Commission who has been employed on regular basis by the Monopolies and Restrictive Trade Practices Commission shall, on its dissolution, become employees of the Competition Commission or the Appellate Tribunal in the manner as may be specified by the Central Government.

FINANCIAL MEMORANDUM

1. Clause 43 of the Bill seeks to establish a Competition Appellate Tribunal with a Chairperson and up to two Members, along with associated staff, whose expenses would be paid from the Consolidated Fund of India. However, clause 6 of the Bill seeks to reduce the strength of the Competition Commission from ten additional Members to six additional Members. Clause 17 of the Bill further provides for Commission to function as a collegium and not through Benches, leading to absence of need for provision of offices to these Benches, and the need for branches of Director General's office at these Benches.
2. The expenditure to be incurred on creation of the Competition Appellate Tribunal would be rupees 109.61 lakh per annum. However, there would be a decrease in expenditure up to an extent of rupees 222.39 lakh in a year due to reduction of strength of Competition Commission of India from ten additional members to six additional members, and by removal of the concept of Benches functioning at different locations, and their associated Director General subordinate offices. Thus, there would be an overall saving of rupees 112.78 lakh per annum.
3. Thus, there would not be any additional financial outgo due to the changes proposed in the amendment Bill.

MEMORANDUM REGARDING DELEGATED LEGISLATION

1. Clause 48 of the Bill seeks to amend section 63 of the Competition Act, 2002. This clause empowers the Central Government to make rules, by notification, to carry out the provisions of the proposed legislation. The matters in respect of which such rules may be made are specified therein. These matters relate to, *inter alia*, provide for (*a*) the term of the Selection Committee and the manner of selection of panel of names under sub-section (2) of section 9; (*b*) the number of Additional, Joint, Deputy or Assistant Directors General or such officers or other employees in the office of Director General and the manner in which such Additional, Joint, Deputy or Assistant Directors General or such officers or other employees may be appointed under sub-section (*1A*) of section 16; (*c*) the salary, allowances and other terms and conditions of service of the Director General, Additional, Joint, Deputy or Assistant Directors General or such officers or other employees under sub-section

(*3*) of section 16; (*d*) the qualifications for appointment of the Director General, Additional, Joint, Deputy or Assistant Directors General or such officers or other employees under subsection (*4*) of section 16; (*e*) the salaries and allowances payable to, and other terms and conditions of service of, the Secretary and officers and other employees of the Commission and the number of such officers and other employees under sub-section (*2*) of section 17; (*f*) the form in which an appeal may be filed before the Appellate Tribunal under sub-section (*2*) of section 53B and the fees payable in respect of such appeal; (g) the term of the Selection Committee and the manner of selection of panel of names under sub-section (*2*) of section 53E; (*h*) the salaries and allowances and other terms and conditions of service of the Chairperson and other Members of the Appellate Tribunal under sub-section (*1*) of section 53G; (*i*) the salaries and allowances and other conditions of service of the officers and other employees of the Appellate Tribunal under sub-section (*3*) of section 53M; (*j*) the fee which shall be accompanied with every application made under subsection (*2*) of section 53N; (*k*) the other matters under clause (*i*) of sub-section (*2*) of section 53-O in respect of which the Appellate Tribunal shall have powers under the Code of Civil Procedure while trying a suit; (*l*) the manner in which the monies transferred to the Competition Commission of India or the Appellate Tribunal, as the case may be, shall be dealt with by the Commission or the Appellate Tribunal under the fourth proviso to sub-section (*2*) of section 66.

2. Clause 49 of the Bill seeks to amend section 64 of the Competition Act, 2002. This clause empowers the Competition Commission of India to make regulations, by notification, to carry out the purposes of the proposed legislation. The matters in respect of which such regulations may be made are specified therein. These matters relate to, *inter alia*, (*a*) the procedure to be followed for engaging the experts and professionals under sub-section (*3*) of section 17; (*b*) the manner and fee which may be determined under clause (*a*) of subsection (1) of section 19; (*c*) the rules of procedure in regard to the transaction of business at the meetings of the Commission under sub-section (*1*) of section 22; (*d*) the manner in which penalty shall be recovered under sub-section (*1*) of section 39; (*e*) any other matter in respect of which provision is to be, or may be, made by regulations.

3. The rules made by the Central Government and the regulations made by the Competition Commission of India shall be laid, as soon as may be after they are made, before each House of Parliament.
4. The matters in respect of which rules and regulations may be made are generally matters of procedure and administrative details and it is not practicable to provide for them in the Bill itself. The delegation of legislative power involved is of a normal character.

Bibliography

Books

Sengupta. N.K. *The Monopolies and Restrictive Practices Act. 1969.* Eastern Law House. 1977.

Hornby. A.S.*Oxford Advanced Learner's Dictionary of Current English.* 6th ed. OUP. 2000.

Roy Abir and Jayant Kumar. *Competition Law in India.* Eastern Law House. 2008.

Kamerling, Alexander and Chris Goodwill. *Restrictive Covenants under Common and Competition Law,* 6th ed. Sweet and Maxwell. 2010.

Jones, Alison and Brenda Sufrin. *EU Competition Law: Text, Cases, and Materials,* 4th ed. OUP. 2011.

Rodger , Barry J. and Angus MacCulloch. *Competition Law and Policy -in the European Community and United Kingdom,* 2nd ed. Cavendish Publishing. 2001.

Chandra, Bipan, Mridula Mukherjee and Aditya Mukherjee. *India After Independence-1947–2000,* Fifth Impression. Penguin Books India. 2002.

Bittker, Boris I. *Bittker on the Regulation of Interstate and Foreign Commerce,* Aspen Publishers. 1999.

Garner, Bryan A. ed. *Black's Law Dictionary.* 8th ed. Thomson West. 2004.

Shaffer, Butler. *In Restraint of Trade-The Business Campaign against Competition 1918–1938.* Associated University Presses. 1997.

Goetz, Charles J. and Fred S. McChesney. *Antitrust Law-Interpretation And Implementation,* 3rd ed. Foundation Press. 2006.

Geisst, Charles R. *Monopolies in America: Empire Builders and their Enemies from Jay Gould to Bill Gates.* OUP. 2000.

Harding, Christopher and Julian Joshua. *Regulating Cartels in Europe-A study of Legal Control of Corporate Delinquency.* OUP. 2003.

Totman, Conrad. *A History of Japan.* Blackwell Publishers. 2001.

Gerber, David J. *Global Competition-Law. Markets and Globalization.* OUP. 2010.

Gerber, David J. *Law and Competition in Twentieth Century Europe- Protection Prometheus.* OUP. 2003.

Debora L. *The Cooperative Edge-The International Politics of International Cartels.* Cornell University Press. 1994.

Sullivan, E. Thomas. ed. *The Political Economy of the Sherman Act-The First One Hundred Years.* OUP. 1991.

Buttigieg, Eugène. *Competition Law: Safeguarding the Consumer Interest: A Comparative Analysis of US Antitrust Law and EC Competition Law.* Kluwer Law International. 2009.

Mckerndrick, Ewan. *Contract Law-Text. Cases. and Materials.* 2nd ed. OUP. 2005.

Scherer, F.M. *Competition Policies for an Integrated World Economy.* The Brookings Institution. 1994.

Frankel, Francine R. *India's Political Economy-1947–2004.* 2nd ed. OUP. 2005.

Treitel, G.H. *The Law of Contract,* 10th ed. Sweet & Maxwell. 1999.

Monti, Giorgio. *EC Competition Law.* CUP. 2007.

Singh, Guru Prasanna. *Principles of Statutory Interpretation.* 12th edn. Lexis Nexis Butterwoths Wadhwa. 2010.

Odagiri, Hiroyuki. *Growth through Competition. Competition through Growth-Strategic Management and the Economy in Japan.* OUP. 2002.

Lianos, Ioannis and Ioannis Kokkoris. eds. *The Reform of EC Competition Law- New Challenges.* Kluwer Law International. 2010.

Ahluwalia, Isher Judge and I.M.D. Little. *India's Economic Reforms And Development-Essays for Manmohan Singh.* OUP. 2001.

Hall, John W., Marius B. Jansen, Madoka Kanai and Denis Twitchett. eds. *The Cambridge History of Japan. Vol. 5: The Nineteenth Century.* CUP. 1996.

Faull, Jonathan and Ali Nickpay. ed. *The EC Law of Competition.* 2nd ed. OUP. 2007.

Blanco, Luiz Ortiz. *EC Competition Procedure.* 2nd ed. OUP. 2006.

Narasimham, M. *Economic Reforms: Development and Finance.* UBSPD. 2002.

Dabbah, Maher M. and Barry E. Hawk. *Anti-Cartel Enforcement Worldwide.* Vol. III. CUP. 2009.

Dabbah, Maher M. *EC and UK Competition Law-Commentary. Cases and Materials.* CUP. 2004.)

Dabbah, Maher M. *International and Comparative Competition Law.* CUP. 2010.

Blackford, Mansel G. *The Rise of Modern Business in Great Britain. The United States. and Japan.* 2nd ed. UNC Press. 1998.

Jansen, Marius B. *The Making of Modern Japan.*Belknap Press. 2002.

Furse, Mark. *Competition Law of the EC and UK.* 6th ed. OUP. 2008.

Joelson, Mark R. *An International Antitrust Primer-A Guide to the Operation of United States. European Union and Other Key Competition Laws in the Global Economy.* 3rd ed. Kluwer Law International. 2006.

LeClair, Mark S. *Cartelization. Antitrust and Globalization in the US and Europe.* Routledge. 2011.

Williams, Mark. *Competition Policy and Law in China. Hong Kong and Taiwan.* Cambridge. 2005.

Motta, Massimo. *Competition Policy-Theory and Practice.* CUP. 2004.

Boyer, Paul S. et al. *The Enduring Vision-A History of the American People.* Vol. 2. 6th ed. Wadsworth Cengage Learning. 2010.

Kornicki, Peter F. ed. *Meiji Japan: Political. Economic and Social History. 1868–1912.* Routledge. 1998.

Koslowski, Peter. ed. *The Theory of Capitalism in the German Economic Tradition-Historism. Ordo-Liberalism. Critical Theory. Solidarism.* Springer. 2000.

Mehta, Pradeep S. ed. *Towards a Functional Competition Policy for India-An Overview.* CUTS International. 2005.

Mason, R. H. P. J. G. Caiger. *A History of Japan.* Tuttle Publishing. 1997.

Guha, Ramachandra. *India after Gandhi.* Picador. 2007.

Sims, Richard. *Japanese Political History since the Meiji Renovation 1868–2000.* Palgrave Macmillan. 2001.

Stone, Richard. *The Modern Law of Contract.* 8th ed. Routledge-Cavendish. 2009.

Whish, Richard. *Competition Law.* 6th ed. OUP. 2009.

Liefmann, Robert. *Cartels, Concerns and Trusts.* Batoche Books. 2001.

Zach, Roger. Andreas Heinemann and Andrea Kellerhals. eds. *The Development of Competition Law- Global Perspectives.* Edward Elgar Publishers. 2010.

Peritz, Rudolph J.R. *Competition Policy in America- History. Rhetoric. Law.* Revised edition. OUP. 2000.

Eiji, Takemae. *The Allied Occupation of Japan.* Continuum International Publishing Group. 2002.

Freyer, Tony A. *Antitrust and Global Capitalism 1930–2004.* CUP. 2009.

Freyer, Tony A. *Regulating Big Business- Antitrust in Great Britain and America 1880–1990.* CUP. 1992.

Korah, Valentine. *An Introductory Guide to EC Competition Law and Practice.* 9th ed. Hart Publishers. 2007.

Bael, Van and Bellis. *Competition Law of the European Community.* 5th ed. Kluwer Law International. 2010.

Dhall, Vinod. ed. *Competition Law Today-Concepts. Issues. and the Law in Practice.* OUP. 2007.

Kumar, Virendra. *Committees and Commissions of India 1947–73.* Vol. 8:1967. Concept Publishing Company. 1979.

Beasley, W. G. *The Rise of Modern Japan-Political. Economic. and Social Change since 1850.* (3rd ed. Palgrave Macmillan. 2000.

Rohl, Wilhelm. ed. *History of Law in Japan since 1868.* Brill. 2005.

Wines, William A. *Ethics. Law and Business.* Routledge. 2006.

Wells, Wyatt. *Antitrust and the Formation of the Postwar World.* Columbia University Press. 2002.

Rab, Suzanne. *Indian Cement Cartel Order- An International Comparative Analysis; Supplement to Indian Competition Law-An International Perspective.* CCH, a Wolters Kluwer Business. 2012.

Articles

Oza, A. N. 'Monopolies and Restrictive Practices Bill'. *EPW*, Annual Number, January (1969): 91–102.

Oza, A. N. 'Monopolies and Restrictive Trade Practices Act'. *EPW*, 5:9 (1970): 413–424.

Oza, A. N. 'Recent Amendments to the MRTP Act'. *EPW*, 17:42 (1982): 1697–1705.

Bhattacharjea, Aditya. 'Competition Policy: India and the WTO'. *EPW*, 36:51 (2001): 4710–4713.

Bhattacharjea, Aditya. 'India's Competition Policy-An Assessment'. *EPW*, 38:34 (2003): 3561–3574.

Bhattacharjea, Aditya. 'India's New Competition Law: A Comparative Assessment'. *J. Competition L. & Econ.* 4 (2008): 609.

Bhattacharjea, Aditya. 'Of Ommissions and Commissions: India's Competition Laws'. *EPW*, 45:35 (2010): 31.

Bhattacharjea, Aditya. 'Protection and the 'Public Interest'. *EPW*, 35:49 (2000); 4327–4336.

Uesugi, Akinori. 'How Japan is Tackling Enforcement Activities against Cartels'. *Geo. Mason L. Rev.* 13 (2005): 349.

Meese, Alan J. 'Liberty and Antitrust in the Formative Era'. *B.U. L. Rev.* 1 (1999): 79.

Seita, Alex Y. and Jiro Tamura. 'The Historical Background of Japan's Antimonopoly Law', *U. Ill. L. Rev.* (1994): 115.

Oza, A.N. 'Putting Teeth into the Monopolies Act'. *EPW*, Special Number (1971): 1703–1708.

Veljanovski, Cento. 'Cartel Fines in Europe-Law. Practice and Deterrence'. *World Competition* 30:1 (2007): 65–86.

Gillis, Diana. 'Closing an Administrative Loophole: Ethics for the Administrative Judiciary'. *Geo. J. Legal Ethics*, 22 (2009): 863.

Schimdt, Dolph. 'Antitrust—Application of Per Se Rule against Price Fixing for Doctors' Maximum Fee Schedules-Arizona v. Maricopa County Medical Society', *U. Kan. L. Rev.* 31 (1983): 479.

Brunet, Edward. 'Streamlining Antitrust Litigation by "Facial Examination" of Restraints: The Burger Court and the Per Se--Rule of Reason Distinction'. *Wsh. L. Rev.* 60 (1984): 1.

Fox, Eleanor M. and Lawrence A. Sullivan. 'Antitrust-Retrospective and Prospective: Where are we Coming from? Where are we Going?'. *N.Y.U. L. Rev.* 62 (1987): 936.

Hughes, G.J. 'The Tort of Conspiracy', MLR, 15:2 Apr. (1952): 209.

Spratling, Gary R. 'Detection and Deterrence: Rewardng Informants for Reporting Violations'. *Geo. Wash. L. Rev.* 69 (2001): 798.

Bader, Gregory K. 'The Keiretsu Distribution System of Japan: Its Steadfast Existence Despite Heightened Foreign and Domestic Pressure for Dissolution'. *Cornell Int'l L.J.* 27 (1994): 365.

Paranjape, H.K. 'The MRTP Amendment Bill: A Trojan Horse'. *EPW*, 19:17 (1984): 715–729.

Hansavivek. 'Companies: Thwarted by MRTP Act?'. *EPW*, 6:23 (1971): 1124–1126.

Iyori, Hiroshi. 'A Comparison of U.S.-Japan Antitrust Law: Looking at the International Harmonization of Competition Law', *Pac. Rim L* (1995): 4 and *Pol'y J.* 59.

Schwartz, Ivo E. 'Antitrust Legislation and Policy in Germany-A Comparative Study' *U. Pa. L. Rev.* 105 (1956–1957): 617.

Bos, Jacqueline. 'Antitrust Treatment of Cartels: A Comparative Survey of Competition Law Exemptions in the United States, the European Union, Australia and Japan'. *Wash. U. Global Stud. L. Rev.* 1 (2002): 415.

Singh, Jaivir. 'Monopolistic Trade Practices and Concentration of Economic Power: Some Conceptual Problems in MRTP Act'. *EPW*, 35:50 (2000): 4437–4444.

Fry, James D. 'Struggling to Teethe: Japan's Antitrust Enforcement Regime'. *Law & Pol'y Int'l Bus.*32 (2001): 825.

Medinger, Jason D. 'Antitrust Leniency Programs: A Call for Increased Harmonization as Proliferating Programs Undermine Deterrence'. *Emory L.J.* 52 (2003): 1439.

Connor, John M. 'Anti-Cartel Enforcement by the DOJ: An appraisal'. *Comp. L. Rev.* 5 (1) (2008): 89.

Brodley, Joseph F. 'The Economic Goals of Antitrust: Efficiency, Consumer Welfare, and Technological Progress'. *N.Y.U.L. Rev.* 62 (1987): 1020.

deFuria. Jr., Joseph W. 'Reasoning Per Se and Horizontal Price Fixing: An Emerging Trend in Antitrust Litigation?'. *Pepperdine. L. Rev.* 14 (1986): 39.

Joshua, Julian. 'The European Cartel Enforcement Regime Post-Modernization: How is it Working?'. *Geo. Mason L. Rev.* 13 (2006): 1247–1271.

Elzinga, Kenneth G. 'The Goals of Antitrust: Other than Competition and Efficiency. What Else Counts?'. *University of Pennsylvania Law Review.* 125:6 (1977): 1191.

Lee, Ki Jong. 'Culture and Competition: National and Regional Levels'. *Loy. Consumer L. Rev.* 21 (2008): 33.

Eisenberg, Melvin Aron. 'The Bargain Principle and its Limits'. *HLR* 95 (1982): 741.

Chen-Wishart, Mindy. 'The O'Brien Principle and Substantive Unfairness'. *The Cambridge law Journal* 56:1 (1997): 60.

Clark, Nolan Ezra. 'Antitrust Comes Full Circle: The Return to the Cartelization Standard'. *Vand. L. Rev.* 38 (1985): 1125.

Rao, P. V. Krishna and K. P. Sastry. 'Restrictive Trade Practices Policy in India'. *The Journal of Industrial Economics.* 37:4 (June 1989) 427–435.

Atiyah, P.S. 'Contract as Promise: A Theory of Contractual Obligation by Charles Fried'. *HLR.* 95(1981): 509.

Carstensen, Peter C. 'Lost in (Doctrinal) Translation: The Misleading Retelling of the Supreme Court's Antitrust decisions on Restraints of Trade'. *SMU L. Rev.* 62 (2009): 525.

Bork, Robert H. 'Legislative Intent and the Policy of the Sherman Act'. *Journal of Law and Economics* 9 (Oct. 1966): 7.

Bork, Robert H. 'The Rule of Reason and the Per Se Concept: Price Fixing and Market Division'. *Yale L. J.* 74(1965): 775.

Lande, Robert H. 'Wealth Transfers as the Original and Primary Concern of Antitrust: The Efficiency Interpretation Challenged'. *Hastings L.J.* 34 (1982–1983): 65.

Spratling, See Gary R. 'Detection and Deterrence: Rewardng Informants for Reporting Violations'. *Geo. Wash. L. Rev.* 69(2001): 798.

Ghosh, Subhadip and Thomas W Ross. 'The Competition (Amendment) Bill 2007: A Review and Critique'. *EPW*, 43:51 (2008. 20th December): 35–40.

Mani, Sunil. 'Concentration and Market Power in Indian Automotive Tyre Industry'. *EPW*, Vol. 20:21 (1985): M 53–64

Lee, Tiffany Lena. 'Anticompetitive Exclusion and the "Inherently Suspect" Framework: The Viability of the Federal Trade Commission's Analysis in Realcomp II'. *U.C. Davis Bus. L.J.* 11 (2011): 375.

Freyer, Tony. 'The Sherman Antitrust Act. Comparative Business Structure. and the Rule of Reason: America and Great Britain. 1880–1920'. *Iowa L. Rev.* 74 (1989): 991.

Takigawa, Toshiaki. 'The Prospect of Antitrust Law and Policy in the Twenty-First Century: In Reference to the Japanese Antimonopoly Law and Japan Fair Trade Commission'. *Wash. U. Global Stud. L. Rev.* 1 (2002): 2.

Mohan, T.T Ram. 'Competition Policy Dilemmas'. *EPW*, 35:28&29 (2000): 2499–2502.

Web sources

[2003] OJ L1/1. COUNCIL REGULATION (EC) No 1/2003 of 16 December 2002 on the Implementation of the Rules on Competition laid down in [Articles 101 and 102] of the Treaty. http://eur-lex.europa.eu/LexUriServ/LexUriServ.do?uri=OJ:L:2003:001:0001:0025:EN:PDF (accessed 3 May 2011).

'GCR EU Cartel Survey-An Analysis of Cartel Fines from 2005–2010' http://www.globalcompetitionreview.com/indepth/444/eu-cartel-survey/ (9 May 2011).

'Jet. Kingfisher Form Alliance to Cut Costs'. (2008). *Reuters*. October 14 http://in.reuters.com/article/2008/10/14/idINIndia-35946620081014 (accessed 16 May 2011).

'Legal Aspects. Industrial Acts and Legislations: Industries (Development and Regulation) Act 1951' http://business.gov.in/legal_aspects/industries_act.php (accessed 25 May 2011)

'Statutory Provisions and Guidelines of the Antitrust Division'. in *Antitrust Division Manual* 4th ed. (US Department of Justice. Antitrust Division. 2008) II-20-II-21 http://www.justice.gov/atr/public/divisionmanual/atrdivman.pdf (accessed 12 October 2011)

Weg, Adam. 'Per Se Treatment: An Unnecessary Relic of Antitrust Litigation'. *Hastings L.J.* 60; 1535. http://www.uchastings.edu/hlj/archive/vol60/Weg_60-HLJ-1535.pdf (accessed 29 August 2011)

Bhattacherjea, Aditya. 'India's Competition Policy- An Assessment'. http://papers.ssrn.com/sol3/papers.cfm?abstract_id=440080 (accessed 4 June 2011).

Administrative Staff College of India. Hyderabad. 'Competition Issues in the Air Transport Sector in India' http://www.cci.gov.in/images/media/completed/transport_20090421133744.pdf (accessed 16 May 2011).

Agri Trade Cartels under Review to Check Inflation'. *Press Trust of India* March 21, 2011. http://profit.ndtv.com/news/show/agri-trade-cartels-under-review-to-check-inflation-145621 (accessed 18 May 2011).

Modi, Ajay. 'CCI Probes Alleged Sugar Cartel'. *Business Standard.* February 8, 2011. http://www.business-standard.com/india/news/cci-probes-allegedsugar-cartel/424361/ (accessed 18 May 2011).

Singh, Ajit. 'Multilateral Competition Policy and Economic Development. A Developing Country Perspective on the European Community Proposals'. (UNCTAD, 2004). http://www.unctad.org/en/docs/ditcclp200310_en.pdf (accessed 12 October 2011).

Singh, Ajit and Rahul Dhumale. 'Competition Policy, Development and Developing Countries'. (1999) http://www.icrier.org/pdf/wto7.pdf (accessed 1 January 2011).

Kapur, Amit, Manas Kumar Chaudhuri and Mansoor Ali Shoket. 'Competition Regulation-History. Insights and Issues for the Way Forward' http://articles.manupatra.com/PopOpenArticle.aspx?ID=ebaae57cb2aa43b7af9fac02df0a35b2&txtsearch= (accessed 23 May 2011).

Kumar, Amitabh. 'Relationship between Competition Authority and Sectoral Regulator'. 2006. http://www.cci.gov.in/images/media/presentations/11lahore_25_26march06_20080410175442.pdf (accessed 23 June 2011).

Antitrust Division (U.S. Department of Justice). 'An Antitrust Primer for Federal Law Enforcement Personnel'. 2005 http://www.justice.gov/atr/public/guidelines/209114.htm (accessed 2 September 2011).

Antitrust Division Manual. 4th ed. Chapter III; Investigation and Case Development- B(3)'. (2009). http://www.justice.gov/atr/public/divisionmanual/chapter3.pdf (accessed 21 October 2011)

Antitrust-An Overview' http://topics.law.cornell.edu/wex/Antitrust (accessed 5 August 2011)

Antitrust Division (Department of Justice). *Grand Jury Manual.* http://www.justice.gov/atr/public/guidelines/4371.htm (accessed 21 October 2011).

Agarwal, Anurag K. 'Competition Law in India- Need to go slow and steady'. http://www.iimahd.ernet.in/publications/data/2005-10-05anurag.pdf (accessed 25 May 2011).

Kapoor, Arjun. 'Competition Law and the Liberalization of Legal Services Sector in India'
http://www.cci.gov.in/images/media/ResearchReports/ArjunIntern280111.pdf (accessed 21 October 2011).

Kevin, Bridget C. 'The Antitrust Criminal Penalty Enhancement and Reform Act of 2003'. http://luc.edu/law/academics/special/center/antitrust/pdfs/b_kevin.pdf (accessed 21 October 2011).

'Competition Policy-Need for an Intentional approach'. *Business Line.* July 6,. 2000. http://www.hindu.com/businessline/2000/07/06/stories/040654ma.htm (accessed 10 June 2011).

Cauffman, Caroline. 'The Interaction of Leniency Programmes and Action for Damages'. *The Competition Law Review* 7:2 (2011); 181–220. http://www.clasf.org/CompLRev/Issues/Vol7Issue2Art1Cauffman.pdf (accessed 26 October 2011).

Cartel Fine Statistics. http://ec.europa.eu/competition/cartels/statistics/statistics.pdf (accessed 9 May 2011).

Kersting, Christian. 'Perspectives for Private Enforcement in European Antitrust Law' http://papers.ssrn.com/sol3/papers.cfm?abstract_id=1161254 (accessed 9 May 2011).

Bellamy, Christopher. 'Some Reflections on Competition Law in the Global Market'. *New England Law Review* 34:1 (2000):15. http://www.nesl.edu/userfiles/file/lawreview/vol34/1/BELLAMY.PDF (accessed 1 July 2011).

COMP/F/38.638 – Butadiene Rubber and Emulsion Styrene Butadiene Rubber. para 249 of the EU Competition Commission's decision. http://

ec.europa.eu/competition/antitrust/cases/dec_docs/38638/38638_826_1.pdf (accessed 4 May 2011).

CUTS International and National Law University. Jodhpur. 'Study of Cartel Case Laws in Select Jurisdictions–Learnings for the Competition Commission of India'. (accessed 25 April 2008) submitted to Competition Commission of India http://www.cci.gov.in/images/media/completed/cartel_report1_20080812115152.pdf (accessed 4 June 2011).

Department of Justice. 'An Antitrust Primer- Price Fixing, Bid Rigging, and Market Allocation Schemes: What They are and What to Look for'. http://www.justice.gov/atr/public/guidelines/211578.pdf (accessed 2 September 2011).

Department of Justice. Corporate Leniency Policy. available at http://www.justice.gov/atr/public/guidelines/0091.htm (accessed 1 September 2011).

Department of Justice. Leniency Policy for Individuals. available at http://www.justice.gov/atr/public/guidelines/0092.htm (accessed 1 September 2011).

EUROPA - Treaty of Lisbon - Taking Europe into the 21st Century'. http://europa.eu/**lisbon_treaty**/take/index_en.htm (accessed 20 September 2010).

Bhatia, G.R. 'Combating Cartel in Markets – Issues and Challenges'. http://www.competition-commission-india.nic.in/speeches_articles_presentations/GR.BhatiaArticle.pdf (accessed 12 October 2011).

Guha, Gautam. Director General of Audit. CAG. 'Collusion in Procurement'. December 8, 2010. available at http://cci.gov.in/images/media/presentations/Guha241210.pdf (accessed 19 May 2011).

http://bookshop.europa.eu/is-bin/INTERSHOP.enfinity/WFS/EU-Bookshop-Site/en_GB/-/EUR/ViewPublication-Start?PublicationKey=FXAC08115 (accessed 20 September 2010).

http://eaindustry.nic.in/handbk/chap001.pdf (accessed 26 May 2011).

http://ec.europa.eu/competition/antitrust/actionsdamages/files_white_paper/impact_study.pdf#page=441 (accessed 9 May 2011).

http://ec.europa.eu/competition/antitrust/cases/dec_docs/37784/37784_8_4.pdf (accessed 4 May 2011).

http://ec.europa.eu/competition/cartels/overview/index_en.html (accessed 20 September 2010).

http://eur-lex.europa.eu/LexUriServ/LexUriServ.do?uri=CELEX:31996Y0718(01):EN:NOT (accessed 9 May 2011).

http://eur-lex.europa.eu/LexUriServ/LexUriServ.do?uri=CELEX:31997Y1209(01):EN:HTML (accessed 20 June 2011).

http://eur-lex.europa.eu/LexUriServ/LexUriServ.do?uri=CELEX:32008R0622:EN:NOT (accessed 9 May 2011).

http://eur-lex.europa.eu/LexUriServ/LexUriServ.do?uri=CELEX:52002XC0219(02):EN:NOT (accessed 9 May 2011).

http://eur-lex.europa.eu/LexUriServ/LexUriServ.do?uri=CELEX:52004XC0427(07):EN:HTML (accessed 2 May 2011).

http://eur-lex.europa.eu/LexUriServ/LexUriServ.do?uri=CELEX:52006XC1208(04):EN:NOT (accessed 9 May 2011).

http://eur-lex.europa.eu/LexUriServ/LexUriServ.do?uri=CELEX:52008SC0404:EN:NOT (accessed 9 May, 2011).

http://eur-lex.europa.eu/LexUriServ/LexUriServ.do?uri=CELEX:52008XC0702(01):EN:NOT (accessed 9 May 2011).

http://eur-lex.europa.eu/LexUriServ/LexUriServ.do?uri=COM:2004:0083:FIN:EN:PDF (accessed 4 May 2011).

http://eur-lex.europa.eu/LexUriServ/LexUriServ.do?uri=COM:2005:0405:FIN:EN:PDF (accessed 4 May 2011).

http://eur-lex.europa.eu/LexUriServ/LexUriServ.do?uri=COM:2008:0165:FIN:EN:PDF (accessed 9 May 2011).

http://eur-lex.europa.eu/LexUriServ/LexUriServ.do?uri=OJ:C:1998:009:0003:0005:EN:PDF (accessed 9 May 2011).

http://eurlex.europa.eu/LexUriServ/LexUriServ.do?uri=OJ:C:2001:368:0013:0015:EN:PDF (accessed 18 June 2011).

http://eurlex.europa.eu/LexUriServ/LexUriServ.do?uri=OJ:C:2006:210:0002:0005:EN:PDF (accessed 9 May 2011).

http://eur-lex.europa.eu/LexUriServ/LexUriServ.do?uri=OJ:L:1999:024:0001:0070:EN:PDF (accessed 5 May 2011).

http://europa.eu/legislation_summaries/competition/firms/l26092_en.htm and http://eur-lex.europa.eu/LexUriServ/LexUriServ.do?uri=OJ:L:2003:001:0001:0025:EN:PDF (accessed 24 October 2011).

http://europa.eu/rapid/pressReleasesAction.do?reference=IP/06/1647&format=HTML&aged=0&language=EN&guiLanguage=en (accessed 4 May 2011).

http://europa.eu/rapid/pressReleasesAction.do?reference=IP/10/586&format=HTML&aged=0&language=EN&guiLanguage=en (accessed 9 May 2011).

http://europa.eu/rapid/pressReleasesAction.do?reference=IP/10/985&format=HTML&aged=0&language=EN&guiLanguage=en (accessed 27 October 2011) ; IP/10/586.

http://europa.eu/rapid/pressReleasesAction.do?reference=IP/11/1214&format=HTML&aged=0&language=EN&guiLanguage=en#footnote-1 (accessed 27 October 2011).

http://europa.eu/rapid/pressReleasesAction.do?reference=IP/11/473&format=HTML&aged=0&language=EN&guiLanguage=en (accessed 27 October 2011).

http://europa.eu/rapid/pressReleasesAction.do?reference=SPEECH/09/454&format=HTML&aged=0&language=EN&guiLanguage=en (accessed 3 May 2011).

http://europa.eu/rapid/pressReleasesAction.do?reference=SPEECH/11/243&format=HTML&aged=0&language=EN&guiLanguage=en (accessed 28 April 2011).

http://indiankanoon.org/doc/1000517/ (accessed 4 June 2011).

http://indiankanoon.org/doc/1075616/ (accessed 4 June 2011).

http://indiankanoon.org/doc/793235/ (accessed 4 June 2011).

http://legaltimes.typepad.com/blt/2010/05/senate-extends-criminal-antitrust-amnesty-law.html (accessed 22 October 2011).

http://planningcommission.nic.in/aboutus/committee/wrkgrp11/wg11_cpolicy.pdf (accessed 25 May 2011).

http://planningcommission.nic.in/plans/planrel/fiveyr/default.html (accessed 31 October 2011)

http://www.bundeskartellamt.de/wEnglisch/download/pdf/GWB/110120_GWB_7_Novelle_E.pdf (accessed 11 October 2011).

http://www.cci.gov.in/images/media/Regulations/engagement.pdf?phpMyAdmin=NMPFRahGKYeum5F74Ppstn7Rf00 (accessed 23 June 2011).

http://www.cci.gov.in/images/media/Regulations/regu_lesser.pdf?phpMyAdmin=NMPFRahGKYeum5F74Ppstn7Rf00 (accessed on 29 June 2011).

http://www.cci.gov.in/images/media/ResearchReports/ArjunIntern280111.pdf (accessed 21 October 2011).

http://www.cci.gov.in/index.php?option=com_content&task=view&id=21 (accessed 14 June 2011).

http://www.epant.gr/img/x2/news/news338_1_1298558886.pdf (accessed 3 May 2011).

http://www.fra.dot.gov/. (accessed 9 April 2010).

http://www.ftc.gov/ (accessed 2 September 2011).
http://www.ftc.gov/bc/index.shtml (accessed 2 September 2011).
http://www.indiankanoon.org/doc/252432/ (accessed 4 June 2011).
http://www.indiankanoon.org/doc/382510/ (accessed 4 June 2011).
http://www.indiankanoon.org/doc/450187/ (accessed 4 June 2011).
http://www.indiankanoon.org/doc/838587/ (accessed v
http://www.lawyersclubindia.com/articles/COMPETITION-LAW-amp-CARTELIZATION-543.asp (accessed 21 November 2011)

Incardona, Rossella. 'The Fight against Hard-core Cartels and the New EU Leniency Notice'. *The European Legal Forum* 1/2 (E) (2007): 39 – 42. at http://www.simonslaw.com/library/pdf/e/686.pdf (accessed 28 April 2011).

India's Commitment under GATS. http://commerce.nic.in/trade/international_trade_tis_gaitis.asp (accessed 9 June 2011).

Indicus Analytics. *Public Enterprises, Government Policy and Impact on Competition-Indian Steel Industry*. (New Delhi, 2009). http://www.cci.gov.in/images/media/completed/Indicussteel_20090420151842.pdf (accessed 18 May 2011).

International Competition Network (ICN) Working Group on Cartels. 'Defining Hard Core Cartel Conduct, Effective Institutions, Effective Penalties'. http://www.internationalcompetitionnetwork.org/uploads/library/doc346.pdf (accessed 28 April 2011).

IP/11/473. Washing Powder Cartel http://europa.eu/rapid/pressReleasesAction.do?reference=IP/11/473&format=HTML&aged=0&language=EN&guiLanguage=en (accessed 9 May 2011).

Kleeberg, John M. 'German Cartels: Myths and Realities'. http://www.econ.barnard.columbia.edu/~econhist/papers/Kleeberg_German_Cartels.pdf (accessed 11 October 2011).

Mariappan, Julie. 'Cartels Kill Purpose of Road Work Bidding'. *The Times of India*. 17 February 2011 http://articles.timesofindia.indiatimes.com/2011-02-17/chennai/28554542_1_contractors-road-works-tender-process (accessed 18 May 2011).

Kampel, Kim. 'The Role of South African Competition Law in Supporting SMEs'. http://www.competition-regulation.org.uk/conferences/southafrica04/kampel.pdf (accessed on 1 October 2011).

Vitzilaiou, Lia. 'Crisis Cartels: For Better or For Worse?'. *Anti-trust Chronicle* (2011) https://www.competitionpolicyinternational.com/crisis-cartels-for-better-or-for-worse/ (accessed 2 May 2011).

Monti, Mario. 'Why should we be Concerned with Cartels and Collusive Behaviour?'. Third Nordic Competition Policy Conference on Fighting Cartels- Why and How. held in Stockholm on 11-12 September 2000. http://www.kkv.se/upload/filer/eng/publications/3rdnordic010412.pdf (accessed 10 October 2010).

Foerster, Morrison. 'Antitrust Report: Department of Justice Amnesty Program Takes Another New Turn' (2005) http://www.mofo.com/pubs/xpqPublicationDetail.aspx?xpST=PubDetail&pub=7064 (accessed 22 October 2011).

Nanda, Nitya and Alice Pham. 'Multilateral Competition Framework: Where and How?'. (CUTS, 2004) www.cuts-international.org/view-2.doc (accessed 12 October 2011).

OECD Policy Brief. 'Hard Core Cartels- Harm and Effective Sanctions' (May 2002). http://www.oecd.org/dataoecd/30/10/2754996.pdf (accessed 2 November 2011).

Opinion of the European Economic and Social Committee on the 'Report from the Commission — Report on Competition Policy' 2008. [2011] C 44/24 http://eur-lex.europa.eu/LexUriServ/LexUriServ.do?uri=OJ:C:2011:044:0143:0147:EN:PDF (accessed 2 May 2011).

Narielvala, P.M. 'Competition Law for the New Millennium'. *The Hindu* June 22, 2000). http://www.hinduonnet.com/thehindu/2000/06/22/stories/0622000d.htm (accessed 7 June 2011).

Youens, Paula. 'Combating Cartels: What are the Real Benefits to the End Consumer?' (19 February 2008) http://www.bowman.co.za/LawArticles/Law-Article~id~2132417247.asp (accessed 2 November 2011).

Misra, Praachi and M.P. Ram Mohan. 'Competition Law and Policy. The Changing Market Structure and the Consequences for the Labour Force: A Perspective from India'http://www.competition-regulation.org.uk/conferences/southafrica04/misra.pdf (accessed 22 May 2011).

Mehta, Pradeep S. 'Competition Law Regime in India: Evolution, Experience and Challenges, Horizons'. *Concurrences* N° 1 (2006):. 150–156. http://www.cuts-ccier.org/pdf/PDF-AR1.pdf (accessed 23 May 2011).

Pant, Manoj. 'Assessing the State of Competition in Indian Manufacturing Sector: Paint and Tyre Industry'. Field Researcher: Rabi Ranjan. Centre for International Trade and Development, School of International Studies, Jawaharlal Nehru University, New Delhi. http://cci.gov.in/images/media/presentations/1_20june08/5assessing_paint_tyre.pdf?phpMyAdmin=NMPFRahGKYeum5F74Ppstn7Rf00 (accessed 13 May 2011).

Pant, Manoj. 'Assessing the State of Competition in Indian Manufacturing Sector: Pesticides and Cement Industries'. Field Researcher: C.G. Hariprasad and Rabi Ranjan. Centre for International Trade and Development, School of International Studies, Jawaharlal Nehru University, New Delhi. The report was commissioned by the Competition Commission of India. http://www.cci.gov.in/images/media/completed/3pesticide_20080508111242.pdf (accessed 13 May 2011).

Khemani, R. Shyam. 'Applications of Competition Law: Exemptions and Exceptions'. (UNCTAD. 2002): 15–16. http://www.unctad.org/EN/docs/ditcclpmisc25_en.pdf (accessed 12 October 2011).

Singh, Rahul. 'The Teeter-Totter of Regulation and Competition: Why Indian Competition Authority must Trump Sectoral Regulators'. 2007 http://www.cci.gov.in/images/media/completed/interface_sr_ca_20080508112129.pdf (accessed 23 June 2011).

Report of the EU submitted to the Organization for Economic Co-operation and Development (OECD) on Crisis Cartels http://www.oecd.org/officialdocuments/publicdisplaydocumentpdf/?cote=DAF/COMP/GF/WD(2011)20&docLanguage=En (accessed 2 May 2011).

Report on Competition Policy 2008. COM (2009) 374 final. para 1 http://eur-lex.europa.eu/LexUriServ/LexUriServ.do?uri=COM:2009:0374:FIN:EN:DOC (accessed 2 May 2011).

Report on Proceedings of the Third Anti-Corruption Summit. 'Chapter 7: Price-Fixing and its Impact on Communities'. http://www.nacf.org.za/anti-corruption-summits/third_summit/UnitedNationsReport_summit3_Chapter7.pdf (accessed 12 October 2011).

Road Goods Transport Industry in India with special reference to The Mumbai Metropolitan Region. available at http://www.cci.gov.in/images/media/completed/1Road-goodstrans_20080508111358.pdf (accessed 12 May 2011).

Dutt, Ruddar. 'Competition Law Report: An evasive document'. *Business Line,* August 1, 2000. http://www.thehindubusinessline.in/businessline/2000/08/01/stories/040120ru.htm (accessed 10 June 2011).

Aggarwal, Sanchit. 'Competition Law and Protection of Consumer Interest'. http://www.cci.gov.in/images/media/ResearchReports/SanchitInt260811.pdf (accessed 20 November 2011).

Das, Sandip and K G Narendranath. 'CCI to Investigate Onion Cartel'. *The Financial Express,* January 7, 2011. http://www.financialexpress.com/news/cci-to-investigate-onion-cartel/734432/ (accessed 18 May 2011).

Baru, Sanjaya. 'Cartels and Competition'. *Business Standard,* December 6, 2010. http://www.business-standard.com/india/news/sanjaya-baru-cartelscompetition/417211/ (accessed 12 May 2011).

Hammond, Scott D. 'An Overview of the Recent Developments in the Antitrust Division's Criminal Enforcement Programme'. (2005) Before the American Bar Association Midwinter leadership Meeting http://www.justice.gov/atr/public/speeches/207226.htm (accessed 21 October 2011).

Hammond, Scott D. and Belinda A. Barnett. 'Frequently Asked Questions Regarding The Antitrust Division's Leniency Program and Model Leniency Letters'. at http://www.justice.gov/atr/public/criminal/239583.pdf (accessed 1 September 2011).

Hammond, Scott D. 'Detecting and Deterring Cartel Activity through an Effective Leniency Program'. http://www.justice.gov/atr/public/speeches/9928.pdf (accessed 1 September 2011).

Hammond, Scott D. 'Measuring the Value of Second in Cooperation in Corporate Plea Negotiations'. (2006) The 54th Annual American Bar Association Section of Antitrust Law Spring Meeting. http://www.justice.gov/atr/public/speeches/215514.htm (accessed 21 October 2011).

Sherman Anti-Trust Act (1890) http://www.ourdocuments.gov/doc.php?flash=old&doc=51# (accessed 13 October 2011).

Mazhuvanchery, Shiju Varghese. 'The Indian Competition Act: A Historical and Developmental Perspective'. *The Law and Development Review* 3: 2 (2010):. 240–270. http://www.bepress.com/ldr/vol3/iss2/art8 (accessed 25 May 2011).

Suman, Sowmya. 'Competition Law and Cartelization' http://www.lawyersclubindia.com/articles/COMPETITION-LAW-amp-CARTELIZATION-543.asp (accessed 21 November 2011).

Speaking Notes for Research Symposium. 'Political Economy Constraints in Regulatory Regimes in Developing Countries'. (22–24 March 2007) Journey of India's New Competition Law through a Practitioner's Eye http://www.circ.in/pdf/INDNewCompetitionLaw.pdf (accessed 7 June 2011).

SPEECH/11/268. Joaquín Almunia. Vice President of the European Commission responsible for Competition Policy. 'Cartels: The Priority in Competition Enforcement' http://europa.eu/rapid/pressReleasesAction.do?reference=SPEECH/11/268&format=HTML&aged=0&language=EN&guiLanguage=en (accessed 9 May 2011).

http://www.merriam-webster.com/dictionary/subpoena (accessed 31 August 2011).

Mani, Sunil and P.K. Michael Tharakan. 'Competitiveness in the Indian Tyre Industry: 1936–1984'. Working Paper No. 203. http://cds.edu/download_files/wp-1971-95/wp203.pdf (accessed 12 May 2011).

T E R I. 2008. Competition Issues in Regulated Industries: Case of the Indian Transport Sector. New Delhi: The Energy and Resources Institute. [Project Report No. 2007CP21] http://www.cci.gov.in/images/media/completed/transport_20090723115524.pdf (accessed 16 May 2011).

Tables of Equivalences Referred to in Article 5 of the Treaty of Lisbon' [2007] OJ 306/13 http://eur-lex.europa.eu/LexUriServ/LexUriServ.do?uri=OJ:C:2007:306:0202:0229:EN:PDF (accessed 24 October 2011).

The 'Pre-insulated Pipes' Judgment: The European Court of Justice Confirms the Legality of the Commission's Guidelines on Fines'. (2005) *Competition Policy Newsletter* ,Vol.3. 78–79. http://ec.europa.eu/competition/publications/cpn/2005_3_78.pdf (accessed 5 May 2011).

The Competition (Amendment) Bill 2009. section 66 (1). (3). (4). (5) and (7) http://www.bareactsonline.com/pdfs/2010/THE%20COMPETITION%20(AMENDMENT).pdf (accessed June 14, 2011).

The FTC website http://www.ftc.gov/bc/about.shtm (accessed 31 August 2011).

The History of Re-unification at http://74.125.153.132/search?q=cache:http://www.cybergerman.addr.com/east_west.html (acessed October 4, 2009). http://www.ftc.gov/ogc/stat1.shtm (accessed 30 August 2011).

The OECD Council Recommendation Concerning Effective Action against Hard Core Cartels. http://acts.oecd.org/Instruments/ShowInstrumentView.aspx?InstrumentID=193&InstrumentPID=189&Lang=en&Book=False (accessed 15 June 2011).

The Statement and Objects of the Competition (Amendment) Bill. 2009. at http://www.prsindia.org/uploads/media/Competition/Competition%20Amendment%20Bill.pdf (accessed 14 June 2011)

Leary, Thomas B. 'A Structured Outline for the Analysis of Horizontal Agreements'. http://www.ftc.gov/speeches/leary/chairsshowcasetalk.pdf (accessed 29 August 2011).

Barnett, Thomas O. 'Seven Steps to Better Cartel Enforcement'. (2006) 11th Annual Competition Law & Policy Workshop European Union Institute Florence. Italy http://www.justice.gov/atr/public/speeches/216453.pdf (accessed 21 October 2011).

TNN. 'Bus Mishap: It's a Cartel Thriving on Parents' Helplessness'. *The Times of India.* April 26, 2009. http://articles.timesofindia.indiatimes.com/2009-04-26/lucknow/28017663_1_cartel-school-bus-bus-mishap (accessed 18 May 2011).

TNN. 'Corporation Commissioner Responds to TOI report'. *The Times of India.* February 17, 2011. http://articles.timesofindia.indiatimes.com/2011-02-17/chennai/28554311_1_bus-route-roads-corporation-commissioner-quality (accessed 18 May 2011).

Mehta, Udai S and Sanjay Pandey. 'Cartels and Other Anticompetitive Agreements'.(14–15 March 2007) Presentation at the Competition Commission Workshop http://www.cci.gov.in/images/workshop/14_15march07/14udai.pdf?phpMyAdmin=NMPFRahGKYeum5F74Ppstn7Rf00 (accessed 3 June 2011).

Dhall, Vinod. Key Note Address at the Seminar on 'Competition Policy and its Impact on Industry' (20 September 2004) Ahmedabad. http://cci.gov.in/images/media/speeches/5policyandimpact_20080411101736.pdf (accessed 10 June 2011).

www.nationalatlas.gov/mld/railrdl.html (accessed 9 November 2010).

Miwa, Yoshiro and J. Mark Ramseyer. 'Does Ownership Matter? Evidence from the Zaibatsu Dissolution Program'. (2001) http://papers.ssrn.com/sol3/papers.cfm?abstract_id=262440 (accessed 10 August 2009).

http://stats.oecd.org/glossary/detail.asp?ID=3157 (accessed 20 August 2013).

List of statutes, orders, reports, guidelines and notices

(2011) OJ C 11/1 (The EU Competition Commission Guidelines on the Applicability of Article 101 of the Treaty on the Functioning of the European Union to Horizontal Co-Operation Agreements).

(2011) OJ C 11/1 (The EU Competition Commission Guidelines on the Applicability of Article 101 of the Treaty on the Functioning of the European Union to Horizontal Cooperation Agreements).

[1996] OJ C 207/4. (Commission Notice on the Non-imposition or Reduction of Fines in Cartel Cases).

[1997] OJ C372/5. (Commission Notice on the Definition of Relevant Market for the Purposes of Community Competition Law).

[1998] OJ C 9/3. (Guidelines on the Method of Setting Fines Imposed Pursuant to Article 15 (2) of Regulation No 17 and Article 65 (5) of the ECSC Treaty).

[2001] OJ C368/13. (Commission Notice on Agreements of Minor Importance which do not Appreciably Restrict Competition under [Article 101 clause (1)] of the Treaty Establishing the European Community (Deminimis)).

[2002] OJ C 45/3. (Commission Notice on Immunity from Fines and Reduction of Fines in Cartel Cases).

[2003] OJ L1/1. (Council Regulation (EC) No 1/2003 of 16 December 2002 on the Implementation of the Rules on Competition Laid down in [Articles 101 and 102] of the Treaty).

[2006] OJ C 210/2. (Guidelines on the Method of Setting Fines Imposed Pursuant to Article 23(2)(a) of Regulation No 1/2003).

[2006] OJ C 298/17. (Commission Notice on Immunity from Fines and Reduction of Fines in Cartel Cases).

[2008] OJ C 167/1. (Commission Notice on the Conduct of Settlement Procedures in View of the Adoption of Decisions Pursuant to Article 7 and Article 23 of Council Regulation (EC) No 1/2003 in Cartel Cases).

[2008] OJ L 171/3. (Commission Regulation (EC) No 622/2008 of 30 June 2008 Amending Regulation (EC) No 773/2004. as Regards the Conduct of Settlement Procedures in Cartel Cases).

Clayton Antitrust Act, 1914.

COM (2004) 83 Final. (The Communication from the Commission-Report on Competition in Professional Services).

COM (2008) 165 Final.(Commission Staff Working Paper Accompanying the White paper on Damages Actions for Breach of the EC Antitrust Rules).

COM(2005) 405 Final. (Communication from the Commission to the Council, the European Parliament, the European Economic and Social Committee and the Committee of the Regions-Professional Services - Scope for more Reform Follow-up to the Report on Competition in Professional Services. COM(2004) 83 of 9 February 2004.

COMP/2006/A3/012. 'Making antitrust damages actions more effective in the EU: Welfare impact and potential scenarios'. A Report Prepared for the EU Competition Commission.

Competition Act, 2002.

Competition Act, 1998 (South Africa).

First Five Year Plan 1951–1956.

Report of the Monopolies Inquiry Commission. 1965.

Report of the Working Group on Competition Policy (Commissioned by the Planning Commission. Government of India. 2007.

Report on Competition Policy 2008. COM (2009) 374 Final.

Sherman Antitrust Act, 1890.

Sports Broadcasting Act, US Code Title 15, Chapter 32 (15 U.S.C 32).

SVS Raghavan Committee Report, 'Report of the High Level Committee on Competition Policy Law, 1999.

The Antitrust Criminal Penalty Enhancement and Reform Act, 2003.

The Antitrust Division Department of Justice Leniency Policy for Individuals.

The Antitrust Division, Department of Justice Corporate Leniency Policy.

The Competition Commission of India (Lesser Penalty) Regulations, 2009.

The Constitution of India, 1950.

The EU Competition Commission Guidelines on the Application of Article 81 clause 3 (Article 101 clause 3) of the Treaty, [2004] OJ C 101/97.

The European Council Regulation [2003] OJ L 1/1.

The Federal Trade Commission Act, 1914.

The Indian Contract Act, 1872.

The Industrial Policy Resolution, 1956.

The Interstate Commerce Act, 1887.

The Monopolies and Restrictive Trade Practices Act, 1969.

The Treaty of Lisbon Article 101–109.

Cases

[1984] OJ L207/17, *Synthetic Fibers* 116;117

[1992] OJ L-68/19, *UK Agricultural Tractor Registration Exchange* ... 128;129

[2005] OJ L 200/92, *Fine Art Auction Houses*.. 124

[2005] OJ L004/10, *Belgian Architects' Association*.............................. 125;126

[2009] IESC 72, *Irish Beef Industry case*.................................... 118;119;120

Addyston Pipe & Steel Company et al. v. United States, 175 U.S. 211, 20 S.Ct. 96 .... 64;65;66;67

American Tobacco Company and Others v. United States Of America, 221 U.S. 106, 31 S.Ct. 632 69

Arizona v. Maricopa County Medical Society et al., 457 U.S. 332, 102 S.Ct. 2466 .... 79;80;81;82;83

Bernard Crehan v. Inntrepreneur Pub Company, CPC[2004] EWCA Civ 637 .... 45;46

Board Of Trade Of City Of Chicago et al. v. United States., 246 U.S. 231, 38 S.Ct. 242 .... 70;71;72

Brahm Dutt v. Union of India, (2005) 2 SCC 431 189

Broadcast Music, Inc., et al.,v. Columbia Broadcasting System, Inc., et al., 441 U.S. 1, 99 S.Ct. 1551 .... 75;76;77;78;81

C-113/07,*SELEX Sistemi Integrati SpA v. Commission of the European Communities and Organisation européenne pour la sécurité de la navigation aérienne (Eurocontrol).* [2009] ECR I-2207 105

Case 246/86, *SC Belasco and others v. Commission of the European Communities*, [1989] ECR 2117 108

Case 41/69, *ACF Chemiefarma NV v. Commission of the European Communities*, [1970] ECR 661 109

Case 48/69, *Imperial Chemical Industries Ltd. v. Commission of the European Communities*, [1972] ECR 619 .... 122;123

Case 5/69, *Franz Volk v. S.P.R.L. Ets J. Vervaecke*, [1969] ECR 295 200

Case C-189/02, *Dansk Rørindustri A/S* (C-189/02 P), *Isoplus Fernwärmetechnik Vertriebsgesellschaft mbH and Others* (C-202/02 P), *KE KELIT Kunststoffwerk GmbH* (C-205/02 P), *LR af 1998 A/S* (C-206/02 P), *Brugg Rohrsysteme GmbH* (C-207/02 P), *LR af 1998 (Deutschland) GmbH* (C-208/02 P) and *ABB Asea Brown Boveri Ltd* (C-213/02 P) *v. Commission of the European Communities*, [2005] ECR I-5425 127

Case C-205/03, *Federación Española de Empresas de Tecnología Sanitaria (FENIN) v Commission of the European Communities*, [2006] ECR I-06295 103

Case C-209/07, *Competition Authority v. Beef Industry Development Society Ltd and Barry Brothers (Carrigmore) Meats Ltd.*, [2008] ECR I-8637 .... 120;121

Case C-309/99, *J. C. J. Wouters, J. W. Savelbergh and Price Waterhouse Belastingadviseurs BV v. Algemene Raad van de Nederlandse Orde van Advocaten*, [2002] ECR I-1577 .... 106;107;125;126

Case C-41/90, *Klaus Höfner and Fritz Elser v. Macrotron GmbH*, [1991] ECR I-1979 102

Case C-439/09, *Pierre Fabre Dermo-Cosmétique SAS v. Président de l'Autorité de la concurrence Ministre de l'Économie, de l'Industrie et de l'Emploi*, [2011] ECR 0000 100

Case C-453/99, *Courage v Crehan*, [2001] ECR I-6297 .... 46;133

Case C-519/04, *David Meca-Medina and Igor Majcen v. Commission of the European Communities*, [2006] ECR I-06991 100

Case T-1/89, *Rhône-Poulenc SA v. Commission of the European Communities*, [1991] ECR II-867 111

Case T-14/89, *Montedipe SpA v. Commission of the European Communities*, [1992] ECR II-115 .... 108;118;123

Case T-155/04, *SELEX Sistemi Integrati SpA v. Commission of the European Communities*, [2006] ECR II-4797 .... 104;105

Case T-17/93, *Hachette SA v. Commission of the European Communities*, [1994] ECR II-59 .... 113; 114

Case T-319/99, *FENIN v. Commission of the European Communities*, [2003] ECR-II 357 103

Case T-374/94, joined with Cases T-375/94, T-384/94 and T-388/94, *the European Night Services Ltd (ENS), Eurostar (UK) Ltd, formerly European Passenger Services Ltd (EPS), Union internationale des chemins de fer (UIC), NV Nederlandse Spoorwegen (NS) and Société nationale des chemins de fer français (SNCF)v Commission of the European Communities*, [1998] ECR II-3141 113

Case T-41/96, *Bayer AG v. Commission of the European Communities*, [2000] ECR II- 3383 109

Case T-44/07, *Kaučuk v Commission*, [2011] ECR 00000 .... 123;124

Central Inland Water Transport Corpn Ltd v. Brojo Nath Ganguly, AIR 1986 SC 1571, (1986) 3 SCC 156 39

COMP/E-2/37.784, *Fine Art Auction Houses* 124

Competition Commission of India v. Steel Authority of India Ltd. and Anr, MANU/SC/0690/201 878

Consumer Online Foundation v. Tata Sky Limited & Ors, Case No. 2 of 2009 .... 17;218;219;220;221

Crofter Hand Woven Harris Tweed Company, Limited, and Others v. Veitch and Another, [1942] A.C. 435 48

Director General Investigations and Registration v. Reliance Industries Ltd. and Anr, l (2003) CPJ 80 MRTP 170;171

Director-General of Investigation and Registration v. Cement Manufacturers Association And Ors., 1991 71 CompCas 46 NULL 169

FICCI-Multiplex Association of India v. United Producers/Distributors Forum and Ors, Case No.01 of 2009 .... 231;232

FTC v Indiana Federation of Dentists, 476 U.S. 447, 106 S.Ct. 2009 .... 86;87

Gujarat Bottling Co. Ltd. and others v. Coca Cola Co and others, (1995) 5 SCC 545 43

Haridas Exports v. All India Float Glass Manufacturers Assn., (2002) 111 Comp Cas 617(SC 169;170;171;181;204

Superintendence Company of India (P) Ltd. v. Sh. Krishan Murgai, MANU/SC/0457/1980 43

Tata Engineering & Locomotive Co. Ltd., Bombay v. The Registrar of the Restrictive Trade Agreement, New Delhi, 1977 SCR (2) 685; AIR 1977 SC 973; (1977) 2 SCC 55 .... 164;165;166;167

The Mogul Steamship Company Limited v. McGregor, Gow, & Co., and Others,[1892] A.C. 25 .... 47;48;52

The Mogul Steamship Company, Limited v. Mcgregor, Gow, & Co., and Others, (1888) L.R. 21 Q.B.D. 544 .... 49;51;52

The Mogul Steamship Company, Limited v. Mcgregor, Gow, & Co., and Others,(1889) L.R. 23 Q.B.D 598 50

The Surinder Bhakoo v. The HDFC Bank Ltd., Case No. 15 of 2009 229

Thorsten Nordenfelt v. The Maxim Nordenfelt Guns and Ammunition Company, Limited, [1894] A.C. 535 .... 41;42

Union of India and Ors v. Hindustan Development Corpn. and others, (1993) SCC 3 499; 1993 SCR (3) 128 4

United States v. Joint-TrafficAss'n, 171 US 505, 19 S.Ct. 25 .... 63;64

United States v. E. C. Knight Co. et al, 156 U.S. 1 (1895), 15 S.Ct. 249 .... 57;58;59

United States v. Trenton Potteries Co. et al., 273 U.S. 392, 47 S.Ct. 377 .... 72;73

United States v. Trans-Missouri Freight Ass'n, 166 U.S. 290, 17 S.Ct. 540 .... 60;61;62;63

Vijay Gupta v. M/s. Paper Merchants Association and others, Case No. 07/2010 228

Yashoda Hospital and Research Centre Ltd. v. Indiabulls Financial Services Limited (IFSL 227;228

Builders Association of India v. Cement Manufacturer's Association and Others Case No. 29/2010 233

Puja Enterprises Ref. Case No. 01 of 2012 232

Jet Airways Case No. 04/2009 .... *230*

Re:Domestic Airlines RTPE 05/2009 of MRTPC/Suo-Motu Case No.02/2010 940

Index